THE FABER BOOK OF LONDON

Once the centre of the greatest mercantile Empire the world has ever known, London remains today one of the major financial hubs of the world. *The Faber Book of London* views this city through the eyes of writers as diverse as Dickens and Joe Orton, Dostoyevsky and Lenin, Boswell and Martin Amis. We see criminal London, low life and high life, beggars and politicians, Royal families, intellectuals and animals. From Black Beauty to Virginia Woolf, from William Wordsworth to Peter Simple, A. N. Wilson has scoured the shelves for a rich pot-pourri of the familiar, diverting and strange.

A. N. Wilson was born in 1950. He was formerly the Literary Editor of the *Evening Standard* and is the author of twelve novels, including *Wise Virgins* (which won the W. H. Smith award) and *The Healing Art*, which won both the Arts Council National Book Award and the Somerset Maugham Prize. He has written biographies of Jesus, St Paul, Milton and Sir Walter Scott, and *Tolstoy* which won the Whitbread Prize for Biography. His most recent book was *God's Funeral* and he is currently writing *A Short History of London*. He is also the editor of *The Faber Book of Church and Clergy*. He lives in London.

The Faber Book of

LONDON

Edited by
A. N. WILSON

faber and faber
LONDON · BOSTON

TO ALGY CLUFF

First published in 1993
by Faber and Faber Limited
3 Queen Square London WC1N 3AU
This paperback edition first published in 2002

Printed in England by Clays Ltd, St Ives plc

A CIP record for this book is available from the British Library

ISBN 0-571-17174-5

4 6 8 10 9 7 5

Contents

Prologue

A Description of London

Houses, churches, mixed together,
Streets unpleasant in all weather;
Prisons, palaces contiguous,
Gates, a bridge, the Thames irriguous.

Gaudy things enough to tempt ye,
Showy outsides, insides empty;
Bubbles, trades, mechanic arts,
Coaches, wheelbarrows and carts.

Warrants, bailiffs, bills unpaid,
Lords of laundresses afraid;
Rogues that nightly rob and shoot men,
Hangmen, aldermen and footmen.

Lawyers, poets, priests, physicians,
Noble, simple, all conditions:
Worth beneath a threadbare cover,
Villainy bedaubed all over.

Women black, red, fair and grey,
Prudes and such as never pray,
Handsome, ugly, noisy, still,
Some that will not, some that will.

Many a beau without a shilling,
Many a widow not unwilling;
Many a bargain, if you strike it:
This is London! How d'ye like it?

John Bancks (1738)

Introduction

I

London has evolved, if not by mistake, then haphazard. It is not a great capital city in the sense that Rome, St Petersburg or Paris are great capitals. There has been no English Peter the Great, or Sixtus the Fifth, or Louis Quatorze, or Napoleon; hence in London no despot was ever in a position to level the place to the ground and start again, or to plan it according to some great design. There are those who deplore this fact. Even in our own day, the Prince of Wales has made a television programme saying that he wished that London was more like Paris – and presumably he would like to be the royal grandee who oversaw the creation of such a grand metropolis. If he were allowed his way he would, for example, destroy the development of buildings on the South Bank that includes the National Theatre, the Hayward Gallery, the Queen Elizabeth Hall and the National Film Theatre. Had he the power of a Napoleon or a Peter the Great, he would probably do so. But by making such a fantasy known, His Royal Highness suggests that he has fundamentally misunderstood the nature of London. As a city, it has not had a very stoutly royalist history. The City of London saw the humiliation of Richard II and the City of Westminster saw the execution of Charles I. Most of the British monarchs have lived in London and some, such as Charles I and George IV, have adorned it. But it was never, like Paris, a royal city. Nor, though many great *palazzi* in London (most of them now destroyed) have housed the aristocracy of Great Britain, has it been of its essence an aristocratic place. Its grandees have been merchants and businessmen; its *raison d'être* has been commerce; its flavour has been unashamedly bourgeois. It is highly appropriate that the first lines which most of us ever hear about London concern the voices of the bells; and it is equally appropriate that the bells of London are not singing an ethereal song, but are tolling out thoughts about money. It would be a naïve child who thought that the oranges and lemons advertised by St Clements were going free – the church bells are not summoning the faithful to worship, but wondering when Old Bailey will be paid and when the Bells of Shoreditch will overcome the under-capitalized position in which the auditors found them at the end of the last financial year.

Though London contains much magnificent architecture, some splendid parks and innumerable wonderful churches, put there by kings, bishops and noble lords, it is chiefly a commercial and bourgeois creation: the merchants have built its streets and squares, and, lacking a tyrant, it has had no over-all plan. Consequently, purists have arisen in every generation to suppose that it has been spoilt beyond redemption. It was not the Prince of Wales but Percy Hunter addressing the architectural association a century earlier, in 1885, who was sad to say that

> the law and order which we boast of in our civil life is absolutely wanting in the architecture of our metropolis. There is absolutely nothing expressive about it, except that of intense selfishness and utter disregard of subordination to general convenience; a reign of anarchy where every man does what is right in his own eyes, and what is wrong in the eyes of all his neighbours . . .*

In fact London has adapted itself and rebuilt itself according to its changing needs, and often in brutal disregard for what would now be described as its 'heritage'.

The Georgians and the Victorians churned up London and rebuilt it according to their own domestic and commercial requirements with as little sensitivity as any modern planner. Much-loved parks, markets, streets and squares in one generation have made way for railways, roads, canals in another. Dickens, in describing Mr Dombey's Georgian house (which most of us today would consider beautiful), sees something soulless and geometrical; but, in the same novel, describing the carving up of Camden Town for the railway, Dickens is as sentimental as any modern conservationist.

I think that the disparate nature of the metropolis has shaped my own sense of London. As a provincial who made frequent visits to the capital, and eventually settled there, I found it difficult to connect the many different Londons which I had come to know – to connect them physically as well as imaginatively. Hence the difficulty felt by many out-of-towners in finding

---

* Donald J. Olsen, *The Growth of Victorian London* (Batsford, 1976), p. 71.

their way about. There is no logic to London. Walk a mile and you can take
in the Reading Room in the British Museum, the seediest pubs in Soho, the
splendours of clubland and the beauties of St James's Park. Walk on another
mile and you can traverse the dingy villages of Victoria and Pimlico, the
grandeur of Belgravia, and then find yourself in Chelsea, with all its mis-
hmash of the magnificent and the raffish – the stately Hospital dividing the
river from the faded modishness of the boutiques in the King's Road.
Nothing but accident explains why one or another of these areas grew up as
it did, so different from its immediate neighbour. London is both a collection
of villages slung chaotically together and it is an idea, almost a metaphysical
entity in the minds of those who contemplate it. London as actually experienced by those who live there is, for most practical purposes, restricted to
the small area where they live and work. There are districts for these
millions of Londoners – Kensington, Balham or Holloway, or Kensal Rise
or Bloomsbury; but London as a unified whole is no more real than Troy.
Perhaps it is fitting that there were those who believed it to be another Troy.

II

On 17 February 1388, Sir Nicholas Brembre, formerly the Lord Mayor of
London, was impeached in the House of Lords at Westminster and condemned to death for treason.* The Lords decreed that he should be taken
back to the Tower of London and 'led from thence through the said city of
London to the place called Tyburn and hanged by the neck'. Brembre had
been on the side of Richard II during the Peasants' Revolt of 1381, when
the City of London was reduced to a state of anarchy by furious mobs.
In the years which followed, the King's enemies (those who would
eventually support Henry Bolingbroke in the rebellion which overthrew
Richard II and placed Henry IV on the throne) had triumphed, and Brembre's severity at the time of the Peasants' Uprising was held against him. He
was accused of taking twenty-two men out of Newgate Prison arbitrarily
and without trial and hanging them 'to encourage the others'. Among the
other crimes laid to the charge of this 'faulx Chevalier de Londres' was that
he had referred to London as the 'new Troy'.† It is hard, at this distance in

* *Dictionary of National Biography.*
† Thomas Walsingham Quondam Monachi S. Albani, *Historia Anglicana*, Rolls Series 28, vol.
II (1864), pp. 173–4.

time, to see why this should have been a hanging offence, but presumably it was deemed unlucky, and therefore treasonable, to associate London with a city which was burned to the ground by its enemies.

History is written by victors, not losers. If we believed Shakespeare's Richard II, we should imagine that all that unhappy monarch's followers were effete, corrupt men – 'the caterpillars of the kingdom'. That is because Shakespeare, writing two hundred years after Richard II's day, was on the side of Bolingbroke, the ancestor of the Tudors. In fact, there would not appear to have been anything more markedly corrupt about Sir Nicholas Brembre than about his enemies. Certainly, as a man with friends in the great city companies, above all the Fishmongers and the Grocers, there was nothing very effete about him. As well as being Lord Mayor from 1377 for two years, he was also, from 1379 to 1386, one of the two collectors of customs for the port of London. His Comptroller of Customs is rather more famous than he is today – a poet called Geoffrey Chaucer.

Chaucer's great poetic contemporary at the court of Richard II was John Gower, whose handsome painted tomb may be seen to this day in South-wark Cathedral. In his Latin poem *Vox Clamantis** – 10,265 lines of elegiacs in imitation of Ovid – Gower, who must have known of the charge against Brembre, takes up the theme of London as a new or 'little Troy', founded by that Trojan refugee Brutus who gave his name to Britain. We do not know where the idea originated, but it first appears in Geoffrey of Monmouth's fanciful history of Britain. As John Stow reminds us, in his *Survey of London*, published towards the close of the sixteenth century,

> As the Romane writers to glorifie the citie of *Rome* drew the originall thereof from Gods and demie Gods, by the Troian progenie: so *Giffrey* of *Monmouth* the Welsh Historian, deduceth the foundation of this famous Citie of *London*, for the greater glorie therof, and emulation of *Rome*, from the very same originall. For he reporteth that *Brute*, lineally descended from the demy god *Eneas*, the sonne of *Venus*, daughter of *Iupiter*, about the yeare of the world 2855, and 1108, before the natiuitie of Christ, builded this city neare vnto the riuer now called *Thames*, and named it *Troynouant* or *Trenouant*.†

---

* *The Complete Works of John Gower*, edited by G.C. Macaulay, vol. 4, *The Latin Works* (Oxford at the Clarendon Press, 1902).
† John Stow, *A Survey of London*, with Introduction and Notes by Charles Lethbridge Kingsford (Oxford at the Clarendon Press, 1908).

The new Troy, London, differs from the old – Gower says in the *Vox Clamantis* – because there are no heroes in it.* It seems an apt description – a city which contains no Hector, and no Priam – nor is it threatened by heroes from without like Agamemnon or Achilles. Yet Gower, like the majority of Londoners, then and now, had a sense of it as a place which was doomed. He feared it would be destroyed by mob violence. Others have feared it would be destroyed by over-population, by pollution, by plague, by fire, by war. All these calamities have befallen it, and yet it survives and grows, an extraordinary and rather monstrous organic entity before which anyone compiling a 'Book of London' must stand in some awe.

In spite of the grandeur of modern London – the great dome of Wren's St Paul's, the wide sweep of the Mall leading down to Buckingham Palace, the great squares of Belgravia, the palatial clubs, the hundreds of churches – it remains a place whose life, when we consider it, seems most memorable in a much smaller scale than these large back-cloths would suggest.

Some years after the death of Chaucer and Gower, Thomas Hoccleve, another poet, tells us how he got up early one morning in his lodgings in Chester Inn (a now defunct Inn of Court, so called because of its proximity to the London residence of the Bishops of Chester) and went walking into the Strand. Hoccleve is one of the most autobiographical of writers. He tells us how much he hated his job at the Privy Seal Office, where his melancholy often descended into depression so acute that he was classified as a lunatic; he tells us about his misspent youth, his excessive drinking, his perpetual hangovers and his addiction to womanizing. As a young man, he liked to patronize the prostitutes who hung about near St Paul's Cathedral, but preferred merely to kiss them. In any case, like many lechers, he was also a prude, and although he himself talks about sex all the time, he blushes when others do so in his presence:

> Had I a kus, I was content ful weel,
> Bettere than I wolde han be with the deede:
> There-on can I but smal; it is no drede
> Whan that men speeke of it in my presence,
> For shame I wexe as reed as is the gleede.†

There is an extraordinary vividness about Hoccleve. He seems as real as one

---

* *Vox Clamantis*, l. 979 ff., e.g. 'Non hic Capaneus valuit, nec et ille Tideus / Non facit excursus iste vel ille ferox; / Non hic Palamades superat, neque nobilis Aiax / Nec regimen gladius Agamemnontis habet.'

† Thomas Hoccleve, *The Regement of Princes* (Early English Text Society, 1899), I. 155.

of the characters evoked by Jeffrey Bernard in his celebrated causeries from modern Soho. When Hoccleve, in the prologue to his long poem *The Regement of Princes*, falls into conversation with a beggar in the street, their conversation seems as real as if it were on a tape recorder, for all the formulaic and clumsy quality of the verse. Hoccleve tactlessly complains to the beggar that he has been working his guts out in the Privy Seal Office for twenty-four years and receives a measly 20 marks a year for his pains. (Actually rather a lot of money! Hoccleve must have had the classic depressive's belief that he was short of cash when he really had plenty.) The beggar tells him that he should count himself lucky he has not had to do manual labour. Hoccleve replies that being a 'writer' – by which he would seem to mean both a pen-pusher in an office and a poet – was no 'game' – it is much harder work than people think. The beggar, a moralist, does not really believe him, nor does he much sympathize with Hoccleve's obsessive dread of poverty, pointing out – not perhaps a very likely thing for a beggar to have at his finger's end, but who knows – that Scipio Africanus did not worry about money. Fame was what the noble Roman cared for – 'I gat Affrik, of that I haue renoun'.*

In the course of their rambling dialogue, we see more of contemporary London than we do in the greater poems of Chaucer (Hoccleve's old boss and literary hero) and Gower. The beggar hates the way that modern people dress. In his younger day, the lords dressed like lords and the middle classes acknowledged their lowlier station by wearing less ostentatious clothes. Now, jumped-up merchants have sleeves as long as great lords – in fact there are so many men in London with aristocratic long sleeves, complains the beggar, that you would hardly need to employ any street-cleaners:

> Now hath this lord but litil neede of broomes,
> To sweepe away the filthe out of the street,
> Syn syde sleves of pennylees gromes
> Wile it up likke, be it drye or wet.†

The beggar's complaint that 'fings ain't wot they used to be' seems to have been repeated by every subsequent generation of Londoners. Likewise, men looking back on their 'misspent youth' in London, probably embroider as much as Hoccleve did, or as Mr Justice Shallow in Shakespeare's *Henry IV* Part II. ('Jesu! Jesu! the mad days that I have spent'.‡)

---

* Hoccleve, *op. cit.*, I. 1163.
† *Ibid.*, 533 ff.
‡ *Henry IV* Part 2, III. ii. 35.

At about the time that Shakespeare's *Henry IV* plays were delighting their first London audiences, John Stow, of an old London family, was seeing his great *Survey* through the presses (first published 1598). By then Stow was an old man of seventy-three. His book is an invaluable source to historians, because, as his twentieth-century editor observes, 'he witnessed the passing of mediaevalism and the birth of the modern capital'.* As a boy he had seen the Dean and Chapter of St Paul's Cathedral, in their copes and vestments, with garlands and roses on their heads, receive a buck at the high altar of the cathedral on the feast of the commemoration of their patron saint. He had witnessed the Reformation, the Marian reaction, the establishment of the Elizabethan settlement; above all, for this obsessive chronicler of London history, he had watched his native town swell. As a boy he had known a London which was a small town surrounded by green fields. Many of its most beautiful buildings had been destroyed to make way for the new capital of an expanding mercantile power. In 1500, the population of London was perhaps no more than 75,000. By 1600, it had swollen to 220,000, and by 1650, it was 450,000. Stow's London threatened by its own commercial success to squash itself to death, as people swarmed into it, not only from disparate parts of the British Isles but also from the European continent. Overcrowding, plague and pestilence, with all their accompanying problems of crime and vagrancy, were to the pattern of London life until it was destroyed by fire in 1666, and it did not take long, after this opportunity to rebuild itself, for all the same problems to be repeated as it became by one and the same relentlessly capitalistic process both grossly richer and miserably poorer, and ever larger. And this process has continued for the subsequent three hundred years, and determined the flavour of life in the capital ever since the days of Pepys. One of the most extraordinary catalogues of urban misery ever compiled is a recent study by the American academic Peter Linebaugh: *The London Hanged: Crime and Civil Society in the Eighteenth Century.*† This book draws with terrifying clarity the world of whose existence we are made aware in Defoe, Gay, Fielding. One wonders, having read such a book, why the very stones of London do not cry out against the oppression under which the working class laboured; one certainly wonders why England escaped a political uprising akin to the French Revolution. There is no ultimate 'explanation' for why certain societies evolve and change as they

---

* Stow, *op. cit.*, xxix.
† Published by Allen Lane, The Penguin Press, 1991.

do; historians like Professor Linebaugh can only lead us by the arm into their particular version of the horror-show. Certainly, an essential ingredient in working-class culture in London, since such a class may be said to have existed, is the hard-edged, cynical quality of its humour. Professor Linebaugh concludes his book with a meditation on Punch and Judy:

> As Punch puts an end to wife and child, black servant and blind beggar, doctor and courtier, constable and hangman, he puts an end to the society that gave rise to the repressions of gender, race, class and law. This, so to speak, is the revolutionary side to Punch. In exercising his murderous rage against women, children, beggars and black people, Punch recapitulates, in the little motions of the puppeteer, larger, actual divisions within the London working class as a whole, in which rape, infanticide and the suppression of slave rebellion were mass experiences, recognizable and undeniable. The media of action in Punch and Judy are the stick and wit. Each could become anything Punch wanted, affirming, as it were, that both the tools and the words of the 1790s were human creations. Action contradicted words – the gallows became the orchard, the fiddle a mortal weapon, the stick became 'physic'. Words mean what those with power say they mean. The stick is Punch's dictionary. Old Nick does appear ('I know you have a great deal of business when you come to London'), a combat ensues, as terrific as Christian's struggle against Apollyon and Punch is triumphant. 'Huzza! Huzza! the Devil's dead!' and the show is over.*

It is perhaps no surprise that those Victorians with the most highly developed social conscience were also those with the most marked loathing of Georgian architecture and Georgian city-planning, just as in the 1960s it was those with the saddest conscience or the bitterest memories of the slums of thirty years previous who felt such hope in their hearts as the concrete tower blocks soared towards the clouds. A modern Londoner must sometimes feel that the place is being destroyed about his ears; but, historically, what is remarkable about the twentieth century (in spite of the Blitz and the architectural expansions and experiments of the late 1960s) is how intensely conservative Londoners have become. When one notes the huge number of Victorian buildings in London – stretching from the Houses of Parliament to the City, railway stations, hotels, blocks of flats,

---

* Linebaugh, *op. cit.*, p. 441.

department stores, government offices, tenements for the poor, churches, warehouses, fire stations, one realizes that Victorian London must have been a permanent building site. With what glee they wrenched out old monuments like Temple Bar across the Strand, and broke up the view of St Paul's Cathedral from that spot by building a cast-iron railway bridge across Ludgate Circus! An architectural historian has written,

> even in the eighteenth century Dr Johnson could exclaim over Lon-
> don's inexhaustible variety. But the variety of the 1890s was different
> in kind from the variety of the 1770s. It derived in large measure,
> paradoxically, from the very techniques of mass-production that
> ought to have imposed a deadening standardisation instead. But by
> making cheap and abundant use of what had once been dear and
> scarce, the new technology made London the prototype of the
> modern consumer society. Vulgar, competitive, raucous, often cruel, it
> yet did more to free than to oppress.*

There has been a perpetual conflict, ever since the growth of London as a great mercantile power, between these two polarities of liberation and oppression. Olsen's American idea that cruel, thrusting capitalistic systems provide an environment in which human beings can find freedom might have conceivably meant something to Charles Lamb, who lamented the decay of London beggars; but it is more questionable whether it would have meant much to those beggars themselves, either in Lamb's day, or Mayhew's, or our own. But the quality of London which Olsen notes – its vulgar cruelty, its hardness – is an essential part of its character, both in the past and in the present. That great London writer V. S. Pritchett once described the capital as a city which was 'as hard as nails'.

III

Anyone who loves London would have welcomed the chance to compile an anthology such as this; and quite inevitably this is a personal selection. The topographical and historical literature relating to London is vast, running to thousands of volumes; nearly all the great writers in the English language have been to London and had something to say about it at some point in

---

* Olsen, *op. cit.*, p. 128.

XV

their writings. So have a great number of non-English writers. It would be possible to compile twenty-five *Faber Books of London*, all as long as this one.

At times, as my boxes filled up with usable extracts, I have wondered whether I was compiling *The Faber Book of London* or *The Faber Book of Londoners*. For in spite of the fact that I delight in London as a place, and love its river, parks, buildings and streets, a large ingredient in my love of the place is its human associations. When Johnson said that when a man was tired of London he was tired of life he was not making a topographical or an architectural statement. I have never myself been bored in London, and I hope it does not sound whimsical to say that this is not merely because of its living population but also because of its dead. One of the pleasures of perambulating the London streets is to pass the large number of houses which carry on their walls a circular blue plaque announcing the former presence of some eminent person. To this day the various bodies who have been responsible for the putting up of these plaques have shown great imagination. In addition to the sort of statesmen who are commemorated in great monuments in Westminster Abbey, the blue plaques recall the presence of poverty-stricken painters like Benjamin Haydon, medical pioneers like Alexander Fleming, poor saints like Father Wainwright and rich philanthropists like Sir Moses Montefiore. I derive great pleasure that I live more or less equidistant from two such plaques, one recalling the presence of Dylan Thomas (his caravan is still in the garden) and the other the studio of Walter Sickert.

Thomas Hardy, when he went to see the Elgin Marbles in the British Museum, was haunted by the fact that these stones had echoed the voice of Paul. I am almost as moved by the fact that they have since echoed the voice of Thomas Hardy – not a famous Londoner, you would have thought, but he once appeared on the West End stage in *Ali Baba and the Forty Thieves*. (He played one of the thieves.) A London walk, for me, almost inevitably summons up the densely populated past. I work in Kensington, just behind the handsome house Thackeray built for himself and his daughters, and which he only lived for a year to enjoy. When I walk to have my lunch, I pass the house of John Stuart Mill, and the flat where T. S. Eliot lived and died. If I go home by bus I alight at the spot in Camden Town where Charles Dickens lived as a child just before the ignominy of the Blacking Factory. If the weather is fine, I walk up to Hampstead Heath – and pass the house where Keats lived. Sometimes, I will wander back by a circuitous route and pass the house where that charming old schoolmaster W. J. Cory lived – best known today for his translation, 'They told me, Heraclitus, they told me you were dead':

> Still are thy pleasant voices, thy nightingales awake
> For Death he taketh all away, but these he cannot take !

The names quoted in the last paragraph are all those of distinguished writers. We remember them because they have managed to articulate what their contemporaries in all probability felt but were unable to write. London, however, has not been, from generation to generation, a community of literate or intellectual men and women. The American poet watching the 'commuters' (as we should call them today) trudge over London Bridge each morning on their way to work in the City was reminded of the streams of departed souls in Dante filing into Purgatory, and exclaimed that he had not thought death had undone so many. There is something terrible about a cemetery in a large town – the graves (and, since cremation became popular, the memorial tablets) stretching as far as the eye can see; and though almost every stone and tablet claims it is erected in memory of someone, or even that it is sacred to the memory of someone else, these monuments, soon to be faded or overgrown, can do no more than postpone the everlasting oblivion into which we all drift. Indeed, when we walk in the older cemeteries of London, the memorial stones to those who died fifty, seventy, a hundred years ago merely emphasize the fact that these names (to whose sacred memory the stones were erected) have been sunk like the shades in the waters of Lethe. It is for that reason that I am so grateful to those writers who have used their gift to immortalize not only their own articulate sense of London but the inarticulate views of others. In the nineteenth century, the man who stands out as an observer of the London poor is Henry Mayhew. Before him in a much less thoroughgoing manner that devoted Londoner and keen Londonophile Charles Lamb was recalling with affection the 'benchers' in the Temple of his childhood and youth, and the beggars on the London streets before they were 'cleaned up' by the Poor Laws. It is very much in the tradition of Lamb and Mayhew that David Thomson wrote his inspired *In Camden Town*, an inspirational book for me, which combines observations of the author's contemporaries in this strange quarter of north London – the tramps, the young punks, the Irish, the Italians, the writers and intellectuals, being for the most part just about distinguishable – with reflections of the past, and with evocations of many lives which would have been unknown to us without this author's requiem: the children who did not even know their own names and were lured into the workhouses of Camden in the early nineteenth century; the Irish navvies who built the railways; the life of the bargees on the Regent's Park canal; the stall-holders in the Inverness Street Market. These were all Londoners, too, as well as the 'famous'. In fact, there is nothing sentimental about David Thomson's book, and there is nothing sentimental about the attempt to recapture the lives of 'nobodies' in London's past, whether it is through the medium of fantasy or through historical research. As I said at the beginning of this introduction, London is not a great 'capital city' in the planned, grandiose sense that this could be said of Paris or St Petersburg. It has very largely been inhabited by nobodies, and made up of nobodies. This is an anthology made up by a nobody – which perhaps explains, if it does not justify, the fact that so many of the following pages are devoted to people and incidents which by some criteria could be deemed 'trivial'. I belong to the school which believes that trivia is, by definition, the stuff of life. A man who is tired of trivia must be tired of London . . .

1

The Face
on Waterloo Steps

This is not a chapter about down-and-outs or destitutes, though they come into it. I have taken my title for the chapter from John Cowper Powys's Wolf Solent. *In that novel, the face of a man glimpsed on Waterloo Steps becomes for the protagonist an archetype, an emblem of all the inexplicable human suffering in the world. Those who would see suffering at first hand could do worse than pace the streets of London. This is not because there are so many poor people: it is simply because there are so many people. Any city as populous as London must bring together a concentration of misery. We are more conscious of this in London than in smaller English towns, because so many of the population are not really at home there: the tourists mingle with a transient population who have drifted to London in search of work, or simply because it seemed like a good place to be.*

The theme of this chapter is desolation of one sort or another – Tennyson standing in Wimpole Street at dawn, grieving for a dead friend; Betjeman's sad couple, round the corner in Devonshire Street, discovering the worst after a cancer test, Ferdinand Mount's bedsit depressives who 'watched the day slip by in a gentle procession of snacks'. T. S. Eliot, while working as a banker, stood on London Bridge watching the commuters, as they would now be called, trudging to and from their dreary jobs, and was reminded of the lost souls in Dante crowding into the Purgatorial realms.

The face on Waterloo Steps

One of the suppressed emotions that had burst forth on that January afternoon had had to do with the appalling misery of so many of his fellow Londoners. He recalled the figure of a man he had seen on the steps outside Waterloo Station. The inert despair upon the face that this figure had turned towards him came between him now and a hillside covered with budding beeches. The face was repeated many times among those great curving masses of emerald-clear foliage. It was an English face; and it was also a Chinese face, a Russian face, an Indian face. It had the variableness of that Protean wine of the priestess Bacbuc. It was just the face of a man, of a mortal man, against whom Providence had grown as malignant as a mad dog. And the woe upon the face was of such a character that Wolf knew at once that no conceivable social readjustments or ameliorative revolutions could ever atone for it – could ever make up for the simple irremediable fact that it *had* been as it had been!

John Cowper Powys, Wolf Solent (1929)

Bedlam

The Hospitals in and about the City of *London*, deserve a little further Observation, especially those more remarkable for their Magnitude, as,

   I. *Bethlem* or *Bedlam*: This and *Bridewell*, indeed, go together, for though they are Two several Houses, yet they are Incorporated together, and have the same Governors; also the President, Treasurer, Clerk, Physician and Apothecary are the same; but the Stewards and the Revenue are different, and so are the Benefactions; but to both very great.

   The Orders for the Government of the Hospital of *Bethlem* are exceeding Good, and a remarkable Instance of the good Disposition of the Gentlemen concerned in it, especially these that follow;

1. That no Person, except the proper Officers who tend them, be allowed to see the Lunaticks of a *Sunday*.
2. That no Person be allowed to give the Lunaticks strong Drink, Wine, Tobacco or Spirits, and to sell any such thing in the Hospital.

3. That no Servant of the House shall take any Money given to any of the Lunaticks to their own Use; but that it shall be carefully kept for them till they are recovered, or laid out for them in such things as the Committee approves.
4. That no Officer or Servant shall beat or abuse, or offer any Force to any Lunatick; but on absolute Necessity. The rest of the Orders are for the good Government of the House.

Daniel Defoe, *A Tour Through the Whole Island of Great Britain* (1724–6)

In a London hospital

At last, after years of trying, I've finally landed the Spring Double. Pneumonia *and* pleurisy. I wonder how much Ladbroke's would have laid me against getting the two? Anyway, I'm back in St Stephens Hospital where I was first shown the yellow card in December 1965. But this is the first time I've ever been in a hospital for something that wasn't self-inflicted and that makes it seem somehow a little unfair. They didn't *conscript* kamikaze pilots.

The ward I'm in is called Ellen Terry and down the corridor there's a ward called Alfred Tennyson. I tried to get moved to Benny Green or Larry Adler but they're completely filled with industrial accidents: people who've fallen into typewriters etc. There are six of us in Ellen Terry. Mr Rice opposite has a dodgy lung and he also has diarrhoea which he reports to me on in graphic detail every 30 minutes or so. I think I hate him. Next to him there lies a sheer hulk, poor Mr Collander, whose bladder is up the spout. Then there's Mr Handley, a costermonger from Fulham, who is rather delightful really and who has cancer of the lung. He quite rightly got a little crotchety with a young doctor last week who told him to give up smoking. As he said, 'A little late for that fucking advice, isn't it?' My chest man and registrar is all right though, even if he has developed the habit of draining my right lung via a needle inserted into it under my shoulder blade. Sadly, his students who play games with me preparatory to taking their finals all suffer from halitosis. A couple of them couldn't diagnose a decapitation but I gather they'll qualify.

Jeffrey Bernard, *Low Life* (1992)

Wentworth Place: Keats Grove

The setting sun will always set me to rights . . .
Keats, to Benjamin Bailey

Keats fancied that the nightingale was happy
Because it sang. So beautiful his garden,
Behind the gate that shuts the present out
With all its greed and grimy noise,
I fall into a like mistake, to think –
Because there are such depths of peace and greenness,
Greenness and peace, because the mulberry
Invites with arms supported like the prophet,
Because the chestnut candles glimmer crimson –
That heartache could not flourish among these flowers,
Nor anguish resist the whisper of the leaves.

Angry for him, blessing his gift, I accuse
The paradise that could not save him,
Sickness and grief that sunsets could not heal.

Anne Ridler, *New and Selected Poems* (1988)

The blind beggar

How oft, amid those overflowing streets,
Have I gone forward with the crowd, and said
Unto myself, 'The face of every one
That passes by me is a mystery!'
Thus have I looked, nor ceased to look, oppressed
By thoughts of what and whither, when and how,
Until the shapes before my eyes became
A second-sight procession, such as glides
Over still mountains, or appears in dreams;
And once, far-travelled in such mood beyond
The reach of common indication, lost

Amid the moving pageant, I was smitten
Abruptly, with the view (a sight not rare)
Of a blind Beggar, who, with upright face,
Stood, propped against a wall, upon his chest
Wearing a written paper, to explain
His story, whence he came, and who he was.
Caught by the spectacle my mind turned round
As with the might of waters; and apt type
This label seemed of the utmost we can know,
Both of ourselves and of the universe;
And, on the shape of that unmoving man,
His steadfast face and sightless eyes, I gazed,
As if admonished from another world.

Though reared upon the base of outward things,
Structures like these the excited spirit mainly
Builds for herself; scenes different there are,
Full-formed, that take, with small internal help,
Possession of the faculties – the peace
That comes with night; the deep solemnity
Of nature's intermediate hours of rest,
When the great tide of human life stands still:
The business of the day to come, unborn,
Of that gone by, locked up, as in the grave;
The blended calmness of the heavens and earth.
Moonlight and stars, and empty streets, and sounds
Unfrequent as in deserts; at late hours
Of winter evenings, when unwholesome rains
Are falling hard, with people yet astir,
The feeble salutation from the voice
Of some unhappy woman, now and then
Heard as we pass, when no one looks about,
Nothing is listened to. But these, I fear,
Are falsely catalogued; things that are, are not,
As the mind answers to them, or the heart
Is prompt, or slow, to feel. What say you, then,
To times, when half the city shall break out
Full of one passion, vengeance, rage, or fear?

5

To executions, to a street on fire,
Mobs, riots, or rejoicings?

William Wordsworth, *The Prelude* (1850)

A Smithfield martyr

Of the long line of sufferers for the Protestant faith, generally on the question of transubstantiation, in the reign of Henry VIII, perhaps the most remarkable was Sir William Askew's beautiful daughter, Anne, whom Wriothesley, the Lord Chancellor, tortured with his own hands, and who lost the use of her feet by her extreme sufferings upon the rack to make her disclose the names of those court ladies of Queen Catherine Parr who shared her opinions. The account in Foxe of her death is too pictorial to omit.

> The day of her execution (1546) being appointed, this good woman was brought into Smithfield in a chair, because she could not go on her feet, by means of her great torments. When she was brought unto the stake, she was tied by the middle with a chain, that held up her body. When all things were thus prepared to the fire, Dr Shaxton,* who was then appointed to preach, began his sermon. Anne Askew, hearing and answering again unto him, when he said well, confirmed the same; when he said amiss, 'There,' said she, 'he misseth, and speaketh without the book.'
>
> The sermon being finished, the martyrs, standing there tied at three several stakes ready to their martyrdom, began their prayers. The multitude and concourse of the people was exceeding; the place where they stood being railed about to keep out the press. Upon the bench under St Bartholomew's Church sate Wriothesley, chancellor of England; the old Duke of Norfolk, the old Earl of Bedford, the Lord Mayor, with divers others. Before the fire should be set unto them, one of the bench, hearing that they had gunpowder about them, and being alarmed lest the faggots, by strength of the gunpowder, would come flying about their ears, began to be afraid; but the Earl of

---

* The renegade Bishop of Salisbury.

6

Bedford, declaring unto him how the gunpowder was not laid under the faggots, but only about their bodies, to rid them out of their pain; which having vent, there was no danger to them of the faggots, so diminished that fear.

Then Wriothesley, lord chancellor, sent to Anne Askew letters, offering her the king's pardon if she would recant; who, refusing once to look upon them, made this answer again, that she came not thither to deny her Lord and Master. Then were the letters likewise offered to the others, who, in like manner, following the constancy of the woman, denied not only to receive them, but also to look upon them. Whereupon the Lord Mayor, commanding fire to be put unto them, cried with a loud voice, 'Fiat Justitia!'

And thus the good Anne Askew, with these blessed martyrs, being troubled so many manner of ways, and having passed through so many torments, now ended the long course of her agonies, being compassed in with flames of fire.

Augustus Hare, *Walks in London* (1878)

A London heart

From the wash the laundress sends
My collars home with ravelled ends:
I must fit, now these are frayed,
My neck with new ones London-made.

Homespun collars, homespun hearts,
Wear to rags in foreign parts.
Mine at least's as good as done,
And I must get a London one.

A. E. Housman, *Collected Poems* (1955)

The Father of the Marshalsea

Thirty years ago there stood, a few doors short of the church of Saint George, in the borough of Southwark, on the left-hand side of the way going southward, the Marshalsea Prison. It had stood there many years before, and it remained there some years afterwards; but it is gone now, and the world is none the worse without it.

It was an oblong pile of barrack building, partitioned into squalid houses standing back to back, so that there were no back rooms; environed by a narrow paved yard, hemmed in by high walls duly spiked at top. Itself a close and confined prison for debtors, it contained within it a much closer and more confined jail for smugglers. Offenders against the revenue laws, and defaulters to excise or customs, who had incurred fines which they were unable to pay, were supposed to be incarcerated behind an iron-plated door, closing up a second prison, consisting of a strong cell or two, and a blind alley some yard and a half wide, which formed the mysterious termination of the very limited skittle-ground in which the Marshalsea debtors bowled down their troubles.

Supposed to be incarcerated there, because the time had rather outgrown the strong cells and the blind alley. In practice they had come to be considered a little too bad, though in theory they were quite as good as ever; which may be observed to be the case at the present day with other cells that are not at all strong, and with other blind alleys that are stone-blind. Hence the smugglers habitually consorted with the debtors (who received them with open arms), except at certain constitutional moments when somebody came from some Office, to go through some form of overlooking something which neither he nor anybody else knew anything about. On those truly British occasions, the smugglers, if any, made a feint of walking into the strong cells and the blind alley, while this somebody pretended to do his something; and made a reality of walking out again as soon as he hadn't done it – neatly epitomising the administration of most of the public affairs in our right little, tight little island.

Charles Dickens, *Little Dorrit* (1857)

Writer without Hands

The next in order are the Writers without Hands and the Chalkers on Flag-stones.

A man of 61, born in the crippled state he described, tall, and with an intelligent look and good manners, gave me this account:

'I was born without hands – merely the elbow of the right arm and the joint of the wrist of the left. I have rounded stumps. I was born without feet also, merely the ankle and heel, just as if my feet were cut off close within the instep. My father was a farmer in Cavan county, Ireland, and gave me a fair education. He had me taught to write. I'll show you how, sir.' (Here he put on a pair of spectacles, using his stumps, and then holding the pen on one stump, by means of the other he moved the two together, and so wrote his name in an old-fashioned hand.) 'I was taught by an ordinary schoolmaster. I served an apprenticeship of seven years to a turner, near Cavan, and could work well at the turning, but couldn't chop the wood very well. I handled my tools as I've shown you I do my pen. I came to London in 1814, having a prospect of getting a situation in the India-house; but I didn't get it, and waited for eighteen months, until my funds and my father's help were exhausted, and then I took to making fancy screens, flower-vases, and hand-racks in the streets. I did very well at them, making 15s. to 20s. a week in the summer, and not half that, perhaps not much more than a third, in the winter. I continue this work still, when my health permits, and I now make handsome ornaments, flower-vases, &c. for the quality, and have to work before them frequently, to satisfy them. I could do very well but for ill-health. I charge from 5s. to 8s. for hand-screens, and from 7s. 6d. to 15s. for flower-vases. Some of the quality pay me handsomely – some are very near. I have done little work in the streets this way, except in very fine weather. Sometimes I write tickets in the street at a halfpenny each. The police never interfere unless the thoroughfare is obstructed badly. My most frequent writing is, "Naked came I into the world, and naked I shall return." "The Lord giveth, and the Lord taketh away; blessed be the name of the Lord." '

Henry Mayhew, *Mayhew's London* (1851)

9

So many destitute people

Monday, 19 January 1981

I have never seen so many destitute people sitting for warmth in Cam. Tn
tube station as this year – not the usual drunks and winos. Last Monday on
my way to meet M. at St Pancras there was one large man in brown tatters
on the platform bench with his head bowed between his knees, motionless.
And on another bench an agitated tatterdemalion who was asking a strolling
passenger for the price of a cup of tea as I passed. He got some money. We
waited a long time for the train and I found it impossible to stop watching
him, his movements were so nervous – feet tapping or jerking, head up,
down and to one side, and all the time he kept wiping his skin, as much of it
as he could reach, with a neatly folded handkerchief – an unrumpled ironed
square which except for its blackish grime could have come straight from
the laundry. With this in the palm of his right hand, he rubbed his forehead
and cheeks, then his neck, shoulder and chest, reaching as far as he could
underneath his clothes. Then he changed hands and without unfolding the
handkerchief or even turning it over, so far as I could see, did the same to
his other side.

I went to give him 15p and felt pretty mean because I had a 10 bob bit in
my pocket not to speak of pound notes in the other, and I sat down beside
him hoping we would talk, but all he said was 'thank you' and, when I said

– How are you, he answered

– Not too bad.

He was thinly dressed, so he can't have been sweating unless from a
nervous habit. The bowed-down man had a heavy overcoat.

David Thomson, In Camden Town (1983)

Bereavement in Wimpole Street

> Dark house, by which once more I stand
>   Here in the long unlovely street,
>   Doors, where my heart was used to beat
> So quickly, waiting for a hand,

A hand that can be clasp'd no more –
Behold me, for I cannot sleep,
And like a guilty thing I creep
At earliest morning to the door.

He is not here; but far away
The noise of life begins again,
And ghastly thro' the drizzling rain
On the bald streets breaks the blank day.

Alfred, Lord Tennyson, *In Memoriam* (1850)

The morning after

The fact that my father should actually be walking past the Safeway Stores on Christmas Eve seemed to me as incredible as the legend of Glastonbury. That my father should walk past the Safeway Stores almost every morning, that his existence was not an occasional intrusion into my life like a comet which passes once in a millennium but rather itself amounted to nothing less than a life was not only incredible but intolerable.

Yet I knew in my mind that Dan and my father set out at half past ten sharp most days, as regular as a postman on his rounds. To start with, they walked briskly, looking neither to right nor to left, no dawdling here in the dry country. There was nothing to see but the occasional twitch of a curtain and a bleared face peering out to see what sort of a day it was or an old woman twirling a mop in a bucket on the doorstep. At best a dog-lover, with curlers veiled, letting her pooch sidle up to a lamp-post, might stir a wordless grimace from Dan and my father, hatred of dogs being one of their few common passions.

Inertia blanketed this dormitory of solitary bourgeois transients: middle-aged women separated from their husbands and behind with the rent, artistic Australians having difficulty with residence permits, thirty-five-year-old public-school men between jobs – will go anywhere, do anything legal – single ladies attending classes in bookbinding, widows come to London to die interestingly, and all sorts of people recovering, convalescing, undergoing treatment, in analysis, taking up theosophy, into encounter groups, taking things easy for a bit, making fresh starts or old endings.

Morning rarely lightened the windows of their dusty basements (or garden flats, as the letting agents liked to call them, though no flowers could have bloomed there since the time when my father's great-grandmother was said to have skated on the Pimlico marshes) and even when a ray of light did manage to straggle through they were not there to greet it. Some had already left in the dark for the travel agencies, photographer's studios and interior decorating shops where they watched the day slip by in a gentle procession of snacks – coffee-and-biscuits, yoghurt-and-salad, tea-and-biscuits and a quick one round the corner on the way home. Others were still savouring their power-assisted sleep, the last traces of mogadon, kif and highland cream sweetly flavouring their dreams of past extravagance and future sobriety. Today they would sand the floor, visit their trustees, get the place really cleaned up, start their exercises, but for the moment they would have one last lie-in.

Ferdinand Mount, The Man Who Rode Ampersand (1975)

Pepys and the Plague

7 June 1665

This day, much against my Will, I did in Drury-lane see two or three houses marked with a red cross upon the doors, and 'Lord have mercy upon us' writ there* – which was a sad sight to me, being the first of that kind that to my remembrance I ever saw. It put me into an ill conception of myself and my smell, so that I was forced to buy some roll=tobacco to smell to and chew – which took away the apprehension.†

8th. About 5 a-clock my wife came home, it having lightened all night hard, and one great shower of rain. She came and lay upon the bed. I up, and to the office, where all the morning. I alone at home to dinner, my wife, mother, and Mercer dining at W. Joyces, I giving her a caution to go round by the Half-Moone to his house, because of the plague.

---

* This proved to be a heavily infected area. The red cross had, by a city regulation, to be one foot high and the houses so marked were shut up (often with the victims inside) for forty days.

† In the Plague tobacco was highly valued. Thomas Hearne (writing in 1721) has the story that no tobacconist in London died of the Great Plague. He adds that at Eton one boy was flogged for being discovered not smoking.

21 August

I was forced to walk it in the dark, at 10 a-clock at night, with Sir J. Mennes's George with me – being mightily troubled for fear of the Dogs at Coome farme, and more for fear of rogues by way, and yet more because of the plague which is there (which is very strange, it being a single house, all alone from the town; but it seems they use to admit beggars (for their own safety) to lie in their barns, and they brought it to them); but I bless God, I got about 11 of the clock well to my wife; and giving 4s. in recompence to George, I to my wife; and having first viewed her last piece of drawing since I saw her (which is seven or eight days), which pleases me beyond anything in the world, I to bed with great content – but weary.

22nd. Up; and after much pleasant talk, and being importuned by my wife and her two maids (which are both good wenches) for me to buy a necklace of pearl for her, and I promising to give her one of 60*l* in two year at furthest, and in less if she pleases me in her painting,* I went away and walked to Greenwich, in my way seeing a coffin with a dead body therein, dead of the plague, lying in an open close belonging to Coome farme, which was carried out last night and the parish hath not appointed anybody to bury it – but only set a watch there day and night, that nobody should go thither or come thence, which is a most cruel thing – this disease making us more cruel to one another then we are [to] dogs.

3 September

Lords day. Up, and put on my colourd silk suit, very fine, and my new periwigg, bought a good while since, but darst not wear it because the plague was in Westminster when I bought it. And it is a wonder what will be the fashion after the plague is done as to periwigs, for nobody will dare to buy any haire for fear of the infection – that it had been cut off the heads of people dead of the plague.

Samuel Pepys, Diary

---

* On 30 April 1666 she bought one costing £80.

Johnson's kindness

His generous humanity to the miserable was almost beyond example. The following instance is well attested: Coming home late one night, he found a poor woman lying in the street, so much exhausted that she could not walk; he took her upon his back, and carried her to his house, where he discovered that she was one of those wretched females who had fallen into the lowest state of vice, poverty, and disease. Instead of harshly upbraiding her, he had her taken care of with all tenderness for a long time, at considerable expence, till she was restored to health and endeavoured to put her into a virtuous way of living.

James Boswell, *Life of Johnson* (1791)

The feet of the woman tramp

The feet of the woman tramp, or street vendor – it is the same thing – are very pitiful to see. They are almost non-human in their shapelessness. Callosities, horny growths, bunions, destroy their contours, running sores are perennial and the efforts of Nature to escape the pain of contact with rough leather, result in distortion of the bone. Ingrowing nails are common; how should it be otherwise? The care of the feet calls for plentiful hot water and requisite toilet accessories; and these women, of whom I write, have not the means to wash their sores. There is, of course, due bathing accommodation in the casual ward of a workhouse, but as I shall show, the thing that survives longest and most fiercely among the destitute, is a passionate fear of restriction, the horror of detention within four walls, under a strange roof. For this reason before they will ask a night's lodging of the Poor Law Guardians they will push endurance to an inhuman limit.

This is especially the case with the outcasts of the London streets. These women who have taken to the road and go out into the country have accustomed themselves to the casual ward, have assimilated every twist and turn of the law, and know to a nicety what they must do, and what the master has not the power to enforce.

Mrs Cecil Chesterton, *In Darkest London* (1926)

Jo, the Crossing-Sweeper

'For *I* don't,' says Jo, '*I* don't know nothink.'

It must be a strange state to be like Jo! To shuffle through the streets, unfamiliar with the shapes, and in utter darkness as to the meaning, of those mysterious symbols, so abundant over the shops, and at the corners of streets, and on the doors, and in the windows! To see people read, and to see people write, and to see the postmen deliver letters and not to have the least idea of all that language – to be to every scrap of it, stone blind and dumb. It must be very puzzling to see the good company going to the churches on Sundays, with their books in their hands, and to think (for perhaps Jo *does* think, at odd times) what does it all mean, and if it means anything to anybody, how comes it that it means nothing to me? To be hustled, and jostled, and moved on; and really to feel that it would appear to be perfectly true that I have no business, here, or there, or anywhere; and yet to be perplexed by the consideration that I *am* here somehow, too, and everybody overlooked me until I became the creature that I am! It must be a strange state, not merely to be told that I am scarcely human (as in the case of my offering myself for a witness), but to feel it of my own knowledge all my life! To see the horses, dogs, and cattle, go by me, and to know that in ignorance I belong to them, and not to the superior beings in my shape, whose delicacy I offend! Jo's ideas of a Criminal Trial, or a Judge, or a Bishop, or a Government, or that inestimable jewel to him (if he only knew it) the Constitution, should be strange! His whole material and immaterial life is wonderfully strange; his death, the strangest thing of all.

Jo comes out of Tom-all-Alone's, meeting the tardy morning which is always late in getting down there, and munches his dirty bit of bread as he comes along. His way lying through many streets, and the houses not yet being open, he sits down to breakfast on the door-step of the Society for the Propagation of the Gospel in Foreign Parts, and gives it a brush when he has finished, as an acknowledgement of the accommodation. He admires the size of the edifice, and wonders what it's all about. He has no idea, poor wretch, of the spiritual destitution of a coral reef in the Pacific, or what it costs to look up the precious souls among the cocoa-nuts and bread-fruit.

He goes to his crossing, and begins to lay it out for the day. The town awakes; the great tee-totum is set up for its daily spin and whirl; all that unaccountable reading and writing, which has been suspended for a few hours, recommences. Jo, and the other lower animals, get on in the unintelligible mess as they can. It is market-day. The blinded oxen, over-goaded, over-driven, never guided, run into wrong places and are beaten out; and plunge, red-eyed and foaming, at stone walls; and often sorely hurt the innocent, and often sorely hurt themselves. Very like Jo and his order; very, very like!

A band of music comes and plays. Jo listens to it. So does a dog – a drover's dog, waiting for his master outside a butcher's shop, and evidently thinking about those sheep he has had upon his mind for some hours, and is happily rid of. He seems perplexed respecting three or four; can't remember where he left them; looks up and down the street, as half expecting to see them astray; suddenly pricks up his ears and remembers all about it. A thoroughly vagabond dog, accustomed to low company and public-houses; a terrific dog to sheep; ready at a whistle to scamper over their backs, and tear out mouthfuls of their wool; but an educated, improved, developed dog, who has been taught his duties and knows how to discharge them. He and Jo listen to the music, probably with much the same amount of animal satisfaction; likewise, as to awakened association, aspiration or regret, melancholy or joyful reference to things beyond the senses, they are probably upon a par. But, otherwise, how far above the human listener is the brute!

Turn that dog's descendants wild, like Jo, and in a very few years they will so degenerate that they will lose even their bark – but not their bite.

The day changes as it wears itself away, and becomes dark and drizzly. Jo fights it out, at his crossing, among the mud and wheels, the horses, whips, and umbrellas, and gets but a scanty sum to pay for the unsavoury shelter of Tom-all-Alone's. Twilight comes on; gas begins to start up in the shops; the lamplighter, with his ladder, runs along the margin of the pavement. A wretched evening is beginning to close in.

Charles Dickens, *Bleak House* (1853)

The Demon Lover

The rain had stopped; the pavements steamily shone as Mrs Drover let herself out by inches from her own front door into the empty street. The unoccupied houses opposite continued to meet her look with their damaged stare. Making towards the thoroughfare and the taxi, she tried not to keep looking behind. Indeed, the silence was so intense – one of those creeks of London silence exaggerated this summer by the damage of war – that no tread could have gained on hers unheard. Where her street debouched on the square where people went on living, she grew conscious of, and checked, her unnatural pace. Across the open end of the square two buses impassively passed each other: women, a perambulator, cyclists, a man wheeling a barrow signalized, once again, the ordinary flow of life. At the square's most populous corner should be – and was – the short taxi rank. This evening, only one taxi – but this, although it presented its blank rump, appeared already to be alertly waiting for her. Indeed, without looking round the driver started his engine as she panted up from behind and put her hand on the door. As she did so, the clock struck seven. The taxi faced the main road: to make the trip back to her house it would have to turn – she had settled back on the seat and the taxi *had* turned before she, surprised by its knowing movement, recollected that she had not 'said where'. She leaned forward to scratch at the glass panel that divided the driver's head from her own.

The driver braked to what was almost a stop, turned round and slid the glass panel back: the jolt of this flung Mrs Drover forward till her face was almost into the glass. Through the aperture driver and passenger, not six inches between them, remained for an eternity eye to eye. Mrs Drover's mouth hung open for some seconds before she could issue her first scream. After that she continued to scream freely and to beat with her gloved hands on the glass all round as the taxi, accelerating without mercy, made off with her into the hinterland of deserted streets.

Elizabeth Bowen, *Collected Stories* (1983)

A wilderness

The maze of little streets threading through the wilderness, the broken walls, the great pits with their dense forests of bracken and bramble, golden ragwort and coltsfoot, fennel and foxglove and vetch, all the wild rambling shrubs that spring from ruin, the vaults and cellars and deep caves, the wrecked guildhalls that had belonged to saddlers, merchant tailors, haberdashers, wax-chandlers, barbers, brewers, coopers, and coachmakers, all the ancient city fraternities, the broken office stairways that spiralled steeply past empty doorways and rubbled closets into the sky, empty shells of churches with their towers still strangely spiring above the wilderness, their empty window arches where green boughs pushed in, their broken pavement floors – St Vedast's, St Alban's, St Anne's and St Agnes's, St Giles Cripplegate, its tower high above the rest, the ghosts of churches burnt in an earlier fire, St Olave's and St John Zachary's, haunting the green-flowered churchyards that bore their names, the ghosts of taverns where merchants and clerks had drunk, of restaurants where they had eaten – all this scarred and haunted green and stone and brambled wilderness lying under the August sun, a-hum with insects and astir with secret, darting, burrowing life, received the returned traveller into its dwellings with a wrecked, indifferent calm. Here, its cliffs and chasms and caves seemed to say, is your home; here you belong; you cannot get away, you do not wish to get away, for this is the maquis that lies about the margins of the wrecked world, and here your feet are set; here you find the irremediable barbarism that comes up from the depth of the earth, and that you have known elsewhere. 'Where are the roots that clutch, what branches grow, out of this stony rubbish? Son of man, you cannot say, or guess. . . .' But you can say, you can guess, that it is you yourself, your own roots, that clutch the stony rubbish, the branches of your own being that grow from it and from nowhere else.

Rose Macaulay, *The World My Wilderness* (1950)

Devonshire Street W1

The heavy mahogany door with its wrought-iron screen
   Shuts. And the sound is rich, sympathetic, discreet.
The sun still shines on this eighteenth-century scene
   With Edwardian faience adornments – Devonshire Street.

No hope. And the X-ray photographs under his arm
   Confirm the message. His wife stands timidly by.
The opposite brick-built house looks lofty and calm
   Its chimneys steady against a mackerel sky.

No hope. And the iron nob of this palisade
   So cold to the touch, is luckier now than he

'Oh merciless, hurrying Londoners! Why was I made
　For the long and the painful deathbed coming to me?'

She puts her fingers in his as, loving and silly,
　At long-past Kensington dances she used to do
'It's cheaper to take the tube to Piccadilly
　And then we can catch a nineteen or a twenty-two.'

John Betjeman, Collected Poems (1970)

Oscar Wilde at Clapham Junction

Everything about my tragedy has been hideous, mean, repellent, lacking in style; our very dress makes us grotesque. We are the zanies of sorrow. We are clowns whose hearts are broken. We are specially designed to appeal to the sense of humour. On November 13th, 1895, I was brought down here from London. From two o'clock till half-past two on that day I had to stand on the centre platform of Clapham Junction in convict dress, and handcuffed, for the world to look at. I had been taken out of the hospital ward without a moment's notice being given to me. Of all possible objects I was the most grotesque. When people saw me they laughed. Each train as it came up swelled the audience. Nothing could exceed their amusement. That was, of course, before they knew who I was. As soon as they had been informed they laughed still more. For half an hour I stood there in the grey November rain surrounded by a jeering mob.

For a year after that was done to me I wept every day at the same hour and for the same space of time. That is not such a tragic thing as possibly it sounds to you. To those who are in prison tears are a part of every day's experience. A day in prison on which one does not weep is a day on which one's heart is hard, not a day on which one's heart is happy.

Oscar Wilde, De Profundis (1949)

A deathly crowd

Unreal City,
Under the brown fog of a winter dawn,
A crowd flowed over London Bridge, so many,
I had not thought death had undone so many.
Sighs, short and infrequent, were exhaled,
And each man fixed his eyes before his feet.
Flowed up the hill and down King William Street,
To where Saint Mary Woolnoth kept the hours
With a dead sound on the final stroke of nine.
There I saw one I knew, and stopped him, crying: 'Stetson!
'You who were with me in the ships at Mylae!
'That corpse you planted last year in your garden,
'Has it begun to sprout? Will it bloom this year?
'Or has the sudden frost disturbed its bed?
'O keep the Dog far hence, that's friend to men,
'Or with his nails he'll dig it up again!
'You! hypocrite lecteur! – mon semblable, – mon frère!'

T. S. Eliot, *The Waste Land* (1922)

2

Out and About

Visitors to London, particularly if they are children, have a tendency to suppose that it is a collection of 'sights', linked together by bus routes or by the underground railway. There is some truth in this. Those, however, who have done no more than dash about from the Tower to Madame Tussaud's, from Trafalgar Square to the Trocadero at Piccadilly Circus, from the Natural History Museum to Westminster Abbey, will not have begun to taste the capital's true flavour. This is best done on foot, and unhurriedly. Then the multiplicity of human life in London and its strangeness will begin to sink in, and the visitor will begin to see some of what fascinated the eighteenth-century poet John Gay in his unforgettable poem Trivia *– 'Of Walking the Streets'. One could fill a book with the 'ordinary' London scene. I have begun this section with the painter Benjamin Haydon's stroll in the Park; I have ended it with the poet John Betjeman, as a child, taking a tram-ride through north London to his parent's house in High-gate. For the architecturally-minded, such journeys will become, as they did for Betjeman when he grew up, or as they were for the Victorian aesthete Augustus Hare, a perpetual journey of discovery. (Some such aestheticism is to be found in Geoffrey Fletcher's ruminations in some of the 'interesting' lavatories of London.) This is not, however, intended to be a chapter of aesthetic appreciation. It is meant, instead, to convey some of the quality of life in the city inhabited by Benjamin Haydon's 'ants' – the street-sellers observed by Mayhew, the market stalls known by Dickens and the department stores beloved of Osbert Lancaster's aunt; the night streets, where Johnson innocently larked about with his much younger friends, and where William Hickey was to make his probably less innocent expeditions in search of amusement; the Turkish baths where Jeff Bernard slept off 'a night on the tiles' or exchanged betting tips with jockeys.*

Perhaps I should have had one extract describing London when it is deserted and empty, but, as Sir Stephen Spender discovers in a memorable entry in his diary here, even when you think yourself alone, walking down a London street, late at night, there might still be an audience in the shadows.

Ants

6 *June 1825*

As I strolled for an hour in the Park today and distantly contemplated the string of fashion – how like ants!, I thought. There goes a little yellow looking box, and two little things with four legs & one little insect driving them, & one behind the box, and something, a living insect, behind inside, and these little boxes & insects constituted superiority! and other little insects that seemed crawling by the side seemed to do so in great ease, for these boxes [and] four legged insects gave evidence of fashion & rank. These were the queen insects, and yet no insect there but had a conscious-ness of existence, as if it was a God! fancied itself born to be immortal! to live in endless bliss, endless torment.

No man can have a just estimation of the insignificance of his species, unless he has been up in an air balloon.

Then came by a two legged insect on a four legged one which seemed to obey it, and behind came another, as if it followed the same path, and the two legged insect before had a sort of command on the two legged insect behind; and it bristled up its little head with a white, tight little thing round its little neck, and a black spot on its head, and immediately the two legged insect behind took off its little black spot and waited. I was very much amused with their curious little manoeuvres, of these little insects, and said to myself, 'I daresay now, these insects have their passions & loves, their hopes & fears, like larger beings.' Wonderful, to be sure. Such is the condescension of the Creator!

Benjamin Haydon, *Diary* (1960–3)

The journey from Deptford

11 April 1661

We waited at Dartford, and thence to London.

But of all the journeys that ever I made, this was the merriest, and I was in a strange moode for mirth. Among other things, I got my Lady to let her maid, Mrs Ann, to ride all the way on horseback – and she rides exceeding well. And so I called [her] my clerk, that she went to wait upon me.

I met two little schoole-boys, going with pichers of ale to their schoolmaster to break up against Easter; and I did drink of some of one of them and give him two pence.

By and by we came to two little girls keeping cowes; and I saw one of them very pretty, so I had a minde to make her aske my blessing. And telling that I was her godfather, she asked me innocently whether I was not Ned Wooding, and I said that I was; so she kneeled down and very simply cried, 'Pray, godfather, pray to God to bless me' – which made us very merry and I gave her twopence.

In several places I asked women whether they would Sell me their children; that they denied me all, but said they would give me one to keep for them if I would.

Mrs Ann and I rode under the man that hangs upon Shooters hill;* and a filthy sight it was to see how his flesh is shrunk to his bones.

So home. And I find all well, and a good deal of work done since I went.

Samuel Pepys, *Diary*

---

* A highwayman: it was common to erect gallows at the scene of the crime. The body of the malefactor would sometimes be soaked in tar to preserve it. Shooter's Hill, about eight miles out of London, was one of the most dangerous points on the Dover Road; the way was steep, narrow and fringed by woods. Many robberies were committed there until, under an act of 1739, a new road was built up the hill.

Outward shows

When we look round us, and behold the strange variety of faces and persons which fill the streets with business and hurry, it is no unpleasant amusement to make guesses at their different pursuits, and judge by their countenances what it is that so anxiously engages their present attention. Of all this busy crowd, there are none who would give a man inclined to such inquiries better diversion for his thoughts, than those whom we call good courtiers, and such as are assiduous at the levées of great men. These worthies are got into a habit of being servile with an air, and enjoy a certain vanity in being known for understanding how the world passes. In the pleasure of this they can rise early, go abroad sleek and well-dressed, with no other hope or purpose, but to make a bow to a man in court favour, and be thought, by some insignificant smile of his, not a little engaged in his interests and fortunes. It is wondrous, that a man can get over the natural existence and possession of his own mind so far as to take delight either in paying or receiving such cold and repeated civilities. But what maintains the humour is, that outward show is what most men pursue, rather than real happiness. Thus both the idol, and idolater, equally impose upon themselves in pleasing their imaginations this way. But as there are very many of her majesty's good subjects who are extremely uneasy at their own seats in the country, where all from the skies to the centre of the earth is their own, and have a mighty longing to shine in courts, or to be partners in the power of the world; I say, for the benefit of these, and others who hanker after being in the whisper with great men, and vexing their neighbours with the changes they would be capable of making in the appearance of a country sessions, it would not methinks be amiss to give an account of that market for preferment, a great man's levée.

For aught I know, this commerce between the mighty and their slaves, very justly represented, might do so much good, as to incline the great to regard business rather than ostentation; and make the little know the use of their time too well to spend it in vain applications and addresses. The famous doctor in Moorfields, who gained so much reputation for his horary predictions, is said to have had in his parlour different ropes to little bells which hung in the room above stairs, where the doctor thought fit to be oraculous. If a girl had been deceived by her lover, one bell was pulled; and if a peasant had lost a cow, the servant rung another. This method was kept in respect to all other passions and concerns, and the skilful waiter below sifted the inquirer, and gave the doctor notice accordingly. The levée of a great man is laid after the same manner, and twenty whispers, false alarms, and private intimations, pass backward and forward from the porter, the valet, and the patron himself, before the gaping crew, who are to pay their court, are gathered together. When the scene is ready, the doors fly open and discover his lordship.

There are several ways of making this first appearance. You may be either half-dressed, and washing yourself, which is indeed the most stately; but this way of opening is peculiar to military men, in whom there is something graceful in exposing themselves naked: but the politicians, or civil officers, have usually affected to be more reserved, and preserve a certain chastity of deportment. Whether it be hieroglyphical or not, this difference in the military and civil list, I will not say; but have ever understood the fact to be, that the close minister is buttoned up, and the brave officer open-breasted on these occasions.

However that is, I humbly conceive the business of a levée is to receive the acknowledgments of a multitude, that a man is wise, bounteous, valiant, and powerful. When the first shot of eyes is made, it is wonderful to observe how much submission the patron's modesty can bear, and how much servitude the client's spirit can descend to. In the vast multiplicity of business, and the crowd about him, my lord's parts are usually so great, that, to the astonishment of the whole assembly, he has something to say to every man there, and that so suitable to his capacity as any man may judge that it is not without talents men can arrive at great employments. I have known a great man ask a flag-officer, which way was the wind; a commander of horse the present price of oats: and a stock-jobber, at what discount such a fund was, with as much ease as if he had been bred to each of those several ways of life. Now this is extremely obliging; for at the same time that the patron informs himself of matters, he gives the person of whom he inquires an opportunity to exert himself. What adds to the pomp of those interviews is, that it is performed with the greatest silence and order imaginable. The patron is usually in the midst of the room, and some humble person gives him a whisper, which his lordship answers aloud, 'It is well. Yes, I am of your opinion. Pray inform yourself further, you may be sure of my part in it.' This happy man is dismissed, and my lord can turn himself to a business of a quite different nature, and off-hand give as good an answer as any great man is obliged to. For the chief point is to keep in generals; and if there be any thing offered that is particular, to be in haste.

But we are now in the height of the affair, and my lord's creatures have all had their whispers round to keep up the farce of the thing, and the dumb-show is become more general. He casts his eye to that corner, and there to Mr Such-a-one; to the other, 'And when did you come to town?' And perhaps just before he nods to another; and enters with him, 'But, Sir, I am glad to see you, now I think of it.' Each of those are happy for the next four-and-twenty hours; and those who bow in ranks undistinguished, and by dozens at a time, think they have very good prospects if they may hope to arrive at such notices half a year hence.

The satirist says, there is seldom common sense in high fortune; and one would think, to behold a levée, that the great were not only infatuated with their station, but also that they believed all below were seized too; else how is it possible they could think of imposing upon themselves and others in such a degree, as to set up a levée for any thing but a direct farce? But such is the weakness of our nature, that when men are a little exalted in their condition, they immediately conceive they have additional senses, and their capacities enlarged not only above other men, but above human comprehension itself. Thus it is ordinary to see a great man attend one listening, bow to one at a distance, and call to a third at the same instant. A girl in new ribands is not more taken with herself, nor does she betray more apparent coquetries, than even a wise man in such a circumstance of courtship. I do not know any thing that I ever thought so very distasteful as the affectation which is recorded of Caesar; to wit, that he would dictate to three several writers at the same time. This was an ambition below the greatness and candour of his mind. He indeed (if any man had pretensions to greater faculties than any other mortal) was the person; but such a way of acting is childish, and inconsistent with the manner of our being. It appears from the very nature of things, that there cannot be any thing effectually dispatched in the distraction of a public levée; but the whole seems to be a conspiracy of a set of servile slaves, to give up their own liberty to take away their patron's understanding.

Richard Steele, *The Spectator*, 11 October 1711

Of Walking the Streets by Night

THE EVENING

When Night first bids the twinkling Stars appear,
Or with her cloudy Vest inwraps the Air,
Then swarms the busie Street; with Caution tread,
Where the Shop-Windows falling threat thy Head;
Now Lab'rers home return, and join their Strength
To bear the tott'ring Plank, or Ladder's Length;
Still fix thy Eyes intent upon the Throng,
And as the Passes open, wind along.

OF THE PASS OF ST CLEMENTS

Where the fair Columns of Saint *Clement* stand,
Whose straiten'd Bounds encroach upon the *Strand*;
Where the low Penthouse bows the Walker's Head,
And the rough Pavement wounds the yielding Tread;
Where not a Post protects the narrow Space,
And strung in Twines, Combs dangle in thy Face;
Summon at once thy Courage, rouze thy Care,
Stand firm, look back, be resolute, beware.
Forth issuing from steep Lanes, the *Collier*'s Steeds
Drag the black Load; another Cart succeeds,
Team follows Team, Crouds heap'd on Crouds appear,
And wait impatient, 'till the Road grow clear.
Now all the Pavement sounds with trampling Feet,
And the mixt Hurry barricades the Street.
Entangled here, the Waggon's lengthen'd Team
Cracks the tough Harness; Here a pond'rous Beam
Lies over-turn'd athwart; For Slaughter fed,
Here lowing Bullocks raise their horned Head.
Now Oaths grow loud, with Coaches Coaches jar,
And the smart Blow provokes the sturdy War;
From the high Box they whirl the Thong around,
And with the twining Lash their Shins resound:

27

Their Rage ferments, more dang'rous Wounds they try,
And the Blood gushes down their painful Eye.
And now on Foot the frowning Warriors light,
And with their pond'rous Fists renew the Fight;
Blow answers Blow, their Cheeks are 'smear'd with Blood,
'Till down they fall, and grappling roll in Mud.
So when two Boars, in wild *Ytene** bred,
Or on *Westphalia*'s fatt'ning Chest-nuts fed,
Gnash their sharp Tusks, and rous'd with equal Fire,
Dispute the Reign of some luxurious Mire;
In the black Flood they wallow o'er and o'er,
'Till their arm'd Jaws distill with Foam and Gore.

OF PICK-POCKETS

Where the Mob gathers, swiftly shoot along,
Nor idly mingle in the noisy Throng.
Lur'd by the Silver Hilt, amid the Swarm,
The subtil Artist will thy Side disarm.
Nor is thy Flaxen Wigg with Safety worn;
High on the Shoulder, in a Basket born,
Lurks the sly Boy; whose Hand to Rapine bred,
Plucks off the curling Honours of thy Head.
Here dives the skulking Thief, with practis'd Slight,
And unfelt Fingers make thy Pocket light.
Where's now thy Watch, with all its Trinkets, flown?
And thy late Snuff-Box is no more thy own.
But lo! his bolder Theft some Tradesman spies,
Swift from his Prey the scudding Lurcher flies;
Dext'rous he scapes the Coach, with nimble Bounds,
Whilst ev'ry honest Tongue *Stop Thief* resounds.
So speeds the wily Fox, alarm'd by Fear,
Who lately filch'd the Turkey's callow Care;
Hounds following Hounds, grow louder as he flies,
And injur'd Tenants joyn the Hunter's Cries.
Breathless he stumbling falls: Ill-fated Boy!
Why did not honest Work thy Youth employ?

* New Forest in Hampshire, anciently so called.

Seiz'd by rough Hands, he's dragg'd amid the Rout,
And stretch'd beneath the Pump's incessant Spout:
Or plung'd in miry Ponds, he gasping lies,
Mud choaks his Mouth, and plaisters o'er his Eyes.

OF BALLAD-SINGERS

Let not the Ballad-Singer's shrilling Strain
Amid the Swarm thy list'ning Ear detain:
Guard well thy Pocket; for these *Syrens* stand,
To aid the Labours of the diving Hand;
Confed'rate in the Cheat, they draw the Throng,
And *Cambrick* Handkerchiefs reward the Song.
But soon as Coach or Cart drives rattling on,
The Rabble part, in Shoals they backward run.
So *Jove*'s loud Bolts the mingled War divide,
And *Greece* and *Troy* retreat on either side.

OF WALKING WITH A FRIEND

If the rude Throng pour on with furious Pace,
And hap to break thee from a Friend's Embrace,
Stop short; nor struggle thro' the Croud in vain,
But watch with careful Eye the passing Train.
Yet I (perhaps too fond) if chance the Tide
A Croud of Lovers follow to her Tomb.
Why is the Herse with 'Scutcheons blazon'd round,
And with the nodding Plume of Ostrich crown'd?
No: The Dead know it not, nor Profit gain;
It only serves to prove the Living vain.
How short is Life! how frail is human Trust!
Is all this Pomp for laying Dust to Dust?

OF AVOIDING PAINT

Where the nail'd Hoop defends the painted Stall,
Brush not thy sweeping Skirt too near the Wall;
Thy heedless Sleeve will drink the colour'd Oil,
And Spot indelible thy Pocket soil.

Has not wise Nature strung the Legs and Feet
With firmest Nerves, design'd to walk the Street?
Has she not given us Hands, to groap aright,
Amidst the frequent Dangers of the Night?
And think'st thou not the double Nostril meant,
To warn from oily Woes by previous Scent?

OF VARIOUS CHEATS FORMERLY IN PRACTICE

Who can the various City Frauds recite,
With all the petty Rapines of the Night?
Who now the *Guinea-Dropper*'s Bait regards,
Trick'd by the Sharper's Dice, or Juggler's Cards?
Why shou'd I warn thee ne'er to join the Fray,
Where the Sham-Quarrel interrupts the Way?
Lives there in these our Days so soft a Clown,
Brav'd by the Bully's Oaths, or threat'ning Frown?
I need not strict enjoyn the Pocket's Care,
When from the crouded *Play* you lead the Fair;
Who has not here, or Watch, or Snuff-Box lost,
Or Handkerchiefs that *India*'s Shuttle boast?

AN ADMONITION TO VIRTUE

O! may thy Virtue guard thee through the Roads
Of *Drury*'s mazy Courts, and dark Abodes,
The Harlots' guileful Paths, who nightly stand,
Where *Katherine-street* descends into the *Strand*.
Say, vagrant Muse, their Wiles and subtil Arts,
To lure the Strangers unsuspecting Hearts;
So shall our Youth on healthful Sinews tread,
And City Cheeks grow warm with rural Red.

HOW TO KNOW A WHORE

'Tis She who nightly strowls with saunt'ring Pace,
No stubborn Stays her yielding Shape embrace;
Beneath the Lamp her tawdry Ribbons glare,
The new-scower'd Manteau, and the slattern Air;

High-draggled Petticoats her Travels show,
And hollow Cheeks with artful Blushes glow;
With flatt'ring Sounds she sooths the cred'lous Ear,
My noble Captain! Charmer! Love! my Dear!
In Riding-hood, near Tavern-Doors she plies,
Or muffled Pinners hide her livid Eyes.
With empty Bandbox she delights to range,
And feigns a distant Errand from the *Change*;
Nay, she will oft' the Quaker's Hood prophane,
And trudge demure the Rounds of *Drury-Lane*.
She darts from Sarsnet Ambush wily Leers,
Twitches thy Sleeve, or with familiar Airs,
Her Fan will pat thy Cheek; these Snares disdain,
Nor gaze behind thee, when she turns again.

John Gay, *Trivia* (1716)

The Turkish baths of London

Ever since Russell Square and Jermyn Street ran out of steam I've despaired of ever getting a Turkish bath again. I much prefer them to saunas, which I find claustrophobic and akin to a punishment box in which you sweat it out metaphorically, so to speak, as well as physically. The Turkish bath is, by comparison, spacious. It's also nicely social. You can walk about and have a chat and all sorts of oddballs loom up in the steam. To my surprise and delight our friendly *Spectator* publican, Dave, introduced me to a steam bath just the other day; it must be one of the very few left in this clapped-out city (name and address withheld for fear of tourist invasion). But what a pleasant afternoon I had and in the best of company. As soon as I'd undressed and left the locker room I was introduced to some very stalwart men who were lolling about and melting in the steam room. 'This is Jeff. I'd like you to meet Freddie. Freddie's one of the most successful bank robbers in the country. This is Jim. Jim's just come out after a seven stretch and here's Tom. He's got a spieler in the Commercial Road.' What a jolly bunch they were and the only one who wasn't smiling was Solly, a 70-year-old taxi driver, who was staring mournfully at his prick and intoning: 'We were born together. We grew up together. We got married together. Why, oh why, did you have to die before me?'

The surprise of the afternoon was the picnic they produced in the locker room. Ice-cold lager, vodka, cold chicken, grouse or what you would and then back to the steam and in and out of the cold plunge. After that, a fairly ancient man with fingers of steel gave me an excellent massage which really toned up the cupboard I live in. Just as I was about to get off the slab he surprised me by pouring shampoo on my nut and giving my scalp a massage. Then he hosed me down. I haven't felt so good since Emprerey won the Derby. In fact I felt five years younger, which brought me down to about 70. I think I'll go regularly from now on, and for all that it's a snip for a fiver. It's also quite safe for me to visit Turkish baths now that I've lost my looks. In my pugilistic days, in the days when I could look a clock that was saying eleven o'clock in the face without breaking into a brisk trot to the nearest pub then I had to repel quite a few would-be boarders. Yes, the sign of being over the hill isn't policemen getting younger as far as I'm concerned, it's not being bought drinks by rich queens; the last time someone tried to drown me on the strength of my being a pretty face must be twenty years ago. The journey to the grave is studded with injuries to one's vanity.

Yes, for my money – and that's a joke – the Turkish variety beats the Swedish one hands down. And saunas can be dangerous. A very well-known friend of mine (name withheld, birds still pining, address Heaven) got into the habit of indulging in sexual intercourse in a sauna in a private house. I caught him at it one day and showed him the yellow card, but he would persist. Ten days later he had a heart attack and dropped dead in the street. Sex at 100 degrees and more Fahrenheit just isn't on and it's a pity, considering the climates of their respective countries, that Khomeini, Amin and Gaddafi don't screw themselves to death.

But there'll never be another Jermyn Street. When the jockeys used to use it to take off pounds after the races and after a session in Jules Bar then that was a night on the tiles. And the stories you heard, never mind the tips. But the Russell Square establishment was the best one for a night's kip, which is exactly what I used it for when I was on the bum. At 10 shillings a night it was the cheapest hotel in London and I was the cleanest man in London. And, as I said, I was pretty good at getting ten bobs in those days. Next week's steam bath will have to be paid for by the sweat of this old brow.

Jeffrey Bernard, *Low Life* (1992)

Some interesting lavatories

It is worth adding that, as the months passed towards the outbreak of the last war, the scribblings in London lavatories gradually became more belligerous. This was most notable in the larger conveniences such as those at Hyde Park Corner, and perhaps represent the folk mind letting loose the dogs of war.

To return to Holborn. I made friends with the attendant while I made the drawing illustrated here, and on my pointing out the resemblance of the water tanks to fish tanks, he told me, to my delight, that a previous attendant had actually used them for this purpose. It seemed to me that the fish must have been surprised to find their breathing space restricted and themselves coming down in the world each time the stalls were flushed, and what they made of the copper ball tap in their water I could not imagine. However, keeping fish in a lavatory tank is a delightfully rococo, or rather *fin de siècle*, idea, and might be copied with decorative results. There is also a certain logic about it which appeals to me, and it is wonderfully intriguing to imagine what the men using the place thought of the fish; more important, what the fish thought of the men. My attendant friend told me that there were very few old lavatories left in London (fewer still even today in the West End where the great landowners frowned on them). He called old conveniences 'Queen Victorias', a somewhat startling terminology. I was told that 'the lavatory in Charing Cross Road was the place to go if you want the writing on the wall . . . make your blood run cold, it would'. Charing Cross Road had been cleaned up before my tour of inspection, and so I found no writing on the wall. This lavatory, on an isolated site, is marked by one of the most splendid gas lamps in London, painted in black and gold and equalled only by the lamp at the back of St Clement Danes in the Strand and the pair in Trafalgar Square; the last, however, are now electrified. Holborn remains one of my favourites, for the gas jets are still intact over the water closets, and there are electric bulbs of Edwardian date which bend over like white tulips. The lavatory at the junction of Kings Cross Road and Pentonville Road was once, I believe, like the one in Rosebery Avenue, a privately owned affair – an odd way to make a living.

Yet another interesting lavatory is the one opposite the Brompton Oratory. From the isolation of the centre of the road, the ironwork makes a foreground to a view of the Italianate Oratory, dating from 1878.

(Brompton Oratory is a sort of pastiche of Italian Baroque, built out of hard stone of an unsympathetic quality, but the front is interesting with its narthex and trumpeting angels. Seen in the fading light of a grey autumn evening with the lavatory rails in front, it creates a curious sensation, but under these conditions, the church is more attractive, a sort of Canaletto-like view strayed somehow into London.) The lavatory is reached by steep, narrow stairs, and the 'conveniences' inside are of boldly marked marble in brown and white. A tiled frieze of yellow-green acanthus runs above the white tile walls. These classical motifs have been made to suit some unusual purposes since they first saw the light of day, purposes that would have caused some consternation to the designers of the Periclean age. The Victorians were strong minded enough not to bother their heads over incongruous ornament, and made the Victorian lavatory, if not a thing of beauty, certainly a joy for ever. This Brompton one has a mosaic floor with a running leaf pattern in the border that gives one the feeling of behaving rather too freely in some corner of the Alhambra or in some delicately glimmering room in old Bagdad.

Other touches that give the place a comfortable period flavour are the cast iron plates fixed in the walls, with a hand pointing the way out. I like those pointing Victorian hands, often showing a nice bit of linen cuff, which showed (or shewed) so many ways to so many Victorians. They invariably occur in advertisements for patent medicines and cocoa, where the hand points to a warning against fraudulent imitations. The attendant's room has the windows covered with that transparent oiled paper in imitation of stained glass which was a characteristic invention of the Victorians who were addicted to semblances and simulations. Over the door is the final touch, a lace curtain – a badge, like the aspidistra, of conformity and utter respectability.

Geoffrey S. Fletcher, *The London Nobody Knows* (1962)

Department stores

It is difficult nowadays to realize how very personal was then the relation-ship, even in London, between shop-keeper and customer and the enor-mous importance, comparable almost to that attained by rival churches, which late Victorian and Edwardian ladies attached to certain stores. All my female relatives had their own favourites, where some of them had been honoured customers for more than half a century and their arrival was greeted by frenzied bowing on the part of the frock-coated shopwalkers, and where certain of the older assistants stood to them almost in the relationship of confessors, receiving endless confidences on the state of their health, the behaviour of their pets and the general iniquity of the Liberal Government. Thus for my Great Aunt Bessie the Army and Navy Stores fulfilled all the functions of her husband's club and her undeviating loyalty was repaid by a respect and consideration which bore little or no relation to the size of her account. My mother's affections were chiefly centred on Harvey Nichols which her family had patronized for many years and which had been finally sanctified by her grandmother having met her death, at the age of ninety, at the wheels of a careless cyclist on leaving that establishment one summer morning in the last year of the old Queen's reign. However, although Harvey Nichols ever retained the first place in my mother's estimation, Knightsbridge was some way off and Queen's Road close at hand, so that Whiteley's had come to play the more important role.

Osbert Lancaster, *All Done from Memory* (1963)

Covent Garden Market

Covent-garden Market, when it was market morning, was wonderful company. The great waggons of cabbages, with growers' men and boys lying asleep under them, and with sharp dogs from market-garden neighbourhoods looking after the whole, were as good as a party. But one of the worst night sights I know in London, is to be found in the children who prowl about this place; who sleep in the baskets, fight for the offal, dart at any object they think they can lay their thieving hands on, dive under the carts and barrows, dodge the constables, and are perpetually making a blunt pattering on the pavement of the Piazza with the rain of their naked feet. A painful and unnatural result comes of the comparison one is forced to institute between the growth of corruption as displayed in the so much improved and cared for fruits of the earth, and the growth of corruption as displayed in these all uncared for (except inasmuch as ever-hunted) savages.

There was early coffee to be got about Covent-garden Market, and that was more company – warm company, too, which was better. Toast of a very substantial quality, was likewise procurable: though the towzled-headed man who made it, in an inner chamber within the coffee-room, hadn't got his coat on yet, and was so heavy with sleep that in every interval of toast and coffee he went off anew behind the partition into complicated cross-roads of choke and snore, and lost his way directly. Into one of these establishments (among the earliest) near Bow-street, there came one morning as I sat over my houseless cup, pondering where to go next, a man in a high and long snuff-coloured coat, and shoes, and, to the best of my belief, nothing else but a hat, who took out of his hat a large cold meat pudding; a meat pudding so large that it was a very tight fit, and brought the lining of the hat out with it. This mysterious man was known by his pudding, for on his entering, the man of sleep brought him a pint of hot tea, a small loaf, and a large knife and fork and plate. Left to himself in his box, he stood the pudding on the bare table, and, instead of cutting it, stabbed it, overhand, with the knife, like a mortal enemy: then took the knife out, wiped it on his sleeve, tore the pudding asunder with his fingers, and ate it all up. The remembrance of this man with the pudding remains with me as the remembrance of the most spectral person my houselessness encountered. Twice only was I in that establishment, and twice I saw him stalk in (as I should say, just out of bed, and presently going back to bed), take out his pudding, stab his pudding, wipe the dagger, and eat his pudding all up. He was a man whose figure promised cadaverousness, but who had an excessively red face, though shaped like a horse's. On the second occasion of my seeing him, he said huskily to the man of sleep, 'Am I red to-night?' 'You are,' he uncompromisingly answered. 'My mother,' said the spectre, 'was a red-faced woman that liked drink, and I looked at her hard when she laid in her coffin, and I took the complexion.' Somehow, the pudding seemed an unwholesome pudding after that, and I put myself in its way no more.

Charles Dickens, *The Uncommercial Traveller* (1861)

Puddings, duffs and milk

OF THE STREET-SELLERS OF BOILED PUDDINGS

The sale of *boiled* puddings, meat and currant – which might perhaps be with greater correctness called dumplings – has not been known in

London, I was informed by one in the trade, more than twelve or fourteen years. The ingredients for the meat puddings are not dissimilar to those I have described as required for the meat pies, but the puddings are boiled, in cotton bags, in coppers or large pans, and present the form of a round ball. The charge is a halfpenny each.

OF THE STREET-SELLERS OF PLUM 'DUFF' OR DOUGH

Plum dough is one of the street-eatables – though perhaps it is rather a violence to class it with the street-pastry – which is usually made by the vendors. It is simply a boiled plum, or currant, pudding, of the plainest description. It is sometimes made in the rounded form of the plum-pudding; but more frequently in the 'roly-poly' style. Hot pudding used to be of much more extensive sale in the streets. One informant told me that twenty or thirty years ago, batter, or Yorkshire, pudding, 'with plums in it', was a popular street business. The 'plums', as in the orthodox plum-puddings, are raisins. The street-vendors of plum 'duff' are now very few, only six as an average, and generally women, or if a man be the salesman he is the woman's husband.

OF THE STREET SALE OF MILK

During the summer months milk is sold in Smithfield, Billingsgate, and other markets, and on Sundays in Battersea-fields, Clapham-common, Camberwell-green, Hampstead-heath, and similar places. About twenty men are engaged in this sale. They usually wear a smock frock, and have the cans and yoke used by the regular milk-sellers; they are not itinerant. The skim milk – for they sell none else – is purchased at the dairies at $1\frac{1}{2}d.$ a quart, and even the skim milk is also further watered by the street-sellers. Their cry is 'Half-penny half-pint! Milk!' The tin measure however in which the milk-and-water is served is generally a 'slang', and contains but half of the quantity proclaimed. The purchasers are chiefly boys and children; rarely men, and never costermongers, I was told, 'for they reckon milk sickly'.

Henry Mayhew, Mayhew's London (1851)

Sitting on pavements

Sitting on pavement – a change I think in Camden Town. Can't remember anyone doing it in our early days here. Now young people do – if waiting for a friend, and outside Spread Eagle drinking (there were no tables in the old days and now the few there are not enough). Old people sit on the market pavement, especially on Sunday mornings and on summer evenings when the shops are closed.

The winos, including Davy and Mary, have found a real 'grandstand' – a huge wooden beam in front of the old ladies lav by the traffic lights at the bottom of Parkway. Here they sit in the middle of the road facing the Camden High Street traffic. When the green man starts walking, two streams of pedestrians cross the road in front of them within touching distance. But they do not touch. They greet me loudly, and I suppose a few others they know. (The lav has been closed for years – some sort of underground work.)

David Thomson, *In Camden Town* (1983)

Impression de Nuit

LONDON

See what a mass of gems the city wears
   Upon her broad live bosom! row on row
   Rubies and emeralds and amethysts glow.
See! that huge circle, like a necklace, stares
With thousands of bold eyes to heaven, and dares
   The golden stars to dim the lamps below,
   And in the mirror of the mire I know
The moon has left her image unawares.

That's the great town at night; I see her breasts,
   Prick'd out with lamps they stand like huge black towers,
   I think they move! I hear her panting breath.
And that's her head where the tiara rests.

And in her brain, through lanes as dark as death,
Men creep like thoughts . . . The lamps are like pale flowers.

Lord Alfred Douglas, Poems (1896)

St James's Street

(A GRUMBLE)

St James's Street, of classic fame,
   The finest people throng it!
St James's Street? I know the name,
   I think I've pass'd along it!
Why, that's where Sacharissa sigh'd
   When Waller read his ditty;
Where Byron loved, and Gibbon died,
   And Alvanley was witty.

A famous street! To yonder Park
   Young Churchill stole in class-time;
Come, gaze on fifty men of mark,
   And then recall the past time!
The *plats* at White's, the play at *Crock's*,
   The bumpers to Miss Gunning;
The *bonhomie* of Charlie Fox,
   And Selwyn's ghastly funning.

The dear old street of clubs and *cribs*,
   As north and south it stretches,
Still seems to smack of Rolliad squibs,
   And Gillray's fiercer sketches;
The quaint old dress, the grand old style,
   The *mots*, the racy stories;
The wine, the dice, the wit, the bile, –
   The hate of Whigs and Tories.

At dusk, when I am strolling there,
   Dim forms will rise around me;

Lepel flits past me in her chair,
   And Congreve's airs astound me!
And once Nell Gwynne, a frail young sprite,
   Look'd kindly when I met her;
I shook my head, perhaps, – but quite
   Forgot to quite forget her.

The street is still a lively tomb
   For rich, and gay, and clever;
The crops of dandies bud and bloom,
   And die as fast as ever.
Now gilded youth loves cutty pipes,
   And slang that's rather scaring;
It can't approach its prototypes
   In taste, or tone, or bearing.

In Brummell's day of buckle shoes,
   Lawn cravats, and roll collars,
They'd fight and woo, and bet – and lose –
   Like gentlemen and scholars:
I'm glad young men should go the pace,
   I half forgive *Old Rapid*;
These louts disgrace their name and race –
   So vicious and so vapid!

Worse times may come. *Bon ton*, indeed,
   Will then be quite forgotten,
And all we much revere will speed
   From ripe to worse than rotten:
Let grass then sprout between yon stones,
   And owls then roost at Boodle's,
For Echo will hurl back the tones
   Of screaming *Yankee Doodles*!

I love the haunts of Old Cockaigne,
   Where wit and wealth were squander'd;
The halls that tell of hoop and train,
   Where grace and rank have wander'd;
The halls where ladies fair and leal
   First ventured to adore me! –

And something of the like I feel
For this old street before me.

Frederick Locker Lampson, London Lyrics (1874)

Victoria Station. 6.58 p.m.

Sudden, beneath the pendant clock arose
Out of the drab and artificial ground
A horse with wings of scarlet, and pale flowers
Glimmered upon his forehead, while around

His neck and mane like wreaths of incense streamed
Young hosts of stars, and as his eyes burned proud,
The men with black umbrellas stood and stared
And nudged each other and then laughed aloud.

Mervyn Peake, Selected Poems (1972)

A night out

A curious circumstance now occurred. I had dined with a jovial set at Wilberforce Bird's in Wood Street, Cheapside, where we drank a large quantity of wine. Soon after midnight, the company breaking up, someone proposed finishing the night at Malby's. A hackney coach being sent for, six of us crammed ourselves into it – Bob Pott, Coombe, Shakespear, Lord Fielding, Vaughan and myself. We had got as far as Ludgate Hill on our way to Covent Garden, when Pott, thinking the coachman did not drive fast enough, damned his blood and bid him move on. Coachie made a gruff answer, which offended Master Bob, who thereupon poked at him through the front window with the hilt of his sword, a salutation John Bull not approving, he instantly returned the compliment by the butt end of his whip. Pott, in a violent rage, crept through the window and began pummelling the fellow with all his might. After a sharp but short conflict, they tumbled together off the box into the street. A mob collecting, the horses were stopped, and we all got out to the assistance of our associate. A kind of general engagement ensued, chiefly between us and the watchmen who had come to support the rights of the brother of the whip. The battle ended, as might be expected it would, by three of us – that is, Vaughan, Pott, and myself – being violently seized and dragged to the watch-house in Fleet Market, Lord Fielding, Shakespear, and Coombe having very prudently made good their retreat, thereby avoiding being taken prisoners by the enemy.

The constable of the night, a respectable-looking person, upon seeing three full-dressed men brought in, all abominably intoxicated, upon the coachman's making his complaint, with great good nature said, 'Come, come, young gentlemen, this is, I perceive, a drunken frolic. You must therefore pay for your folly, and go quietly home to sleep off the effects of too much wine.' While the constable was speaking, a good fat-looking body, who declared himself to be a peaceable citizen and pastrycook in Fleet Street, came up, the blood streaming from his nose, protesting against the unjustifiable conduct and violence of our party, who had assailed and maltreated him merely because he had stepped forward and exerted himself to rescue them out of the hands of an offending mob, rendered more angry by the appearance of, and story told by, the coachman, who certainly had sustained some injury in the affray. Although my head was by no means clear, I, nevertheless, felt the full force of the kind constable's very sensible advice, and putting my hand into my pocket was about to make a pecuniary recompense for our transgression, when Pott, who was in one of his wicked and facetious fits, and resolved to have some fun before he paid, cried out, 'No! No! I protest against the doling out of cash. So, old Bollocks, (to the constable) proceed, sir, to do your duty. Observe, I am a profound lawyer, deeply read in the statutes since the establishment of Englishmen's pride and glory, *Magna Charta*. So stand by, my old cock, and let me see that I do not catch you tripping; for blood and zounds, if I do I'll circumfloborate you and all your base understrappers.'

The constable looked with some symptoms of surprise at Pott, and, after hemming once or twice, said, 'I think, young gentleman, that after the experience of thirty years I do pretty well know my duty. I will convince you that I do know it by clapping you for the remainder of the night into the black hole, young gentleman, do you see, and have no doubt but the air of that agreeable apartment will restore your senses.' 'Black hole!' repeated Pott. 'Take care, old Dogberry, you are upon the edge of a precipice, into which if you fall, the devil himself will not be able to relieve you, though I can. Proceed, therefore, with caution. You talk of black holes without a trial! You are a pretty son-of-a-bitch of a judge. Come, proceed. Ascend your magisterial chair and take down depositions; otherwise you will be all at sea, and cast away upon the rocks of error and ignorance. Proceed, I say!'

'Very well! very well! young sir, I believe you may be right in this notion, and I will act comfortably.' While preparing to take his seat, Pott slipped behind him and occupied it, to the great entertainment of the bystanders. Again the black hole was alluded to; Bob therefore relinquished the chair, which the humble representative of justice immediately filled, and taking up his pen, prepared his book. Bob, in the meantime, got behind him and twirled his wig round, putting the back part in front. Again a burst of laughter broke forth, and again the black hole was threatened. The constable then demanded to know his name. 'George,' answered Pott. 'That's not true,' observed the constable, 'for I just now heard that gentleman (pointing to me) call you Bob.' 'That gentleman,' said Bob, 'is too drunk to tell his own name, and I am sure cannot distinguish any other person's. So get on, most upright judge, you second Daniel.'

'Well, sir,' asked the constable, 'who are you?' 'A son of the King's,' said Bob. The man stared, and in a hesitating voice said, 'I do not exactly understand what you are at, young sir. I wish you would act like a reasonable creature.' 'Proceed, thou mirror of all that's just, or by the mighty Jupiter I'll jumble you to mincemeat.' The constable, losing his temper at being made a laughing stock, ordered the door of the black hole to be opened; whereupon Vaughan with vast solemnity addressed him, saying, 'I have hitherto, sir, been a quiet spectator of all that has passed and, although wrongfully brought and detained here as a prisoner, have not uttered a syllable; but, when I hear you talk of more rigorous confinement of my friend, I consider it right to caution you as to your proceedings, for which, if wrong, depend upon it you shall be made responsible. And give me leave further to inform you that I am the more competent to caution you as to your measures from myself having the honour to be in His Majesty's commission of the peace for the County of Middlesex. I, therefore, once more recommend you to take care what you are about.' 'I am sorry to hear you are yourself a magistrate, sir,' said the constable, 'because, if that be the case, you ought to know better than to commit a breach of the peace by kicking up a broil and riot in the streets at midnight. However, sir, that matter you shall settle before the sitting alderman in the morning.'

William Hickey, Memoirs, 1749–1809 (1960)

Another night out

One night when Beauclerk and Langton had supped at a tavern in London, and sat till about three in the morning, it came into their heads to go and knock up Johnson, and see if they could prevail on him to join them in a ramble. They rapped violently at the door of his chambers in the Temple, till at last he appeared in his shirt, with his little black wig on the top of his head, instead of a nightcap, and a poker in his hand, imagining, probably, that some ruffians were coming to attack him. When he discovered who they were, and was told their errand, he smiled, and with great good humour agreed to their proposal: 'What, is it you, you dogs! I'll have a frisk with you.' He was soon drest, and they sallied forth together into Covent-Garden, where the greengrocers and fruiterers were beginning to arrange their hampers, just come in from the country. Johnson made some attempts to help them; but the honest gardeners stared so at his figure and manner, and odd interference, that he soon saw his services were not relished. They then repaired to one of the neighbouring taverns, and made a bowl of that liquor called *Bishop*, which Johnson had always liked; while in joyous contempt of sleep, from which he had been roused, he repeated the festive lines,

> 'Short, O short then be thy reign,
> And give us to the world again!'

They did not stay long, but walked down to the Thames, took a boat, and rowed to Billingsgate. Beauclerk and Johnson were so well pleased with their amusement, that they resolved to persevere in dissipation for the rest of the day: but Langton deserted them, being engaged to breakfast with some young Ladies. Johnson scolded him for 'leaving his social friends, to go and sit with a set of wretched *un-idea'd* girls'. Garrick being told of this ramble, said to him smartly, 'I heard of your frolick t'other night. You'll be in the Chronicle.' Upon which Johnson afterwards observed, '*He* durst not do such a thing. His *wife* would not *let* him!'

James Boswell, *Life of Johnson* (1791)

In Long Acre

26 January

Got my pay cheque today. Thought I would celebrate by taking myself to a good restaurant. Walked home; thought about so many things. One of them was how some weeks ago in London I walked along Long Acre from Covent Garden where I had seen *Götterdämmerung* – alone as I thought, along the street I farted. It was much louder, after five hours of Wagner, than I had dreamed it could possibly be! Some boys and girls, rather charming, whom I had scarcely noticed, overheard me, or it, and started cheering. In the darkness I was more amused than embarrassed. Then a self-important thought came in my mind. Supposing they knew that this old man walking along Long Acre and farting was Stephen Spender? What would they think? Anyway, for some reason a bit difficult for me to analyse, it would be embarrassing. Then I saw how an incident like this divides people one knows into categories – those who would laugh and those who would be shocked (shocked anyway at me writing this down). I don't think F. R. Leavis would have been amused. But Forster, Auden, Isherwood, Connolly, Ackerley, and Matthew, my son, would be.

Stephen Spender, Journals, 1939–1983 (1985)

Punk girls

26 September

On our way home from Mornington Crescent we stopped to look at the old Camden Theatre which was renamed the Music Machine when it became a pop music centre about five years ago. Its old green dome and yellow pillars are unchanged but above and around the doors there are psychedelic lights and lettering, which make it look like an old lady, in stately hat and bodice, who has stepped into a young girl's glittering mini.

Said to M. as we walked on how glad I am that it has been opened for people's pleasure again after all those private years as a BBC studio.

Several punk girls came walking fast towards us, and it struck me again how like space fiction their get-up is; their make-up is inhuman too; some give the impression of *Grand Guignol*. The first we saw took long strides in long legs closely fitted with yellow stockings to the knee and tight black satin breeches to above the waist. A top of some bright colour, hair cropped and scraped with top knots sticking up. She had passed us in a flash, and as I looked back I had the impression that she was wearing a sword at her waist. It may have been a long cane, or an umbrella as tightly rolled as herself. Then a few yards behind her came the others straggling but with rapid steps like speckled glaring lights.

In spite of the bright clothes and the greens, yellows, scarlets of the hair in streaks, in patches or whole – sometimes a blotch of white on dark hair reminds me of a long-healed saddle sore on an old horse – in spite of the showy flash, there is a puritanical severity about the punk look, male and female. The skimpy scrimp of the boys' clothes – tight jeans often not long enough to cover their shins, jackets pinched at the armpits and chest with sleeves stopping short of the wrist – give them a poor and meagre look, especially if you compare them with the long-haired boys of a few years ago whose clothes were more amply cut. Then, since facial expressions can be designed and worn to fashion, the majority look as grim as any Wee Free Minister. It is startling to see such a look of severity, especially on the girls' faces in the evening outside a pleasure dome, but this I guess is fashion too.

David Thomson, *In Camden Town* (1983)

Driving in London

Algernon Stitch went to his office in a sombre and rather antiquated Daimler; Julia always drove herself, in the latest model of mass-produced baby car; brand-new twice a year, painted an invariable brilliant black, tiny and glossy as a midget's funeral hearse. She mounted the kerb and bowled rapidly along the pavement to the corner of St James's, where a policeman took her number and ordered her into the road.

'Third time this week,' said Mrs Stitch. 'I wish they wouldn't. It's such a nuisance for Algy.'

Once embedded in the traffic block, she stopped the engine and turned her attention to the crossword.

'It's "detonated",' she said, filling it in.

East wind swept the street, carrying with it the exhaust gas of a hundred motors and coarse particles of Regency stucco from a once decent Nash façade that was being demolished across the way. John shivered and rubbed some grit further into his eye. Eight minutes' close application was enough to finish the puzzle. Mrs Stitch folded the paper and tossed it over her shoulder into the back seat; looked about her resentfully at the stationary traffic.

'This is too much,' she said; started the engine, turned sharp again on to the kerb and proceeded to Piccadilly, driving before her at a brisk pace, until he took refuge on the step of Brooks's, a portly, bald young man; when he reached safety, he turned to remonstrate, recognized Mrs Stitch, and bowed profoundly to the tiny, black back as it shot the corner of Arlington Street. 'One of the things I like about these absurd cars,' she said, 'is that you can do things with them that you couldn't do in a real one.'

From Hyde Park Corner to Piccadilly Circus the line of traffic was continuous and motionless, still as a photograph, unbroken and undisturbed save at a few strategic corners where barricaded navvies, like desperate outposts of some proletarian defence, were rending the road with mechanical drills, mining for the wires and tubes that controlled the life of the city.

'I want to get away from London,' said John Boot.

Evelyn Waugh, *Scoop* (1938)

Parliament Hill Fields

Rumbling under blackened girders, Midland, bound for Cricklewood,
Puffed its sulphur to the sunset where that Land of Laundries stood.
Rumble under, thunder over, train and tram alternate go,
Shake the floor and smudge the ledger, Charrington, Sells, Dale and Co.,
Nuts and nuggets in the window, trucks along the lines below.

When the Bon Marché was shuttered, when the feet were hot and tired,
Outside Charrington's we waited, by the 'STOP HERE IF
    REQUIRED',
Launched aboard the shopping basket, sat precipitately down,
Rocked past Zwanziger the baker's, and the terrace blackish brown,

And the curious Anglo–Norman parish church of Kentish Town.

Till the tram went over thirty, sighting terminus again,
Past municipal lawn tennis and the bobble-hanging plane;
Soft the light suburban evening caught our ashlar-speckled spire,
Eighteen-sixty Early English, as the mighty elms retire
Either side of Brookfield Mansions flashing fine French-window fire.

Oh the after-tram-ride quiet, when we heard a mile beyond,
Silver music from the bandstand, barking dogs by Highgate Pond;
Up the hill where stucco houses in Virginia creeper drown –
And my childish wave of pity, seeing children carrying down
Sheaves of drooping dandelions to the courts of Kentish Town.

John Betjeman, *Collected Poems* (1970)

3

Monuments

Were this a guide-book to London, it would have been necessary to have a passage, preferably 'literary', descriptive of all the great monuments of London. Starting with the arrival of Julius Caesar, and taking in monuments which date from historical periods just as remote, but which have been imported since (such as the Elgin Marbles and Cleopatra's Needle), I should have felt obliged to provide a sort of literary-historical guide to London. At one stage of this book's composition, indeed, I found that this was what I had done, and I was including passages merely because they mentioned Temple Bar or the statue of Handel in Vauxhall Gardens.

My idea of what this chapter should be like changed when, on the same afternoon, I found I had copied and placed on my 'monuments' pile two of the items which follow: Thomas Hardy's terse but elegant poem about the Elgin Marbles, and David Thomson's observations about the ladies lavatory in Parkway, Camden Town. Until reading David Thomson's book In Camden Town, I had taken the existence of these lavatories for granted, even though I pass them each day on my way to work, or to the shops. The women of Camden Town, many of them running market stalls all day long, had nowhere to relieve themselves until that humane feminist George Bernard Shaw campaigned for their lavatory. Thomson's description of that campaign, and the fierce opposition Shaw encountered, was alas too long to include here in its entirety. But, having copied it out and placed it (perhaps incongruously) beside Thomas Hardy's poem, I discovered what was my chief concern in this collection of 'monuments'. Hardy was moved by the Elgin Marbles because they had 'echoed the voice of Paul'. Some time in the first century, the Apostle spoke on the Areopagus to the

49

wise men of Athens. Nineteen hundred years later, the stones which had heard his voice were transported to Bloomsbury.

There is hardly any area of London which is not rich in monuments that tug at us in some way and remind us of our past. The crowd who flowed over London Bridge in Eliot's poem are all 'undone' by death, and the stones of the bridge outlast them. But it is chiefly because of the crowd that we revere the bridge.

Any walk through London in the company of a well-informed person produces a mood of elegy and sadness. So many great monuments and buildings have gone – wilfully demolished like the arch at Euston Station, removed, like Temple Bar, or destroyed by fire or Blitzkrieg. I had a shock not long ago walking up Drury Lane and seeing that they were ploughing up 'Tom-All-Alones', the paupers' burial ground in Bleak House *where little Jo the crossing-sweeper is buried. After it ceased to be a cemetery, it became a small public garden. I do not know what its fate will be now. Perhaps it will remain a garden, and they were merely relaying the turf. The shock was not merely visual, though. I felt that the bulldozers were interfering with our memories, and that was why the sight caused pain. Londoners have been having such sad thoughts ever since the place was built, and there has never been a generation (even in times where architects were more skilful than those of the 1960s and 1970s) which did not regret the demolition and passing away of the monuments that had 'heard the voices' of our ancestors.*

Cleopatra's Needle

Here, I that stood in On beside the flow
Of sacred Nile, three thousand years ago! –
A Pharaoh, kingliest of his kingly race,
First shaped, and carved, and set me in my place.
A Caesar of a punier dynasty
Thence haled me toward the Mediterranean sea,
Whence your own citizens, for their own renown,
Through strange seas drew me to your monster town.
I have seen the four great empires disappear.
I was when London was not. I am here.

Alfred, Lord Tennyson (1878)

Great Men are the Property of the Nation

'It being in the contemplation of some persons to bestow a considerable sum of money in erecting a monument, in the parish church of St Giles, Cripplegate, to the memory of Milton, and the particular spot of his interment in that church having for many years past been ascertained only by tradition, several of the principal parishioners have, at their meetings, frequently expressed a wish that his coffin should be dug for, that incontestable evidence of its exact situation might be established, before the said monument should be erected. The entry, among the burials, in the register-book, twelfth of November, 1674, is "John Milton, Gentleman, consumption, chancell". The church of St Giles, Cripplegate, was built in 1030, was burnt down (except the steeple) and rebuilt in 1545; was repaired in 1682; and again in 1710. In the repair of 1782, an alteration took place in the disposition of the inside of the church; the pulpit was removed from the second pillar, against which it stood, north of the chancel, to the south side of the present chancel, which was then formed, and pews were built over the old chancel. The tradition has always been that Milton was buried in the chancel, under the clerk's desk; but the circumstance of the alteration in the church, not having, of late years, been attended to, the clerk, sexton, and other officers of the parish have misguided inquirers, by showing the spot under the clerk's desk, in the present chancel, as the place of Milton's interment. I have twice, at different periods, been shown that spot as the place where Milton lay. Even Mr Baskerville, who died a few years ago, and who had requested, in his will, to be buried by Milton, was deposited in the above-mentioned spot of the present chancel, in pious intention of compliance with his request. The church is now, August, 1790, under a general repair, by contract, for £1,350, and Mr Strong, Mr Cole, and other parishioners, having very prudently judged that the search would be made with much less inconvenience to the parish at this time, when the church is under repair, than at any period after the said repair should be completed, Mr Cole, in the last days of July, ordered the workmen to dig in search of the coffin. Mr Ascough, his father, and grandfather, have been parish clerks of St Giles for upwards of ninety years past. His grandfather, who died in February 1759–60, aged eighty-four, used often to say that Milton had been buried under the clerk's desk in the chancel. John Poole, aged seventy, used to hear his father talk of Milton's person, from those who had seen him; and also, that he lay under the common-councilmen's pew. The common-councilmen's pew is built over that very part of the old chancel, where the former clerk's desk stood. These traditions in the parish reported to Mr Strong and Mr Cole readily directed them to dig from the present chancel, northwards, towards the pillar, against which the former pulpit and desk had stood. On Tuesday afternoon, August 3rd, notice was brought to Messrs Strong and Cole that the coffin was discovered. They went immediately to the church, and, by help of a candle, proceeded under the common-councilmen's pew to the place where the coffin lay. It was in a chalky soil, and directly over a wooden coffin, supposed to be that of Milton's father; tradition having always reported that Milton was buried next to his father. The registry of the father of Milton, among the burials, in the parish-book, is "John Melton, Gentleman, 15th of March 1646–7". In digging through the whole space from the present chancel, where the ground was opened, to the situation of the former clerk's desk, there was not found any other coffin, which could raise the smallest doubt of this being Milton's. The two oldest found in the ground had inscriptions, which Mr Strong copied; they were of as late dates as 1727 and 1739. When he and Mr Cole had examined the coffin, they ordered water and a brush to be brought, that they might wash it, in search of an inscription, or initials, or date; but, upon its being carefully cleansed, none was found.

'The following particulars were given me in writing by Mr Strong, and they contain the admeasurement of the coffin, as taken by him, with a rule. "A leaden coffin, found under the common-councilmen's pew, on the north side of the chancel, nearly under the place where the old pulpit and clerk's desk stood. The coffin appeared to be old, much corroded, and without any inscription or plate upon it. It was, in length, five feet ten inches, and in width, at the broadest part, over the shoulders, one foot four inches." Conjecture naturally pointed out, both to Mr Strong and Mr Cole, that, by moving the leaden coffin, there would be a great chance of finding some inscription on the wooden one underneath; but, with a just and laudable piety, they disdained to disturb the sacred ashes, after a requiem of one hundred and sixteen years; and having satisfied their curiosity, and ascertained the fact, which was the subject of it, Mr Cole ordered the ground to be closed. This was on the afternoon of Tuesday, August the 3rd; and, when I waited on Mr Strong, on Saturday morning, the 7th, he informed me that the coffin had been found on the Tuesday, had been examined, washed, and measured by him and Mr Cole; but that the ground had been immediately closed, when they left the church – not doubting that Mr Cole's order had been punctually obeyed. But the direct contrary appears to have been the fact.

'On Tuesday evening the 3rd, Mr Cole, Messrs Laming & Taylor, Holmes, &c., had a merry meeting, as Mr Cole expresses himself, at Fountain's house; the conversation there turned upon Milton's coffin having been discovered; and, in the course of the evening, several of those present expressing a desire to see it, Mr Cole assented that, if the ground was not already closed, the closing of it should be deferred until they should have satisfied their curiosity. Between eight and nine on Wednesday morning, the 4th, the two overseers (Laming and Fountain) and Mr Taylor, went to the house of Ascough, the clerk, which leads into the church-yard, and asked for Holmes; they then went with Holmes into the church, and pulled the coffin, which lay deep in the ground, from its original station to the edge of the excavation, into daylight. Mr Laming told me that, to assist in thus removing it, he put his hand into a corroded hole, which he saw in the lead, at the coffin foot. When they had thus removed it, the overseers asked Holmes if he could open it, that they might see the body. Holmes immediately fetched a mallet and a chisel, and cut open the top of the coffin, slantwise from the head, as low as the breast; so that the top, being doubled backward, they could see the corpse; he cut it open also at the foot. Upon first view of the body, it appeared perfect, and completely enveloped in the shroud, which was of many folds; the ribs standing up regularly. When they disturbed the shroud, the ribs fell. Mr Fountain told me that he pulled hard at the teeth, which resisted, until some one hit them a knock with a stone, when they easily came out. There were but five in the upper jaw, which were all perfectly sound and white, and all taken by Mr Fountain; he gave one of them to Mr Laming; Mr Laming also took one from the lower jaw; and Mr Taylor took two from it. Mr Laming told me that he had, at one time, a mind to bring away the whole under-jaw, with the teeth in it; he had it in his hand, but tossed it back again. Also that he lifted up the head, and saw a great quantity of hair, which lay straight and even behind the head, and in the state of hair which had been combed and tied together before interment; but it was wet, the coffin having considerable corroded holes, both at the head and foot, and a great part of the water with which it had been washed on the Tuesday afternoon having run into it. The overseers and Mr Taylor went away soon afterwards, and Messrs Laming and Taylor went home to get scissors to cut off some of the hair: they returned about ten, when Mr Laming poked his stick against the head, and brought some of the hair over the forehead; but, as they saw the scissors were not necessary, Mr Taylor took up the hair, as it lay on the forehead, and carried it home. The water, which had got into the coffin on the Tuesday afternoon, had made a sludge at the bottom of it, emitting a nauseous smell, which occasioned Mr Laming to use his stick to procure the hair, and not to lift up the head a second time. Mr Laming also took out one of the leg-bones, but threw it in again. Holmes went out of church, whilst Messrs Laming, Taylor, and Fountain were there the first time, and he returned when the two former were come the second time. When Messrs Laming and Taylor had finally quitted the church, the coffin was removed from the edge of the excavation back to its original station; but was no otherwise closed than by the lid, where it had been cut and reversed, being bent down again. Mr Ascough, the clerk, was from home the greater part of that day, and Mrs Hoppey, the sexton, was from home the whole day. Elizabeth Grant, the grave-digger, who is servant to Mrs Hoppey, therefore now took possession of the coffin; and, as its situation under the common-councilmen's pew would not admit of its being seen without the help of a candle, she kept a tinder-box in the excavation, and, when any persons came, struck a light, and conducted them under the pew, where, by reversing the part of the lid which had been cut, she exhibited the body, at first for sixpence, and afterwards for threepence and twopence each person. The workers in the church kept the doors locked to all those who would not pay the price of a pot of beer for entrance, and many, to avoid that payment, got in at a window at the west end of the church, near to Mr Ascough's counting-house.

'I went on Saturday, the 7th, to Mr Laming's house, to request a lock of the hair; but, not meeting with Mr Taylor at home, went again on Monday, the 9th, when Mr Taylor gave me part of what hair he had reserved for himself. Hawkesworth having informed me, on the Saturday, that Mr Ellis, the player, had taken some hair, and that he had seen him take a rib-bone, and carry it away in paper under his coat, I went from Mr Laming's on Monday to Mr Ellis, who told me that he had paid 6*d*. to Elizabeth Grant for seeing the body; and that he had lifted up the head, and taken from the sludge under it a small quantity of hair, with which was a piece of the shroud, and, adhering to the hair, a bit of the skin of the skull, of about the size of a shilling. He then put them all into my hands, with the rib-bone, which appeared to be one of the upper ribs. The piece of shroud was of coarse linen. The hair which he had taken was short; a small part of it he had washed, and the remainder was in the clotted state in which he had taken it. He told me that he had tried to reach down as low as the hands of

54

the corpse, but had not been able to effect it. The washed hair corresponded exactly with that in my possession, and which I had just received from Mr Taylor. Ellis is a very ingenious worker in hair, and he said that, thinking it would be of great advantage to him to possess a quantity of Milton's hair, he had returned to the church on Thursday, and had made his endeavours to get access a second time to the body; but had been refused admittance. Hawkesworth took a tooth, and broke a bit off the coffin; of which I was informed by Mr Ascough. I purchased them both of Hawkesworth, on Saturday the 7th for 2s.; and he told me that, when he took the tooth out, there were but two more remaining; one of which was afterwards taken by another of Mr Ascough's men. And Ellis informed me that, at the time when he was there, on Wednesday, the teeth were all gone; but the overseers say they think that all the teeth were not taken out of the coffin, though displaced from the jaws, but that some of them must have fallen among the other bones as they very readily came out, after the first were drawn. Haslib, son of William Haslib, of Jewin Street, undertaker, took one of the small bones, which I purchased of him, on Monday the 9th, for 2s.

'With respect to the identity of the person; anyone must be a skeptic against violent presumptions to entertain a doubt of its being that of Milton. The parish traditions of the spot; the age of the coffin – none other found in the ground which can at all contest with it, or render it suspicious – Poole's tradition that those who had conversed with his father about Milton's person always described him to have been thin, with long hair; the entry in the register-book that Milton died of consumption, are all strong confirmations, with the size of the coffin, of the identity of the person. If it be objected that, against the pillar where the pulpit formerly stood, and immediately over the common-councilmen's pew, is a monument to the family of Smith, which shows that "near that place" were buried, in 1653, Richard Smith, aged 17; in 1655, John Smith, aged 32; and in 1664, Elizabeth Smith, the mother, aged 64; and in 1675, Richard Smith, the father, aged 85; it may be answered that, if the coffin in question be one of these, the others should be there also. The corpse is certainly not that of a man of 85; and, if it be supposed one of the first named males of the Smith family, certainly the two later coffins should appear; but none such were found, nor could that monument have been erected until many years after the death of the last person mentioned in the inscription; and it was then placed there, as it expresses, not by any of the family, but at the expense of friends. The flatness of the pillar, after the pulpit had been removed, offered an advantageous situation for it; and "*near this place*", upon a mural monument, will always admit of a liberal construction. Holmes, who is much respected in that parish, and very ingenious and intelligent in his business, says that a leaden coffin, when the inner wooden case is perished, must, from pressure and its own weight, shrink in breadth, and that, therefore, more than the present admeasurement of this coffin across the shoulders must have been its original breadth. There is evidence, also, that it was incurvated, both on the top and at the sides, at the time when it was discovered. But the strongest of all confirmations is the hair, both in its length and colour. Behold Fairthorne's quarto-print of Milton, taken *ad vivum* in 1760, five years before Milton's death. Observe the short locks growing towards the forehead, and the long ones flowing from the same place down the sides of the face. The whole quantity of hair which Mr Taylor took was from the forehead, and all taken at one grasp. I measured on Monday morning, the 9th, that lock of it which he had given to Mr Laming, six inches and a half by a rule; and the lock of it which he gave to me, taken at the same time, and from the same place, measures only two inches and a half. In the reign of Charles II how few, besides Milton, wore their own hair! Wood says Milton had light-brown hair, the very description of that which we possess; and, what may seem extraordinary, it is yet so strong that Mr Laming, to cleanse it from its clotted state, let the cistern-cock run on it for near a minute, and then rubbed it between his fingers without injury.

'Milton's coffin lay open from Wednesday morning, the 4th, at 9 o'clock, until 4 o'clock in the afternoon of the following day, when the ground was closed.

'With respect to there being no inscriptions on the coffin, Holmes says that inscription-plates were not used, nor invented at the time when Milton was buried; that the practice then was to paint the inscription on the outside wooden coffin, which in this case was entirely perished.

'It has never been pretended that any hair was taken except by Mr Taylor and by Ellis the player; and all which the latter took would, when cleansed, easily lie in a small locket. Mr Taylor has divided his share into many small parcels; and the lock which I saw in Mr Laming's hands on Saturday morning, the 7th, and which then measured six inches and a half, had been so cut and reduced by divisions among Mr Laming's friends, at noon, on Monday, the 9th, that he thus possessed only a small bit, from two to three inches in length.

'All the teeth are remarkably short, below the gums. The five which were in the upper jaw, and the middle teeth of the lower, are perfect and white. Mr Fountain took the five upper jaw teeth; Mr Laming one from the lower jaw, Mr Taylor two from it; Hawkesworth one; and another of Mr Ascough's men one; besides these, I have not been able to trace any, nor have I heard that any more were taken.'

Notes and Queries (1852) quoted in Edith Sitwell, *The English Eccentrics* (1933)

The Great Fire

6 September 1666

A sad sight to see how the River looks – no houses nor church near it to the Temple – where it stopped. At home did go with Sir W. Batten and our neighbour Knightly (who, with one more, was the only man of any fashion left in all the neighbourhood hereabouts, they all removing their goods and leaving their houses to the mercy of the fire) to Sir R. Ford's, and there dined, in an earthen platter a fried breast of mutton, a great many of us. But very merry; and endeed as good a meal, though as ugly a one, as ever I had in my life. Thence down to Deptford, and there with great satisfaction landed all my goods at Sir G. Carteret's,* safe, and nothing missed I could see, or hurt. This being done to my great content, I home; and to Sir W. Batten's, and there with Sir R. Ford, Mr Knightly, and one Withers,† a professed lying rogue, supped well; and mighty merry and our fears over. From them to the office and there slept, with the office full of labourers, who talked and slept and walked all night long there. But strange it was to see Cloathworkers-hall on fire these three days and nights in one body of Flame – it being the cellar, full of Oyle.

7th. Up by 5 a-clock and, blessed be God, find all well, and by water to Paul's wharfe. Walked thence and saw all the town burned, and a miserable sight of Pauls church, with all the roofs fallen and the body of the Quire fallen into St Fayths‡ – Paul's school also – Ludgate – Fleet street – my father's house, and the church, and a good part of the Temple the like. So to

* He had an official residence there, as Navy Treasurer.
† Probably Robert Withers, shipbuilder, of Bolton-le-Sands, Lancs.
‡ 'St Faith's-under-St Paul's' was the popular name for the crypt under the choir of the cathedral.

Creeds lodging near the New Exchange, and there find him laid down upon a bed – the house all unfurnished, there being fears of the fire's coming to them.

Samuel Pepys, *Diary*

Toad in the hole

This is a letter which Huish quotes – it is supposed to be an epistle addressed by a French architect in London to his friend in Paris, but Huish takes it so seriously that one is reluctantly forced to believe that the eminent historian must have been the subject of some mild 'leg-pulling'.

My dear Sair – I shall now give you some account of de royal Palace here, called de Buck-and-Ham palace, which is building for de English King in de spirit of John Bull, plum-pudding and roast beef taste, for which de English are so famous. It is great curiosity. In de first place, de pillars of de palace are made to represent English vegitable, as de sparrowgrass, de leek, and onion; then de entablatures or friezes are vary mouch enriched with leg of mutton, and de pork, with vat dey call de garnish, all vary beautiful carved: then, on de impediment of the front, stand colossal figure of de man-cook with de large English toasting-fork in his hand, ready to put into de pot a vary large plum pudding behind him, which is vary fine pudding, not de colour of black Christmas pudding, because de architect say it would not look vell in summair time; it is vary plain pudding. Then de small windows of de kitchen, on each side de impediment at top story of de palace, have before dem trophy of de kitchen, such as pot and de pan, and othare thing, which look well at de distance, except that de poker and de tong are too big. On de wing of de palace, called de gizzard wing (de othare wing was cut off), stand de domestique servant, in neat dress, holding in de trays biscuit and tart, and othare ding. The name of de architect is Mistaire Hash, de King's architect, who, I was informed, was roasted vary much. (The term I did not comprehend.) De English people seem vary much to like dis palace for de King, and do laugh vary much. There is to be in de front of de palace vary large kitchen range, made of white marble, vich I was told would contain

von hundred of goose at von time. De palace, ven complete, will be
called after von famous English dish, de Toad-in-de-Hole!

Bruce Graeme, *The Story of Buckingham Palace* (1928)

On the Tombs in Westminster Abbey

Mortality, behold and fear!
What a change of flesh is here!
Think how many royal bones
Sleep within this heap of stones,
Hence remov'd from beds of ease,
Dainty fare, and what might please,
Fretted roofs, and costly shows,
To a roof that flats the nose:
Which proclaims all flesh is grass,
How the world's fair glories pass;
That there is no trust in health,
In youth, in age, in greatness, wealth:
For if such could have reprived,
Those had been immortal lived.
Know from this the world's a snare,
How that greatness is but care,
How all pleasures are but pain,
And how short they do remain:
For here they lie had realms and lands,
That now want strength to stir their hands;
Where from their pulpits seal'd with dust
They preach, 'In greatness is no trust.'
Here's an acre sown indeed
With the richest royal seed
That the earth did e'er suck in
Since the first man died for sin;
Here the bones of birth have cried
'Though Gods they were, as men have died.'
Here are sands, ignoble things,

59

Drop'd from the ruin'd sides of Kings;
With whom the poor man's earth being shown,
The difference is not easily known.
Here's a world of pomp and state
Forgotten, dead, disconsolate.
Think then this scythe that mows down kings,
Exempts no meaner mortal things.
Then bid the wanton lady tread
Amid these mazes of the dead;
And these, truly understood,
More shall cool and quench the blood
Than her many sports a day,
And her nightly wanton play:
Bid her paint till day of doom,
To this favour she must come.
Bid the merchant gather wealth;
The usurer exact by stealth;
The proud man beat it from his thought –
Yet to this shape all must be brought.

Anon. (?William Basse)

Westminster Abbey

When I am in a serious humour, I very often walk by myself in Westmin-ster-abbey: where the gloominess of the place, and the use to which it is applied, with the solemnity of the building, and the condition of the people who lie in it, are apt to fill the mind with a kind of melancholy or rather thoughtfulness that is not disagreeable. I yesterday passed a whole after-noon in the church-yard, the cloisters, and the church, amusing myself with the tombstones and inscriptions that I met with in those several regions of the dead. Most of them recorded nothing else of the buried person, but that he was born upon one day, and died upon another; the whole history of his life being comprehended in those two circumstances that are common to all mankind. I could not but look upon these registers of existence, whether of brass or marble, as a kind of satire upon the departed persons; who had left no other memorial of them, but that they were born, and that they died. They put me in mind of several persons mentioned in the battles of heroic poems, who have sounding names given them, for no other reason but that they may be killed, and are celebrated for nothing but being knocked on the head.

Glaucumque, Medontaque, Thersilochumque. – VIRGIL
Glaucus, and Melon, and Thersilochus.

The life of these men is finely described in holy writ by 'the path of an arrow', which is immediately closed up and lost.

Upon my going into the church, I entertained myself with the digging of a grave; and saw in every shovel-full of it that was thrown up, the fragment of a bone or skull intermixed with a kind of fresh mouldering earth that some time or other had a place in the composition of a human body. Upon this I began to consider with myself what innumerable multitudes of people lay confused together under the pavement of that ancient cathedral; how men and women, friends and enemies, priests and soldiers, monks and prebendaries, were crumbled amongst one another, and blended together in the same common mass; how beauty, strength, and youth, with old age, weakness, and deformity, lay undistinguished in the same promiscuous heap of matter.

After having thus surveyed the great magazine of mortality, as it were, in the lump, I examined it more particularly by the accounts which I found on several of the monuments which are raised in every quarter of that ancient fabric. Some of them were covered with such extravagant epitaphs, that if it were possible for the dead person to be acquainted with them, he would blush at the praises which his friends have bestowed upon him. There are others so excessively modest, that they deliver the character of the person departed in Greek or Hebrew, and by that means are not understood once in a twelve-month. In the poetical quarter, I found there were poets who had no monuments, and monuments which had no poets. I observed, indeed, that the present war has filled the church with many of these uninhabited monuments, which had been erected to the memory of persons whose bodies were perhaps buried in the plains of Blenheim, or in the bosom of the ocean.

I could not but be very much delighted with several modern epitaphs, which are written with great elegance of expression and justness of thought, and therefore do honour to the living as well as the dead. As a foreigner is very apt to conceive an idea of the ignorance or politeness of a nation from the turn of their public monuments and inscriptions, they should be submitted to the perusal of men of learning and genius before they are put in execution. Sir Cloudesly Shovel's monument has very often given me great offence. Instead of the brave rough English admiral, which was the distinguishing character of that plain gallant man, he is represented on his tomb by the figure of a beau, dressed in a long periwig, and reposing himself upon velvet cushions, under a canopy of state. The inscription is answerable to the monument; for instead of celebrating the many remarkable actions he had performed in the service of his country, it acquaints us only with the manner of his death, in which it was impossible for him to reap any honour. The Dutch, whom we are apt to despise for want of genius, show an infinitely greater taste of antiquity and politeness in their buildings and works of this nature than what we meet with in those of our own country. The monuments of their admirals, which have been erected at the public expense, represent them like themselves, and are adorned with rostral crowns and naval ornaments, with beautiful festoons of sea-weed, shells, and coral.

But to return to our subject. I have left the repository of our English kings for the contemplation of another day, when I shall find my mind disposed for so serious an amusement. I know that entertainments of this nature are apt to raise dark and dismal thoughts in timorous minds and gloomy imaginations; but for my own part, though I am always serious, I do not know what it is to be melancholy; and can therefore take a view of nature in her deep and solemn scenes with the same pleasure as in her most gay and delightful ones. By this means I can improve myself with those objects which others consider with terror. When I look upon the tombs of the great, every motion of envy dies in me; when I read the epitaphs of the beautiful, every inordinate desire goes out; when I meet with the grief of parents upon a tombstone, my heart melts with compassion; when I see the tomb of the parents themselves, I consider the vanity of grieving for those whom we must quickly follow. When I see kings lying by those who deposed them, when I consider rival wits placed side by side, or the holy men that divided the world with their contests and disputes, I reflect with sorrow and astonishment on the little competitions, factions, and debates of mankind. When I read the several dates of the tombs, of some that died yesterday, and some six hundred years ago, I consider that great day when we shall all of us be contemporaries, and make our appearance together.

Joseph Addison, *The Spectator*, 30 March 1711

Monuments in the Abbey

I am just returned from Westminster-abbey, the place of sepulture for the philosophers, heroes, and kings of England. What a gloom do monumental inscriptions and all the venerable remains of deceased merit inspire! Imagine a temple marked with the hand of antiquity, solemn as religious awe, adorned with all the magnificence of barbarous profusion, dim windows, fretted pillars, long colonades, and dark cielings. Think then, what were my sensations at being introduced to such a scene. I stood in the midst of the temple, and threw my eyes round on the walls filled with the statues, the inscriptions, and the monuments of the dead.

Alas, I said to myself, how does pride attend the puny child of dust even to the grave! Even humble as I am, I possess more consequence in the present scene than the greatest heroe of them all; they have toiled for an hour to gain a transient immortality, and are at length retired to the grave, where they have no attendant but the worm, none to flatter but the epitaph.

As I was indulging such reflections, a gentleman dressed in black, perceiving me to be a stranger came up, entered into conversation, and politely offered to be my instructor and guide through the temple. If any monument, said he, should particularly excite your curiosity, I shall endeavour to satisfy your demands. I accepted with thanks the gentleman's offer, adding, that 'I was come to observe the policy, the wisdom, and the justice of the English, in conferring rewards upon deceased merit. If adulation like this, continued I, be properly conducted, as it can no way injure those who are flattered, so it may be a glorious incentive to those who are now capable of enjoying it. It is the duty of every good government to turn this monumental pride to its own advantage, to become strong in the aggregate from the weakness of the individual. If none but the truly great have a place in this awful repository, a temple like this will give the finest lessons of morality, and be a strong incentive to true ambition. I am told, that none have a place here but characters of the most distinguished merit.' The man in black seemed impatient at my observations, so I discontinued my remarks, and we walked on together to take a view of every particular monument in order as it lay.

As the eye is naturally caught by the finest objects, I could not avoid being particularly curious about one monument, which appeared more beautiful than the rest; that, said I to my guide, I take to be the tomb of some very great man. By the peculiar excellence of the workmanship, and the magnificence of the design, this must be a trophy raised to the memory of some king who has saved his country from ruin, or law-giver, who has reduced his fellow-citizens from anarchy into just subjection. It is not requisite, replied my companion smiling, to have such qualifications in order to have a very fine monument here. More humble abilities will suffice. *What, I suppose then the gaining two or three battles, or the taking half a score towns, is thought a sufficient qualification?* Gaining battles, or taking towns replied the man in black, may be of service; but a gentleman may have a very fine monument here without ever seeing a battle or a siege. *This then is the monument of some poet, I presume, of one whose wit has gained him immortality?* No, sir, replied my guide, the gentleman who lies here never made verses; and as for wit, he despised it in others, because he had none himself. *Pray tell me then in a word, said I peevishly, what is the great man who lies here particularly remarkable for?* Remarkable, sir! said my companion; why, sir, the gentleman that lies here is remarkable, very remarkable – for a tomb in Westminster-abbey. *But, head of my Ancestors! how has he got here; I fancy he could never bribe the guardians of the temple to give him a place? Should he not be ashamed to be seen among company, where even moderate merit would look like infamy?* I suppose, replied the man in black, the gentleman was rich, and his friends, as is usual in such a case, told him he was great. He readily believed them; the guardians of the temple, as they got by the self delusion, were ready to believe him too; so he paid his money for a fine monument; and the workman, as you see, has made him one of the most beautiful.

Oliver Goldsmith, *The Citizen of the World* (1762)

Sir Thomas More's head

His discourse was extraordinary facetious. Riding one night, upon the suddaine he crossed himselfe *majori cruce*, crying out Jesu Maria! doe not you see that prodigious Dragon in the skye? They all lookt up, and one did not see it, and nor the tother did not see it. At length one had spyed it, and at last all had spied. Whereas there was no such phantome, only he imposed on their phantasies.

After he was beheaded, his trunke was interred in Chelsey chuch, neer the middle of the South wall, where was some slight Monument erected.

His head was upon London bridge. There goes this story in the family, viz. that one day as one of his daughters was passing under the Bridge, looking on her father's head, sayd she, That head haz layn many a time in my Lapp, would to God it would fall into my Lap as I passe under. She had her wish, and it did fall into her Lappe, and is now preserved in a vault in the Cathedral Church at Canterbury.

John Aubrey, Brief Lives (1693)

On the Demolition of the Odeon Cinema, Westbourne Grove

Never one for the flicks,* I did not frequent the place:
Though I recall the *Voyage of the Argonauts*,
And a second feature – some twaddle about
A daughter of King Arthur, otherwise unrecorded
By history or tradition. Now, each day,
I pass it, and I hear the brutal noise
Of demolition: clatter of falling masonry,
Machines that seem to grit and grind their teeth,
And munch in gluttony of destruction.

Its soft innards, I guess, are gone already:
The screen, the lighting, the plush seats; the ghosts likewise –
Shadows of shadows, phantoms of phantoms,
The love goddesses, the butcher boy heroes,
The squawking cartoon-animals.

This odeon – I should regret it? –
In which no ode has ever been recited.
Yet there's a pang – for I've lived long enough
To know that every house of dreams
Must be torn down at last.

John Heath-Stubbs, Collected Poems (1988)

* The poet is blind.

The Soane Museum

On the north side of Lincoln's Inn Fields, beyond the handsome *Inns of Court Hotel*, is (No. 13) the eccentric *Soane Museum*, formed in his own house and bequeathed to the nation by Sir John Soane (*ob.* 1837), who was the son of a bricklayer at Reading, but, being distinguished as a student in the Royal Academy, and sent to Rome with the Academy pension, lived to become the architect of the Bank of England. The museum, which Mrs Jameson calls 'a fairy palace of *virtu*', was especially intended by its founder to illustrate the artistic and instructive purposes to which it is possible to devote an English private residence, and is open to the public from eleven to five on Tuesdays and Thursdays in February and March; and on Tuesdays, Wednesdays, Thursdays, and Saturdays in April, May, June, July, and August. Few people know of it, and fewer visit it, which is much to be regretted, since, though, as Dr Waagen says, the overcrowded and labyrinthine house leaves an impression as of a feverish dream, it contains, together with much rubbish, several most interesting pictures.

Augustus Hare, *Walks in London* (1878)

Railway Stations

The serious scholar of London railway stations will make the historical approach. I unfold the map of my *Bradshaw's Railway Companion* for 1841. London shrinks to its size a hundred and nine years ago. I notice that there were fields beyond Regent's Park and Pentonville and Islington and Hackney. Bethnal Green was in London, Stratford was not. Southeast of Bermondsey and south of Walworth there were still fields between terraces and squares, fields that in two years were to be filled with either Italianate merchants' houses amid laurel shrubbery or with rows of two-storey artisans' dwellings. Chelsea and Brompton and Kensington still had separate personalities. No railways dared to invade the centre of London. Westminster was even more sacred than the City. There they are on the map, little pink lines, pushing tentatively towards the heart of the metropolis.

These early stations, you must remember, are part of the Georgian age. They are stately but not sumptuous. They are spreading but not soaring. They suggest coaches pulled by iron horses. They are merely another sort of posting inn, not something private, railed off and of another world, which railways have now become. They are the stables of the iron horses and they blend naturally with the drays which clatter over cobbles towards them and the carriages which are unloaded from them and pulled away by horses to the noblemen's houses of Mayfair. Euston (1837), London Bridge (1838), Paddington (1839) are still on their original sites. Philip Hardwick's magnificent Doric Arch of granite (1837) at Euston originally had two lodges flanking each side and was visible from the Euston road; the outer pairs of these have been destroyed. It was the gateway not only to all the country houses of the North, but also to a new age. The little iron sheds of the station behind it, so ridiculed by Pugin, are rather an anti-climax. Successive generations have treated this noble arch scurvily and its glory has been hidden by the Euston Hotel. As an essay of the Greek Revival, I consider the arch even now, almost shorn of its lodges, the noblest thing in London, nobler even than St Pancras church or the British Museum or the Hyde Park Screen. Only one building rivalled it and that was Rennie's Waterloo Bridge. The L.M.S. made determined efforts to remove Euston Arch altogether. British Railways will probably succeed in doing so, for no one, except you and me, dear reader, yet believes that there can be anything beautiful about a railway station.

John Betjeman, *First and Last Loves* (1952)

Monody on the Death of Aldersgate Street Station

Snow falls in the buffet of Aldersgate station,
   Soot hangs in the tunnel in clouds of steam.
City of London! before the next desecration
   Let your steepled forest of churches be my theme.

Sunday Silence! with every street a dead street,
   Alley and courtyard empty and cobbled mews,
Till 'tingle tang' the bell of St Mildred's Bread Street
   Summoned the sermon taster to high box pews,

And neighbouring towers and spirelets joined the ringing
    With answering echoes from heavy commercial walls
Till all were drowned as the sailing clouds went singing
    On the roaring flood of a twelve-voiced peal from Paul's.

Then would the years fall off and Thames run slowly,
    Out into marshy meadow-land flowed the Fleet,
And the walled-in City of London, smelly and holy,
    Had a tinkling mass house in every cavernous street.

The bells rang down and St Michael Paternoster
    Would take me into its darkness from College Hill,
Or Christ Church Newgate Street (with St Leonard Foster)
    Would be late for Mattins and ringing insistent still.

Last of the east wall sculpture, a cherub gazes
    On broken arches, rosebay, bracken and dock,
Where once I heard the roll of the Prayer Book phrases
    And the sumptuous tick of the old west gallery clock.

Snow falls in the buffet of Aldersgate station,
    Toiling and doomed from Moorgate Street puffs the train,
For us of the steam and the gas-light, the lost generation,
    The new white cliffs of the City are built in vain.

John Betjeman, *Collected Poems* (1970)

A memorial to G.B.S.

Thursday, 27 August

In the middle of Parkway, at its junction with Camden High Street, there stands an island which divides the one-way traffic into two streams. It is fenced on three sides by iron railings ornamented at the top with hoops in groups of four enclosed by horizontal bars. From its open end, which faces the crossroads, a steep flight of marbled stairs leads to a lower world beneath the street. It is, so far as I know, the only memorial a grudging Camden Town ever raised to George Bernard Shaw (though there is a plaque on his house at 29 Fitzroy Square). His name is not on it. It has one inscription only, the word 'Ladies' in bold black letters on white plates, one on either side below the hoops. This island has been boarded up for five years or more. Huge beams of wood, one of which forms the winos' grandstand, facing the High Street and backing on to the stairs, lie on the ground all round it. A hoarding painted red and white encloses the memorial but wire-netting windows have been made in it through which you can see a part of the sloping banisters which were once gleaming brass and are now painted black. Mary and all the other ladies have for all these years, in peril of their lives, had to cross the main road and enter an orange coloured horsebox or showman's van which blocks the way into the tube station.

How can it take five years to refurbish a lavatory? It took less than a year to build it, once that dreaded decision was reached, to excavate the site by spade, before mechanical diggers hastened that kind of work, to fit it up and tile it. But more than six years of angry argument, in which Shaw took a strong and humorous part, preceded the decision. In 1927, at a meeting on behalf of the Cecil Houses Fund, for dosshouses for women, Shaw said

> When I went into active municipal life, and became a member of the Health Committee of a London Borough Council (St Pancras), the question of providing accommodation for women, which was part of our business, was one which I conceived to be pressingly important. And you can have no idea of the difficulty I had in getting that notion, to a limited extent, into the heads of the gentlemen who were working with me on the Committee ... I talked and talked to get proper sanitary accommodation for women, I found it impossible for a long time to get over the opposition to it as an indecency. A lavatory for women was described as an abomination. Exactly the same feeling stands in the way of providing for women what is popularly known as a 'doss-house'.

Such notions stay for years and years. We accept women's lavatories in the middle of our streets just as we accept pedestrian crossings and traffic lights, but nothing so far has persuaded us to provide for homeless women. Lord Rowton thought only of men. And so do all of us, except for a few devotees of small and impoverished charities.

Bernard Shaw was not the first person to advocate the building of public lavatories for women. There were a few in St Pancras and in other parts of London before he was made a member of St Pancras vestry in the spring of 1897. In October he became a member of the health committee, on which he served for a second time after the vestry became St Pancras Borough Council.

David Thomson, *In Camden Town* (1983)

The Elgin Marbles

The Elgin Room is almost entirely devoted to the precious marbles removed by Lord Elgin from the Parthenon in 1801, lost by shipwreck, recovered by divers, and purchased by Government, after long controversy, in 1816. It is almost forgotten now with what vituperation the marbles were assailed on their arrival in England; they were 'not originals', they were 'of the time of Hadrian', they were the 'works of journeymen, not deserving the name of artists', they were 'too much broken to be of any value'. The sum paid to Lord Elgin was less than he had expended upon the marbles, and far less than Napoleon was willing to pay for them. Yet now they are recognized as the greatest masterpieces of Greek art in this or any other country. A model of the Parthenon (the Temple of Athene) here shows their original position. Around the room are the glorious frieze and metopes of the temple (their subjects are described beneath): we must remember that here they are, as it were, turned inside out. The frieze represents the procession which took place every five years in honour of the goddess. The south side is the least perfect, having been injured by the winds from the sea: it is chiefly occupied by the victims, who made this procession a kind of cattle-show, as each of the Athenian colonies contributed, and, by their anxiety to shine in this, Athens knew the disposition of her colonies. Here also we see the maidens carrying the sacrificial vessels, the flat vessels being used for libations. To meet this procession comes from the north side a long cavalcade of chariots and horsemen, many of the latter most glorious. From the east end of the temple, where the processions united, are representations of the gods, without whose presence no Greek festival was considered complete, and of the delivery of the *peplos*, the embroidered veil of Athene, given every five years.

Augustus Hare, *Walks in London* (1878)

In the British Museum

'What do you see in that time-touched stone,
    When nothing is there
But ashen blankness, although you give it
    A rigid stare?

'You look not quite as if you saw,
    But as if you heard,
Parting your lips, and treading softly
    As mouse or bird.

'It is only the base of a pillar, they'll tell you,
    That came to us
From a far old hill men used to name
    Areopagus.'

– 'I know no art, and I only view
    A stone from a wall,
But I am thinking that stone has echoed
    The voice of Paul;

'Paul as he stood and preached beside it
    Facing the crowd,
A small gaunt figure with wasted features,
    Calling out loud

'Words that in all their intimate accents
    Pattered upon
That marble front, and were wide reflected,
    And then were gone.

'I'm a labouring man, and know but little,
    Or nothing at all;
But I can't help thinking that stone once echoed
    The voice of Paul.'

Thomas Hardy, *Collected Poems* (1974)

The beauty of the Elgin Marbles

13 May 1815

I came home from the Elgin Marbles melancholy. I almost wish the French had them; we do not deserve such productions. There they lie, covered with dust & dripping with damp, adored by the Artists, admired by the People, neglected by the Government, doubted by Payne Knight, because to doubt them is easier than to feel them, & reverenced & envied by Foreigners, because they do not possess them. What new idea of the perfection of Art God Almighty has pleased to inspire this Man's imagination with – Heaven knows! But I begin to believe with Soame Jennings in his 'Origin of Evil', that these beings who delight & exist in miseries, the diseases, the follies of Man, and as Johnson said in his Review, perhaps some of these mischievous creatures induced Jennings to write an essay on evil that he might revel in his absurdity, and I have not the slightest doubt the descendants of the same branch of little demons are now enjoying the success of their whisperings that like ignes fatui have set visions before the eyes & have bewildered the imaginations of Payne Knights to doubt the beauty of the Elgin Marbles. Poor man, there is nothing more miserable than to think men are the instruments of organizations or infatuation or fancy. Whatever takes away from the power of reasoning on differences & seeing distinctions & arriving at conclusions deprives a human being of half his dignity.

Benjamin Haydon, *Diary* (1960–3)

On the Statue of King Charles I at Charing Cross

That the first Charles does here in triumph ride,
See his son reign'd where he a martyr died,
And people pay that rev'rence as they pass,
(Which then he wanted) to the sacred brass,
Is not th' effect of gratitude alone,
To which we owe the statue and the stone;
But Heav'n this lasting monument has wrought,

That mortals may eternally be taught,
Rebellion, though successful, is but vain,
And kings so kill'd rise conquerors again.
This truth the royal image does proclaim,
Loud as the trumpet of surviving Fame.

Edmund Waller, *Complete Poetical Works* (1953)

A bungler

No. 63 St Martin's-lane formerly led to Roubilliac's studio. Here, in 1828, the Sunday paper, 'The Watchman', was printed.

It must have been here, in the sculptor's time, that Garrick, coming to see how his Shakspere statue progressed, drew out a two-foot rule, and put on a tragic and threatening face to frighten a great red-headed Yorkshireman who was sawing marble for Roubilliac; but who, to his surprise, merely rolled his quid, and coolly said, 'What trick are you after next, my little master?' Upon the honest sculptor's death, Read, one of his pupils, a conceited pretender, took the premises in 1762, and advertised himself as 'Mr Roubilliac's successor'.

This bungler executed the monuments of the Duchess of Northumberland and of Admiral Tyrrell, now disgracing Westminster Abbey. His master used to say to Read when he was bragging, 'Ven you do de monument, den de varld vill see vot von d— ting you vill make.' Nollekens used to say of the admiral's monument, 'That figure going to heaven out of the sea looks for all the world as if it were hanging from a gallows with a rope round its neck.'

Walter Thornbury, *Haunted London* (1865)

A Description of the Boatmen's Chapel
(the Paddington One) by Tom

Last Sunday our boat lay in the basin and in the morning some persons came and asked us if we could read; we said, yes, some of us, Master, then they left us some of their books, and asked us to go to their Chapel . . . The front was just like our Master's stables, only 'Boatman's Chapel' was written on at the top . . . I had a good look at the place; there were some benches for the gentlemen and ladies and some plank ends for us to sit upon . . . After a bit the place got nearly full and then some one got up and read a little, then we all stood up and they began singing, but were soon tired . . . Then a nice old gentleman in black said 'Let us Pray' and he asked the good God to look down from heaven on the boatmen who were present; then I was afraid, but he soon prayed to God to give us new hearts, and after death to take us to heaven. When he had said 'Amen' he sat down, and the people opened their eyes again: and all looked so comfortable. He said we were all great sinners. Thinks I, some of the fine people won't like that; but they all kept quiet.

Quoted in David Thomson, *In Camden Town* (1983)

The Knights of the Temple

Colleges, schools, and Inns of Court still have some respect for antiquity, and maintain a great number of the customs and institutions of our ancestors, with which those persons who do not particularly regard their forefathers, or perhaps are not very well acquainted with them, have long since done away. A well-ordained workhouse or prison is much better provided with the appliances of health, comfort, and cleanliness, than a respectable Foundation School, a venerable College, or a learned Inn. In the latter place of residence men are contented to sleep in dingy closets, and to pay for the sitting-room and the cupboard, which is their dormitory, the price of a good villa and garden in the suburbs, or of a roomy house in the neglected squares of the town. The poorest mechanic in Spitalfields has a cistern and an unbounded supply of water at his command; but the gentlemen of the Inns of Court, and the gentlemen of the Universities, have their supply of this cosmetic fetched in jugs by laundresses and bedmakers, and live in abodes which were erected long before the custom of cleanliness and decency obtained among us. There are individuals still alive who sneer at the people, and speak of them with epithets of scorn. Gentlemen, there can be but little doubt that your ancestors were the great unwashed; and in the Temple especially, it is pretty certain that, only under the greatest difficulties and restrictions, the virtue which has been pronounced to be next to godliness could have been practised at all.

Old Grump, of the Norfolk Circuit, who had lived for more than thirty years in the chambers under those occupied by Warrington and Pendennis, and who used to be awakened by the roaring of the shower-baths which those gentlemen had erected in their apartments – part of the contents of which occasionally trickled through the roof into Mr Grump's room – declared that the practice was an absurd, new-fangled, dandified folly, and daily cursed the laundress who slopped the staircase by which he had to pass. Grump, now much more than half a century old, had indeed never used the luxury in question. He had done without water very well, and so had our fathers before him. Of all those knights and baronets, lords and gentlemen, bearing arms, whose escutcheons are painted upon the walls of the famous hall of the Upper Temple, was there no philanthropist good-natured enough to devise a set of Hummums for the benefit of the lawyers, his fellows and successors? The Temple historian makes no mention of such a scheme. There is Pump Court and Fountain Court, with their hydraulic apparatus; but one never heard of a bencher disporting in the fountain, and can't but think how many a counsel learned in the law of old days might have benefited by the pump.

Nevertheless, those venerable Inns which have the Lamb and Flag and the Winged Horse for their ensigns have attractions for persons who inhabit them, and a share of rough comforts and freedom, which men always remember with pleasure. I don't know whether the student of law permits himself the refreshment of enthusiasm, or indulges in poetical reminiscences as he passes by historical chambers, and says, 'Yonder Eldon lived – upon this site Coke mused upon Lyttleton – here Chitty toiled – here Barnwell and Alderson joined in their famous labours – here Byles composed his great work upon bills, and Smith compiled his immortal leading cases – here Gustavus still toils, with Solomon to aid him'; but the man of letters can't but love the place which has been inhabited by so many of his brethren, or peopled by their creations, as real to us at this day as the authors whose children they were – and Sir Roger de Coverley walking in the Temple Garden, and discoursing with Mr Spectator about the beauties in hoops and patches who are sauntering over the grass, is just as lively a figure to me as old Samuel Johnson rolling through the fog with the Scotch gentleman at his heels on their way to Dr Goldsmith's chambers in Brick Court; or Harry Fielding, with inked ruffies and a wet towel round his head, dashing off articles at midnight for the *Covent Garden Journal*, while the printer's boy is asleep in the passage.

William Makepeace Thackeray, Pendennis (1850)

St Paul's Cathedral

Sir *Christopher's* Design was, indeed, very unhappily baulked in several Things at the beginning, as well in the Situation as in the Conclusion of this Work, which, because very few may have heard of, I shall mention in Publick, from the Mouth of its Author.

1. In the Situation: He would have had the Situation of the Church removed a little to the *North*, that it should have stood just on the Spot of Ground which is taken up by the Street called *Pater-noster-Row*, and the Buildings on either Side; so that the *North* Side of the Church should have stood open to the Street now called *Newgate-street*, and the *South* Side, to the Ground on which the Church now stands.

By this Situation, the *East* End of the Church, which is very beautiful, would have looked directly down the main Street of the City, *Cheapside*; and for the *West* End, *Ludgate* having been removed a little *North*, the main Street called *Ludgate-street* and *Ludgate-Hill*, would only have sloped a little *WSW* as they do now irregularly Two Ways, one within, and the other without the Gate, and all the Street beyond *Fleet-Bridge* would have received no Alteration at all.

By this Situation, the common Thorough-fare of the City would have been removed at a little farther Distance from the Work, and we should not then have been obliged to walk just under the very Wall as we do now, which makes the Work appear quite out of all Perspective, and is the chief Reason of the Objections I speak of; whereas, had it been viewed at a little Distance, the Building would have been seen infinitely to more Advantage.

Had Sir *Christopher* been allowed this Situation, he would then, also, have had more Room for the Ornament of the *West* End, which, tho' it is a most beautiful Work, as it now appears, would have been much more so then, and he would have added a Circular Piazza to it, after the Model of that at *Rome*, but much more Magnificent, and an Obelisk of Marble in the Center of the Circle, exceeding any Thing that the World can now shew of its kind, I mean of Modern Work.

But the Circumstance of Things hindered this Noble Design, and the City being almost rebuilt before he obtained an Order and Provision for laying the Foundation; he was prescribed to the narrow Spot where we see it now stands, in which the Building, however Magnificent in itself, stands with the infinite Disadvantage as to the Prospect of it; the Inconveniencies of which was so apparent when the Church was finished, that Leave was at length, tho' not without difficulty, obtained, to pull down one whole Row of Houses on the *North* Side of the Body of the Church, to make Way for the Ballister that surrounds the Cimetry or Church-yard, and, indeed, to admit the Light into the Church, as well as to preserve it from the Danger of Fire.

Another Baulk which, as I said, Sir *Christopher* met with, was in the Conclusion of the Work, namely, the covering of the Dome, which Sir *Christopher* would have had been of Copper double Gilded with Gold; but he was over-ruled by *Party*, and the City thereby, deprived of the most glorious Sight that the World ever saw, since the Temple of *Solomon*.

Yet with all these Disadvantages, the Church is a most regular Building, Beautiful, Magnificent, and beyond all the Modern Works of its Kind in *Europe*, St *Peter*'s at *Rome*, as above, only excepted.

It is true, St *Peter*'s, besides its Beauty in Ornament and Imagery, is beyond St *Paul*'s in its Dimensions, is every way larger; but it is the only Church in the World that is so; and it was a merry Hyperbole of Sir *Christopher Wren*'s, who, when some Gentlemen in Discourse compared the Two Churches, and in Compliment to him, pretended to prefer St *Paul*'s, and when they came to speak of the Dimensions, suggested, that St *Paul*'s was the biggest: *I tell you*, says Sir *Christopher*, *you might set it in St* Peter*'s, and look for it a good while, before you could find it.*

Daniel Defoe, *A Tour Through the Whole Island of Great Britain* (1724–6)

77

The achievement of Sir Christopher Wren

On July 7, 1713, was the thanksgiving for the Peace of Utrecht. Both Houses of Parliament attended in full state. The Queen signified her pleasure not to go to S. Paul's, but designed to return thanks to God for peace in her own closet.

On this day was the first spectacle of the Charity Children in the streets, not yet in the Cathedral. They were said to be 4,000 in number, and to occupy a space of 620 feet, eight rows, one behind the other.

Before this last great festival, about three years, the exterior of the Cathedral was adjudged to be complete. It stood with its perfect dome and encircling colonnades, its galleries and ball, and surmounting cross. In the year 1710, Sir Christopher Wren, by the hands of his son, attended by Mr Strong, the master mason who had executed the whole work, and the body of Freemasons, of which Sir Christopher was an active member, laid the last and highest stone of the lantern of the cupola, with humble prayers for the Divine blessing on his work.

If ever there was an occasion on which the heart of man might swell with pardonable pride, it was the heart of Wren at that hour, whether he himself was actually at the giddy summit of the building, or watched his son's act from below. The architect looked down, or looked up and around, on this great and matchless building, the creation of his own mind, the achievement of his sole care and skill. The whole building stretching out in all its perfect harmony, with its fine horizontal lines, various yet in perfect unison, its towers, its unrivalled dome, its crowning lantern and cross. All London had poured forth for the spectacle, which had been publicly announced, and were looking up in wonder to the old man, or his son if not the old man himself, who was, on that wondrous height, setting the seal, as it were, to his august labours. If in that wide circle (let us, however doubtful, lift the old man to that proud eminence), which his eye might embrace, there were various objects for regret and disappointment; if instead of beholding the spacious streets of the city, each converging to its centre, London had sprung up and spread in irregular labyrinths of close, dark, intricate lanes; if even his own Cathedral was crowded upon and jostled by mean and unworthy buildings; yet, on the other hand, he might survey, not the Cathedral only, but a number of stately churches, which had risen at his command and taken form and dignity from his genius and skill. On one

side the picturesque steeple of S. Mary-le-Bow, on the other the exquisite
tower of S. Bride's, with all its graceful gradually diminishing circles, not
yet shorn of its full and finely proportioned height. Beyond and on all sides,
if more dimly seen, yet discernible by his partial eyesight (he might even
penetrate to the inimitable interior of S. Stephen's, Walbrook), church after
church, as far as S. Dunstan-in-the-East, perhaps Greenwich may have
been vaguely made out in the remote distance. And all this one man
had been permitted to conceive and execute; a man not originally destined
or educated for an architect, but compelled, as it were, by the public
necessities to assume the office, and so to fulfil it, as to stand on a level with
the most consummate masters of the art in Europe, and to take his stand on
an eminence which his English successors almost despair of attaining.

H. H. Milman, *Annals of St Paul's Cathedral* (1868)

Bunhill Fields

Beyond Finsbury Square, by the *Finsbury Pavement* – once the only firm
path in the marshy district of Moorfields – we reach, in the *City Road* (left),
the modern castellated buildings of the *Militia Barracks*, which are the
headquarters of the London Militia – the 'London Trained Bands' of our
Civil Wars, which were the mainstay of the Parliamentary army. . . .

Just beyond the Barracks (divided by the street) is the vast burial-ground
of *Bunhill Fields*, Anthony Wood's 'fanatical burial-place', and Southey's
'Campo Santo of the Dissenters', originally called 'Bone-hill Fields', probably from the vast quantities of bones which Maitland mentions as having
been transported here (*c.* 1540).

> Open, *Week-days*, 9 to 7 in summer, 9 to 4 in winter.
> *Sundays*, 1 to 7 in summer, 1 to 4 in winter.

The burial-ground is now closed as a cemetery, but the forest of tombs
on the left, shaded by young trees, remains a green oasis in one of the
blackest parts of London. Near the centre of 'the Puritan Necropolis' a
white figure, lying aloft upon a high (modern) altar-tomb, marks the *Grave
of John Bunyan* (1628–88), whither all will at once direct their steps, for
who does not, with Cowper –

Revere the man whose pilgrim marks the road,
And guides the progress of the soul to God.

Bunyan wrote as many books as the sixty years of his life, but is chiefly honoured as the author of 'The Pilgrim's Progress', which was written during his imprisonment as a dissenter in Bedford jail, where, 'with only two books – the Bible and "Foxe's Book of Martyrs" – he employed his time for twelve years and a half in preaching to, and praying with, his fellow-prisoners, in writing several of his works, and in making tagged laces for the support of himself and his family.' . . .

George Whitefield preached in Bunhill Fields (April 30, 1760) at the grave of Robert Tilling, who was hung at Tyburn for the murder of his master, Mr Lloyd, a Bishops-gate merchant. He frequently preached in the open air in Moorfields to congregations of from twenty to thirty thousand persons, and it was there especially, as he wrote to Lady Huntingdon, that 'he went to meet the devil'. In 1741 a wooden tabernacle was built for him, which was superseded by a brick building in 1753, but he continued, when the weather allowed, to address in the open air larger congregations than any building would contain. His open-air church was like a battle-field, merry-andrews exhibiting their tricks close by to draw off his congregations, recruiting sergeants with their drums marching through the midst of his hearers, showers of dirt, eggs, &c., being perpetually hurled at him.

Augustus Hare, *Walks in London* (1878)

Blake's Chaucer

An Original Engraving by him from his Fresco Painting of Sir Jeffery Chaucer and his Nine and Twenty Pilgrims setting forth from Southwark on their Journey to Canterbury.

Three Feet 1 Inch long, and 1 Foot high;
Price Three Guineas

THE time chosen is early morning before sun-rise when the Jolly Company are just quitting the Tabarde Inn. The Knight and Squire with the Squire's Yeoman lead the Procession; then the youthful Abbess, her Nun and three Priests: her Grey-hounds attend her.

> Of small hounds had she, that she fed
> With roast flesh, milk and wastel bread.

Next follow the Friar and Monk, then the Tapiser, the Pardoner, the Sompnour and the Manciple. After these 'Our Host', who occupies the Center of the Cavalcade, directs them to the Knight as the person who will be likely to commence their Task of each telling a Tale in their order. After the Host follow the Shipman, the Haberdasher, the Dyer, the Franklin, the Physician, the Plowman, the Lawyer, the Parson, the Merchant, the Wife of Bath, the Cook, the Oxford Scholar, Chaucer himself, and the Reeve comes as Chaucer has described:

> And ever he rode hinderest of the rout.

These last are issuing from the Gateway of the Inn. The Cook and the Wife of Bath are both taking their morning's draught of comfort. Spectators stand at the Gateway of the Inn, and are composed of an Old Man, a Woman and Children.

This Inn is yet extant under the name of the Talbot; and the Landlord, Robert Bristow, Esq. of Broxmore near Rumsey, has continued a Board over the Gateway, inscribed 'This is the Inn from which Sir Jeffery Chaucer and his Pilgrims set out for Canterbury.'

St Thomas's Hospital which is situated near to it, is one of the most amiable features of the Christian Church; it belonged to the Monastery of St Mary Overies and was dedicated to Thomas a Becket. The Pilgrims, if sick or lame, on their Journey to and from his Shrine, were received at this House. Even at this day every friendless wretch who wants the succour of it, is considered as a Pilgrim travelling through this Journey of Life.

The Landscape is an eastward view of the Country from the Tabarde Inn in Southwark as it may be supposed to have appeared in Chaucer's time, interspersed with Cottages and Villages. The first beams of the sun are seen above the horizon: some Buildings and Spires indicate the situation of the Great City. The Inn is a Gothic Building which Thynne in his Glossary says was the Lodging of the Abbot of Hyde by Winchester. On the Inn is inscribed its Title, and a proper advantage is taken of this circumstance to describe the subject of the Picture. The words written in Gothic Letters over the Gateway of the Inn are as follow: 'The Tabarde Inn by Henry Bailly. The Lodging House for Pilgrims who Journey to St Thomas's Shrine at Canterbury.'

Of Chaucer's Characters as described in his Canterbury Tales, some of the names are altered by Time, but the Characters themselves for ever remain unaltered and consequently they are the Physiognomies or Lineaments of Universal Human Life beyond which Nature never steps. The Painter has consequently varied the heads and forms of his Personages into all Nature's varieties; the Horses he has varied to accord to their riders, the Costume is correct according to authentic Monuments.

Subscriptions received at No. 28, Corner of Broad Street, Golden Square.

A Descriptive Catalogue of Pictures, Poetical and Historical Inventions,
Painted by William Blake (1809)

Albert Grant, Esq., MP

On reaching Leicester Square Kingsmill asked Pearson if he knew the statue of Albert Grant. No, said Pearson; so Kingsmill led him to the centre of the Square and pointed at an Elizabethan figure in doublet and hose who was resting his elbow on a volume and trying to look thoughtful.

PEARSON: But, damn it, that's Shakespeare! I've known it as long as I've known London. Everyone knows it. It's the most familiar statue in the world.

KINGSMILL: Well, let's read the inscription. That should settle it.

Approaching the statue they read –

This enclosure was purchased, laid out and decorated as a garden by ALBERT GRANT, Esq., MP and conveyed by him on 2nd July, 1874, to the Metropolitan Board of Works to be preserved for ever for the free use and enjoyment of the public.

KINGSMILL: As you see, there's no mention of Shakespeare anywhere on the monument; and I therefore infer that the man up there is Albert Grant, a scrupulous company promoter, whose maiden name, I understand, was Gottheimer. Have you any comments to make?

PEARSON: None.

Hesketh Pearson and Hugh Kingsmill, *Talking of Dick Whittington* (1947)

A London pleasure garden

The event of 1775 was the Ranelagh Regatta and Ball, which took place on June 23rd. Early in the afternoon of that day the whole river from London Bridge to Millbank was covered with pleasure boats, and scaffold erections were to be seen on the banks, and even on the top of Westminster Hall. Gambling tables lined the approaches to Westminster Bridge: men went about selling indifferent liquor, Regatta songs and Regatta cards. The river banks now resembled a great fair, and the Thames itself a floating town. Wild calculations fixed the number of the spectators at 200,000, or 'at least' three millions. At 7.30 a cannon signalled the start of the racing-boats, and about 8.30, when the prizes had been awarded, the whole procession began to move 'in a picturesque irregularity towards Ranelagh'. The Directors' barge, with its band playing and gold REGATTA ensign flying, led the way, and the fortunate persons who had ball-tickets landed at Ranelagh Stairs at nine o'clock.

Dancing took place in the Temple of Neptune, a temporary octagon erection in the grounds. Mrs Cornelys had been given seven hundred guineas (it is said) to supply the supper, and it is lamentable to reflect that the supper was 'indifferent, and the wine very scarce'. However, there was a great company: the Duke of Gloucester, the Duke of Northumberland, Lord North, the Duchess of Devonshire, Sir Joshua Reynolds, Garrick, Colman, Samuel Foote. A band of two hundred and forty instrumentalists, under Giardini, performed in the Rotunda, and there was singing by Vernon and Reinhold, including the cheering ballad:

> Ye lords and ye ladies who form this gay throng,
> Be silent a moment, attend to our song,
> And while you suspend your fantastical round,
> Come, bless your sweet stars that you're none of you drowned.

. . .

On 1 June, 1803, a ball in commemoration of the Installation of the Knights of the Bath took place and proved one of the finest of the entertainments. Yet these were only 'struggles for happiness', and attempts to galvanize a nearly lifeless Ranelagh. The unending promenade, with its sentimental songs and elegant regale of tea and coffee, had ceased to attract, and the lamp-hung trees, the Chinese House and the music on the Canal had lost their ancient charm. On 8 July, 1803, the Rotunda of Ranelagh was opened for the last time as a place of amusement.

On 30 September, 1805, the proprietors gave directions for the demolition of Ranelagh House and the Rotunda; the furniture was sold by auction shortly afterwards, and the buildings were removed. The organ was bought for Tetbury Church, Gloucestershire, where it remained till 1863, when it was purchased by a builder.

The Ranelagh grounds had extended from the old Burial Ground (east of Chelsea Hospital) to the river-marshes on the south, and the Chelsea Bridge Road now crosses their eastern boundary. When the buildings were removed the grounds were, by degrees, purchased of the shareholders by General Richard R. Wilford to add to his property adjoining. A poet of the *Gentleman's Magazine* in June 1807 laments the Fall of Ranelagh, and the site already overgrown with weeds. The foundation walls of the Rotunda and the arches of some of the cellars could, however, be traced as late as 1813, and part of the site was a favourite playground for Chelsea children. By 1826, the Ranelagh grounds had become by purchase the property of Chelsea Hospital and were parcelled out into allotments. The ground is, at the present time, once more a 'Ranelagh Garden', in which the public are admitted, as the old advertisements would say, 'to walk gratis'.

All traces of Ranelagh have been thus obliterated, and a London historian (Jesse, *London*, iii, 420) on visiting the site in 1871, could find as its memorial only a single avenue of trees with one or two of the old lamp-irons – the 'firetrees' of the early advertisements – still attached.

Warwick Wroth, *The London Pleasure Gardens in the Eighteenth Century* (1896)

4

The Place

Districts, places, street names

There are worlds of differences every half mile or so in London. The strangely seedy, treeless regions around Paddington Station give place almost imperceptibly to the great creamy stucco houses and leafy squares of Bayswater. Only a short walk northwards takes you to the nondescript regions described by house agents as 'North Kensington'; westwards you enter Notting Hill, which varies almost from street to street between palatial splendour and bohemian chic, rubbing shoulders with the no less fashionable Afro-Caribbean quarter around All Saints Road, with its interesting bars, restaurants and mildly druggy music shops. All this contained in one or two postal districts, W2 and W11. Any part of London could claim a similarly marked social, racial and cultural mix, and it was nearly always so.

Since the British are snobs, they like to suggest by their London address that they are the sort of people whom their interlocutor would admire. Thus, if you lived somewhere in the regions I have just described, you could describe your domicile variously as 'Kensington', 'Bayswater' or 'Notting Hill' depending upon whom you wished to impress. We have all got lost on the way to suppers with new friends or acquaintances, and have said, as we peered at our street maps, 'But they said they lived in Hampstead.' 'Well, West Hampstead is sort of Hampstead, I suppose.'

Only the vulgar would speak about, or covet, what the Edwardians would have called a 'good' address. In fact, it is hard to say what the modern equivalent of a good address would be in today's London. (Until the Second World War, you could not have a good address north of Hyde Park.) There remains a great importance in London places, place names and street names; and it is an importance whose labyrinthine strands of meaning or assonance in a fellow-Londoner's

*mind would be all but untranslatable to an outsider. It is partly a matter of
chance that Parson's Green, let us say, should have been fashionable among the
yuppies of the 1980s. (Their parents, had they been reduced to living there,
would have said they lived in Chelsea.) Likewise, it was modishness which
destroyed 'Fitzrovia', the region of Soho which stayed north of Oxford Street
and which no longer provides a refuge for the bohemian crowd of poets and
painters who patronized its largely homosexual pubs in the 1950s. But fashion
alone does not explain our complicated feelings about the place names and street
names of London. There is, as G. K. Chesterton conveys in his reverie about the
street names of Notting Hill, a whole buried world of history and association in
almost every street and square.*

King's Cross

'You see, it's a *queer* neighbourhood.'

'Queer?' He was shocked, perhaps a little hurt, but his calm tone dis-
closed nothing of that. He had a desire to explain to Mrs Arb at great length
that the neighbourhood was one of almost unique interest.

'Well, you know what I mean. You see, I come from Fulham – Chelsea
you might call it. I'm not saying that when I lived in this shop before –
eighteen years ago, is it? – I'm not saying I thought it was a queer neighbourhood then. I didn't – and I was here for over a year, too. But I do now.'

'I must confess it hasn't struck me as *queer*.'

'You know this King's Cross Road?' Mrs Arb proceeded with increased
ardour. 'You know it? You've walked all along it?'

'Yes.'

'So have I. Oh! I've looked about me. Is there a single theatre in it? Is
there one music-hall? Is there one dance-hall? Is there one picture theatre?
Is there one nice little restaurant? Or a tea-shop where a nice person could
go if she'd a mind? . . . And yet it's a very important street; it's full of
people all day. And you can walk for miles round here and see *nothing*. And
the dirt and untidiness! Well, I thought Fulham was dirty. Now look at this
Riceyman Square place, up behind those funny steps! I walked *through*
there. And I lay there isn't one house in it – not one – without a broken
window! The fact is, the people about here don't want things nice and
kept. . . . I'm not meaning you – certainly not! But people in general. And

they don't want anything fresh, either. They only want all the nasty old things they've always had, same as pigs. And yet I must say I admire pigs, in a way. Oh, dear!' She laughed, as if at herself, a tinkling laugh, and looked down, with her steady agreeable hand still on the door.

Arnold Bennett, *Riceyman Steps* (1923)

Rights of way, 1360

Time out of mind the commonalty of the city have been wont to have free ingress and egress with horses and carts from sunrise to sunset for carrying and carting all manner of victuals and wares therefrom to the water of Thames and from the said water of Thames to the city aforesaid, through the great gate of the Templars, situate within Temple Bar, in the ward [of Farringdon Without], in the suburb of London; and the possessors of the Temple were wont and by right ought to maintain a bridge* at the water aforesaid and a common latrine there, well covered and with four apertures therein over the same water. And the possessors of a certain structure in Fleet Street in the suburb of London ought to pave the road on either side of that structure. Also, the Prior of St John of Jerusalem in England, who is the possessor of the Temple aforesaid, molests the citizens of the said city so that they cannot have their free ingress and egress through the gate aforesaid as of old . . . and . . . by default of the said Prior . . . the pavement . . . is worn out and broken and dangerous to all persons passing or riding thereby.

Quoted in Edith Rickert, *Chaucer's World* (1948)

---

* A pier, or jetty, for landing, called Templebridge.

London Misnomers

From Park Lane to Wapping, by day and by night,
    I've many a year been a roamer,
And find that no lawyer can London indict,
    Each street, ev'ry lane's a misnomer.
I find Broad Street, St Giles's, a poor narrow nook,
    Battle Bridge is unconscious of slaughter,
Duke's Place cannot muster the ghost of a duke,
    And Brook Street is wanting in water.

I went to Cornhill for a bushel of wheat,
    And sought it in vain ev'ry shop in,
The Hermitage offered a tranquil retreat
    For the jolly Jack hermits of Wapping.
Spring Gardens, all wintry, appear on the wane,
    Sun Alley's an absolute blinder,
Mount Street is a level, and Bearbinder Lane
    Has neither a bear nor a binder.

No football is kicked up and down in Pall Mall,
    Change Alley, alas! never varies,
The Serpentine river's a straitened canal,
    Milk Street is denuded of dairies.
Knight's bridge, void of tournaments, lies calm and still,
    Butcher Row cannot boast of a cleaver,
And (tho' it abuts on his garden) Hay Hill
    Won't give Devon's duke the hay fever.

The Cockpit's the focus of law, not of sport,
    Water Lane is affected with dryness,
And, spite of its gorgeous approach, Prince's Court
    Is a sorry abode for his Highness.
From Baker Street North all the bakers have fled,
    So, in verse not quite equal to Homer,
Methinks I have proved what at starting I said,
    That London's one mighty misnomer.

James Smith, Comic Miscellanies (1873)

Necessary or contingent

There are some parts of London which are necessary and others which are contingent. Everywhere west of Earls Court is contingent, except for a few places along the river. I hate contingency. I want everything in my life to have a sufficient reason. Dave lived west of Earls Court, and this was another thing I had against him. He lived off the Goldhawk Road, in one of those reddish black buildings which for some reason are called mansions. It was in such contexts, in my dark London childhood, that I first learnt the word, and it has ruined many pieces of prose for me since, including some Biblical ones. I think that Dave doesn't mind much about his surroundings. Being a philosopher, he is professionally concerned with the central knot of being (though he would hate to hear me use this phrase), and not with the loose ends that most of us have to play with. Also, since he is Jewish he can feel himself to be a part of History without making any special effort. I envy him that. For myself, I find I have to work harder and harder every year to keep in with History. So Dave can afford to have a contingent address. I wasn't sure that I could.

Iris Murdoch, Under the Net (1954)

A vanished class

I had never gone out of my way to investigate this Alsatia of North Kensington. Now, when it seemed probable that the more enterprising thugs would be exercising their calling, thanks to the favourable conditions provided by the blackout, in the profitable districts of W1, and the more nervous would be deep in the Tube shelters, was surely the ideal time for this long postponed exploration.

The deeper I penetrated into the stucco wilderness, deserted save for an occasional pathetic figure weighed down by bedding hurrying through the drizzle to the Shepherd's Bush Tube Station, the more insistent did the past become. A certain plenitude of frosted glass and bold Victorian display-types, still characteristic of Dublin and the lower East Side of New York, but elsewhere in London long since submerged beneath a flood of chromium plate and modernistic sans-serif, was doubtless chiefly responsible, but in addition long buried memories of streets half-seen in the distance from my pram, as nurse cautiously skirted the fringe of this City of the Plain on our way to Wormwood Scrubs in the hope of seeing Mr Graham White go up in his new flying machine, played their part. As I drifted on in a vaguely north-eastern direction, ears cocked for overhead chugging, the sense of familiarity deepened and finally achieved its maximum intensity at the end of a curving street of dilapidated semi-detacheds, all peeling paint and crumbling volutes.

As I paused to take in this panorama of decay my attention was irresistibly, but apparently illogically, drawn to a house immediately opposite across the street. Separated from the pavement by a few square feet of trampled grass and sooty laurels, the brickwork of the low wall still bearing scars that marked the recent out-wrenching of railings for the armaments drive, it in no way differed from any of its neighbours; the pillared portico and debased but still classical mouldings marked it as having been originally intended for some solid family of the Victorian *bourgeoisie*; the marked disparity of the window-curtains on the various floors, all subtly different in their general cheapness and vulgarity, indicated that it now sheltered three or perhaps four separate establishments. My glance travelling disdainfully across this depressing façade, marking the broken balustrade above the cornice, the hacked and blackened lime-trees, the half erased 79 on the dirty umber of the door-pillars that had once been cream, came finally and shockingly to rest on the street name attached to the garden wall – Elgin Crescent. This, I suddenly realized, was my birthplace.

In my subconscious eagerness to prolong my evening stroll, I must have walked right through the haunted district I had set out to explore and emerged into the once familiar playground of my childhood on the slopes of Notting Hill. The fact that I had done so all unawares, that I had passed the formerly so firmly established boundary line without for a moment realizing it, spoke far more clearly of what had happened here in the last thirty years than could many volumes of social history. As I walked on up the hill, regardless for once of a flying-bomb now following the course of Ladbroke Grove seemingly only just above the chimney-pots, I noticed with a certain proprietary satisfaction that the progress of decay had not been halted at Elgin Crescent; that the squares and terraces that had once formed the very Acropolis of Edwardian propriety grouped round the church had suffered a hardly less severe decline. Some of the most obvious signs of degradation were certainly the result of five years of war and common to all parts of

London, but here this enforced neglect was clearly but a temporary acceleration of a continuous process. The vast stucco palaces of Kensington Park Road and the adjoining streets had long ago been converted into self-contained flats where an ever-increasing stream of refugees from every part of the once civilized world had found improvised homes, like the dark-age troglodytes who sheltered in the galleries and boxes of the Colosseum. Long, long before the outbreak of war these classical façades had already ceased to bear any relevance to the life that was lived behind them; the eminent KCs and the Masters of City Companies had already given place to Viennese professors and Indian students and bed-sitter business girls years before the first siren sounded. And yet I who was only on the threshold of middle-age could clearly remember the days when they flourished in all their intended glory. At that house on the corner I used to go to dancing classes; outside that imposing front-door I had watched the carriages setting down for a reception; and in that now denuded garden I had once played hide and seek.

Many times since that wet wartime evening I have pondered on the implications of the dismal transformation then so suddenly brought home to me. This was not, it seemed to me, just a case of a once fashionable district declining slowly into slumdom but rather the outward and visible sign of the disappearance of a whole culture; a disappearance, moreover, which no one seems to have noticed and for which no tears had been shed. For it is a curious fact the term 'upper-middle-class' used as a social classification should only have achieved its maximum currency at a time when that class, or rather the cultural pattern which it established, had completely vanished.

Osbert Lancaster, *All Done from Memory* (1963)

Feeding Tudor London

The feeding of Tudor London governed the agricultural policy of the home counties, and the same influence was felt in varying degrees further afield. Food was wanted in the capital, in vast quantity for the population, and of the best quality for the richest tables of the kingdom. Kent with its enclosed fields, already called 'the garden of England', was specifically London's fruit-garden, rich with 'apples beyond measure and also with cherries'.

The barley of East Anglia, coming through brewing towns like Royston, quenched the daily thirst of the Londoner; while Kent and Essex were learning to train hops to flavour his beer. For the rest, the wheat and rye that made London's bread, were grown all over the south-eastern counties.

Thus the great market of the capital helped to change agricultural methods, by inducing districts best fitted for one particular crop to specialize on that. Near London, Norden the topographer noticed 'another sort of husbandman, or yeoman rather, who wade in the weeds of gentlemen, . . . who having great feedings for cattle', sell their fat stock at Smithfield, 'where also they store themselves with lean. There are also those that live by carriage for other men, and to that end they keep carts and carriages, carry milk, meal and other things to London, whereby they live very gainfully.' In regions so fortunately situated, the pressure to enclose the land was strong.

G. M. Trevelyan, *English Social History* (1944)

The railway comes to north London

The first shock of a great earthquake had, just at that period, rent the whole neighbourhood to its centre. Traces of its course were visible on every side. Houses were knocked down; streets broken through and stopped; deep pits and trenches dug in the ground; enormous heaps of earth and clay thrown up; buildings that were undermined and shaking, propped by great beams of wood. Here, a chaos of carts, overthrown and jumbled together, lay topsy-turvy at the bottom of a steep unnatural hill: there, confused treasures of iron soaked and rusted in something that had accidentally become a pond. Everywhere were bridges that led nowhere; thoroughfares that were wholly impassable; Babel towers of chimneys, wanting half their height; temporary wooden houses and enclosures, in the most unlikely situations; carcases of ragged tenements, and fragments of unfinished walls and arches, and piles of scaffolding, and wildernesses of bricks, and giant forms of cranes, and tripods straddling above nothing. There were a hundred thousand shapes and substances of incompleteness, wildly mingled out of their places, upside down, burrowing in the earth, aspiring in the air, mouldering in the water, and unintelligible as any dream. Hot springs and fiery eruptions, the usual attendants upon earthquakes, lent their contributions of confusion to the scene. Boiling water hissed and heaved within dilapidated walls; whence, also, the glare and roar of flames came issuing forth; and mounds of ashes blocked up rights of way, and wholly changed the law and custom of the neighbourhood.

In short, the yet unfinished and unopened Railroad was in progress; and, from the very core of all this dire disorder, trailed smoothly away, upon its mighty course of civilization and improvement.

Charles Dickens, *Dombey and Son* (1848)

By land

Long after the railway was made which passed by Whitmore (within a long drive of Stoke), we continued to go in our own carriage, posting, to Shropshire. Gradually my mother consented to go in her own carriage, on a truck, by rail as far as Birmingham; farther she could not endure it. Later still, nearly the whole journey was effected by rail, but in our own chariot. At last we came to use the ordinary railway carriages, but then, for a long time, we used to have post-horses to meet us at some station near London: my mother would not be known to enter London in a railway carriage – 'it was so excessively improper' (the sitting opposite strangers in the same carriage); so we entered the metropolis 'by land', as it was called in those early days of railway travelling.

Augustus Hare, *The Story of My Life* (1896)

Under the Leaves

For all my dislike of Hampstead thinkers and their thoughts, I have lived in Hampstead twice myself. I too have walked her winding streets and lanes and peered into her umbrageous gardens where rich progressive ladies sit under the trees and plan to overwhelm South Africa with blood and fire.

I too have tramped her noted heath in all weathers and listened darkling as groups of Indian economics students, among the most gifted bores in the world, passed nattering like clouds of flies with many a fine-wrought gesture of dissent.

I have hated Hampstead for her Left-wingery, but I have loved her for her strange, secret, leafy soul. Nowhere in London are green thoughts so green, especially in a rainy June, when the grass grows high in her innumerable gardens tamed or wild.

As 'Wayfarer' says in his book 'Afoot in London' (in the chapter called 'Hampstead Heritage'), 'a man may walk with stick and knapsack, map and compass a livelong summer's day from Archway to Finchley Road Underground Station, and so be he can read a map and have an eye for country, need scarce once put foot on tarmac'.

I have often thought of trying this out, following the hidden, half-overgrown paths between garden fences, sometimes crossing the gardens themselves or even passing through houses when no other way seems open.

What adventures I might have in those damp and leafy solitudes! 'Wayfarer', in the book I have mentioned, says there are parts of Hampstead which have never been fully explored; in one densely-wooded stretch, between the garden of Mrs Dutt-Pauker's Queen Anne house Marxmount and the Heath, there is a tribe of Left-wing pygmies of cannibal habits and strong views on racial integration.

That would be among the least of the perils I might have to face as I pushed on through the dense foliage or paused to eat my bread and cheese by some gay flowerbed, watched by indignant progressive eyes from a book-lined study or seized and dragged indoors to take part in a discussion on comprehensive education and the need for Socialist play-groups.

Peter Simple (Michael Wharton), The Stretchford Chronicles (1980)

The origin of Squares

The City of London enjoyed complete self-government in an unusually democratic form. At that time very few boroughs in England were so free of the element of oligarchy, unless it were Ipswich and Norwich. In London as many as 12,000 ratepaying householders voted in their respective Wards to elect the 26 Aldermen and 200 Common Councillors. These ratepayers of the Wards were almost identical with the Liverymen of the 89 Gilds and

Companies: in their double capacity they controlled by their votes the antique and complicated machinery of London self-government.

The electorate of shopkeepers chose men of their own class to represent them on the Common Council, rather than the great merchant princes known in the world of high finance and politics. The City magnates were more often chosen as Aldermen. Common pride in the privileges and power of London, and jealous care for her independence, prevented a serious breach between the great men of the Exchange and the shopkeeping democracy. But there was sometimes friction, and in the course of Anne's reign a tendency became apparent for the democratic Common Council to be Tory, and for the Mayor, Aldermen and wealthy City magnates to be Whig.

The jurisdiction of London's elected magistrates was not confined to the area of their own City. Their power stopped short of Westminster, but they clipped it in on every side. They possessed the Shrievalty of Middlesex and the Bailiwick of Southwark. They administered and taxed the port of London. The Lord Mayor was Conservator of the river from Gravesend and Tilbury up to a point just above Staines Bridge – a course of over sixty miles. London levied coal duties in a radius of twelve miles, and enforced her monopoly of markets in a radius of seven.

The City proper was the most densely populated acreage in England. It was not, as in later times, abandoned to 'cats and caretakers' at nightfall; the merchant prince and the shopkeeper slept, each with his family, over his place of business – servants and prentices above in the garrets, and porters and messengers packed away anywhere in cellarage and warehouse. Old Jewry and Basinghall Street, in particular, were reputed to contain the homes of some of the richest men in England. But the nobility of the realm had already deserted their ancestral palaces in the crowded City and the Strand, whence gardens were vanishing apace: the grandees resided, during the season, round Covent Garden, Piccadilly, Bloomsbury. or St James's Square, or in some part of Westminster. And gentlemen from the country, civil servants, members of Parliament and professional men had smaller houses in these same regions, clustering round the mansions of the nobility. Such is the origin of many famous London 'Squares'.

G. M. Trevelyan, English Social History (1944)

London cabs

London was Kipps' third world. There were, no doubt, other worlds, but Kipps knew only these three; firstly, New Romney and the Emporium, constituting his primary world, his world of origin, which also contained Ann; secondly, the world of culture and refinement, the world of which Coote was chaperon, and into which Kipps was presently to marry, a world, it was fast becoming evident, absolutely incompatible with the first; and thirdly, a world still to a large extent unexplored, London. London presented itself as a place of great grey spaces and incredible multitudes of people, centering about Charing Cross station and the Royal Grand Hotel, and containing at unexpected arbitrary points shops of the most amazing sort, statuary, squares, restaurants – where it was possible for clever people like Walshingham to order a lunch item by item to the waiters' evident respect and sympathy – exhibitions of incredible things – the Walshinghams had taken him to the Arts and Crafts and to a Picture Gallery – and theatres. London, moreover, is rendered habitable by hansom cabs. Young Walshingham was a natural cab-taker; he was an all-round, large-minded young man, and he had in the course of their two days' stay taken Kipps into no less than nine, so that Kipps was singularly not afraid of these vehicles. He knew that wherever you were, so soon as you were thoroughly lost, you said 'Hi!' to a cab, and then 'Royal Grand Hotel'. Day and night these trusty conveyances are returning the strayed Londoner back to his point of departure, and were it not for their activity, in a little while the whole population, so vast and incomprehensible is the intricate complexity of this great city, would be hopelessly lost for ever. At any rate, that is how the thing presented itself to Kipps, and I have heard much the same from visitors from America.

H. G. Wells, *Kipps* (1905)

Spitalfields

'Spitalfields': the *consiglieri* liked the sound of it, the authentic whiff of heritage, drifting like cordite from the razed ghetto. But, please, do not call it 'Whitechapel', or whisper the dreaded 'Tower Hamlets'. Spitalfields meant Architecture, the Prince, Development Schemes: it meant gay vicars swishing incense, and charity-ward crusaders finding the peons to refill the poor benches, and submit to total-immersion baptism. It meant Property Sharks, and New Georgians promoting wallpaper catalogues. It meant video cams tracking remorselessly over interior *detail*, and out, over lamp-holders, finials, doorcases, motifs, cast-iron balconies; fruity post-synch, lashings of Purcell. And bulldozers, noise, dust; snarling angry machines. Ball-and-chain demolitions. *Sold!* There's nothing the cutting-room boys like as much as a good ball-and-chain: especially with some hair-gelled noddy in a pin-stripe suit at the controls. Skin-deep Aztec fantasies of glass and steel lifting in a self-reflecting glitter of irony from the ruins. Spitalfields was this week's buzz-word.

Iain Sinclair, Downriver (1991)

Fleet Street

Closes and courts and lanes,
　　Devious, clustered thick,
The thoroughfare, mains and drains,
　　People and mortar and brick,
Wood, metal, machinery, brains,
　　Pen and composing-stick:

　　　　Fleet Street, but exquisite flame
　　　　　　In the nebula once ere day and night
　　　　Began their travail, or earth became,
　　　　　　And all was passionate light.

Networks of wire overland,
　　Conduits under the sea,

Aerial message from strand to strand
  By lightning that travels free,
Hither in haste to hand
  Tidings of destiny:

      These tingling nerves of the world's
        affairs
        Deliver remorseless, rendering still
      The fall of empires, the price of shares,
        The record of good and ill.

Tidal the traffic goes
  Citywards out of the town;
Townwards the evening ebb o'erflows
  This highway of old renown,
When the fog-woven curtains close,
  And the urban night comes down,

      Where souls are spilt and intellects spent
        O'er news vociferant near and far,
      From Hesperus hard to the Orient,
        From dawn to the evening star.

This is the royal refrain
  That burdens the boom and the thud
Of omnibus, mobus, wain,
  And the hoofs on the beaten mud,
From the Griffin at Chancery Lane
  To the portal of old King Lud –

      Fleet Street, diligent night and day,
        Of news the mart and the burnished
        hearth,
      Seven hundred paces of narrow way,
        A notable bit of the earth.

        John Davidson, *Fleet Street and Other Poems* (1909)

George
Who Played with a Dangerous Toy, and
Suffered a Catastrophe of Considerable Dimensions

When George's Grandmamma was told
That George had been as good as Gold,
She Promised in the Afternoon
To buy him an Immense BALLOON.
And so she did; but when it came,
It got into the candle flame,
And being of a dangerous sort
Exploded with a loud report!

The Lights went out! The Windows broke!
The Room was filled with reeking smoke.
And in the darkness shrieks and yells
Were mingled with Electric Bells,
And falling masonry and groans,
And crunching, as of broken bones,
And dreadful shrieks, when, worst of all,
The House itself began to fall!
It tottered, shuddering to and fro,
Then crashed into the street below –
Which happened to be Savile Row.

. . .

When Help arrived, among the Dead
Were Cousin Mary, Little Fred,
The Footmen (both of them), The Groom,
The man that cleaned the Billiard-Room,
The Chaplain, and the Still-Room Maid.
And I am dreadfully afraid
That Monsieur Champignon, the Chef,
Will now be permanently deaf –
And both his Aides are much the same;
While George, who was in part to blame,
Received, you will regret to hear,
A nasty lump behind the ear.

99

MORAL

The moral is that little Boys
Should not be given dangerous Toys.

Hilaire Belloc, *Complete Verse* (1991)

London in the 1840s

But the growth of London in the 1840s was westward. By 1846 Bayswater
was wholly built up as far as Stanhope Gate, though there were still some
open fields west of there and north of the Bayswater Road, then the
Uxbridge Road. All this newly built area drained into the Serpentine, and
such was the effect that people still could catch a lethal fever if they took an
evening stroll by its waters.

This was Haydon's neighbourhood. His house was in Burwood Place, a
little street running from the Edgware Road (then still called Connaught
Terrace at its southern end) to Norfolk Crescent. The house, which has also
vanished now, was four-storied with iron railings round the area and pretty
little balconies at each of the tall first-floor windows. It was on the south
side of the street on the corner of the Edgware Road, overlooking a stream
of traffic which sometimes included Queen Victoria on her way from Buckingham Palace to Paddington Station. It was one of the noisiest situations in
London, but when Haydon was painting he became so absorbed in his work
that nothing penetrated to his consciousness of all the uproar of carts,
carriages, barking dogs, street cries, banging door knockers.

West of the new Bayswater terraces, Notting Hill was still fields, with just
a fringe of houses along the north side of the Uxbridge Road and along
Moscow Road. Then you came to leafy Campden Hill, and Holland House
with its great green oblong of park, and so south to the village of Kensington, at whose western end Leigh Hunt lived in a pretty but sadly smelly
house in Edwardes Square, while at its eastern end Thackeray had just
moved into a bow-windowed little house in Young Street. South from there
were fields and lanes and market gardens, and a few new streets and terraces
in Brompton and the King's Private Road, until you reached the village of
Chelsea, and the Carlyles' house in Great Cheyne Row, and Turner's secret
and poorly-furnished hide-out in Cremorne Road. If you wanted to get

from the Carlyles' to New Cross, where Browning lived, you would have to take a river boat from the Cadogan Steam Boat Pier a few yards east from the Carlyles' house along Cheyne Walk, or have a long ride or drive, due east, crossing the river at Vauxhall Bridge, through built-up Kennington and Walworth to where the fringes of the Rotherhithe and Deptford dockland faded out into open fields. Except for Mrs Jameson, far away to the westward in the distant village of Ealing, Browning lived the furthest from the centre of London of any of this group of friends and acquaintances. Only the rich banker Samuel Rogers and the well-to-do Member of Parliament Monckton Milnes had houses right in the centre, in St James's Place and Pall Mall, which in 1846 was still where the Establishment lived.

Alethea Hayter, *A Sultry Month* (1965)

In Trafalgar Square

It is recorded that late one night in Trafalgar Square an old gentleman, slightly the worse for drink, was observed apparently searching for something on the pavement. A constable approached and said: 'What's the matter, sir? Have you lost something?'

'Yes,' said the old gentleman feebly, 'I've lost my purse.'

It seemed rather an odd place to lose a purse and the constable said: 'Are you sure you lost it hereabouts?'

'Oh no,' replied the old gent, 'I lost it in Dover Street, but Trafalgar Square is so much better lighted.'

H. M. Howgrave-Graham, *Light and Shade at Scotland Yard* (1947)

Kensington place names

Almost all that district of Kensington was and is laid out like a chart or plan to illustrate Macaulay's Essays. Of course we read Macaulay's Essays; and in our simple isolation, often even believed them. We knew all the great names of the Whig aristocrats who had made the Revolution (and incidentally their own fortunes) and those names were written conspicuously all over the Kensington estates. Every day we passed Holland House, that opened its hospitality to Macaulay, and the statue of Lord Holland inscribed with the boast that he was the nephew of Fox and the friend of Grey. The street opposite where we came to live bore the name of Addison; the street of our later sojourn the name of Warwick the step-son of Addison. Beyond was a road named after the house of Russell, to the south another with the name of Cromwell. Near us, on our original perch in Campden Hill, was the great name of Argyll. Now all these names thrilled me like trumpets, as they would any boy reading Macaulay. But it never so much as crossed my mind that we should ever know any people who bore them, or even especially want to. I remember making my father laugh very much by telling him of the old Scots ballad with the line,

> There fell about a great dispute between Argyle and Airlie.

For he knew, as a house-agent, that Lord Airlie's house was actually quite close to Argyll Lodge; and that nothing was more likely than that there might fall about a great dispute, directly affecting his own line of business. He knew the old Duke of Argyll in purely business relations, and showed me a letter from him as a curiosity; but to me it was like a delightful curiosity in a museum. I no more thought of expecting McCallum More to come in any way into my own social existence, than I expected Graham of Claverhouse to ride up on his great black horse to the front-door, or Charles the Second to drop in to tea. I regarded the Duke living at Argyll Lodge as an historical character. My people were interested in an aristocracy because it was still an historical thing. The point is worth mentioning, because it is exactly this difference, whether for good or evil, that justifies a fight or feud of which I shall have to write on a later page. Long afterwards, I had the luck to figure in a political row about the Sale of Peerages; and many said that we were wasting our energies in denouncing it. But we were not. The treatment of a title did make a difference; and I am just old enough to be able to measure the difference it has really made. If, regarding Lord Lorne with historical respect, I had been introduced to an unknown Lord Leatherhead, I should have respected him also as something historical. If I were to meet him now, I should know he might be any pawnbroker from any gutter in Europe. Honours have not been sold; they have been destroyed.

G. K. Chesterton, *Autobiography* (1936)

Wapping

The gloom of the secluded wharves and muddy banks had always attracted him and, when he came to Wapping Reach, he stared down at the shadows of the clouds moving quickly over the surface of the water. But when he removed his glasses and again looked down, it seemed to him that the river itself was perpetually turning and spinning: it was going in no certain direction, and Hawksmoor felt for a moment that he might fall into its darkness. Two men passed on a small boat – one of them was laughing or grimacing, and seemed to be pointing at Hawksmoor, but his voice did not carry over the water; Hawksmoor watched this dumb-show pass until it turned the bend towards Tower Bridge and vanished as suddenly as it had arrived.

It had started to rain and he began walking along the river-bank away from Wapping and towards Limehouse. He turned left down Butcher Row, for he could see now the tower of St Anne's Limehouse ahead of him, and he entered that area of abandoned houses and derelict land which still divides the city from the river. Then he stopped suddenly in confusion: the dampness had released a close, rank smell from the lush vegetation which spread over the stones and sprang up between wires, and he could see a vagrant squatting on the ground with his face turned up to catch the rain. So he turned away from this waste-land and crossed into Shoulder-of-Mutton Alley, and there was silence by the time he came to the front of St Anne's.

Hawksmoor could have produced a survey of the area between the two churches of Wapping and Limehouse, and given at the same time a precise account of the crimes which each quarter harboured. This had been the district of the CID to which he had been attached for some years, before he was assigned to the Murder Squad, and he had come to know it well: he knew where the thieves lived, where the prostitutes gathered, and where the vagrants came. He grew to understand that most criminals tend to remain in the same districts, continuing with their activities until they were arrested, and he sometimes speculated that these same areas had been used with similar intent for centuries past: even murderers, who rapidly became Hawksmoor's speciality, rarely moved from the same spot but killed again and again until they were discovered. And sometimes he speculated, also, that they were drawn to those places where murders had occurred before.

In his own time in this district, there had been a house in Red Maiden Lane in which three separate murders had been perpetrated over a period of eight years, and the building itself gave such an impression to those who entered it that it had stayed unoccupied since the last killing. In Swedenborg Gardens Robert Haynes had murdered his wife and child, and it was Hawksmoor who was called when the remains were found beneath the floorboards; in Commercial Road there had been the ritual slaying of one Catherine Hayes, and then only last year a certain Thomas Berry had been stabbed and then mutilated in the alley beside St George's-in-the-East. It had been in this district, as Hawksmoor knew, that the Marr murders of 1812 had occurred – the perpetrator being a certain John Williams, who, according to De Quincey whose account Hawksmoor avidly read, 'asserted his own supremacy above all the children of Cain'. He killed four in a house by Ratcliffe Highway – a man, wife, servant and child – by shattering their skulls with a mallet and then gratuitously cutting their throats as they lay dying. Then, twelve days later and in the same quarter, he repeated his acts upon another family. He was transformed, again according to De Quincey, into a 'mighty murderer' and until his execution he remained an object of awe and mystery to those who lived in the shadow of the Wapping church. The mob tried to dismember his body when eventually it was brought in a cart to the place of burial – at the conflux of four roads in front of the church, where he was interred and a stake driven through his heart. And, as far as Hawksmoor knew, he lay there still: it was the spot where he had this morning seen the crowd pressing against the cordon set up by the police. And it did not take any knowledge of the even more celebrated Whitechapel murders, all of them conducted in the streets and alleys around Christ Church, Spitalfields, to understand, as Hawksmoor did, that certain streets or patches of ground provoked a malevolence which generally seemed to be quite without motive. And he knew, also, how many murders go undetected and how many murderers remain unknown.

Peter Ackroyd, *Hawksmoor* (1985)

5

London Molehills

In his last great novel, Resurrection, *Tolstoy begins his story of corruption and prostitution with the words,*

> *Though hundreds of thousands had done their very best to disfigure the small piece of land on which they were crowded together, by paving the ground with stones, scraping away every vestige of vegetation, cutting down the trees, turning away the birds and beasts, and filling the air with the smoke of naphtha and coal, still spring was spring, even in the town.*

This is very much the countryman's attitude to a great city – the attitude, imbibed from reading Rousseau at a formative age, would imply that paving stones were somehow less innocent than mud. Yet it would be wrong, in trying to build up an anthology-picture of London, to be purely anthropocentric. The paradox is that one can be just as aware of nature, and in particular of the passing seasons, in the midst of London as in the countryside. Dr Watson, listening to the wind howl outside the apartments of his friend Mr Sherlock Holmes, observes that

> *It was strange there in the very depths of the town, with ten miles of man's handiwork on every side of us, to feel the iron grip of Nature, and to be conscious that to the huge elemental forces all London was no more than the molehills that dot the fields.*

Certainly, for my part, many of my most intense experiences of 'Nature' have come not in open fields or country lanes (where I am likely to be bored) but in London, a city as rich in small domestic gardens and well-planted squares as it is in parks. Before I lived in London, I would visit it as often as possible. I remember remarking to an old Londoner at that period that whenever I was up in town, I felt an increased appetite, a phenomenon for which I found it difficult to account. 'It's the sea air,' he said.

Coleridge, in 'This Lime Tree Bower My Prison', saluted his old friend Charles Lamb, and told Lamb that

> *thou hast pined*
> *And hungered after Nature, many a year,*
> *In the great City pent.*

The truth of the matter is to be found in one of Lamb's letters to Wordsworth where that passionate Londoner says,

> *Have I not enough, without your mountains? . . . My attachments are all local, purely local. I have no passion for groves and valleys . . . The rooms where I was born, the furniture which has been before my eyes all my life, a bookcase . . . old chairs, old tables, streets, squares, where I have sunned myself, my old school – these are my mistresses.*

As Lamb was well aware (Wordsworth, too, in his most famous sonnet), we can feel the rays of the sun even in the middle of London.

A wild night

It was a wild, tempestuous night towards the close of November. Holmes and I sat together in silence all the evening, he engaged with a powerful lens deciphering the remains of the original inscription upon a palimpsest, I deep in a recent treatise upon surgery. Outside the wind howled down Baker Street, while the rain beat fiercely against the windows. It was strange there in the very depths of the town, with ten miles of man's handiwork on every side of us, to feel the iron grip of Nature, and to be conscious that to the huge elemental forces all London was no more than the molehills that dot the fields. I walked to the window and looked out on the deserted street. The occasional lamps gleamed on the expanse of muddy road and shining pavement. A single cab was splashing its way from the Oxford Street end.

'Well, Watson, it's as well we have not to turn out tonight,' said Holmes, laying aside his lens and rolling up the palimpsest. 'I've done enough for one sitting. It is trying work for the eyes. So far as I can make out, it is nothing more exciting than an Abbey's accounts dating from the second half of the fifteenth century. Halloa! halloa! halloa! What's this?'

Amid the droning of the wind there had come the stamping of a horse's hoofs and the long grind of a wheel as it rasped against the kerb. The cab which I had seen had pulled up at our door.

'What can he want?' I ejaculated, as a man stepped out of it.

'Want! He wants us. And we, my poor Watson, want overcoats and cravats and goloshes, and every aid that man ever invented to fight the weather. Wait a bit, though! There's the cab off again! There's hope yet. He'd have kept it if he had wanted us to come. Run down, my dear fellow, and open the door, for all virtuous folk have been long in bed.'

Arthur Conan Doyle, 'The Adventure of the Golden Pince-Nez' in *The Return of Sherlock Holmes* (1905)

Westminster Bridge

Earth has not anything to show more fair:
Dull would he be of soul who could pass by
A sight so touching in its majesty:
This City now doth, like a garment, wear
The beauty of the morning; silent, bare,
Ships, towers, domes, theatres, and temples lie
Open unto the fields, and to the sky;
All bright and glittering in the smokeless air.
Never did sun more beautifully steep
In his first splendour, valley, rock, or hill;
Ne'er saw I, never felt, a calm so deep!
The river glideth at his own sweet will:
Dear God! the very houses seem asleep;
And all that mighty heart is lying still!

William Wordsworth, *Poetical Works* (1903)

A snowstorm

Syme sprang erect upon the rocking car, and after staring wildly at the wintry sky, that grew gloomier every moment, he ran down the steps. He had repressed an elemental impulse to leap over the side.

Too bewildered to look back or to reason, he rushed into one of the little courts at the side of Fleet Street as a rabbit rushes into a hole. He had a vague idea, if this incomprehensible old Jack-in-the-box was really pursuing him, that in that labyrinth of little streets he could soon throw him off the scent. He dived in and out of those crooked lanes, which were more like cracks than thoroughfares; and by the time that he had completed about twenty alternate angles and described an unthinkable polygon, he paused to listen for any sound of pursuit. There was none; there could not in any case have been much, for the little streets were thick with the soundless snow. Somewhere behind Red Lion Court, however, he noticed a place where some energetic citizen had cleared away the snow for a space of about twenty yards, leaving the wet, glistening cobble-stones. He thought little of this as he passed it, only plunging into yet another arm of the maze. But when a few hundred yards farther on he stood still again to listen, his heart stood still also, for he heard from that space of rugged stones the clinking crutch and labouring feet of the infernal cripple.

The sky above was loaded with the clouds of snow, leaving London in a darkness and oppression premature for that hour of the evening. On each side of Syme the walls of the alley were blind and featureless; there was no little window or any kind of eye. He felt a new impulse to break out of this hive of houses, and to get once more into the open and lamplit street. Yet he rambled and dodged for a long time before he struck the main thoroughfare. When he did so, he struck it much farther up than he had fancied. He came out into what seemed the vast and void of Ludgate Circus, and saw St Paul's Cathedral sitting in the sky.

G. K. Chesterton, *The Man Who Was Thursday* (1908)

The Great Frost

Sunday, 1 January 1684

The weather continuing intolerably severe, streetes of booths were set upon the Thames; the air was so very cold and thick, as of many yeares there had not ben the like. The small pox was very mortal. . . .

9th. I went crosse the Thames on the ice, now become so thick as to beare not onely streetes of boothes, in which they roasted meate, and had divers shops of wares, quite acrosse as in a towne, but coaches, carts and horses, passed over. So I went from Westminster Stayres to Lambeth, and din'd with the Archbishop. . . .

16th. The Thames was fill'd with people and tents, selling all sorts of wares as in the Citty.

24th. The frost continuing more and more severe, the Thames before London was still planted with boothes in formal streetes, all sortes of trades and shops furnish'd and full of commodities, even to a printing presse, where the people and ladyes tooke a fancy to have their names printed, and the day and yeare set down when printed on the Thames: this humour tooke so universally, that 'twas estimated the printer gain'd £5 a day, for printing a line onely, at sixpence a name, besides what he got by ballads, &c. Coaches plied from Westminster to the Temple, and from several other staires to and fro, as in the streetes, sleds, sliding with skeetes, a bull-baiting, horse and coach races, puppet plays and interludes, cookes, tipling, and other lewd places, so that it seem'd to be a bacchanalian triumph or carnival on the water, whilst it was a severe judgement on the land, the trees not onely splitting as if lightning-struck, but men and cattle perishing in divers places, and the very seas so lock'd up with ice, that no vessels could stir out or come in. The fowles, fish, and birds, and all our exotiq plants and greenes universally perishing. Many parkes of deer were destroied, and all sorts of fuell so deare that there were great contributions to preserve the poore alive. Nor was this severe weather much less intense in most parts of Europe, even as far as Spaine and the most southern tracts. London, by reason of the excessive coldnesse of the aire hindering the ascent of the smoke, was so filled with the fuliginous steame of the sea-coale, that hardly could one see crosse the streets, and this filling the lungs with its grosse particles, exceedingly obstructed the breast, so as one could hardly breath.

Here was no water to be had from the pipes and engines, nor could the brewers and divers other tradesmen worke, and every moment was full of disastrous accidents.

4 February

I went to Says Court to see how the frost had dealt with my garden, where I found many of the greenes and rare plantes utterly destroied. The oranges and mirtalls very sick, the rosemary and laurells dead to all appearance, but yᵉ cypress likely to indure it.

5th. It began to thaw, but froze againe. My coach crossed from Lambeth to the Horseferry at Millbank, Westminster. The booths were almost all taken downe, but there was first a map or landskip cut in copper representing all the manner of the camp, and the several actions, sports, and pastimes thereon, in memory of so signal a frost. . . .

8th. The weather was set in to an absolute thaw and raine, but yᵉ Thames still frozen.

John Evelyn, Diary (1971)

The great frost

AN EPISODE OF THE GREAT FROST

O roving Muse, recal that wond'rous Year,
When Winter reign'd in bleak *Britannia*'s Air;
When hoary *Thames*, with frosted Oziers crown'd,
Was three long Moons in icy Fetters bound.
The Waterman, forlorn along the Shore,
Pensive reclines upon his useless Oar,
Sees harness'd Steeds desert the stony Town;
And wander Roads unstable, not their own:
Wheels o'er the harden'd Waters smoothly glide,
And rase with whiten'd Tracks the slipp'ry Tide.
Here the fat Cook piles high the blazing Fire,
And scarce the Spit can turn the Steer entire.
Booths sudden hide the *Thames*, long Streets appear,

And num'rous Games proclaim the crouded Fair.
So when a Gen'ral bids the martial Train
Spread their Encampment o'er the spatious Plain;
Thick-rising Tents a Canvas City build,
And the loud Dice resound thro' all the Field.
'Twas here the Matron found a doleful Fate:
Let Elegiac Lay the Woe relate,
Soft, as the Breath of distant Flutes, at Hours,
When silent Ev'ning closes up the Flow'rs;
Lulling, as falling Water's hollow noise;
Indulging Grief, like *Philomela*'s Voice.

 Doll ev'ry Day had walk'd these treach'rous Roads;
Her Neck grew warpt beneath autumnal Loads
Of various Fruit; she now a Basket bore,
That Head, alas! shall Basket bear no more.
Each Booth she frequent past, in quest of Gain,
And Boys with pleasure heard her shrilling Strain.
Ah *Doll!* all Mortals must resign their Breath,
And Industry it self submit to Death!
The cracking Crystal yields, she sinks, she dyes,
Her Head, chopt off, from her lost Shoulders flies:
Pippins she cry'd, but Death her Voice confounds,
And Pip-Pip-Pip along the Ice resounds.
So when the *Thracian* Furies *Orpheus* tore,
And left his bleeding Trunk deform'd with Gore,
His sever'd Head floats down the silver Tide,
His yet warm Tongue for his lost Consort cry'd;
Eurydice, with quiv'ring Voice, he mourn'd,
And *Heber*'s Banks *Eurydice* return'd.

A THAW

 But now the western Gale the Flood unbinds,
And black'ning Clouds move on with warmer Winds,
The wooden Town its frail Foundation leaves,
And *Thames*' full Urn rolls down his plenteous Waves:
From ev'ry Penthouse streams the fleeting Snow,
And with dissolving Frost the Pavements flow.

John Gray, Trivia (1716)

London Snow

When men were all asleep the snow came flying,
In large white flakes falling on the city brown,
Stealthily and perpetually settling and loosely lying,
    Hushing the latest traffic of the drowsy town;
Deadening, muffling, stifling its murmurs failing;
Lazily and incessantly floating down and down:
    Silently sifting and veiling road, roof and railing;
Hiding difference, making unevenness even,
Into angles and crevices softly drifting and sailing.
    All night it fell, and when full inches seven
It lay in the depth of its uncompacted lightness,
The clouds blew off from a high and frosty heaven;
    And all woke earlier for the unaccustomed brightness
Of the winter dawning, the strange unheavenly glare:
The eye marvelled – marvelled at the dazzling whiteness;
    The ear hearkened to the stillness of the solemn air;
No sound of wheel rumbling nor of foot falling,
And the busy morning cries came thin and spare.
    Then boys I heard, as they went to school, calling,
They gathered up the crystal manna to freeze
Their tongues with tasting, their hands with snowballing;
    Or rioted in a drift, plunging up to the knees;
Or peering up from under the white-mossed wonder,
'O look at the trees!' they cried, 'O look at the trees!'
    With lessened load a few carts creak and blunder,
Following along the white deserted way,
A country company long dispersed asunder:
    When now already the sun, in pale display
Standing by Paul's high dome, spread forth below
His sparkling beams, and awoke the stir of the day.
    For now doors open, and war is waged with the snow;
And trains of sombre men, past tale of number,
Tread long brown paths, as toward their toil they go:
    But even for them awhile no cares encumber
Their minds diverted; the daily word is unspoken,

The daily thoughts of labour and sorrow slumber
At the sight of the beauty that greets them, for the charm they
   have broken.

Robert Bridges, Poetical Works (1912)

Description of a City Shower

   Careful Observers may foretell the Hour
(By sure Prognosticks) when to dread a Show'r:
While Rain depends, the pensive Cat gives o'er
Her Frolicks, and pursues her Tail no more.
Returning Home at Night, you'll find the Sink
Strike your offended Sense with double Stink.
If you be wise, then go not far to Dine,
You'll spend in Coach-hire more than save in Wine.
A coming Show'r your shooting Corns presage,
Old Aches throb, your hollow Tooth will rage.
Saunt'ring in Coffee-house is *Dulman* seen;
He damns the Climate, and complains of Spleen.

   Mean while the South rising with dabbled Wings,
A Sable Cloud a-thwart the Welkin flings,
That swill'd more Liquor than it could contain,
And like a Drunkard gives it up again.
Brisk *Susan* whips her Linen from the Rope,
While the first drizzling Show'r is born aslope,
Such is that Sprinkling which some careless Quean
Flirts on you from her Mop, but not so clean.
You fly, invoke the Gods; then turning, stop
To rail; she singing, still whirls on her Mop.
Not yet, the Dust had shunn'd th'unequal Strife,
But aided by the Wind, fought still for Life;
And wafted with its Foe by violent Gust,
'Twas doubtful which was Rain, and which was Dust.
Ah! where must needy Poet seek for Aid,
When Dust and Rain at once his Coat invade;

113

His only Coat, where Dust confus'd with Rain,
Roughen the Nap, and leave a mingled Stain.

Now in contiguous Drops the Flood comes down,
Threat'ning with Deluge this *Devoted* Town.
To Shops in Crowds the dagged Females fly,
Pretend to cheapen Goods, but nothing buy.
The Templer spruce, while ev'ry Spout's a-broach,
Stays till 'tis fair, yet seems to call a Coach.
The tuck'd-up Sempstress walks with hasty Strides,
While Streams run down her oil'd Umbrella's Sides.
Here various Kinds by various Fortunes led,
Commence Acquaintance underneath a Shed.
Triumphant Tories, and desponding Whigs,
Forget their Feuds, and join to save their Wigs.

Box'd in a Chair the Beau impatient sits,
While Spouts run clatt'ring o'er the Roof by Fits;
And ever and anon with frightful Din
The Leather sounds, he trembles from within.
So when *Troy* Chair-men bore the Wooden Steed,
Pregnant with *Greeks*, impatient to be freed,
(Those Bully *Greeks*, who, as the Moderns do,
Instead of paying Chair-men, run them thro'.)
Laoco'n struck the Outside with his Spear,
And each imprison'd Hero quak'd for Fear.

Now from all Parts the swelling Kennels flow,
And bear their Trophies with them as they go:
Filth of all Hues and Odours seem to tell
What Street they sail'd from, by their Sight and Smell.
They, as each Torrent drives, with rapid Force
From *Smithfield*, or St *Pulchre*'s shape their Course,
And in huge Confluent join at *Snow-Hill* Ridge,
Fall from the *Conduit* prone to *Holborn-Bridge*.
Sweepings from Butchers' Stalls, Dung, Guts, and Blood,
Drown'd Puppies, stinking Sprats, all drench'd in Mud,
Dead Cats and Turnip-Tops come tumbling down the Flood.

Jonathan Swift (October 1710)

Autumn in a bomb-site

Richie, on the last afternoon of his vacation, walked home from Moorgate station across the ruins. Pausing at the bastion of the Wall near St Giles's, he looked across the horrid waste, for horrid he felt it to be; he hated mess and smashed things; the squalor of ruin sickened him; like Flaubert, he was aware of an irremediable barbarism coming up out of the earth, and of filth flung against the ivory tower. It was a symbol of loathsome things, war, destruction, savagery; an earnest, perhaps, of the universal doom that stalked, sombre and menacing, on its way.

Autumn now lay sodden, with its drifting mists and quiet sunshine, on the broken city, on the companies' halls, where Michaelmas daisies, milky ways of tiny blue stars, crowded among the withered rose-bay, the damp brown bracken, the sprawling nightshade and the thistles. Excavators had begun their tentative work, uncovering foundations, seeking the Middle Ages, the Dark Ages, Londinium, Rome. The Wall was being examined, its great bastions identified and cleared, their tiles and brickwork dated. Roman and medieval pots and coins were gathered up and housed; civilized intelligence was at work among the ruins. Before long, cranes and derricks would make their appearance, sites would be cleared for rebuilding, tottering piles would be laid low, twisting flights of steps destroyed. One day the churches would be dealt with, taken down, or mended and built up. The fireweed, the pink rose-bay, that had seeded itself in the burnt soil and flowed and blossomed everywhere where bombs had been, would take fright at the building and drift back on the winds to the open country whence it came, together with the red campion, the yellow charlock, the bramble, the bindweed, the thorn-apple, the thistle, and the vetch. The redstarts and the wheatears, the woodpeckers and the hooting owls, would desert this wilderness too, and take wing for woods and fields. In place of the fireweed, little garden plots would flourish, gay with vegetables and flowers; the fire brigade already had one, trim and neat, with trenches of scarlet tomatoes, outside the Wall, and close to the old Jews' burying ground, which fair gardens and houses had covered four centuries ago. Beside the tomato garden a bonfire of weeds burned; sticks crackled and blue smoke drifted, smelling of incense and autumn.

So men's will to recovery strove against the drifting wilderness to halt and tame it; but the wilderness might slip from their hands, from their spades and trowels and measuring rods, slip darkly away from them, seeking the primeval chaos and old night which had been before Londinium was, which would be when cities were ghosts haunting the ancestral dreams of memory.

Rose Macaulay, *The World My Wilderness* (1950)

Cheerless Soho

Crossing the road by the bombed-out public house on the corner and pondering the mystery which dominates vistas framed by a ruined door, I felt for some reason glad the place had not yet been rebuilt. A direct hit had excised even the ground floor, so that the basement was revealed as a sunken garden, or site of archaeological excavation long abandoned, where great sprays of willow herb and ragwort flowered through cracked paving stones; only a few broken milk bottles and a laceless boot recalling contemporary life. In the midst of this sombre grotto five or six fractured steps had withstood the explosion and formed a projecting island of masonry on the summit of which rose the door. Walls on both sides were shrunk away, but along its lintel, in niggling copybook handwriting, could still be distinguished the word *Ladies*. Beyond, on the far side of the twin pillars and crossbar, nothing whatever remained of that promised retreat, the threshold falling steeply to an abyss of rubble; a triumphal arch erected laboriously by dwarfs, or the gateway to some unknown, forbidden domain, the lair of sorcerers.

Then, all at once, as if such luxurious fantasy were not already enough, there came from this unexplored country the song, strong and marvellously sweet, of the blonde woman on crutches, that itinerant prima donna of the highways whose voice I had not heard since the day, years before, when Moreland and I had listened in Gerrard Street, the afternoon he had talked of getting married; when we had bought the bottle labelled *Tawny Wine (port flavour)* which even Moreland had been later unwilling to drink. Now once more above the rustle of traffic that same note swelled on the grimy air, contriving a transformation scene to recast those purlieus into the vision of an oriental dreamland, artificial, if you like, but still quite alluring under the shifting clouds of a cheerless Soho sky.

'Pale hands I loved beside the Shalimar,
Where are you now? Who lies beneath your spell?'

Anthony Powell, *Casanova's Chinese Restaurant* (1960)

April

I opened my window to an April night and, looking down into the London square, saw that new leaves were silver-white in the lamplight. Into my room came an earthy smell and the freshness of new grass. The top boughs of the trees were etched against the saffron stain of a London sky, but their boles descended into a pool of darkness, silent and remote as the primeval forest. The fretful traffic sped left and right against the railings, and beyond lay that patch of stealthy vitality older than London. What an amazing thing is the coming of spring to London. The very pavements seem ready to crack and lift under the denied earth; in the air is a consciousness of life which tells you that if traffic stopped for a fortnight grass would grow again in Piccadilly and corn would spring in pavement cracks where a horse had spilt his 'feed'. And the squares of London, so dingy and black since the first October gale, fill week by week with the rising tide of life, just as the sea, running up the creeks and pushing itself forward inch by inch towards the land, comes at last to each remote rock pool.

The squares of London, those sacred little patches of the country-side preserved, perhaps, by the Anglo-Saxon instinct for grass and trees, hold in their restricted glades some part of the magic of spring. I suppose many a man has stood at his window above a London square in April hearing a message from the lanes of England. The Georgians no doubt fancied that Aegipans and Centaurs kicked their hoofs in Berkeley Square, and I, above my humbler square, dreamt a no less classic eclogue of hedges lit with hawthorn, of orchards ready for their brief wave of pink spray, of fields in which smoky-faced lambs pressed against their dams, of new furrows over which moved slowly the eternal figure bent above a plough.

H. V. Morton, *In Search of England* (1927)

Carlyle in his garden

At the back of Carlyle's house in Cheyne Row is a strip of garden, a grass plot, a few trees and flowerbeds along the walls, where are (or were) some bits of jessamine and a gooseberry-bush or two, transported from Haddington and Craigenputtock. Here, when spring came on, Carlyle used to dig and plant and keep the grass trim and tidy. Sterling must have seen him with his spade there when he drew the picture of Collins in the 'Onyx Ring', which is evidently designed for Carlyle. The digging must have been more of a relaxation for him than the walks, where the thinking and talking went on without interruption.

J. A. Froude, *Carlyle's Life in London, 1834–81* (1885)

The River's Tale

(PREHISTORIC)

Twenty bridges from Tower to Kew –
(Twenty bridges or twenty-two) –
Wanted to know what the River knew,
For they were young and the Thames was old,
And this is the tale that the River told:

'I walk my beat before London Town,
Five hours up and seven down.
Up I go till I end my run
At Tide-end-town, which is Teddington.
Down I come with the mud in my hands
And plaster it over the Maplin Sands.
But I'd have you know that these waters of mine
Were once a branch of the River Rhine,
When hundreds of miles to the East I went
And England was joined to the Continent.

I remember the bat-winged lizard-birds,
The Age of Ice and the mammoth herds,
And the giant tigers that stalked them down
Through Regent's Park into Camden Town.
And I remember like yesterday
The earliest Cockney who came my way,
When he pushed through the forest that lined the Strand,
With paint on his face and a club in his hand.
He was death to feather and fin and fur.
He trapped my beavers at Westminster.
He netted my salmon, he hunted my deer,
He killed my heron off Lambeth Pier.
He fought his neighbour with axes and swords,
Flint or bronze, at my upper fords,
While down at Greenwich, for slaves and tin,
The tall Phoenician ships stole in,
And North Sea war-boats, painted and gay,
Flashed like dragon-flies, Erith way;
And Norseman and Negro and Gaul and Greek
Drank with the Britons in Barking Creek,
And life was gay, and the world was new,
And I was a mile across at Kew!
But the Roman came with a heavy hand,
And bridged and roaded and ruled the land,
And the Roman left and the Danes blew in –
And that's where your history-books begin!'

Rudyard Kipling, *Rudyard Kipling's Verse* (1940)

A London particular

I made myself sob less, and persuaded myself to be quiet by saying very
often, 'Esther, now you really must! This *will not* do!' I cheered myself up
pretty well at last, though I am afraid I was longer about it than I ought to
have been; and when I had cooled my eyes with lavender water, it was time
to watch for London.

I was quite persuaded that we were there, when we were ten miles off;

and when we really were there, that we should never get there. However, when we began to jolt upon a stone pavement, and particularly when every other conveyance seemed to be running into us, and we seemed to be running into every other conveyance, I began to believe that we really were approaching the end of our journey. Very soon afterwards we stopped.

A young gentleman who had inked himself by accident, addressed me from the pavement, and said, 'I am from Kenge and Carboy's, miss, of Lincoln's Inn.'

'If you please, sir,' said I.

He was very obliging; and as he handed me into a fly, after superintending the removal of my boxes, I asked him whether there was a great fire anywhere? For the streets were so full of dense brown smoke that scarcely anything was to be seen.

'O dear no, miss,' he said. 'This is a London particular.'

I had never heard of such a thing.

'A fog, miss,' said the young gentleman.

'O indeed!' said I.

We drove slowly through the dirtiest and darkest streets that ever were seen in the world (I thought), and in such a distracting state of confusion that I wondered how the people kept their senses, until we passed into sudden quietude under an old gateway, and drove on through a silent square until we came to an odd nook in a corner, where there was an entrance up a steep, broad flight of stairs, like an entrance to a church. And there really was a churchyard, outside under some cloisters, for I saw the gravestones from the staircase window.

Charles Dickens, *Bleak House* (1853)

The sultry month

This June was the hottest summer month that anyone could remember. For the first twenty-two days of the month the average day temperature was 84° in the shade, 105° in the sun. Kent had had six weeks without rain and midday temperatures of 104° to 116°. On the morning of Friday 19th June the temperature in some parts of the country reached 96° in the shade. The heat had begun in the very first days of the month. Already by 2nd June Browning was complaining that it was very warm, and warning Elizabeth

Barrett to be careful of her health. By the 5th the temperature in her room was 80°, and though she loved the heat she could do nothing but lie on the sofa and drink lemonade and read *Monte Cristo*. 'Oh – it is so hot,' she wrote to Browning. 'There is a thick mist lacquered over with light – it is cauldron-heat, rather than fire-heat.' He meanwhile was at Church, and seeing people faint with the heat. A week later it was still 'too hot to laugh'; even the mornings burned and dazzled in white heat; it was so overcoming that even Flush was cross, and Miss Barrett had to take him out in the carriage at half-past seven in the evening to get a breath of coolness by the silvery water of the Serpentine in the dusk of Hyde Park.

It was murderous weather. Wherrymen, out in boats on the Thames all day, died of sunstroke; farm-labourers died of heatstroke after a day's mowing; many people all over the country were drowned while bathing. There were rumours of Asiatic cholera at Hull and Leeds, there were typhus outbreaks in London. There were proclamations that dogs must go muzzled, for fear of rabies. Anyone not in robust health suffered and sickened in the stifling weather. 'The great heat of London . . . made me quite ill again,' complained Mrs Carlyle, and from Manchester she heard from Geraldine Jewsbury, 'The Heat is terrible, for our air is so thick and heavy that, when heated, it is like a casing of hot lead.'

For the hay harvest the weather was a boon, and by the third week in June the hay in the south of England was all cut, and much of it stacked. The wheat crop was doing well, but the prolonged drought was destroying the barley and oats, there were heath fires all over the country, and the gardeners were in despair. Grass everywhere was burnt brown, the peas and beans were wilting, the mignonette in the London window-boxes was withered and dry. It was a wonderful year for roses, though; Browning brought Elizabeth Barrett bunches of them from his parents' garden in New Cross, and she herself actually drove out to Hampstead Heath and picked a dog rose there, quite early in the month. Everything was early – Miss Mitford's famous strawberry parties at Three Mile Cross were already collecting all her neighbours. But hot and fine as it was, one could not reckon safely on the weather for outdoor parties; there were sudden and violent storms all over the country, many people were killed by lightning, in some places the very air smelt of fire, and the raindrops that fell were the largest ever seen. Dickens, who left England with his family on 31st May and travelled up the Rhine in a heat 'more intense than any I have ever felt', described the huge thunderstorms that boomed and rumbled among the Swiss mountains. The wooden walls and floor of the pretty lake-side house which he had taken at Lausanne were hot to the touch all the night through, and his children were so tanned that they looked 'as if they were in one perpetual sunset'.

The stored-up heat of the houses caused many fires in London, and there were other disagreeable effects of town life in the heat. On this 19th June 'a correspondent requests us to call the attention of the authorities to the offensive condition of the sewers, the effluvia from which, in this hot weather, is most offensive' announced the *Daily News*, the paper which Dickens had founded a few months earlier. The rapid development of London in recent years had overstrained the sewers, as everyone could now perceive. 'The Heat has been so savage that not only we Italians, but the East Indians, have suffered much from it. I never knew hot nights so oppressive and hot days so little agreeable,' wrote Milnes to a friend, while his future wife Annabel Crewe, whose spelling was not always perfectly reliable, recorded in her diary on 19th June, 'Heat of weather quite unparralled in England.'

The only pleasant thing to contemplate was ice. A ship called the *Ilizaide* came into St Katharine's Docks with 664 tons of ice in large blocks; little boys hung all day round the depots of the Wenham Lake ice, as though the mere sight of the great white blocks would cool them; sherry coblers with ice (and no doubt quantities of typhoid germs) in them were a favourite drink. But it was impossible to keep cool, or look as if you were cool. 'This hot weather puts us all into Falstaff's state,' wrote Wordsworth to Crabb Robinson, conjuring up an unlikely vision of the stately old poet 'larding the lean earth' with his sweat as he pottered about Rydal Mount. The papers were full of advertisements for clothes to keep cool in. 'The Delightful Coolness of the Golden Flax Cravat Collar, together with its perfect fit, however loosely tied on, recommend it especially during this weather.' For the women 'dresses of the most aerial textures, tulles, barèges, muslinés, organdies, tarlatans, and Chinese Batiste were alone wearable during the late insupportable heat'. If you had lost a relation within the year, you could go to Jay's, or The London General Mourning Warehouse as it was then called, and get 'Muslin Dresses for Half-Mourning. The extreme heat of the season has given an extraordinary impetus to the sale of PRINTED MUSLINS.' In a world without refrigerators, it was also useful to be told of Carson's Meat Preservers, by which meat could be cured in twelve or fifteen minutes and 'all taints avoided, even in the hottest weather', or of 'Lemon and Kali, a cooling beverage' advertised by a chemist in Cornhill as 'of inestimable value to those whose duties oblige them to perambulate the crowded streets of large towns in hot weather'.

Alethea Hayter, *A Sultry Month* (1965)

6

London Animals

Modern Londoners might be tempted to hold the arrogant belief that they were the only, or the most important, creatures in the metropolis. I am lucky enough to live near Regent's Park Zoo. Only a short walk from my house, wolves prowl (and howl), lions roar and vultures hover. The threat to our Zoo was distressing, but it now looks as if it will survive, though in much reduced form.

The Zoo was, and is, a most important centre of scientific research. Many of the endangered species of the world have been preserved entirely because of the skills of zoologists, and those skills can only be perfected in zoos. It is quite wrong to think of zoos purely as politically 'incorrect' museums where human beings are encouraged to laugh at animals through the bars.

I can not endure the sight of the big cats in cages – but I enjoy canal walks on summer evenings, knowing that a llama or a giraffe or a camel might cast me a disdainful glance from the opposite bank.

Zoos are all the more important now that animals have by and large vanished from the London streets. In Mayhew's pages (1851) there are as many extraordinary animals as there are human beings – ranging from performing mice to costermongers' donkeys to the poor caged goldfinches.

Above any changes which have taken place to London in this century, surely the greatest is the arrival of the motor-car and the subsequent banishment of the horse. Now their mews are pieds-à-terre for businessmen living in the country and their livery stables have become antique supermarkets or fashion warehouses. Generations of children brought up on Black Beauty *had a keen sense of the lives of London horses; and no child had a more marked sympathy with the plight of beleaguered drays and over-worked cart-horses than the little girl described by Marion Crawford.*

If I am ever Queen

One of Lilibet's favourite games that went on for years was to harness me with a pair of red reins that had bells on them, and off we would go, delivering groceries. I would be gentled, patted, given my nosebag, and jerked to a standstill, while Lilibet, at imaginary houses, delivered imaginary groceries, and held long and intimate conversations with her make-believe customers.

Sometimes she would whisper to me, 'Crawfie, you must pretend to be impatient. Paw the ground a bit.' So I would paw.

Frosty mornings were wonderful, for then my breath came in clouds, 'just like a proper horse', said Lilibet contentedly. Or she herself would be the horse, prancing around, sidling up to me, nosing in my pockets for sugar, making convincing little whinnying noises.

Besides the toy horses there were other four-legged friends in the world outside. A brewer's dray with a fine pair often pulled up in Piccadilly just below, stopped by the traffic lights. There they would stand, steaming, on winter nights. The little girls, their faces pressed to the nursery window, would watch for them fondly, anxious if they were late. On wet streets anything might happen to big dray horses. And many a weary little pony trotting home at the end of the day in its coster's cart little dreamed of the wealth of Royal sympathy it roused, from that upper window.

From another side of the house we could see the riding schools going along Rotten Row. At the end of the track they would turn, and start off again, the same horse appearing several times a day with different riders.

'If I am ever Queen,' said Lilibet firmly, 'I shall make a law that there must be no riding on Sundays. Horses should have a rest too. And I shan't let anyone dock their pony's tail.'

Marion Crawford, *The Little Princesses* (1950)

Horses in London

I saw a great deal of trouble amongst the horses in London, and much of it that might have been prevented by a little common sense. We horses do not mind hard work if we are treated reasonably; and I am sure there are many driven by quite poor men who have a happier life than I had when I used to go in the Countess of W—'s carriage, with my silver-mounted harness and high feeding.

It often went to my heart to see how the little ponies were used, straining along with heavy loads, or staggering under heavy blows from some low cruel boy. Once I saw a little grey pony with a thick mane and a pretty head, and so much like Merrylegs, that if I had not been in harness, I should have neighed to him. He was doing his best to pull a heavy cart, while a strong rough boy was cutting him under the belly with his whip, and chucking cruelly at his little mouth. Could it be Merrylegs? It was just like him; but then Mr Blomefield was never to sell him, and I think he would not do it; but this might have been quite as good a little fellow, and had as happy a place when he was young.

I often noticed the great speed at which butchers' horses were made to go, though I did not know why it was so, till one day when we had to wait some time in 'St John's Wood'. There was a butcher's shop next door, and, as we were standing, a butcher's cart came dashing up at a great pace. The horse was hot, and much exhausted; he hung his head down, while his heaving sides and trembling legs showed how hard he had been driven. The lad jumped out of the cart and was getting the basket, when the master came out of the shop much displeased. After looking at the horse, he turned angrily to the lad:

'How many times shall I tell you not to drive in this way? You ruined the last horse and broke his wind, and you are going to ruin this in the same way. If you were not my own son, I would dismiss you on the spot; it is a disgrace to have a horse brought to the shop in a condition like that; you are liable to be taken up by the police for such driving, and if you are, you need not look to me for bail, for I have spoken to you till I am tired; you must look out for yourself.'

During this speech, the boy had stood by, sullen and dogged, but when his father ceased, he broke out angrily. It wasn't his fault, and he wouldn't take the blame, he was only going by orders all the time.

'You always say, "Now be quick; now look sharp!" and when I go to the houses, one wants a leg of mutton for an early dinner, and I must be back with it in a quarter of an hour. Another cook had forgotten to order the beef; I must go and fetch it and be back in no time, or the mistress will scold; and the housekeeper says they have company coming unexpectedly and must have some chops sent up directly; and the lady at No. 4, in the Crescent, *never* orders her dinner till the meat comes in for lunch, and it's nothing but hurry, hurry, all the time. If the gentry would think of what they want, and order their meat the day before, there need not be this blow up!'

'I wish to goodness they would,' said the butcher; ''twould save me a wonderful deal of harass, and I could suit my customers much better if I knew beforehand – but there – what's the use of talking – who ever thinks of a butcher's convenience, or a butcher's horse? Now then, take him in, and look to him well: mind, he does not go out again today, and if anything else is wanted, you must carry it yourself in the basket.' With that he went in, and the horse was led away.

But all boys are not cruel. I have seen some as fond of their pony or donkey as if it had been a favourite dog, and the little creatures have worked away as cheerfully and willingly for their young drivers as I work for Jerry. It may be hard work sometimes, but a friend's hand and voice make it easy.

Anna Sewell, Black Beauty (1877)

An immense brute of an elephant

[My grandchildren and I] were then driven to the Zoological Gardens, a place which I often like to visit (keeping away from the larger beasts, such as the bears, who I often fancy may jump from their poles upon certain unoffending Christians; and the howling tigers and lions, who are continually biting the keepers' heads off), and where I like to look at the monkeys in the cages (the little rascals!) and the birds of various plumage.

Fancy my feelings, Sir, when I saw in these gardens – in these gardens frequented by nursery-maids, mothers, and children – an immense brute of an elephant, about a hundred feet high, rushing about with a wretched little child on his back, and a single man vainly endeavouring to keep him back! I uttered a shriek; I called my dear children round about me. And I am not ashamed to confess it, Sir, I ran. I ran for refuge into a building hard by, where I saw – ah, Sir, I saw an immense boa constrictor swallowing a live rabbit – swallowing a live rabbit, Sir, and looking as if he would have swallowed one of my little boys afterwards. Good heavens! Sir, do we live in a Christian country, and are parents and children to be subjected to sights like these?

W. M. Thackeray, *Contributions to Punch* (1846)

The Zoo

The lion sits within his cage,
Weeping tears of ruby rage,
He licks his snout, the tears fall down
And water dusty London town.

He does not like you, little boy,
It's no use making up to him,
He does not like you any more
Than he likes Nurse, or Baby Jim.

Nor would you do if you were he,
And he were you, for dont you see
God gave him lovely teeth and claws
So that he might eat little boys.

So that he might
In anger slay
The little lambs
That skip and play
Pounce down upon their placid dams
And make dams flesh to pad his hams.

So that he might
Appal the night
With crunching bones
And awful groans
Of antelope and buffalo,
And the unwary hunter whose 'Hallo'

Tells us his life is over here below.
There's none to help him, fear inspired,
Who shouts because his gun misfired.

All this the lion sees, and pants
Because he knows the hot sun slants
Between the rancid jungle-grass,
Which never more shall part to let him pass
Down to the jungle drinking-hole,
Whither the zebra comes with her sleek foal.

The sun is hot by day and has his swink,
And sops up sleepy lions' and tigers' stink,
But not this lion's stink, poor carnivore,
He's on the shady shelf for ever more.

His claws are blunt, his teeth fall out,
No victim's flesh consoles his snout,
And that is why his eyes are red
Considering his talents are misusèd.

Stevie Smith, *Collected Poems* (1975)

Of the Donkeys of the Costermongers

The costermongers almost universally treat their donkeys with kindness.
Many a costermonger will resent the ill-treatment of a donkey, as he would
a personal indignity. These animals are often not only favourites, but pets,
having their share of the costermonger's dinner when bread forms a portion
of it, or pudding, or anything suited to the palate of the brute. Those well-
used, manifest fondness for their masters, and are easily manageable; it is,
however, difficult to get an ass, whose master goes regular rounds, away
from its stable for any second labour during the day, unless it has fed and
slept in the interval. The usual fare of a donkey is a peck of chaff, which
costs 1*d*., a quart of oats and a quart of beans, each averaging 1½*d*., and
sometimes a pennyworth of hay, being an expenditure of 4*d*. or 5*d*. a day;
but some give double this quantity in a prosperous time. Only one meal a

day is given. Many costermongers told me, that their donkeys lived well when they themselves lived well.

'It's all nonsense to call donkeys stupid,' said one costermonger to me; 'them's stupid that calls them so: they're sensible. Not long since I worked Guildford with my donkey-cart and a boy. Jack (the donkey) was slow and heavy in coming back, until we got in sight of the lights at Vauxhall-gate, and then he trotted on like one o'clock, he did indeed! just as if he smelt it was London besides seeing it, and knew he was at home. He had a famous appetite in the country, and the fresh grass did him good. I gave a country lad 2*d*. to mind him in a green lane there. I wanted my own boy to do so, but he said, "I'll see you further first." A London boy hates being by himself in a lone country part. He's afraid of being burked; he is indeed. One can't quarrel with a lad when he's away with one in the country; he's very useful. I feed my donkey well. I sometimes give him a carrot for a luxury, but carrots are dear now. He's fond of mashed potatoes, and has many a good mash when I can buy them at 4 lb a penny.'

Henry Mayhew, *Mayhew's London* (1851)

The songbird trade

The *Goldfinch* is also in demand by street customers, and is a favourite from its liveliness, beauty, and sometimes sagacity. It is, moreover, the longest lived of our caged small birds, and will frequently live to the age of fifteen or sixteen years. A goldfinch has been known to exist twenty-three years in a cage. Small birds, generally, rarely live more than nine years. This finch is also in demand because it most readily of any bird pairs with the canary, the produce being known as a 'mule', which, from its prettiness and powers of song, is often highly valued.

Goldfinches are sold in the streets at from 6*d*. to 1*s*. each, and when there is an extra catch, and they are nearly all caught about London, and the shops are fully stocked, at 3*d*. and 4*d*. each. The yearly catch is about the same as that of the linnet, or 70,000, the mortality being perhaps 30 per cent. If any one casts his eye over the stock of hopping, chirping little creatures in the window of a bird-shop, or in the close array of small cages hung outside, or at the stock of a street-seller, he will be struck by the preponderating number of goldfinches. No doubt the dealer, like any other shopkeeper, dresses his window to the best advantage, putting forward his smartest and prettiest birds. The demand for the goldfinch, especially among women, is steady and regular. The street-sale is a tenth of the whole.

The *Chaffinch* is in less request than either of its congeners, the bullfinch or the goldfinch, but the catch is about half that of the bullfinch, and with the same rate of mortality. The prices are also the same.

Greenfinches (called *green birds*, or sometimes *green linnets*, in the streets) are in still smaller request than are chaffinches, and that to about one-half. Even this smaller stock is little saleable, as the bird is regarded as 'only a middling singer'. They are sold in the open air, at 2*d*. and 3*d*. each, but a good 'green bird' is worth 2*s*. 6*d*.

Larks are of good sale and regular supply, being perhaps more readily caught than other birds, as in winter they congregate in large quantities. It may be thought, to witness the restless throwing up of the head of the caged sky-lark, as if he were longing for a soar in the air, that he was very impatient of restraint. This does not appear to be so much the fact, as the lark adapts himself to the poor confines of his prison – poor indeed for a bird who soars higher and longer than any of his class – more rapidly than other wild birds, like the linnet, &c. The mortality of larks, however, approaches one-third.

The yearly 'take' of larks is 60,000. This includes sky-larks, wood-larks, tit-larks, and mud-larks. The sky-lark is in far better demand than any of the others for his 'stoutness of song', but some prefer the tit-lark, from the very absence of such stoutness. 'Fresh-catched' larks are vended in the streets at 6*d*. and 8*d*., but a seasoned bird is worth 2*s*. 6*d*. One-tenth is the street-sale.

The larks for the supply of fashionable tables are never provided by the London bird-catchers, who catch only 'singing larks', for the shop and street-traffic. The edible larks used to be highly esteemed in pies, but they are now generally roasted for consumption. They are principally the produce of Cambridgeshire, with some from Bedfordshire, and are sent direct (killed) to Leadenhall-market, where about 215,000 are sold yearly, being nearly two-thirds of the gross London consumption.

It is only within these twelve or fifteen years that the London dealers have cared to trade to any extent in *Nightingales*, but they are now a part of the stock of every bird-shop of the more flourishing class. Before that they were merely exceptional as cage-birds. As it is, the 'domestication', if the word be allowable with reference to the nightingale, is but partial. Like all migratory birds, when the season for migration approaches, the caged nightingale shows symptoms of great uneasiness, dashing himself against the wires of his cage or his aviary, and sometimes dying in a few days.

Ibid.

Exhibitors of Trained Animals

THE HAPPY FAMILY EXHIBITOR

'Happy Families,' or assemblages of animals of diverse habits and propensities living amicably, or at least quietly, in one cage, are so well known as to need no further description here. Concerning them I received the following account:

'I have been three years connected with happy families, living by such connexion. These exhibitions were first started at Coventry, sixteen years ago, by a man who was my teacher. He was a stocking-weaver, and a fancier of animals and birds, having a good many in his place – hawks, owls, pigeons, starlings, cats, dogs, rats, mice, guinea-pigs, jackdaws, fowls, ravens, and monkeys. He used to keep them separate and for his own amusement, or would train them for sale, teaching the dogs tricks, and such-like. He found his animals agree so well together, that he had a notion – and a snake-charmer, an old Indian, used to advise him on the subject – that he could show in public animals and birds, supposed to be one another's enemies and victims, living in quiet together. He did show them in public, beginning with cats, rats, and pigeons in one cage; and then kept adding by degrees all the other creatures I have mentioned. He did very well at Coventry, but I don't know what he took. His way of training the animals is a secret, which he has taught to me. It's principally done, however, I may tell you, by continued kindness and petting, and studying the nature of the creatures. Hundreds have tried their hands at happy families, and have failed. The cat has killed the mice, the hawks have killed the birds, the dogs the rats, and even the cats, the rats, the birds, and even one another; indeed, it was anything but a happy family. By our system we never have a mishap; and have had animals eight or nine years in the cage – until they've died of age, indeed. In our present cage we have 56 birds and animals, and of 17 different kinds; 3 cats, 2 dogs (a terrier and a spaniel), 2 monkeys, 2 magpies, 2 jackdaws, 2 jays, 10 starlings (some of them talk), 6 pigeons, 2 hawks, 2 barn fowls, 1 screech owl, 5 common-sewer rats, 5 white rats (a novelty), 8 guinea-pigs, 2 rabbits (1 wild and 1 tame), 1 hedgehog, and 1 tortoise. Of all these, the rat is the most difficult to make a member of a happy family; among birds, the hawk. The easiest trained animal is a monkey, and the easiest trained bird a pigeon. They live together in their cages all night, and sleep in a stable, unattended by any one. They were once thirty-six hours, as a trial, without food – that was in Cambridge; and no creature was injured; but they were very peckish, especially the birds of prey.'

EXHIBITOR OF BIRDS AND MICE

A stout, acute-looking man, whom I found in a decently-furnished room with his wife, gave me an account of this kind of street exhibition:

'I perform,' said he, 'with birds and mice, in the open air, if needful. I was brought up to juggling by my family and friends, but colds and heats brought on rheumatism, and I left juggling for another branch of the profession; but I juggle a little still. My birds are nearly all canaries – a score of them sometimes, sometimes less. I have names for them all. I have Mr and Mrs Caudle, dressed quite in character: they quarrel at times, and that's self-taught with them. Mrs Caudle is not noisy, and is quite amusing. They ride out in a chariot drawn by another bird, a goldfinch mule. I give him any name that comes into my head. The goldfinch harnesses himself to a little wire harness. Mr and Mrs Caudle and the mule is very much admired by people of taste. Then I have Marshal Ney in full uniform, and he fires a cannon, to keep up the character. I can't say that he's bolder than others. I have a little canary called the Trumpeter, who jumps on to a trumpet when I sound it, and remains there until I've done sounding. Another canary goes up a pole, as if climbing for a leg of mutton, or any prize at the top, as they do at fairs, and when he gets to the top he answers me. He climbs fair, toe and heel – no props to help him along. These are the principal birds, and they all play by the word of command, and with the greatest satisfaction and ease to themselves. I use two things to train them – kindness and patience, and neither of these two things must be stinted.'

Ibid.

A bombed-out zebra in Camden Town

8 October 1940

Go round to see Julian Huxley* at the Zoo. He is in an awkward position since he is responsible for seeing that his animals do not escape. He assures me that the carnivores are perfectly safe, although a zebra got out the other day when its cage was bombed and bolted as far as Camden Town. While we are at supper a fierce raid begins and the house shakes. We go on discussing war aims. He feels that the future of the world depends upon the organization of economic resources and the control by the USA and ourselves of raw materials. The raid gets very bad, and at 8.30 he offers to drive me back. It is a heavenly moonlit night, and the searchlights are swaying against a soft mackerel sky and a great calm moon. The shells light up their match-flares in the sky. A great star-shell creeps slowly down over the city under a neat parachute. We hear loud explosions all round as he drives me bravely back to the Ministry.

Harold Nicolson, *Diaries and Letters 1939-45* (1967)

London Tom-Cat

Look at the gentle savage, monstrous gentleman
With jungles in his heart, yet metropolitan
As we shall never be; who – while his human hosts,
Afraid of their own past and its primaeval ghosts,
Pile up great walls for comfort – walks coquettishly
Through their elaborate cares, sure of himself and free
To be like them, domesticated, or aloof!
A dandy in the room, a demon on the roof,
He's delicately tough, endearingly reserved,
Adaptable, fastidious, rope-and-fibre-nerved.
Now an accomplished Yogi good at sitting still
He ponders ancient mysteries on the window-sill,

* The scientist and author. He was Secretary of the Zoological Society, 1935-42.

Now stretches, bares his claws and saunters off to find
The thrills of love and hunting, cunningly combined.
Acrobat, diplomat, and simple tabby cat,
He conjures tangled forests in a furnished flat.

Michael Hamburger

The Phoenix and the High Priest

Presently the children came to a great house in Lombard Street, and there, on each side of the door, was the image of the Phoenix carved in stone, and set forth on shining brass were the words:

PHOENIX FIRE OFFICE

'One moment,' said the bird. 'Fire? For altars, I suppose?'

'*I* don't know,' said Robert; he was beginning to feel shy, and that always made him rather cross.

'Oh, yes, you do,' Cyril contradicted. 'When people's houses are burnt down the Phoenix gives them new houses. Father told me; I asked him.'

'The house, then, like the Phoenix, rises from its ashes? Well have my priests dealt with the sons of men!'

'The sons of men pay, you know,' said Anthea; 'but it's only a little every year.'

'That is to maintain my priests,' said the bird, 'who, in the hour of affliction, heal sorrows and rebuild houses. Lead on; inquire for the High Priest. I will not break upon them too suddenly in all my glory. Noble and honour-deserving are they who make as nought the evil deeds of the lame-footed and unpleasing Hephaestus.'

'I don't know what you're talking about, and I wish you wouldn't muddle us with new names. Fire just happens. Nobody does it – not as a deed, you know,' Cyril explained. 'If they did the Phoenix wouldn't help them, because it's a crime to set fire to things. Arsenic, or something, they call it, because it's as bad as poisoning people. The Phoenix wouldn't help *them* – father told me it wouldn't.'

'My priests do well,' said the Phoenix. 'Lead on.'

'I don't know what to say,' said Cyril; and the others said the same.

'Ask for the High Priest,' said the Phoenix. 'Say that you have a secret to

135

unfold that concerns my worship, and he will lead you to the innermost sanctuary.'

So the children went in, all four of them, though they didn't like it, and stood in a large and beautiful hall adorned with Doulton tiles, like a large and beautiful bath with no water in it, and stately pillars supporting the roof. An unpleasing representation of the Phoenix in brown pottery disfigured one wall. There were counters and desks of mahogany and brass, and clerks bent over the desks and walked behind the counters. There was a great clock over an inner doorway.

'Inquire for the High Priest,' whispered the Phoenix.

An attentive clerk in decent black, who controlled his mouth but not his eyebrows, now came towards them. He leaned forward on the counter, and the children thought he was going to say, 'What can I have the pleasure of showing you?' like in a draper's; instead of which the young man said:

'And what do *you* want?'

'We want to see the High Priest.'

'Get along with you,' said the young man.

E. Nesbit, The Phoenix and the Carpet (1904)

The death of Mrs Carlyle at Hyde Park Corner

Nero lay under a stone in the garden at Cheyne Row, but she loved all kinds of animals, dogs especially, and had found another to succeed him. Near Victoria Gate she had put the dog out to run. A passing carriage went over its foot, and, more frightened than hurt, it lay on the road on its back crying. She sprang out, caught the dog in her arms, took it with her into the brougham, and was never more seen alive. The coachman went twice round the drive, by Marble Arch down to Stanhope Gate, along the Serpentine and round again. Coming a second time near to the Achilles statue, and surprised to receive no directions, he turned round, saw indistinctly that something was wrong, and asked a gentleman near to look into the carriage. The gentleman told him briefly to take the lady to St George's Hospital, which was not 200 yards distant. She was sitting with her hands folded on her lap *dead*.

I had stayed at home that day, busy with something, before going out in the evening. A servant came to the door, sent by the housekeeper at Cheyne

Row, to say that an accident had happened to Mrs Carlyle, and to beg me to go at once to St George's. Instinct told me what it must be. I went on the way to Geraldine; she was getting ready for the party, and supposed that I had called to take her there. I told her the message which I had received. She flung a cloak about her, and we drove to the hospital together. There, on a bed in a small room, we found Mrs Carlyle, beautifully dressed, dressed as she always was, in quietly perfect taste. Nothing had been touched. Her bonnet had not been taken off. It was as if she had sate upon the bed after leaving the brougham, and had fallen back upon it asleep. But there was an expression on her face which was not sleep, and which, long as I had known her, resembled nothing which I had ever seen there. The forehead, which had been contracted in life by continued pain, had spread out to its natural breadth, and I saw for the first time how magnificent it was. The brilliant mockery, the sad softness with which the mockery alternated, both were alike gone. The features lay composed in a stern majestic calm. I have seen many faces beautiful in death, but never any so grand as hers. I can write no more of it. I did not then know all her history. I knew only how she had suffered, and how heroically she had borne it. Geraldine knew everything. Mrs Carlyle, in her own journal, calls Geraldine her *Consuelo*, her chosen comforter. She could not speak. I took her home. I hurried down to Cheyne Row, where I found Forster half-distracted, yet, with his vigorous sense, alive to what must immediately be done. Mr Blunt, the Rector of Chelsea, was also there; he, too, dreadfully shaken, but collected and considerate. Two points had immediately to be considered: how to communicate the news to Carlyle; and how to prevent an inquest and an examination of the body, which Forster said would kill him. Forster undertook the last. He was a lunacy commissioner, and had weight with official persons.

J. A. Froude, *Carlyle's Life in London, 1834–81* (1885)

Bear-baiting

Generally the bears were set upon by several dogs at once, and they were further handicapped by having their teeth ground down so that they were dependent entirely upon their powerful forepaws. Bulls were generally matched with one highly trained dog at a time. The German Thomas

Platter describes a fight he saw where a great white bull tossed dog after dog, attendants catching them on sticks to break their fall so that they would not be killed but could be nursed back to health for further fighting. It is reminiscent of the remark of a master of staghounds who is reported to have said, 'I would not tolerate any cruelty . . . the same stag is never hunted more than three times in one season.'*

Sometimes fights were staged between men instead of animals. In one of these gladiatorial shows Jorevin de Rocheford saw one combatant with his wrist nearly severed and the other with his ear cut off. 'For my part,' he said, 'I think there is an inhumanity, a barbarity, and cruelty, in permitting men to kill each other for diversion.' At much the same date John Evelyn went, after an absence of twenty years, to the Bear-garden to see 'cock-fighting, dog-fighting, beare and bull baiting, it being a famous day for all these butcherly sports'. He added that he, for one, was 'heartily weary of the rude and dirty pastime'. There were few who thought as he did, and fewer still who would admit their disgust. Bear-baiting did, however, begin to die out towards the end of the seventeenth century, and by the time of Queen Anne the three bear gardens that still existed were ill-attended. It was not made illegal, however, until 1835. Cock-fighting continued to be popular for many years, though it was practised more frequently outside than inside London's boundaries.

R. J. Mitchell and M. R. D. Leys, *A History of London Life* (1958)

Dog stealers

The following extraordinary circumstances respecting this species of depredation were yesterday related in evidence against Jane Sellwood and Thomas Pallett, who were brought before the sitting magistrates on suspicion of having stolen and killed a large number of dogs for the sake of their skins:

Robert Townsend, one of the patrol, said, that having received information that a large number of stolen dogs were concealed in the prisoner Sellwood's house, near the back of the Philanthropic Society, St George's

* *The Times*, January 1956.

Fields, he went there yesterday morning; and in a back room, found about thirty carcases of dogs piled one on another; and under the floor of the same room and that adjoining, many more, the ground having been dug to receive them, and most of them were in a state of putridity.

William Bagshaw, of Earl Street, London Road, deposed that on the 14th December last, he lost a pug bitch, which he had every reason to suppose was stolen from him; that on hearing yesterday morning of a number of dead dogs being found in the prisoner Sellwood's house, he went there, and among the carcases discovered that of his pug bitch, which he was enabled to swear to from a particular mark in its mouth.

In the course of the examination it appeared that it was a common mode among the dog stealers to take small houses for the purpose of carrying on this abominable trade, and when they had collected as many carcases as they could bury, and the house would contain, to abscond without paying any rent; a circumstance of this nature having happened a short time since in Webber Row, St George's Fields, where the neighbours were almost poisoned by the stench.

The prisoner Sellwood is an old woman, Pallett is a boy. Neither of them having anything satisfactory to urge in their defence they were committed for further examination.

During the time the prisoners were at the bar, a man came to give them a character, when three dogs in the office immediately fondled about him; and had they not been prevented would have followed him away; from which circumstance, and his appearance, there was every reason to suppose he was one of the gang. Mr Ford therefore ordered him out of the office.

Morning Herald, 28 January 1801

Twilight Barking

From the first, it was quite clear the dogs knew just where they wanted to go. Very firmly, they led the way right across the park, across the road, and to the open space which is called Primrose Hill. This did not surprise the Dearlys as it had always been a favourite walk. What did surprise them was the way Pongo and Missis behaved when they got to the top of the hill. They stood side by side and they barked.

They barked to the north, they barked to the south, they barked to the east and west. And each time they changed their positions, they began the barking with three very strange, short, sharp barks.

'Anyone would think they were signalling,' said Mr Dearly.

But he did not really mean it. And they *were* signalling.

Many people must have noticed how dogs like to bark in the early evening. Indeed, twilight has sometimes been called 'Dogs' Barking Time'. Busy town dogs bark less than country dogs, but all dogs know all about the Twilight Barking. It is their way of keeping in touch with distant friends, passing on important news, enjoying a good gossip. But none of the dogs who answered Pongo and Missis expected to enjoy a gossip, for the three short, sharp barks meant: 'Help! Help! Help!'

No dog sends that signal unless the need is desperate. And no dog who hears it ever fails to respond.

Within a few minutes, the news of the stolen puppies was travelling across England, and every dog who heard at once turned detective. Dogs living in London's Underworld (hard-bitten characters; also hard-biting) set out to explore sinister alleys where dog thieves lurk. Dogs in Pet Shops hastened to make quite sure all puppies offered for sale were not Dalmatians in disguise. And dogs who could do nothing else swiftly handed on the news, spreading it through London and on through the suburbs, and on, on to the open country: 'Help! Help! Help! Fifteen Dalmatian puppies stolen. Send news to Pongo and Missis Pongo, of Regent's Park, London. End of Message.'

Pongo and Missis hoped all this would be happening. But all they really knew was that they had made contact with the dogs near enough to answer them, and that those dogs would be standing by, at twilight the next evening, to relay any news that had come along.

One Great Dane, over towards Hampstead, was particularly encouraging.

'I have a chain of friends all over England,' he said, in his great, booming bark. 'And I will be on duty day and night. Courage, courage, O Dogs of Regent's Park!'

Dodie Smith, *The Hundred and One Dalmatians* (1956)

Blackbird in Fulham

A John the Baptist bird which comes before
The light, chooses an aerial
Toothed like a garden rake, puts a prong at each shoulder,
Opens its beak and becomes a thurifer
Blessing dark above dank holes between the houses,
Sleek patios or rag-and-weed-choked messes.

Too aboriginal to notice these,
Its concentration is on resonance
Which excavates in sleepers memories
Long overgrown or expensively paved-over,
Of innocence unmawkish, love robust.
Its sole belief, that light will come at last.

The point is proved and, casual, it flies elsewhere
To sing more distantly, as though its tune
Is left behind imprinted on the air,
Still legible, though this the second carbon.
And puzzled wakers lie and listen hard
To something moving in their minds' backyard.

P. J. Kavanagh, *Collected Poems* (1992)

Dog shit

One thing about London: not so much dogshit everywhere. A lot still. Compared to New York, even old New York, it's the cloaca maxima. But nothing like it used to be, when the streets of London were *paved* with dogshit.

Explanation. The English still love their dogs, for some reason. But the dogs aren't living as long as they used to. Nothing is. It's weird. I mean, one expects snow-leopards and cockatoos and tsessebes to buy the farm eventually. But *dogs*? I have an image of fat Clive, sitting in a zoo.

How will we teach the children to speak when all the animals are gone?

Because animals are what they want to talk about first. Yes, and buses and food and Mama and Dada. But animals are what they break their silence for.

Martin Amis, *London Fields* (1989)

A London turkey

Turkeys, I suppose, spend the major part of their lives being lulled into a false sense of security and well-being. Their final demand, so to speak, comes but once and lack of rehearsals must make the final crunch an unexpected and painless event. No, I can't feel sorry for them en masse but I couldn't help shedding a tear for the one I nibbled at in the Park Lane Hilton on Christmas Day. The idea of being stuffed daily only to end up being eaten by me and an assorted bunch of fairly revolting Arabs and Iranians makes me feel that a turkey's life lacks meaning. And, talking of getting stuffed, it occurred to me as I eyed the menu that had the Last Supper been held in the Hilton the bill would have come to £500, VAT and tip included.

Jeffrey Bernard, *Low Life* (1992)

7

Characters

*If the crowd flowing over London Bridge makes the populace seem like a
collection of anonymous wage-slaves, that is perhaps one reason why London is
so full of exhibitionists, eccentrics and 'characters'. Sometimes consciously, sometimes unconsciously, they treat the streets, pubs, libraries and offices of London as
a stage on which they play out the roles they have composed for themselves.
Mayhew and Dickens made it their business as writers to record as many of these
'characters' as they could. I can remember when I used to work near Dickens's
house in Doughty Street, near Gray's Inn. The walk from the office to the bus
would nearly always involve passing at least half a dozen oddities – a dwarf,
shouting in fury at passing traffic; an ancient nun, appearing quite lost and
pacing round Mecklenburgh Square as if in search of belongings lost in the Blitz;
learned eccentrics on their way to the British Museum; punks with hair styled
like that of Mohican Indians. One did not feel that Dickens had exaggerated in
his visions of the human side-show.*

An Ode for Ben Jonson

Ah Ben!
Say how, or when
Shall we thy guests
Meet at those lyric feasts,
Made at the Sun,

The Dog, the Triple Tun?
Where we such clusters had,
As made us nobly wild, not mad;
And yet each verse of thine
Out-did the meat, out-did the frolic wine.

My Ben!
Or come again:
Or send to us
Thy wit's great overplus;
But teach us yet
Wisely to husband it,
Lest we that talent spend:
And having once brought to an end
That precious stock; the store
Of such a wit the world should have no more.

Robert Herrick, *Hesperides* (1648)

On the University Carrier, who Sickened in the Time of his Vacancy, being Forbid to go to London by Reason of the Plague

Here lies old Hobson; Death hath broke his girt,
And here, alas, hath laid him in the dirt,
Or else, the ways being foul, twenty to one,
He's here stuck in a slough, and overthrown.
'Twas such a shifter, that if truth be known,
Death was half glad when he had got him down;
For he had any time this ten years full
Dodged with him, betwixt Cambridge and the Bull.
And surely Death could never have prevail'd
Had not his weekly course of carriage fail'd;
But lately finding him so long at home,
And thinking now his journey's end was come,
And that he had ta'en up his latest inn,
In the kind office of a chamberlain,
Shew'd him his room where he must lodge that night,

144

Pull'd off his boots, and took away the light:
If any ask for him, it shall be said,
Hobson has supp'd, and's newly gone to bed.

John Milton, Minor Poems (1645)

Coleridge in Highgate

Coleridge sat on the brow of Highgate Hill, in those years, looking down on London and its smoke-tumult, like a sage escaped from the inanity of life's battle; attracting towards him the thoughts of innumerable brave souls still engaged there. His express contributions to poetry, philosophy, or any specific province of human literature or enlightenment, had been small and sadly intermittent; but he had, especially among young inquiring men, a higher than literary, a kind of prophetic or magician character. He was thought to hold, he alone in England, the key of German and other Transcendentalisms; knew the sublime secret of believing by 'the reason' what 'the understanding' had been obliged to fling out as incredible; and could still, after Hume and Voltaire had done their best and worst with him, profess himself an orthodox Christian, and say and print to the Church of England, with its singular old rubrics and surplices at Allhallowtide, *Esto perpetua*. A sublime man; who, alone in those dark days had saved his crown of spiritual manhood; escaping from the black materialisms, and revolutionary deluges, with 'God, Freedom, Immortality' still his: a king of men. The practical intellects of the world did not much heed him, or carelessly reckoned him a metaphysical dreamer: but to the rising spirits of the young generation he had this dusky sublime character; and sat there as a kind of *Magus*, girt in mystery and enigma; his Dodona oak-grove (Mr Gilman's house at Highgate) whispering strange things, uncertain whether oracles or jargon.

The Gilmans did not encourage much company, or excitation of any sort, round their sage; nevertheless access to him, if a youth did reverently wish it, was not difficult. He would stroll about the pleasant garden with you, sit in the pleasant rooms of the place, – perhaps take you to his own peculiar room, high up, with a rearward view, which was the chief view of all. A really charming outlook, in fine weather. Close at hand, wide sweep of flowery leafy gardens, their few houses mostly hidden, the very chimney-pots veiled under blossomy umbrage, flowed gloriously down hill; gloriously issuing in wide-tufted undulating plain-country, rich in all charms of field and town. Waving blooming country of the brightest green; dotted all over with handsome villas, handsome groves; crossed by roads and human traffic, here inaudible or heard only as a musical hum: and behind all swam, under olive-tinted haze, the illimitable limitary ocean of London, with its domes and steeples definite in the sun, big Paul's and the many memories attached to it hanging high over all. Nowhere, of its kind, could you see a grander prospect on a bright summer day, with the set of the air going southward, – southward, and so draping with the city-smoke not *you* but the city. Here for hours would Coleridge talk, concerning all conceivable things; and liked nothing better than to have an intelligent, or failing that, even a silent and patient human listener. He distinguished himself to all that ever heard him as at least the most surprising talker extant in this world, – and to some small minority, by no means to all, as the most excellent.

The good man, he was now getting old, towards sixty perhaps; and gave you the idea of a life that had been full of sufferings; a life heavy-laden, half-vanquished, still swimming painfully in seas of manifold physical and other bewilderment. Brow and head were round, and of massive weight, but the face was flabby and irresolute. The deep eyes, of a light hazel, were as full of sorrow as of inspiration; confused pain looked mildly from them, as in a kind of mild astonishment. The whole figure and air, good and amiable otherwise, might be called flabby and irresolute; expressive of weakness under possibility of strength. He hung loosely on his limbs, with knees bent, and stooping attitude; in walking, he rather shuffled than decisively stept; and a lady once remarked, he never could fix which side of the garden-walk would suit him best, but continually shifted, in corkscrew fashion, and kept trying both. A heavy-laden, high-aspiring and surely much-suffering man. His voice, naturally soft and good, had contracted itself into a plaintive snuffle and singsong; he spoke as if preaching, – you would have said, preaching earnestly and also hopelessly the weightiest things. I still recollect his 'object' and 'subject', terms of continual recurrence in the Kantean province; and how he sung and snuffled them into 'om-m-mject' and 'sum-m-mject', with a kind of solemn shake or quaver, as he rolled along. No talk, in his century or in any other, could be more surprising.

Thomas Carlyle, The Life of John Sterling (1851)

Lord Archibald Douglas

The Reverend Lord Archibald Douglas was a conscientious, if somewhat unorthodox, Catholic priest. Like the rest of his family, Archie had a marked streak of independence which, at times, must have caused his superiors some concern. This, however, was not noticeable during the early years of his career. As long as he remained in charge of the St Vincent's Home for Boys – the post to which he had been appointed by Cardinal Manning after his ordination – his career appears to have been conventional enough. That St Vincent's became the centre of what many people considered a 'scandal' was not his fault.

St Vincent's Home was in Woodfield Terrace, a dingy side-street off the Harrow Road in Paddington. By Victorian standards, it was an extremely worthy institution. Largely self-supporting – although aided by various Catholic lay societies – its main concern was in rescuing orphaned and destitute Catholic boys from the streets, teaching them a trade and finding them employment. (In time the work of St Vincent's was to develop into a well-known Catholic organization known as the Crusade of Rescue.) In 1882 a substantial portion of its income came from the sale of bread which, baked on the premises, was sold to local Catholic families. The brightly coloured, hand-pulled carts marked 'St Vincent's Bread' were a familiar sight in the Paddington streets. There were between 70 and 80 youngsters resident in the Home and for several years they ran the establishment themselves under the supervision of Archie and a married couple who acted as caretaker and housekeeper. It was a highly commendable but somewhat spartan arrangement. Only by rigorous cheese-paring and by his talent for improvisation was Archie able to keep the Home going.

Brian Roberts, *The Mad Bad Line* (1981)

Haydon's suicide

'We regret to state that Mr B. R. Haydon, the historical painter, died suddenly at his residence in Burwood-place, yesterday morning. The unfortunate gentleman was in his usual health on the previous evening, and it is believed that his decease was hastened by pecuniary embarrassment.'

This paragraph in *The Times* of Tuesday 23rd June caught the eye of Elizabeth Barrett's brother Alfred at Paddington Station that morning; he copied it out and sent it by post to his sister. Browning saw it too that morning, and after some hesitation wrote to Elizabeth Barrett to tell her. He thought she might not have had the news yet; he knew she did not see a newspaper in the mornings. If she had not yet heard, his letter might seem brutal, but he could not write without mentioning such a tragedy at all. He thought more of the effect on Miss Barrett than of the news itself; he knew Haydon very slightly, had not much admired what he had heard about him, and now deduced from the wording of *The Times* announcement that Haydon must have killed himself. It was the shock to Elizabeth Barrett that mattered to Browning, especially after the storm the previous night – storms always made her ill. But perhaps she would not feel it as much as he feared; she and Haydon had never actually met, after all – she might regard him as a mere acquaintance.

Elizabeth Barrett felt a good deal more than that. From the moment when she first learned the news, when she got her brother's letter, she was overcome with sadness, and with a feeling of guilt too – could she have averted Haydon's suicide if she had offered to lend him money? She had assumed, when Haydon sent her his pictures and journals for safe-keeping, that it was just one of his usual recurring financial crises. Everybody had warned her that lending money to Haydon was like dropping it into a hole in the ground, and at that particular moment she had no money of her own in hand, and would have had to apply to her father for a loan – which would not have been granted. But all these excuses seemed poor enough now. '*Would* it have availed, to have dropped something into that "hole in the ground"? Oh, to imagine *that*! Yet a little would have been as nothing! – and he did not ask even for a little – and I should have been ashamed to have offered but a little. Yet I cannot turn the thought away – *that I did not offer.*'

She was sure that Haydon had killed himself on a sudden insane impulse. He could not have been meditating suicide when he wrote the letters she had had from him last week, though she could see now that there was a note of desperate feeling in them. 'Oh that a man so high hearted and highly endowed . . . a bold man, who has thrown down gauntlet after gauntlet in the face of the world – that such a man should go mad for a few paltry pounds! For he was *mad* if he killed himself! of that I am as sure as if I knew it. If he killed himself, he was mad first.'

She got her brother Henry to go round to Burwood Place that afternoon, telling him to make a general inquiry after the family. Frank Haydon came to the door and said that 'Mr Haydon was dead, and that his family were quite as well as could be expected.'

The news of Haydon's suicide spread round London. One of the first to react to it was the Prime Minister. Haydon's farewell letter had been left at Downing Street by Coulton on the Monday afternoon; Peel endorsed it – 'Last letter from Haydon. It must have been written a few minutes before he deprived himself of life. Observe the word "wife" had been originally written "widow", and been altered by him.' Peel wrote at once to Coulton, saying how painfully shocked he was to hear the news, and enclosing a cheque for £200 from the Royal Bounty Fund for the immediate relief of Haydon's family. He added that when a subscription was opened he would contribute to that from his private purse.

Wellington's reaction was different. On the morning after Haydon's death, as soon as he saw the news in *The Times*, he sent a servant round to Burwood Place to recover his hat, which Haydon had borrowed for painting the Duke's portrait.

Alethea Hayter, A Sultry Month (1965)

The Duke of Wellington fights a duel

The Duke's doctor, John Hume, was surprised to receive a request from Hardinge on the Friday night to attend a duel between unnamed 'persons of rank and consequence' and to meet Hardinge at his house at 6.45 a.m. on Saturday for instructions, bringing with him a case of pistols. Hume duly appeared; and, instructed in all but the names, was taken alone in a carriage through Pimlico, along the King's Road and over Battersea Bridge, while Hardinge rode off to collect his 'friend'. Hume's carriage stopped at a crossroads half a mile beyond the river. Next moment he was astonished to see Hardinge riding up with the Duke of Wellington.

'Well, I daresay you little expected it was I who wanted you to be here,' said the Duke cheerfully. Hume shuddered.

'Indeed, my Lord, you certainly are the last person I should have expected here.'

'Ah! perhaps so; but it was impossible to avoid it, and you will see by and by that I had no alternative, and could not have acted otherwise than I have done.'

The party proceeded into Battersea Fields. Hume carried the pistols under his greatcoat and hid them beneath a hedge. They waited about.

At last Winchilsea and his second arrived, Falmouth apologizing because his coachman had taken them to Putney by mistake.

'Oh, no; it is no matter,' said Hardinge. This was not the apology his principal wanted, and Hardinge proceeded to berate the agitated Falmouth for letting things reach '*this extremity*'. The party moved forward into the field, but catching sight of some farm-workers jumped a ditch into a second field, where they found suitable ground. Hume then loaded his two pistols for the one-armed Hardinge and almost had to load Falmouth's also, since Winchilsea's second was shaking so much with cold and the effect of Hardinge's continued reproaches.

'Now then, Hardinge,' called the Duke, 'look sharp and step out the ground. I have no time to waste.' Hardinge hastily marked out the Duke's position with his heel and then stepped out twelve paces towards the ditch where Winchilsea was standing. Again the Duke called to him.

'Damn it! don't stick him up so near the ditch. If I hit him he will tumble in.' The Duke intended to lame his traducer with a bullet in his leg but not to stop his mouth for ever with ditch-water.

Before giving the Duke his pistol Hardinge unfolded a piece of paper and from it read Winchilsea and Falmouth a lecture which drew tears to Falmouth's eyes. The Duke stood with a good-natured expression during this performance. Finally the two pistols were in the principals' hands and cocked.

'Then gentlemen, I shall ask you if you are ready,' said Hardinge, 'and give the word fire without any further signal or preparation.' There was an instant's pause. 'Gentlemen, are you ready? *Fire!*' Hume's eyes were fixed in agony on his friend, whose blood he might in another moment be staunching, and he did not notice that Winchilsea kept his right arm glued to his side. The Duke noticed, and instead of hitting Winchilsea's leg fired wide. With a seraphic smile Winchilsea then raised his pistol as if in blessing and fired it off into the air. (Before acting as his second Falmouth had made Winchilsea promise on his honour, if he survived the Duke's shot, not to fire back. Falmouth had always considered him to be 'completely in the wrong'.)

Having stood the Duke's fire, Winchilsea now felt that honour permitted him to apologize for the *Standard* letter. Falmouth produced a draft apology which he read aloud to the Duke.

'This won't do,' said the Duke in a low voice to Hardinge; 'it is no apology.' For though the word 'regret' appeared the word 'apology' did not. Hume promptly pencilled in the words 'in apology' and initialled them, 'J.R.H.'. This the Duke accepted. He bowed coldly to the two peers and interrupted another stream of anguished personal explanation from Falmouth.

'My Lord Falmouth, I have nothing to do with these matters.' Then he touched the brim of his hat with two fingers. 'Good morning, my Lord Winchilsea; good morning, my Lord Falmouth' – and cantered off the field. It had been a good morning for a Prime Minister.

Elizabeth Longford, Wellington, Pillar of State (1972)

Ode on the Death of the Duke of Wellington

I

Bury the Great Duke
   With an empire's lamentation,
Let us bury the Great Duke
   To the noise of the mourning of a mighty nation,
Mourning when their leaders fall,
Warriors carry the warrior's pall,
And sorrow darkens hamlet and hall.

II

Where shall we lay the man whom we deplore?
Here, in streaming London's central roar.
Let the sound of those he wrought for,
And the feet of those he fought for,
Echo round his bones for evermore.

III

Lead out the pageant: sad and slow,
As fits an universal woe,

Let the long long procession go,
And let the sorrowing crowd about it grow,
And let the mournful martial music blow;
The last great Englishman is low.

IV

Mourn, for to us he seems the last,
Remembering all his greatness in the Past.
No more in soldier fashion will he greet
With lifted hand the gazer in the street.
O friends, our chief state-oracle is mute:
Mourn for the man of long-enduring blood,
The statesman-warrior, moderate, resolute,
Whole in himself, a common good.
Mourn for the man of amplest influence,
Yet clearest of ambitious crime,
Our greatest yet with least pretence,
Great in council and great in war,
Foremost captain of his time,
Rich in saving common-sense,
And, as the greatest only are,
In his simplicity sublime.
O good gray head which all men knew,
O voice from which their omens all men drew,
O iron nerve to true occasion true,
O fall'n at length that tower of strength
Which stood four-square to all the winds that blew!
Such was he whom we deplore.
The long self-sacrifice of life is o'er.
The great World-victor's victor will be seen no more.

V

All is over and done:
Render thanks to the Giver,
England, for thy son.
Let the bell be toll'd.
Render thanks to the Giver,
And render him to the mould.
Under the cross of gold
That shines over city and river,

There he shall rest for ever
Among the wise and the bold.
Let the bell be toll'd:
And a reverent people behold
The towering car, the sable steeds:
Bright let it be with its blazon'd deeds,
Dark in its funeral fold.
Let the bell be toll'd:
And a deeper knell in the heart be knoll'd;
And the sound of the sorrowing anthem roll'd
Thro' the dome of the golden cross;
And the volleying cannon thunder his loss;
He knew their voices of old.
For many a time in many a clime
His captain's-ear has heard them boom
Bellowing victory, bellowing doom:
When he with those deep voices wrought,
Guarding realms and kings from shame;
With those deep voices our dead captain taught
The tyrant, and asserts his claim
In that dread sound to the great name,
Which he has worn so pure of blame,
In praise and in dispraise the same,
A man of well-attemper'd frame.
O civic muse, to such a name,
To such a name for ages long,
To such a name,
Preserve a broad approach of fame,
And ever-echoing avenues of song.

Alfred, Lord Tennyson (1852)

The Carlyles at home

These were times when Carlyle was like a child, and like a very naughty one.

During the three months of his absence the house in Cheyne Row had undergone a 'thorough repair'. This process, which the dirt of London makes necessary every four or five years, is usually undergone in the absence of the owners. Mrs Carlyle, feeble and out of health as she was, had remained, to spare her husband expense, through the paint and noise, directing everything herself, and restoring everything to order and cleanliness at a minimum of cost. The walls had been painted or papered, the floors washed, the beds taken to pieces and remade, the injured furniture mended. With her own hands she had newly covered chairs and sofas, and stitched carpets and curtains; while for Carlyle himself she had arranged a library exactly in the form which he had declared before that it was essential to his peace that his own working-room should have. For three days he was satisfied, and acknowledged 'a certain admiration'. Unfortunately when at heart he was really most gratified, his acknowledgments were limited; he was shy of showing feeling, and even those who knew him best and understood his ways were often hurt by his apparent indifference. He had admitted that the house had been altered for the better, but on the fourth morning the young lady next door began upon her fatal piano, and then the tempest burst out which Mrs Carlyle describes with such pathetic humour. First he insisted that he would have a room made for himself on the roof where no sound could enter. When shown how much this would cost, he chose to have his rooms altered below – partitions made or taken down – new fireplaces introduced. Again the house was filled with dust and workmen; saws grating and hammers clattering, and poor Carlyle in the midst of it, 'wringing his hands and tearing his hair at the sight of the uproar which he had raised'. And after all it was not the piano, or very little the piano. It is in ourselves that we are this or that, and the young lady might have played her fingers off, and he would never have heard her, had his work once been set going, and he absorbed in it. But go it would not, except fitfully and unsatisfactorily; his materials were all accumulated; he had seen all that he needed to see, yet his task still seemed impossible. The tumult in the house was appeased: another writing-room was arranged; the unfortunate young lady was brought to silence. 'Past and Present' was done and out of the way. The dinner-hour was changed to the middle of the day to improve the biliary condition. No result came. He walked about the streets to distract himself. His mind wandered to other subjects as one thing or another suggested itself.

J. A. Froude, *Carlyle's Life in London, 1834–81* (1885)

Silas Wegg

Over against a London house, a corner house not far from Cavendish Square, a man with a wooden leg had sat for some years, with his remaining foot in a basket in cold weather, picking up a living on this wise: Every morning at eight o'clock, he stumped to the corner, carrying a chair, a clothes-horse, a pair of trestles, a board, a basket, and an umbrella, all strapped together. Separating these, the board and trestles became a counter, the basket supplied the few small lots of fruit and sweets that he offered for sale upon it and became a foot-warmer, the unfolded clothes-horse displayed a choice collection of halfpenny ballads and became a screen, and the stool planted within it became his post for the rest of the day. All weathers saw the man at the post. This is to be accepted in a double sense, for he contrived a back to his wooden stool by placing it against the lamp-post. When the weather was wet, he put up his umbrella over his stock-in-trade, not over himself; when the weather was dry, he furled that faded article, tied it round with a piece of yarn, and laid it cross-wise under the trestles: where it looked like an unwholesomely-forced lettuce that had lost in colour and crispness what it had gained in size.

He had established his right to the corner by imperceptible prescription. He had never varied his ground an inch, but had in the beginning diffidently taken the corner upon which the side of the house gave. A howling corner in the winter time, a dusty corner in the summer time, an undesirable corner at the best of times. Shelterless fragments of straw and paper got up revolving storms there, when the main street was at peace; and the water-cart, as if it were drunk or short-sighted, came blundering and jolting round it, making it muddy when all else was clean.

On the front of his sale-board hung a little placard, like a kettle-holder, bearing the inscription in his own small text:

Errands gone
On with fi
Delity By
Ladies and Gentlemen
I remain
Your humble Servt.
Silas Wegg.

He had not only settled it with himself in the course of time, that he was errand-goer by appointment to the house at the corner (though he received such commissions not half-a-dozen times in a year, and then only as some servant's deputy), but also that he was one of the house's retainers and owed vassalage to it and was bound to leal and loyal interest in it. For this reason, he always spoke of it as 'Our House', and, though his knowledge of its affairs was mostly speculative and all wrong, claimed to be in its confidence. On similar grounds he never beheld an inmate at any one of its windows but he touched his hat. Yet, he knew so little about the inmates that he gave them names of his own invention: as 'Miss Elizabeth', 'Master George', 'Aunt Jane', 'Uncle Parker' – having no authority whatever for any such designations, but particularly the last – to which, as a natural consequence, he stuck with great obstinacy.

Over the house itself, he exercised the same imaginary power as over its inhabitants and their affairs. He had never been in it, the length of a piece of fat black water-pipe which trained itself over the area door into a damp stone passage, and had rather the air of a leech on the house that had 'taken' wonderfully; but this was no impediment to his arranging it according to a plan of his own. It was a great dingy house with a quantity of dim side window and blank back premises, and it cost his mind a world of trouble so to lay it out as to account for everything in its external appearance. But, this once done, was quite satisfactory, and he rested persuaded that he knew his way about the house blindfold: from the barred garrets in the high roof, to the two iron extinguishers before the main door – which seemed to request all lively visitors to have the kindness to put themselves out, before entering.

Assuredly, this stall of Silas Wegg's was the hardest little stall of all the sterile little stalls in London. It gave you the face-ache to look at his apples, the stomach-ache to look at his oranges, the tooth-ache to look at his nuts. Of the latter commodity he had always a grim little heap, on which lay a little wooden measure which had no discernible inside, and was considered to represent the penn'orth appointed by Magna Charta. Whether from too much east wind or no – it was an easterly corner – the stall, the stock, and the keeper, were all as dry as the Desert. Wegg was a knotty man, and a close-grained, with a face carved out of very hard material, that had just as much play of expression as a watchman's rattle. When he laughed, certain jerks occurred in it, and the rattle sprung. Sooth to say, he was so wooden a man that he seemed to have taken his wooden leg naturally, and rather suggested to the fanciful observer, that he might be expected – if his development received no untimely check – to be completely set up with a pair of wooden legs in about six months.

Charles Dickens, *Our Mutual Friend* (1865)

The Arrest of Oscar Wilde at the Cadogan Hotel

He sipped at a weak hock and seltzer
    As he gazed at the London skies
Through the Nottingham lace of the curtains
    Or was it his bees-winged eyes?

To the right and before him Pont Street
    Did tower in her new built red,
As hard as the morning gaslight
    That shone on his unmade bed,

'I want some more hock in my seltzer,
    And Robbie, please give me your hand –
Is this the end or beginning?
    How can I understand?

'So you've brought me the latest *Yellow Book*:
    And Buchan has got in it now:
Approval of what is approved of
    Is as false as a well-kept vow.

'More hock, Robbie – where is the seltzer?
    Dear boy, pull again at the bell!
They are all little better than *cretins*,
    Though this *is* the Cadogan Hotel.

'One astrakhan coat is at Willis's –
    Another one's at the Savoy:
Do fetch my morocco portmanteau,
    And bring them on later, dear boy.'

A thump, and a murmur of voices –
    ('Oh why must they make such a din?')
As the door of the bedroom swung open
    And TWO PLAIN CLOTHES POLICEMEN came in:

'Mr Woilde, we 'ave come for tew take yew
    Where felons and criminals dwell:
We must ask yew tew leave with us quoietly
    For this *is* the Cadogan Hotel.'

He rose, and he put down *The Yellow Book*.
    He staggered – and, terrible-eyed,
He brushed past the palms on the staircase
    And was helped to a hansom outside.

                John Betjeman, *Collected Poems* (1970)

Swinburne at Putney

I left my house on a bicycle about 12.0 and rushed up town after an unsatisfactory morning of odds and ends. I had been received by Mr Watts-Dunton with a great amount of epistolary ceremony, many courteous letters arranging my visit, written by a secretary. The day was dark and gloomy. I got to Putney about 1.15 and walked into the street; I asked my way to the house expecting it to stand high up. I was standing in a very common suburban street, with omnibuses and cabs, and two rows of semi-detached houses going up the gentle acclivity of the hill. I suddenly saw I was standing opposite the house, a perfectly commonplace bow-windowed yellow-brick house, with a few shrubs in the tiny garden. I went up to the door, and was at once taken in by a maid. The house was redolent of cooking, dark, not very clean-looking, but comfortable enough – the walls crowded everywhere with pictures, mostly Rossetti's designs in pen and ink or chalk. I was taken into a dining-room on the right looking out at the back. To the left the tall backs of yellow-brick houses; the gardens full of orchard trees in bloom. A little garden lay beneath with a small yew hedge and a statue of a nymph, rather smoke-stained, some tall elms in the background.

Mr Watts-Dunton came out and greeted me with great cordiality. He seemed surprised at my size, as I was similarly surprised at his – and had not remembered he was so small. He was oddly dressed in waistcoat and trousers of some greenish cloth and with a large heavy blue frock-coat, too big for him with long cuffs. He was rather bald, with his hair grown rather thick and long and a huge moustache which concealed a small chin. He had lost his teeth since I saw him and looked an old man, though healthily bronzed and with firm small hands. After a compliment or two he took me upstairs. There lay a pair of elastic-sided boots outside a door, the passage thickly carpeted and pictures everywhere. He went quickly in, the room being over the dining-room.

There stood before me a little pale, rather don-like man, quite bald, with a huge head and domelike forehead, a ragged red beard in odd whisks, a small aquiline red nose. He looked supremely shy but received me with a distinguished courtesy, drumming on the ground with his foot and utter-ing strange little whistling noises. He seemed very deaf. The room was crammed with books; bookcases all about – a great sofa entirely filled with stacked books – books on the table. He bowed me to a chair, 'Will you sit?' On the fender was a pair of brown socks. W.D. said to me 'he has just come in from one of his long walks', took up the socks and put them behind a coal scuttle. 'Stay!' said Swinburne, and took them out carefully holding them in his hand, 'they are drying.' W.D. murmured something to me about his fearing they would get scorched, and we sate down. Swinburne sate down concealing his feet behind a chair and proceeded with strange motions to put the socks on out of sight. 'He seems to be changing them,' said W.D. Swinburne said nothing but continued to whistle and drum.

Then he rose and bowed me down to lunch, throwing the window open. We went down and solemnly seated ourselves, W.D. at the head, back to light; Swinburne opposite to me. We had soup, chickens, many sweets, plovers' eggs. Swinburne had a bottle of beer which he drank. He was rather tremulous with his hands and clumsy. At first he said nothing, but gazed at intervals out of the window with a mild blue eye, and a happy sort of look. Watts-D. and I talked gravely, W.D. mumbling his food with difficulty. When he thought that Swinburne was sufficiently refreshed he drew him gracefully into the conversation. I *could* not make Swinburne hear, but W.D. did so without difficulty. He began to talk about Hawthorne;

he said that *The Scarlet Letter* was a great book, but that any book *must* be a bathos after such a first chapter. 'I want more catastrophe for my money.' He smiled at me. Then he went on to speak of *The House with Seven Gables*, and then of certain dramas which were names to me – *Le Tourneur* etc. He waxed very enthusiastic over Elizabeth Arden(?), which he said was as great as Shakespeare, greater than Romeo and Juliet or the early plays. He said it was published in 1598(?) and that if it was *not* by Shakespeare there was the extraordinary fact of a dramatist living at the same time as Shakespeare who could create and embody a perfectly natural supreme woman.*

He seemed content to be silent, and I was struck with his great courtesy, esp. to W.D. This was very touching. W.D. made some criticism on Scott (Swinburne having said the *Bride of Lammermuir* was a *perfect* story) about the necessity when Scott became bookish of translating him into patois. 'Very beautiful and just,' said Swinburne, looking affectionately and grate-fully at W.D. 'I have never heard that before and it is just. You must put that down.' W.D. smiled and bowed. Later on W.D. attributed some opinion to Rossetti – 'Gabriel thought etc.' Swinburne smiled and said, 'I have often heard you say that, but' (he turned smiling to me) 'Mr Benson, there is no truth in it. Rossetti had no opinions when I first knew him on Chatterton and many other subjects – and our friend here had merely to say a thing to him and it was absolutely adopted and fixed in the firmament.' W.D. stroked Swinburne's small pink hand which lay on the table and Swinburne gave a pleased schoolboy smile.

Lunch being over, Swinburne looked revived, and talked away merrily. He bowed me out of the room with ceremony. W.D. seemed to wish me to stay and Swinburne looked concerned, drew nearer to him and said, 'Mr Benson must come and sit a little in my room' – so we went up. Swinburne began pulling down book after book and showed them to me, talking delightfully. As he became more assured he talked rhetorically. He has a full firm beautiful pronunciation, and talks like one of his books. Occasionally his voice went into a little squeak. He suddenly rose and went and drank some medicine in a corner. He had on an odd black tail-coat, a greenish waistcoat and slippers; low white collar, made-up tie – very shabby indeed. There was an odd bitter bookish scent about the room, which hung I noticed about him too.

He talked a little about Eton and Warre, saying 'he sate next me many a

---

* It seems likely that the play to which Swinburne was referring was *Arden of Feversham* published in 1592 and attributed by some to Shakespeare.

half and he was a good friend of mine'. Then W.D. proposed that I should go, when Swinburne said, half timidly, 'I hope there is time just to show Mr Benson one of these scenes.' – 'Well, one scene,' said W.D., 'but we have a lot of business to talk. You read it to him.' He took the book I was holding – the Arden play – and read very finely and dramatically, with splendid inflections, a fine scene; his little feet kicked spasmodically under his chair and he drummed on the table. He was pleased at my pleasure; and then took up some miracle plays, and told me a long story of the Annunciation of the Nativity in it – the sheep-stealer, called Mack, who steals a sheep and puts it into the child's cradle; the shepherds come to find it and laugh; then the angel appears. 'Do you think Mr Benson will be shocked if I show him what Cain says?' he said, and showed me giggling a piece of ancient school-boy coarseness. W.D. smiled indulgently.

Then at last W.D. took me away. Swinburne shook hands with great cordiality, and a winning shy kind of smile lighting up his pale eyes. I was haunted by a dim resemblance to William Sidgwick. W.D. led me off, saying, 'I like him to get a good siesta. He is such an excitable fellow. He is like a schoolboy – unfailing animal spirits, always pleased with everything; but he has to take care.' He was much amused at Swinburne asking me if I was his contemporary at Eton.

I was somehow tremendously touched by these two old fellows living together (Swinburne must be 66 and W.D. about 72?), and paying each other these romantic compliments and displaying distinguished consider-ation; as though the world was young. I imagine that the secret of W.D.'s influence is that he is ready to take all the trouble off the shoulders of these eminent men; that he is very sedulous, complimentary, gentle – and that he is at the same time just enough of an egotist to require and draw out some sympathy.

He is certainly a *great* egotist, and not, in any technical sense, a gentle-man. He drops his h's; he pronounces 'prowl' '*proal*', 'cloud' '*clowd*', 'round' '*roaned*' etc. He leads the talk back and back to himself. I will give some instances of this first. He kept on saying that he didn't say and didn't do this or that. 'Good God, the world's a great whispering gallery' and he seemed to have quite a disproportionate sense of the place he occupied in the world's eye. Here is this kind old gentleman, living in the glow of the embers of two great literary friendships, in a comfortable frowsy kind of house at Putney, and thinking that he is a kind of pivot on which the world turns. But then he has excuses. His absurd book (*Aylwin*) flies into a twentieth edition. Rossetti tells him that the figure of 'Rosabell' in *The*

Coming of Love is the most living breathing vital thing since Shakespeare. *I* should believe myself a great and inspired poet on much less. And after all, what harm does it do? To take oneself seriously is the great happiness of life.

W.D. kept – all through our long talk (we sate from 2.30 to 5.0) – reverting to himself: how *he* was the only man not dominated by Rossetti; how dogs wouldn't bite him; how as a boy at school, *he* dominated all the school, so that no boy ever got a hamper without bringing it to W.D. for him to choose what he liked best (he called it a very big fashionable private school) and would have carried him about all day on their shoulders if he had desired it; and how no edict of the masters would have availed, if he had given contrary orders.

He sighed heavily at one time and said that he had himself not done what he ought to have done in literature. At this I poured in a good deal of rather rancid oil and ginger-wine. He smiled indulgently and deprecatingly, and then said that the charge of Rossetti had been very anxious – the strategems to reduce chloral, the dancing attendance on his whims. But he said: 'In his friendship and the friendship of Swinburne I find my consolation.' This I did not think sincerely said.

'Swinburne,' he said several times over, 'is a mere boy still – and must be treated like one – a simple schoolboy, full of hasty impulses and generous thought – like April showers.' He added, 'His mental power grows stronger every year – everybody's does – he is now a pure and simple improvisatore.'

W.D. sipped a little whisky and water and smoked a cigarette. He sometimes reclined in an armchair; sometimes came and sate near me. I sate in a great carved chair of Rossetti's (very fine – Indian) facing the light. There were fine pictures everywhere: a *most* interesting one of Rossetti reading poetry to Watts-Dunton in the Green Room at 16 Cheyne Walk, by Dunn. He gave me a reproduction of this; a Shakespeare in a heavy frame; beautiful witches of Rossetti, in crayons, pale red, peeping out of great gold frames. Outside [were] the white orchard blooms and trees – and I arranged myself so that I could see no house-backs, and we might have been at Kelmscott.

I now transcribe as accurately as I can what he told me about Rossetti, in answer to many questions.

Rossetti was *not* a hard worker. He had *no* permanent quarrel with Morris. Mackail's book, he said, was a mere *joke*. Morris had a peculiar dislike to Mackail, and it was as Burne Jones's friend that Mackail did it. It was not what Rossetti *did* that impressed you. It was what he *was*. His work was nothing. It came streaming out irrepressibly as heat from radium. He had an extraordinary effect on everyone (except W.D.) and dominated them. 'Look at Swinburne's poetry. Swinburne has no animal nature at all – a mere bookman and a schoolboy. *The feminine and sensuous element in Swinburne's poetry was entirely under Rossetti's influence.*'

Mystical passion, he said, was the root idea of Rossetti's life. 'That was his life – yes, that was his life,' he said very gravely and impressively. He was *very* susceptible to female charm; and women fell wildly in love with him. W.D. had refused to introduce a lady-friend of his to Rossetti. She kept on asking why. 'Because you are a married woman – a beautiful woman – and if he falls in love with you, I won't answer for the consequences.' He had no *conscience* in the matter, though superstitious and in other ways much troubled by conscience. The odd Holman Hunt quarrel was this: Holman Hunt had a young model, Annie Miller, a simple pretty girl, to whom he was engaged. When he went out to the East, he committed her to Rossetti's charge. 'Good God,' said W.D., 'the folly of committing such a girl to so susceptible and so dominant a man!' However, Rossetti did *not* fall in love with her (and when W.D. once questioned him as to whether he had in any way played Holman Hunt false about it, he answered very angrily that he would not have behaved so to H.H., and moreover that he had never any temptation to act otherwise). But he saw a great deal of the girl; took her about to restaurants and music-hall. Holman Hunt heard of all this, when he came back; was very angry, broke off with the girl and married someone else and broke with Rossetti – 'very unfairly', said Watts-Dunton.

Rossetti's engagement to Miss Siddal was too long protracted (ten years – I found I knew all the dates better than W.D.). She was *sewing* in a back shop when Deverell saw her. She was indescribably lovely, but not very clever (tho' Swinburne thought so), but about 55? Rossetti fell in love with Mrs Morris, then a girl, daughter of an Oxford tradesman (W.D. would not mention her name, but said 'a dear friend of mine' represented 'in that picture behind you' – afterwards saying 'this is Mrs Morris'). But Morris was also in love; and Rossetti, between friendship to Morris and loyalty to Miss Siddal, gave her up. Miss Siddal was fiercely in love with Rossetti. Rossetti was good and kind to her, but neglected her a good deal. Mrs Rossetti was very unhappy.

He went on to talk of his humour – not *delicate*, but *fancy in rapid evolution*. He was never tolerant of any subject he did not feel interested in and used to put it indignantly or contemptuously away. He would talk of art, poetry, people, life, character; loathed politics.

He did not re-touch his poems much; but was a great corrector *in print*. Like Tennyson, he did not seem to realize what a poem was, until he saw it in print.

These really interesting things were sandwiched in with a lot of rot – about a girls' school at New York and a girl of Caribbean origin etc. He said to me very gravely, 'I shall *not* write the life of Gabriel. I cannot. I knew him *too well*. He told me too much about himself – day after day, year after year.'

I had intended to go earlier but we talked on. Occasionally he went to his secretaries. Before I went, we had some tea; and then he brought in two little framed pictures (Rossetti in Green Room and Kelmscott), prepared for his illustrated *Aylwin* – and the illustrated edition of *Aylwin* itself, and gave them to me, with many expressions of kindness and cordial offers of help. '*Come* and see me,' he said. 'Don't write. My correspondence is a simple curse. I have thirty letters a post' (I wonder what about?).

He wrote my name in the book. He talked a good deal about Lord de Tabley, or rather a good deal of the influence he had over de Tabley! I can't understand this enigma – how this egotistical, ill-bred, little man can have established such relations with Rossetti and Swinburne. There must be something fine about him, and his extraordinary kindness is perhaps the reason. But his talk, his personal habits (dripping moustache etc.) and his egotism would grate on me at every hour of the day. And yet 'he is a hero of friendship' said Rossetti.

I went out with my precious parcel; back by train in driving rain to Windsor.

A. C. Benson, *Edwardian Excursions* (1981)

Gilbert the Filbert

I am known around town as a fearful blood,
For I come straight down from the dear old flood,
And I know who's who and I know what's what,
And between the two I'm a trifle hot.
For I set the tone as you may suppose,
For I stand alone when it comes to clo'es,

And as for gals just ask my pals, why ev'rybody knows:
I'm Gilbert, the Filbert, the Knut with a 'K',
The pride of Piccadilly, the blasé roué.
Oh, Hades, the ladies, who leave their wooden huts
For Gilbert the Filbert, the Colonel of the Knuts.
You may look on me as a waster, what?
But you ought to see how I fag and swot,
For I'm called by two, and by five I'm out,
Which I couldn't do if I slacked about.
Then I count my ties, and I change my kit,
And the exercise keeps me awfully fit,
Once I begin, I work like sin,
I'm full of go and grit.
I'm Gilbert, the Filbert, etc. . . . .

Arthur Wimperis (1914)

Street characters in Ladbroke Grove

A few additional figures there were who stood in a rather closer relation to the small world of Number 79 than the anonymous ranks of passers-by I observed from my pram: they, while obviously debarred from the full club privileges of Kate, the cook, my parents and the boot-boy, yet enjoyed, as it were, the facilities of country membership. The Italian organ-grinder, a martyr to gastric troubles, who regularly appeared every Thursday afternoon; the crossing-sweeper in Ladbroke Grove whose function the internal combustion engine was even then rapidly rendering as decorative as that of the King's Champion; the muffin man, the lamplighter and the old gentleman who came out on winter evenings to play the harp by the foggy radiance of the street lamp – Dickensian figures who have obviously no rôle to play in the Welfare State and have left no successors. Doubtless their disappearance should be welcomed, and yet they did not appear to be either downtrodden or exploited: indeed, the impression they gave was chiefly of a proper consciousness of the important rôle in the social fabric played by muffin men, lamplighters and organ-grinders. Certainly their spirits seemed higher and their manners were undoubtedly better than those of the majority of the present-day beneficiaries of enlightened social legislation. Even the crossing-sweeper, despite his ostentatious rags and traditional whine, displayed a certain individuality and professional pride which one seldom observes in the hygienically-uniformed Municipal Refuse Disposal Officer.

Osbert Lancaster, *All Done from Memory* (1963)

Kate Meyrick

Kate Meyrick, who became London's 'Night-Club Queen' in the twenties, managed the mixture better. She was the daughter of a well-to-do family in County Clare and something of a rebel – she was the first woman in Ireland to ride a bicycle – but she had married a doctor and disappeared into dull and dreary respectability in Basingstoke. Fabian of the Yard described her as a neat, stern little woman, dressed in blacks and greys, 'who might easily have run a first-class seminary for well-brought-up young ladies'.

By the end of the war she was on her own and had eight children to support. She answered an advertisement for someone to help run 'tea dances'. She was not at all put off when she discovered she would be required to run something less genteel and a few months later she opened Dalton's Club, next door to the Alhambra in Leicester Square. The gangsters who infested the West End provided colour and excitement and, as she ingenuously explained: 'An evening-dress constituted no guarantee at all of its wearer's credentials: a party of apparently quite decent men might easily – only too often did – turn out to be one of the numerous gangs of bullies or racecourse terrorists who held sway.' With their continual demand for free drinks they were a drain on resources but Kate's club did a roaring trade and made a healthy profit. After seven weeks, however, the police raided Dalton's, and at the resulting trial Kate was fined and her club anathematized as 'a hell of iniquity'. Having been 'robbed for ever' of her good name, she threw caution to the winds and opened a succession of clubs.

Robert Murphy, *Smash and Grab* (1993)

Reading Room eccentrics

I think some readers were, quite simply, tramps who came in for warmth and shelter, tramps of a special kind who loved to be surrounded by books and to see people studying, even if they didn't do much reading themselves. There were not many of them, and it was cheering to see how this great institution was open to them in this rough competitive world; no one interfered with them, they were treated with as much respect as anyone else. I think of one man in particular. There is a swing-door entrance opening into a corridor leading to another swing-door into the Reading Room. In this corridor there used to be hot-water pipes. One of the readers took up a position there for a great deal of the time, gazing down at the pipes as if carefully examining them. He was quite broken down in person and dress. He was slight and small with almost no shoulders, and with decayed trousers creased concertina-fashion from thigh to foot. A long piece of string always dangled from the pocket of a miserable overcoat. He had so little face and so much battered hat that it was like a mouse wearing a hat. Occasionally he would sit in the Reading Room, but nearly always he would be found standing in the corridor carefully studying the pipes.

There were strange characters not always easy to make out. Once when having obtained a place at one of the crowded seats in the aisles between the main desks, I sat opposite a man who was writing very fast in an exercise book. He was not copying anything, but wrote very fast in his book, paused for a second or so, and then pushed forward again. I had seen him before rather vaguely and had noticed a certain abstracted air about him which did not seem congruous with composition. Now sitting opposite him I became amazed not only at his ceaseless writing but at his manner of writing which seemed to me sheer *scribbling*. I got up and walked about a little and finally stood behind him. I knew that he was unaware of me and that it would be safe to observe what he was writing. On he went, at a great pace, his pen racing across the paper, writing – *nothing*. It was just like this⹁⹁⹁⹁⹁⹁⹁, line after line with almost no variation, no letters formed. When he came to the end of his page he turned over and feverishly started on the next. I think he has been doing this for some time; he is doing it still, for I had another look only the other day, and there he was, in a kind of enchantment, still bent on this strange task.

When I first went to the Reading Room, I was attracted by one particular man who was always there. He was tall, dark-haired, and moved in a very calm, slightly lounging manner which argued an inner serenity which I thought was reflected in the expression of his face upon which there rested always the foundation of a smile. He came early and stayed till closing time. I never went to the Reading Room without seeing him there. The twenties passed, and still he took up his position at a certain part of the circle near the door leading to the North Library. He always had a pile of books beside him from which he took notes. One day when he was out at lunch I looked at the titles of his books. I even wrote them down, but have lost the list; books such as 'New Aspects of Evolution'; 'The Future of Psychoanalysis'; 'Moral Force in Sociological Idealism'; 'The Philosophical Significance of Comparative Religion' and so on. His notes were written on rather small sheets of paper, and his handwriting was very small indeed and the letters crushed together. More years passed. I would be away for some time. I would return, and there he was; never, on any single occasion, absent from his station. He must, I felt, be writing a major work; he must have published some books. In the late thirties I noticed his name on one of his book-slips, and decided to see if I could find him in the catalogue. Yes, there he was, two or three books to his credit. I filled in a slip and got them out. They were on Evolution and Religion and Morals; but they were very short and slight, and I had never seen a single review of any of them at any time. Still, I thought to myself, perhaps these are mere notes for the major work he is preparing. Again the years went by. The war came howling down, and like a great storm passed over, and when it had gone, the Museum was seen to be still standing – and there was my friend as before, still studying, still taking his notes. More years passed. Now his dark hair had become grey and his movements slow, but something of the old dignity remained. We entered the fifties, and still he came. When we entered the sixties I went to the catalogue again to see what was now listed in his name. But *nothing* more was there. He had added nothing to his published output for thirty years. His hair was now white, straggling untidily over the collar of an overcoat which he never removed; his beard was ragged; his pale face had turned grey-green; and now he wore black gloves, keeping them on when reading and even when writing his notes.

John Stewart Collis, *Bound Upon a Course* (1971)

A Forgotten Man of the Thirties

Porteus made his reputation first of all in the *Twentieth Century*, one of the oddest and most interesting magazines of the time (not to be confused with the magazine of the same name that was the successor to the *Nineteenth Century*). It was the journal of the Promethean Society, a group that might be called the forerunners of today's feminist, green and anti-racist movements. The Prometheans favoured sexual freedom, a world commonwealth and a 'peace-mind'. They held weekly meetings at Conway Hall, and the small original membership proliferated into branches covering most social activities. Porteus was in charge of the Arts group, and was responsible for the poems and articles dealing with the arts, the former including the first, complete and later much truncated poem by Auden, 'A Communist to Others'. In the magazine's four years of life, he contributed to almost every issue, writing about the new poets and the new art, Pound and Huxley and Julien Benda, Middleton Murry and Faulkner and Svevo, Auden and Eliot and Hulme – and, of course, Lewis.

He wrote long pieces in two-thirds of the magazine's three dozen numbers, and by the time it closed down in 1934 had become known as a critic with a sharply vivid turn of phrase, distrustful like his master Lewis of left-wing literary politicos, and again like Lewis passionately secretive, with a distinct tendency towards paranoia. Porteus's background was ordinary enough – he was born in Leeds in 1906, attended various schools including an art school in Huddersfield, came to London and worked in advertising – but he concealed it, in part perhaps because of its very ordinariness. The flip side of this secretiveness was extreme indiscretion, and a tendency to fantasize about himself and everybody he met.

My first meeting with him had typical Porteusian elements. I went up the front steps of a house in Pimlico's Warwick Way, rang the bell and got no reply, then became aware that I was being watched by a man below me who had been investigating the contents of a dustbin. He asked who I wanted, then my name. On hearing it, he straightened up, smiled, abandoned his dustbin, and led the way up to a room at the top of the house crowded with books, newspapers, magazines, and pictures on and propped against the walls. The room also contained a table, two or three chairs, and a remarkable typewriter with eight rows of keys instead of the usual four, the extra rows having upper-case letters and some unusual keys that typed accents, umlauts and cedillas. Typing on it must have been the slowest possible work, but Porteus explained that time and trouble were saved because he had, as he put it, figures of every kind at his fingertips without the need of using a shift key. He immediately agreed to write for the magazine I was starting (the purpose of the visit), and we went round the corner to a pub called the Monster. Porteus talked amusingly about artists and writers who were only names to me, and deftly probed into my background and, in particular, my politics. He said he read a different party paper every day since none of them was to be trusted, and that I must meet Zenka with whom he shared the attic apartment. We parted on friendly terms, and he produced in good time a review of Auden's *Look, Stranger*.

Zenka, when met, was charming, small, dark and neat, a Ukrainian Jewess by origin, but born in England. Porteus first saw her at one of the Promethean Society gatherings, 'a rather striking small girl who at once sat near me on an empty table, pulling up a short skirt to show her ballet legs, speaking very passionately her Left-wing women's lib views'. Zenka was not intellectual but intelligent, seemed to enjoy the company of poets, was introduced by Porteus to Eliot and wrote reviews of books of ballet for the *Criterion*. She cooked bacon, sausages and odd mix-ups over a gas-ring for me, George Barker, Bernard Spencer, Ruthven Todd, and one or two youthful admirers and protégés of Hugh, as I soon called him.

My office was a five-minute bus ride from the Porteus attic, and once or twice a week I would meet him for lunchtime drinking in the Monster or another local, plus chat about the state of current poetry and prose, literary and international politics. He had almost no interest in British politics, didn't care who was Prime Minister or who led the Labour Party, but was deeply concerned by what he regarded as the general left-wing deviousness and occasional villainy of Victor Gollancz, whose Left Book Club was almost at the height of its popularity. The editor of the *Twentieth Century* was Gollancz's chief reader, Jon Randell Evans, and Hugh had a theory that the whole Promethean Society had been what he called a 'game' of Gollancz's, a sort of dry run for the Left Book Club which the publisher abandoned when he found most of the Society's members were not gulled by his left-wing intentions.

This idea, which he never gave up, was typical of the fantasies with which he improved reality. Most of them were based on his feeling of persecution, like the tale of the lost gold watch. It was lost by someone during a party at John and Myfanwy Piper's home, by a guest who took it off while washing his hands, forgot to put it on again, and then – well, when he looked for it, the watch had vanished, obviously picked up by somebody. Stolen, in a word. No accusation was made, but Hugh became convinced by the Pipers' manner that they believed him to be the thief. Two or three weeks later, a man rang Porteus's bell at the Warwick Way house, and said he could offer good prices for any old trinkets, china, ornaments . . . No, Hugh said, nothing. The man was undeterred. Jewellery, perhaps . . . *watches*? And in his guise as the man, Hugh stuck out his neck, narrowed his eye and said: 'Any gold watches? Any *gold* watches? I'd give a good price.'

The surrealist illogic of this outrageous story was typical. (Was he suggesting the Pipers had sent the street hawker? No, nothing so rational.) Yet to give an impression of mere crankiness would be quite wrong, even though in one letter to me he called himself a madman. . . .

Although Porteus had no interest in local politics, one couldn't be in his company for long without hearing him express strong right-wing views about the proper ordering of society, which involved rule by an aristocracy of intellect. Many were indignant or infuriated. 'Porteus is just a nudist fascist with a borrowed overcoat of complexity,' Roy Fuller wrote to me. 'A pity, because he is an acute critic.' (In the 1930s, Marxists were able to acknowledge that fascists might be acute critics.) On meeting the nudist fascist, Roy found him agreeable, although the feeling may not have been reciprocated. After an evening with the two of us that ended with drinks and argument in the Café Royal, Porteus went as we presumed to the lavatory and never returned. At my next meeting with him a few days later, he said ambiguously that he needed air, but it is quite possible that he found the assumptions shared by two left-wingers more than he could bear.

In any event, Roy was mistaken. Porteus was no kind of fascist, but a believer in the virtues and strengths of a calm hierarchical society, hence in part his lasting interest in Chinese history and admiration for Chinese literature. This found expression chiefly in his poems, some almost translations of Chinese characters, all deliberately stylized in a way unfashionable and untypical in the 1930s and today. He had also a natural courtesy at times so elaborate that it could seem exaggerated.

Julian Symons, *Times Literary Supplement*, 26 March 1993

Ramsay MacDonald

28 January 1931

Down to the House to see the division on the second reading of the Trade Disputes Bill. Churchill has just finished the wittiest speech of his life and the House is still chuckling. The division bell rings and they troop out. Pause of suspense while sounds of singing from the lobbies: 'Auld Lang Syne' and the 'Red Flag'. Troop back and figure announced. Unexpected Government majority. People troop out. I follow.

Walking across St Stephen's Yard I observe a small figure in front of me with collar turned up. He turns to see who is behind him and I see it is Ramsay MacDonald. I say, 'Hullo, sir. How are you?' He greets me warmly. We walk across to Downing Street and people take off their hats as he passes. The traffic is stopped. He talks about Vita's broadcast on Persia: the best he has ever heard. He asks me to come in and have a drink. We reach the door of No. 10. He knocks. The porter opens and stands to attention. Ramsay asks him, 'Is Berry in?' 'No, sir, he has gone.' 'Is Ishbel in?' (not 'Miss Ishbel'). 'Yes, sir.' 'Would you ask her to bring two glasses to my room?' We then go upstairs. The room has an unlived-in appearance. Turners over the fireplace. Ishbel is there. He asks her to get us a drink. She goes out and returns with two tooth-glasses and a syphon. Says she can't find any whisky. Ramsay says it is in the drawer of his table. He finds it. 'What about some champagne', he says, 'to celebrate the victory?' I say I will not have champagne. Malcolm [MacDonald] comes in. 'A cigarette?' I say I will. 'Malcolm, we have got cigarettes, haven't we – in that Egyptian box?' Malcolm goes to search for the Egyptian box. Then there are no matches.

He shows me the Turners. There is also a De Wint and a Wilson, both his own. And an early Turner also his own. He is pleased. He then says that he has made a deal with Lloyd George to score off the Tories. The Liberal resolution about unemployment has been so drafted that it forestalls any similar resolution by the Tories and is yet not a vote of censure. He tells me that Winston on leaving the House met him behind the Speaker's Chair. 'You'll get three months hard for tonight's work,' he said. At which Ramsay raised his glass: 'Here's to our three months hard.' He complains of over-work and bother. He sees me out. Nothing will convince me that he is not a fundamentally simple man. Under all his affectation and vanity there is a core of real simplicity.

Harold Nicolson, *Diaries and Letters 1930–39* (1966)

Phyllis

'Phyllis', also known as 'Rosie' because he wore a rose behind each ear, had been thrown out of the French earlier that day. He darted into the pubs of Soho in order to create a scene. Later, in a very rash moment I gave him half a crown, which meant that forever after if he saw me he made a dash towards me with a cry of joyful recognition: 'Mr Farson, Mr Farson, *dear*! Give me the price of a drink. Oh, well, give me the kiss of life.' He had a knack of appearing when I was trying to impress someone. His devastating screams and comments were broken off abruptly as he was thrown out, but at least the atmosphere had been enlivened.

Phyllis's real name with Timothy Cotter. Sometimes he'd appear horribly beaten up and people whispered that this had happened when he was arrested. This was not necessarily true, but his only 'fixed address' was Brixton Police Station and it was here that he died after one of his bouts of drunkenness. As he had no relatives and no friends, a pauper's funeral was imminent, but then a wonderful thing happened. The street traders of Berwick Street market took over the responsibility, decorating their stalls with flowers and photographs of Phyllis in order to raise the money to 'send him off' in style. 'The stalls were startling,' Deakin told me, 'like primitive Greek shrines.' Two hundred pounds were raised and Phyllis enjoyed a moment of posthumous approval as the *Daily Mirror* described him as 'an incredibly kind man and well-loved by everybody. His endless kindness, especially to children, made him a very popular figure.'

How death transforms! Phyllis ran errands for the traders and may have presented a different face to them, but he was a fearful nuisance too, barred from most of the pubs in Soho, and also rather frightening. I began to feel that behind the madness lay a devilish perception, that a sane man lurked inside the freak. On hangover mornings, I am ashamed to admit that I crossed the street to avoid him, warned by his shrill progress towards me. Yet he was so eccentric, with every shred of conventionality abandoned, that he was admirable too. No one wanted to know him when he made his screaming appearance in the doorway but they wanted to be in at the death. Two thousand people turned up for the funeral, lavishly organized by the traders as if he was the last Chicago gangster, and doffed their hats as the flower-laden coffin passed by *en route* to the cemetery. One news photo showed a tiresome adversary, who also wore flowers in his ears, saluting both the cortège and the camera. 'We won't see the like of him again,' the crowd said, uttering all the usual dishonest euphemisms when someone disconcerting dies.

Daniel Farson, Soho in the Fifties (1987)

A peppery magistrate

Mr Rowland Thomas served at Marlborough Street for only two years (just before my police service in the area) but left an indelible mark, nonetheless. First of all it was evident that Mr Thomas ('a Welsh terrier', as one onlooker describes him), was not over-keen on foreigners of any kind or dark-skinned persons with British passports, added to which his ideas were rather behind the times – as was his *Boy's Own Paper* language, full of 'rotters' and 'cads'. But no one could call him a coward. He always said what he thought. 'Well, really that was because he was never sober,' comments one lawyer who knew him.

He publicly regretted not being able to give corporal punishment to a man who, while living on the immoral earnings of a woman, had also assaulted a policeman; Mr Thomas was very pro-police. 'FLOGGING NEEDED!' yelled the headline.

A black man who was found guilty of having three grains of Indian hemp about his person was treated to a harangue about the appalling effect that that 'wicked drug' had on white girls who mixed with these coloured men. Rowland vowed that he would like to deport all those found 'in possession'. Sometimes even the police or prosecution felt the need to protect the accused against Rowly's wilder flights, and in this case the detective sergeant assured Mr Thomas that, although the accused was a 'stowaway', he had worked well since he had arrived.

'That,' agreed Rowly, 'is very much in his favour. As a rule these stowaways from Africa have only one port of call here – the public assistance!'

It was not just black people who earned his contempt. Once a Pole who had, as the contemporary parlance put it, 'associated' with another man's wife who was now up on a charge of soliciting, was given the full treatment.

'Fellows like you should be horse-whipped,' he was told. 'If there were not rotten fellows like you about, these girls would stick to their husbands. It is time some of you learned the law. A large number of you do nothing good in this country. Keep away from this woman and clear out!' Rowland concluded by adding, to the woman, that he would save her from this 'wastrel and scallywag'.

Being white and British through and through was no guarantee of escape, but the language employed was liable to be more 'boy scout'. 'You young bloods try to be clever,' he told a couple of young men who had been accosting women in the park, 'but you are nothing but a couple of cads.'

Sometimes even the beloved police felt the edge of his tongue.

'Who,' he asked one day, 'is responsible for this magnificent prosecution?' A man had been brought before him for stealing, by finding, five bars of chocolate from a carton outside a kiosk at Hyde Park Corner. 'If this man had eaten the rest of the chocolate,' he declared with undeniable logic, 'there would be no prosecution!' Then he gave the man an absolute discharge, telling him, 'You should have eaten the other four bars.'

To see him perform was, I understand, the most unbelievable experience. Instead of listening impassively, as most magistrates do, to the tale of evil doings of the person in the dock, he would react with tutting, exclamations and facial expressions of disgust and anger and even (people insist) jump up and down in his chair in a fury.

Joan Lock, *Marlborough Street: The Story of a London Court* (1980)

Joe Orton and the library books

The English public first learned of Orton and Halliwell in 1962. It was not exactly the debut they'd dreamt of. On 15 May the *Daily Mirror* devoted a banner headline to a story about a mischievous form of literary vandalism. Books from the Islington and Hampstead libraries were appearing on the shelves with photographs and book jackets humorously altered. The *Mirror* story was headed 'GORILLA IN THE ROSES', which referred to a monkey's head pasted in the middle of a rose on the cover of the *Collins Guide to Roses*. . . .

Orton, aged twenty-nine and described as a 'lens cleaner', had been arraigned with Kenneth Halliwell, aged thirty-five and a 'cleaner', at Old Street Magistrates' Court for stealing seventy-two library books and 'wilfully' (the word was carefully typed over 'unlawfully' in the court citation) damaging a number of books, which included the removal of 1,653 plates from art books. Total damage was estimated at £450. They had been sentenced to six months in jail. . . .

Orton's jacket designs didn't stop at gardening books. In a critical study of the poet, a pot-bellied old man tattooed from head to toe and clothed only in a skimpy swim-suit stood stiffly beside the name JOHN BETJEMAN. The first volume of Emyln Williams's collected plays had a curious repertoire of 'Knickers Must Fall', 'Up the Front', 'Up the Back', 'Olivia Prude', 'He Was Born Grey', 'Mr Winifred', and 'Fucked by Monty'. Instead of their photograph a biography of the Lunts had tacky Christmas figurines including a stuffed snowman, red and white reindeer, and two red and white does called Jill and Judy. In Alec Clunes's biography his face was replaced by a skull with a hole in the cranium. *Glok*, an American novel by Richard G. Stern, had its author as Hedda Hopper in one of her preposterous feathered *chapeaux*. . . .

'I used to write false blurbs on the inside of Gollancz books,' Orton remembered. 'Because I discovered that Gollancz books had blank yellow flaps and I used to type false blurbs on the inside.' Halliwell told the police: 'I saw Orton typing on the covers of books. I read what he typed, and I considered it a criticism of what the books contained.' The target for most of this mischief was Dorothy Sayers's Lord Peter Wimsey whodunits:

When little Betty Macdree says that she has been interfered with, her mother at first laughs [Orton wrote on the flap for *Clouds of Witness*]. It is only something that the kiddy had picked up off television. But when, sorting through the laundry, Mrs Macdree discovers that a new pair of knickers are missing she thinks again. On being questioned, Betty bursts into tears. Mrs Macdree takes her to the police station and to everyone's surprise the little girl identifies P.C. Brenda Coolidge as her attacker. Brenda, a new recruit, denies the charge. A search is made of the Women's Police Barracks. What is found there is a seven inch phallus and a pair of knickers of the kind used by Betty. All looks black for kindly P.C. Coolidge . . . What can she do? This is one of the most enthralling stories ever written by Miss Sayers.

It is the only one in which the murder weapon is concealed, not for reasons of fear but for reasons of decency!

READ THIS BEHIND CLOSED DOORS. And have a good shit while you are reading!

'My blurbs were mildly obscene,' Orton admitted. 'Even at the trial they said they were only mildly obscene. When I put the plastic covers back over the jackets you couldn't tell that the blurbs weren't printed. I used to stand in corners after I'd smuggled the doctored books back into the library and then watch the people read them. It was very funny, very interesting.'

John Lahr, *Prick up Your Ears* (1978)

London restaurateur

Jean-Pierre O'Higgins, I was later to discover, was the product of an Irish father and a French Mother. He spoke in the tones of those Irishmen who come up in a menacing manner and stand far too close to you in pubs. He was well known, I had already heard it rumoured, for dominating both his kitchen and his customers; his phenomenal rudeness to his guests seemed to be regarded as one of the attractions of his establishment. The gourmets of London didn't feel that their dinners had been entirely satisfactory unless they were served up, by way of a savoury, with a couple of insults from Jean-Pierre O'Higgins. . . .

O'Higgins had clearly never heard of the old adage about the customer always being right. 'And are you the joker that requested mash?'

'Am I to understand you to be saying,' I inquired as politely as I knew how, 'that there are to be no mashed spuds for my delight?'

'Look here, my friend. I don't know who you are . . .' Jean-Pierre went on in an unfriendly fashion and Everard did his best to introduce me. 'Oh, this is Horace Rumpole, Jean-Pierre. The *criminal* lawyer.'

'*Criminal* lawyer, eh?' Jean-Pierre was unappeased. 'Well, don't commit your crimes in my restaurant. If you want "mashed spuds", I suggest you move down to the working-men's caff at the end of the street.'

'That's a very helpful suggestion.' I was, as you see, trying to be as pleasant as possible.

'You might get a few bangers while you're about it. And a bottle of OK sauce. That suit your delicate palate, would it?'

'Very well indeed! I'm not a great one for wafer-thin slices of anything.'

'You don't look it. Now, let's get this straight. People who come into my restaurant damn well eat as I tell them to!'

'And I'm sure you win them all over with your irresistible charm.' I gave him the retort courteous. As the chef seemed about to explode, Hilda weighed in with a well-meaning 'I'm sure my husband doesn't mean to be rude. It's just, well, we don't dine out very often. And this is such a delightful room, isn't it?'

'Your husband?' Jean-Pierre looked at She Who Must Be Obeyed with deep pity. 'You have all my sympathy, you unfortunate woman. Let me tell you, Mr Rumpole, this is La Maison Jean-Pierre. I have three stars in the Michelin. I have thrown out an Arabian king because he ordered filet mignon well cooked. I have sent film stars away in tears because they dared to mention Thousand Island dressing. I am Jean-Pierre O'Higgins, the greatest culinary genius now working in England!'

I must confess that during this speech from the patron I found my attention straying. The other diners, as is the way with the English at the trough, were clearly straining their ears to catch every detail of the row whilst ostentatiously concentrating on their plates. The pale, bespectacled girl making up the bills behind the desk in the corner seemed to have no such inhibitions. She was staring across the room and looking at me, I thought, as though I had thoroughly deserved the O'Higgins rebuke. And then I saw two waiters approach Erskine-Brown's table with domed dishes, which they laid on the table with due solemnity.

'And let me tell you,' Jean-Pierre's oration continued, 'I started my career with salads at La Grande Bouffe in Lyons under the great Ducasse. I was rôtisseur in Le Crillon, Boston. I have run this restaurant for twenty years and I have never, let me tell you, in my whole career, served up a mashed spud!'

The climax of his speech was dramatic but not nearly as startling as the events which took place at Erskine-Brown's table. To the count of '*Un, deux, trois!*' the waiters removed the silver covers and from under the one in front of Tricia Benbow sprang a small, alarmed brown mouse, perfectly visible by the light of a table candle, which had presumably been nibbling at the *poésie*. At this, the elegant lady solicitor uttered a piercing scream and leapt on to her chair. There she stood, with her skirt held down to as near her knees as possible, screaming in an ever-rising scale towards some ultimate crescendo. Meanwhile the stricken Claude looked just as a man who'd planned to have a quiet dinner with a lady and wanted to attract no one's attention would look under such circumstances. 'Please, Tricia,' I could hear his plaintive whisper, 'don't scream! People are noticing us.'

'I say, old darling,' I couldn't help saying to that three-star man O'Higgins, 'they had a mouse on that table. Is it the *spécialité de la maison?*'

John Mortimer, *Rumpole à la Carte* (1991)

8

Royal London

Westminster Abbey is where nearly all the English monarchs have been crowned, and the throne of Edward the Confessor occupies a focal place in the sanctuary of that church. At the other end of the city, in the Tower, are deposited the crown jewels, seemingly attracting more and more visitors each year. London is a royal city – its parks are royal, some of its finest domestic architecture belongs to the crown estates. And, of course, it is the place where the royal palaces may be found: Kensington Palace, where Queen Victoria was born, and the marriage of the present Prince of Wales came unstuck; Clarence House, home of the Queen Mother; St James's Palace, with its marvellously subdued old brick elevations; Buckingham Palace itself. One of the great sadnesses for an architectural historian must be that George IV, having spent a fortune on his residence in Carlton House (a few hundred yards from St James's Palace), had the place demolished. A recent exhibition in the Queen's Gallery at Buckingham Palace revealed to us some of the splendours of Carlton House.

From William the Conqueror's coronation to the execution of Charles I in Whitehall, from the grisly fate of Henry VIII's brides on Tower Green to the marriage of Lady Diana Spencer to Prince Charles in St Paul's Cathedral, London has been the background to the greater part of our royal history, in all its poetry, pageantry and squalor.

The Execution of Lady Jane Grey

The Monday, being the 12th of February [1554], about ten of the clock, there went out of the Tower to the scaffold on Tower Hill, the Lord Guildford Dudley, son to the late Duke of Northumberland, husband to the Lady Jane Grey, daughter to the Duke of Suffolk, who at his going out took by the hand Sir Anthony Browne, master John Throgmorton, and many other gentlemen, praying them to pray for him; and without the bulwark Offley the Sheriff received him and brought him to the scaffold, where, after a small declaration, having no ghostly father with him, he kneeled down and said his prayers; and then holding up his eyes and hands to God many times, he laid himself along, and his head upon the block, which was at one stroke of the axe taken from him.

Note, the lord Marquis (Northampton) stood upon the Devil's tower, and saw the execution. His carcass thrown into a cart, and his head in a cloth, he was brought into the chapel within the Tower, where the Lady Jane, whose lodging was in Partridge's house, did see his dead carcass taken out of the cart, as well as she did see him before on life going to his death – a sight to her no less than death.

By this time was there a scaffold made upon the green over against the White Tower, for the said Lady Jane to die upon. Who with her husband was appointed to have been put to death the Friday before, but was stayed till then, for what cause is not known, unless it were because her father was not then come into the Tower. The said lady, being nothing at all abashed, neither with fear of her own death, which then approached, neither with the sight of the dead carcass of her husband, when he was brought into the chapel, came forth, the lieutenant leading her, in the same gown wherein she was arraigned, her countenance nothing abashed, neither her eyes anything moistened with tears, although her two gentlewomen, mistress Elizabeth Tilney and mistress Eleyn, wonderfully wept, with a book in her hand, whereon she prayed all the way till she came to the said scaffold, whereon . . . she was mounted.

Camden Society, The Chronicle of the Years of Queen Mary (1849)

The execution of Charles I

It was nearly two o'clock in the afternoon before Hacker knocked for the last time on the King's door. Charles had waited calmly, sometimes in silence, sometimes talking with Bishop Juxon. He had eaten nothing since the previous night, intending that no food should pass his lips, on his last day, except the Sacrament. The kindly sensible Bishop dissuaded him from this plan, and Herbert fetched a small loaf of white bread and a glass of claret. The King drank the wine and ate a small piece of the bread.

At the last summons he rose calmly, although Juxon and Herbert immediately fell on their knees, tearfully kissing his hands. He helped Juxon to his feet and asked Herbert to open the door and tell Hacker to lead the way. He followed along the corridors of his palace and through the great Banqueting Hall, going all the way between two lines of soldiers, shoulder to shoulder. In the last hours, the people had crowded into the palace, and behind the soldiers they pressed and struggled to get a sight of the King, some of them loudly calling out prayers and blessings as he passed. No one stopped them. The soldiers were themselves silent and dejected.

It was seven years since Charles had fled from Whitehall and the riots of the London apprentices; during that time his once beautiful palace had stood half-empty, had been used for its own purpose by Parliament and later occupied by the Army. For reasons of defence the seven noble windows of the Banqueting House had been partly blocked by boards or masonry. The light and gorgeous hall that the King remembered was now dark and bare. Far above his head, the great ceiling by Rubens, representing the triumph of wisdom and justice over rebellion and falsehood, can hardly have been visible in the grey light.

The King passed through the hall, and so out to the scaffold which was built against the palace wall and approached through one of the windows which had been enlarged for the purpose. The scaffold was covered in black and near to the block three or four staples had been driven into the wood so that the King could be bound if he refused to submit. The small platform was already crowded with people – the executioner and his assistant, not only masked, as was usual, but disguised beyond recognition in thick close-fitting frieze-coats with hair and beards that were evidently not their own. Colonel Tomlinson was there and Colonel Hacker, several soldiers on guard (among them John Harris the Leveller journalist), and two or three shorthand writers with note-books and ink-horns. Herbert remained inside the palace but Juxon came with the King.

Charles looked towards the axe and the block, and asked Hacker if no higher one could be provided. It was extremely low, not more than ten inches from the ground. Coming farther on to the scaffold he noticed the mounted troops drawn up between it and the crowds who filled the street. He had probably expected this, but he saw at a glance that it would be impossible and undignified to attempt to speak to the people. He took out of his pocket and unfolded a piece of paper about four inches square on which he had made a few notes, then addressed himself to the group round him on the scaffold, and more especially to Colonel Tomlinson.

'I shall be very little heard of anybody here,' he said. 'I shall therefore speak a word unto you here. Indeed I could hold my peace very well, but I think it is my duty, to God first, and to my country, for to clear myself both as an honest man, a good King and a good Christian.'

He began by briefly attesting his innocence: 'I think it is not very needful for me to insist long upon this, for all the world knows that I never did begin a war first with the two Houses of Parliament. . . .'

He gave his own brief, and convinced, account of how the troubles had begun, with Parliament, as he saw it, the aggressor, but added: 'God forbid I should lay it on the two Houses of Parliament. . . . I do believe that ill instruments between them and me have been the chief cause of all this bloodshed.'

Yet if, as a King, he denied the justice of the sentence against him, he added that as a Christian he saw his fate as God's judgment on him: 'An unjust sentence that I suffered to take effect, is punished now by an unjust sentence on me.'

He did not speak the name of Strafford; for most of those who heard, or afterwards read, his words there was no need to be more explicit.

Passing now to his duties as a Christian he declared that he had forgiven all the world, 'and even those in particular that have been the chief causers of my death: who they are, God knows, I do not desire to know, I pray God forgive them.' It was a strange statement to make, but true. During these last weeks he had never seen or spoken to any of the chief commanders of the Army. Fairfax and Cromwell and Ireton, the three whom he had come to know eighteen months before when he had negotiated with them at Hampton Court had not confronted him since he became their prisoner. He had been a prisoner, cut off from the world, communicating only with lesser men and underlings, Ewer and Rolfe, Harrison and Whichcot,

Tomlinson and Hacker. At his trial he had been judged and prosecuted by Bradshaw and Cook, two obscure lawyers neither of whom he had ever heard of before. 'The chief causers of my death, who they are, God knows. . . .' He could have made a very good guess, but it was true that he did not, absolutely, *know*. All these men who stood round him now, and would in a few minutes, in cold blood, murder him – they were instruments merely. But the hidden enemies who had finally destroyed him, who and where were they? Fairfax? Cromwell? Ireton?

He went on: 'I wish that they may repent, for indeed they have committed a great sin in that particular; I pray God, with St Stephen, that this be not laid to their charge. Nay, not only so, but that they may take the right way to the peace of the Kingdom: for my charity commands me not only to forgive particular men, but my charity commands me to endeavour to the last gasp the peace of the Kingdom. So, Sirs, I do wish with all my soul, (and I do hope there is some here will carry it further) that they may endeavour the peace of the Kingdom.'

He looked towards the clerks who were busy taking notes, then went on with great composure to instruct his enemies in politics. They would achieve nothing by unjust conquest; they must learn to know their duty to God, the King – 'that is, my successors' – and the people. They should call a national council to settle the affairs of the Church. As for the King— He broke off short, for one of the officers on the scaffold, happened by accident to touch the axe. 'Hurt not the axe,' said the King, 'that may hurt me.'

He resumed. Their duty to the king was clearly laid down in the known laws of the land. Then he came to the people: 'Truly I desire their liberty and freedom as much as anybody whomsoever; but I must tell you their liberty and freedom consists in having of government, those laws by which their life and their goods may be most their own. It is not for having a share in government, Sir, that is nothing pertaining to them. A subject and a sovereign are clear different things. . . . Sirs, it was for this that now I am come here. If I would have given way to an arbitrary way, for to have all laws changed according to the power of the sword, I needed not to have come here; and therefore I tell you (and I pray God it be not laid to your charge) that I am the Martyr of the people.'

He added a regret that he had had so little time to put his thoughts into better order, and would have concluded there, had not Juxon reminded him that 'for the world's satisfaction' he should make some statement about his religion. It was true that in putting forward this last eloquent claim that he died for the liberties of his people, he had 'almost forgotten' (his own words) to vindicate himself and his Church from the accusation of Popery. He now solemnly attested 'that I die a Christian according to the profession of the Church of England, as I found it left me by my father. . . . I have a good Cause and I have a gracious God; I will say no more.'

He turned now to speak to the grotesque figures by the block. For some reason, perhaps out of nervous forgetfulness, the executioner did not go through the usual formula of asking for, and receiving, the forgiveness of his victim. There is, in no account, any indication that these words were said. The King explained that he would pray briefly and then sign for him to strike. He also asked how he should arrange his hair not to impede the axe. Then with the help of Juxon, he put on his cap and pushed his hair underneath it.

'There is but one stage more,' said Juxon, 'which though turbulent and troublesome, yet it is a very short one; you may consider it will soon carry you a very great way; it will carry you from Earth to Heaven; and there you shall find, to your great joy, the prize you hasten to, a Crown of Glory.'

The King replied: 'I go from a corruptible to an incorruptible Crown, where no disturbance can be, no disturbance in the world.'

He now took off his George, the insignia of the Garter, the last of his jewels and gave it to the Bishop with the one word 'Remember.'

He took off his doublet, and for a moment resumed his cloak, against the bitter cold. Looking at the block he asked if it was set fast, and again regretted that it was no higher. The reason for the low block was to make the execution easier to perform if he had offered any resistance. The executioner was, naturally, unwilling to explain this. 'It can be no higher, Sir,' was all he said.

The King stood for a moment raising his hands and eyes to Heaven and praying in silence, then slipped off his cloak and lay down with his neck on the block. The executioner bent down to make sure that his hair was not in the way, and Charles, thinking that he was preparing to strike, said, 'Stay for the sign.'

'I will, an' it please Your Majesty,' said the executioner.

A fearful silence had now fallen on the little knot of people on the scaffold, on the surrounding troops, and on the crowd. Within a few seconds the King stretched out his hands and the executioner on the instant and at one blow severed his head from his body.

A boy of seventeen, standing a long way off in the throng, saw the axe fall. He would remember as long as he lived the sound that broke from the crowd, 'such a groan as I never heard before, and desire I may never hear again'.

C. V. Wedgwood, *The Trial of Charles I* (1964)

Cromwell's corpse at Somerset House

About the same time the House of Peers permitted the Protestant service to be held in Somerset House instead of Durham House. This drove out the Quakers and Anabaptists, and prevented the pulling down of the palace and the making of a street from the garden through the chapel and back-yard up into the Strand.

The Protector's palace was the scene of a great and sad event in November 1658; for the body of Cromwell, who had died at Whitehall, lay in state here for several days. He lay in effigy on a bed of royal crimson velvet, covered with a velvet gown, a sceptre in his hand, and a crown upon his head. The Cavaliers, whose spirits were recovering, were very angry at this foolish display, forgetting that it was not poor Oliver's own doing; and the baser people, who follow any impulse of the day, threw dirt in the night upon the blazoned escutcheon that was displayed over the great gate of Somerset House.

Walter Thornbury, *Haunted London* (1865)

Charles II plays tennis

2 September 1667

I dined with Sir G. Carteret, with whom dined Mr Jack Ashburnham. In discourse at dinner concerning the change of men's humours and fashions touching meats, Mr Ashburnham told us that he remembers since the only fruit in request, and eaten by the King and Queen at table as the best fruit, was the Katharine payre, though they knew at the time other fruits of France and our own country. After dinner comes in Mr Townsend, and there I was witness of a horrid rateing, which Mr Ashburnham, as one of the Grooms of the King's Bedchamber, did give him for want of linen for the King's person; which he swore was not to be endured, and that the King would not endure it, and that the King his father, would have hanged his Wardrobe-man should he have been served so, the King having at this day no handkerchers, and but three bands to his neck, he swore. Mr Townsend answered want of money, and the owing of the linen-draper £5,000; and that he hath of late got many rich things made, beds and sheets and saddles, and all without money, and he can go no further: but still this old man, indeed like an old loving servant, did cry out for the King's person to be neglected. But when he was gone Townsend told me that it is the grooms taking away the King's linen at the quarter's end as their fees which makes this great want; for whether the King can get it or no they will run away at the quarter's end with what he hath had, let the King get more as he can.

From him I went to see a great match at tennis between Prince Rupert and one Captain Cooke against Bab. May and the elder Chichly,* where the King was, and Court; and it seems are the best players at tennis in the nation. But this puts me in mind of what I observed in the morning, that the King, playing at tennis, had a steele-yard carried to him, and I was told it was to weigh him after he had done playing; and at noon Mr Ashburnham told me that it is only the King's curiosity which he usually hath of weighing himself before and after his play to see how much he loses in weight by playing, and this day he lost $4\frac{1}{2}$ lbs. Thence home and took my wife out to Mile End Green, and there I drank, and so home, having a very fine evening.

Samuel Pepys, Diary

The German invasion

Delightful as London city was, King George I liked to be out of it as much as ever he could; and when there, passed all his time with his Germans. It was with them as with Blücher, a hundred years afterwards, when the bold old Reiter looked down from St Paul's, and sighed out, 'Was für Plunder!'

---

* Captain Thomas Cooke, Master of the Tennis Court at Whitehall; Baptist May, Keeper of the Privy Purse; Sir Thomas Chicheley, Master of the Ordnance.

The German women plundered; the German secretaries plundered; the German cooks and intendants plundered; even Mustapha and Mahomet, the German negroes, had a share of the booty. Take what you can get, was the old monarch's maxim. He was not a lofty monarch, certainly: he was not a patron of the fine arts; but he was not a hypocrite, he was not revengeful, he was not extravagant. Though a despot in Hanover, he was a moderate ruler in England. His aim was to leave it to itself as much as possible, and to live out of it as much as he could. His heart was in Hanover. When taken ill on his last journey, as he was passing through Holland, he thrust his livid head out of the coach-window, and gasped out, 'Osnaburg, Osnaburg!' He was more than fifty years of age when he came amongst us: we took him because we wanted him, because he served our turn; we laughed at his uncouth German ways, and sneered at him. He took our loyalty for what it was worth; laid hands on what money he could; kept us assuredly from Popery and wooden shoes. I, for one, would have been on his side in those days. Cynical, and selfish, as he was, he was better than a king out of St Germains with the French King's orders in his pocket, and a swarm of Jesuits in his train.

William Makepeace Thackeray, The Four Georges (1860)

George II 'mugged' in Kensington Gardens

Duncannon in the evening told me the story of George II's robbery in Kensington Gardens, which I had heard before, but remembered imperfectly. He was walking with William IV, he said, in Kensington Gardens one day, and when they got to a certain spot the King said to him, 'It was here, my Lord, that my great-grandfather, King George II, was robbed. He was in the habit of walking every morning alone round the garden, and one day a man jumped over the wall, approached the King, but with great respect, and told him he was in distress, and was compelled to ask him for his money, his watch, and the buckles in his shoes. The King gave him what he had about him, and the man knelt down to take off his buckles, all the time with profound respect. When he had got everything, the King told him that there was a seal on the watch–chain of little or no value, but which he wished to have back, and requested he would take it off the chain and restore it. The man said, "Your Majesty must be aware that we have already been here some time, and that it is not safe for me to stay longer, but if you will give me your word not to say anything of what has passed for twenty-four hours, I will place the seal at the same hour to-morrow morning on that stone," pointing to a particular place. The King promised, went the next morning at the appointed hour, the man appeared, brought the seal, and then jumped over the wall and went off. His Majesty,' added King William, 'never afterwards walked alone in Kensington Gardens.' His Majesty's attendants must have been rather surprised to see him arrive at the palace *minus* his shoe-buckles!

Charles Cavendish Fulke Greville, *Leaves from the Greville Diary* (1929)

A royal divorce

HENRY BROUGHAM, MP, TO MR CREEVEY

London, 19 July 1821

Dear C.,

This town is in a state of general lunacy beginning most certainly with the Illustrious Person on the throne. Geo. 3 was an ill used man to be shut up for 10 years. His son has slept none, I believe, since you left town; nor will, till it is over. Yesterday he went for near 3 hours to Buckingham House, where Lawrence was painting Lady Conynghame. He then came back and had another row with his ministers, having been all Saturday and half of Sunday in a squabble with them; and, soon after he was housed, there drove along the Mall furiously a carriage and four, which was followed by my informant and found to contain old Wellesley in person. He was actually traced into Carlton House by the back door. You may make what you please of this,* but the fact is undoubted, as Duncannon and Calcraft were the persons who saw him.

To-day the Q.'s being allowed to enter the Abbey is doubted . . . but I still think it possible the Big Man may have gout and not be up to it.†

Yours,
H.B.

---

* The inference was that the Cabinet was jibbing about the Queen's exclusion, and that the King contemplated laying his commands on Wellesley to form an administration.
† The Coronation.

20 July

... The paroxysm rather encreases than diminishes, and literally extends to all classes. There never was a more humbling sight in this world. The Ministers are still sitting and squabbling; nor have they to this hour (5) made up their minds whether to stop her or not. My belief is they will let her pass, and also admit her at the Abbey if she persists. She is quite resolved to do so, and comes to sleep at Cambridge House for the purpose. But she is sure to blunder about the hour, and to give them excuses for turning her back by being late. . . . We [Brougham and Denman] thought at one time she meant to command our attendance, which we had resolved, of course, to refuse, as no more in our department than going to Astley's; but she did not venture. She has turned off the poor Chaplain Fellowes, who wrote all the balderdash answers, to make room for Wood's son; but the Alderman has failed in an attempt to turn off Hieronymus, the Major-domo, in order to put some friend of his in the place. Dr Parr has written a vehement letter to advise against her going, and certainly this is the prevailing opinion among her friends. I suppose I must be wrong, but I still cannot see it in the same light; and of this I am quite sure, that she would have been quite as much blamed had she stayed away. It is also certain that nothing short of a quarrel and resigning would have stopped her: perhaps not even that; . . . but to take such a step, one ought to have been much more positive against the measure than I have ever been from the first.

Thursday

Dear C.,

The Qn (as I found on going to her house at 20 minutes before six this morning) started at a quarter past five, and drove down Constitution Hill in the mulberry – Lady A[nne] H[amilton] and Lady Hood sitting opposite. Hesse (in uniform) and Lord H[ood] in another carriage went before. I followed on foot and found she had swept the crowd after her: it was very great, even at that hour. She passed thro' Storey's Gate, and then round Dean's Yard, where she was separated from the crowd by the gates being closed. The refusal was peremptory at all the doors of the Abbey when she tried, and one was banged in her face. . . . She was saluted by all the soldiery, and even the people in the seats, who had paid 10 and 5 guineas down, and might be expected to hiss most at the untimely interruption, hissed very little and applauded loudly in most places. In some they were silent, but the applause and waving handkerchiefs prevailed. I speak from hearsay of various persons of different parties, having been obliged to leave it speedily, being recognized and threatened with honors.

About $\frac{1}{2}$ past six [a.m.] she had finished her walks and calls at the doors, and got into the carriage to return. She came by Whitehall, Pall Mall and Piccadilly. The crowd in the Broad Street of Whitehall was immense (the barriers being across Parlt St and King St). All, or nearly all followed her and risked losing their places. They crammed Cockspur Street and Pall Mall, &c., hooting and cursing the King and his friends, and huzzaing her. A vast multitude followed her home, and then broke windows. But they soon (in two or three hours) dispersed or went back.

I had just got home and she sent for me, so I went and breakfasted with her, and am now going to dine, which makes me break off; but I must add that the King was *not* well received at all – silence in many places, and a mixture of hisses and groans in others. However, there were some bounds kept with him. For Wood and Waithman – a division of hissing and shouting – for the Atty and Solr Gen. an unmixed hissing of the loudest kind. *This* verdict is really of some moment, when you consider that the jury was very much a special, if not a packed, one. The general feeling, even of her own partisans, was very much agt her going; but far more agt their behaviour to her. I still can't see it in that light; and as she will go quietly back to B[randenburg] House,* avoiding all mob most carefully, she gains more than she loses, and I think her very lucky in being excluded. They put it on not being at liberty to recognize her or any one, except as ticket-bearers. Lord H[ood] shewed me one which they said of course would pass *any one* of the party, but she refused to go in except as Q. and without a ticket. The one Lord H. shewed me was the Beau's,† and I have it as a memorial of the business. . . .

Brougham now made plans to rouse the North in the Queen's favour, though he appears to have opposed Her Majesty going there in person. His

---

* She had come to Cambridge House for the Coronation.
† The Duke of Wellington's.

plans, here characteristically sketched in a letter to Creevey, were never carried into effect, death intervening mercifully to remove Queen Caroline from the troubled scene – the scene which her continued presence could only have rendered still more troubled. The appalling severity of the remedies administered can scarcely have failed to accelerate her release.

Thomas Creevey, *Diaries* (1923)

George IV buys a picture

18 April 1828

This morning, to my unexpected surprize, the King, George IVth (whom God preserve), sent Seguier to say he would wish to see the Mock Election! For my part I am so used to be one day in a Prison, and the other in [a] Palace, that it scarcely moved me. God only have mercy on the Art, & make me a great instrument in advancing it by any means, suffering or happiness. Oh have mercy, & grant this bit of Fortune, under thy mercy, may turn out profitable to my Creditors. Amen.

19th. This morning I moved the Mock Election to St James' Palace. I rang the bell, and out came a respectable man, dressed in black silk stockings, &c. I was shewn into a back room, & the Picture moved in.

In a short time Livery Servants, Valets, & the devil knows who crowded around it. At XI Seguier came; the Picture was moved up into the State apartments. I went into the City to my old Friend Kearsey, one of those who had supported me during the struggle. He was gone to a *Funeral*! 'Man groweth up & is cut down like a flower.' 'Dust to dust, ashes to ashes' was a very proper rap to me in my superhuman *elevation*! This is life.

When I came back Seguier was at Le Thiere's bricky Picture of Virginius! He called me aside. The room was in a bustle. 'Well,' said he, 'the King is delighted with your Picture. When the Picture was brought in, he looked at it & said, "This is a very fine thing." To the Figures on the left hand he said, "This is our Friend Wilkie out & out." He then turned to Campbell in the corner. "That's a fine head; it's like Buonaparte." "Your Majesty, Mr Haydon thinks it's like Buonaparte & Byron!" "Can I have it left to day?" "Mr Haydon will leave it with your Majesty as long as you desire." '

Seguier said the King was highly delighted, & said, 'Come to me tomorrow.' Seguier said he really was astonished at the tact of the King. He told some stories about his Father, G. III, so exquisitely & laughed so heartily, that the Pages were obliged to go out of the room. (Exquisite flattery of the Pages!)

Seguier said, 'Can the King have it directly?' 'Directly,' said I. 'Meet me at the British Gallery at 12 on Monday!' 'That I will, my hero,' said I. What destinies hang on 12 on Monday! . . .

20th. I thought in the morning, Shall I go to Church and pour forth my gratitude? Will it not be cant? Will it not be more in hopes for what is coming, than in gratitude for what is past? Yes. But my Creator is merciful. He knows the weaknesses of human nature. . . .

21st. Today has been a bright day in the annals of my life. The King has purchased my Picture, and paid my money. I went to the British Gallery at $^1/_2$ past eleven; at twelve Seguier came, with a face bursting, and coming up to me, said, 'Get a 7/6 penny stamp.' 'My dear fellow, I have only got 5/ in my pocket.' Looked Seguier mischievously arch as he took out 2/6. Away I darted for a stamp. '3*d.* more,' said the Girl! In I ran again and got the stamp, signed it, and received the money.

Seguier was really rejoiced, and verily I believe to him I owe this honor!

To my Merciful Creator I bow & bend & beg his acceptance of my gratitude, & that he will bless my next Picture of Chairing the Members, and that I may do nothing to incur his anger, but be good & virtuous, grateful & humble. Amen.

Benjamin Haydon, Diary (1960–3)

One king drops another at his hotel

24 July 1830

Yesterday the King went to the House of Lords, and was admirably received. I can fancy nothing like his delight at finding himself in the state coach surrounded by all his pomp. He delivered the Speech very well, they say, for I did not go to hear him. He did not wear the crown, which was carried by Lord Hastings. Etiquette is a thing he cannot comprehend. He wanted to take the King of Würtemberg with him in his coach, till he was told it was out of the question. In his private carriage he continues to sit backwards, and when he goes with men makes one sit by him and not opposite to him. Yesterday, after the House of Lords, he drove all over the town in an open calèche with the Queen, Princess Augusta and the King of Würtemberg, and coming home he set down the King (*dropped him*, as he calls it) at Grillon's Hotel. The King of England dropping another king at a tavern! It is impossible not to be struck with his extreme good-nature and simplicity, which he cannot or will not exchange for the dignity of his new situation and the trammels of etiquette; but he ought to be made to understand that his simplicity degenerates into vulgarity, and that without departing from his natural urbanity he may conduct himself so as not to lower the character with which he is invested, and which belongs not to him, but to the country. . . .

30th. The King has been to Woolwich, inspecting the artillery, to whom he gave a dinner, with toasts and hip, hip, hurrahing and three times three, himself giving the time. I tremble for him; at present he is only a mountebank, but he bids fair to be a maniac.

Charles Cavendish Fulke Greville, Leaves from the Greville Diary (1929)

Que pensez-vous de cela?

17 September 1831

The talk of the town has been about the King and a toast he gave at a great dinner at St James's the other day. He had ninety guests – all his Ministers, all the great people, and all the foreign Ambassadors. After dinner he made a long rambling speech in French, and ended by giving as 'a sentiment', as he called it, 'The land we live in.' This was before the ladies left the room. After they were gone he made another speech in French, in the course of which he travelled over every variety of topic that suggested itself to his excursive mind, and ended with a very coarse toast and the words 'Honi soit qui mal y pense.' Sefton, who told it me, said he never felt so ashamed; Lord Grey was ready to sink into the earth; everybody laughed of course, and Sefton, who sat next to Talleyrand, said to him, 'Eh bien, que pensez-vous de cela?' With his unmoved, immoveable face he answered only, 'C'est bien remarquable.'

Ibid.

The cost of kingship, 1836

LORD CHAMBERLAIN'S DEPT., 1836

	£
Upholsterers and cabinet-makers	11,381
Joiners and blind-makers	1,038
Carpet manufacturers	225
Turners, mat-layers, etc.	690
Locksmiths, etc.	4,119
Clock-makers, etc.	895
Pianoforte-makers, etc.	356
Or-mulu restorers, etc.	391
Japanners	654
Lamp and lustre manufacturers	268
Plate-glass men	26
China-men	201
Paper-hangers	898
Silk-mercers	16
Linen-drapers	1,962
Woollen-drapers	348
Furniture-printers	12
Sempstress	284
Tailors	25
Hatters	14
Hosiers and glovers	97
Stationers, etc.	1,080
Card-makers	118
Modellers and floor-chalkers	137
Washing	3,014
Dyers	74
Soap	479
Chimney-sweepers	150
Surgeons, etc.	1,957
Artists, etc.	400
Masons, etc.	18
Allowances	4,631

,,	1,578
Sundry payments	1,365
Messengers' bills	2,997
TOTAL	£41,898

LORD STEWARD'S DEPT., 1836

	£
Bread	2,050
Butter, etc.	4,976
Milk, etc.	1,478
Meat	9,472
Poultry	3,633
Fish	1,979
Grocery	4,644
Oilery	1,793
Fruit	1,741
Vegetables	487
Wine	4,850
Liqueurs	1,843
Ale	2,811
Candles (wax)	1,977
,, (tallow)	679
Lamps	4,660
Fuel	6,846
Stationery	824
Turnery	376
Brazier	890
China, glass	1,328
Linen	1,085
Washing table-linen	3,130
Plate	355
Royal gardens	10,569
Maundy expenses	276
Royal yachts	45
Board wages	3,615
Travelling expenses	1,050
Allowances	764
Hired persons	3,646

Yeomen	2,230
Compensation	1,244
Sundries	4,719
TOTAL .	£92,065

MASTER OF THE HORSE DEPT., 1836

	£
Liveries	6,208
Forage	5,308
Farriery	102
Horses	3,345
Carriages	4,825
Harness	567
Saddlery	577
Bits and spurs	30
Whips	46
Lamps	642
Coal	954
Stationery	48
Candles	214
Turnery	176
Washing	84
Ironmongery	182
Allowance	590
Sundries	2,822
Travelling	1,846
Post horses	1,402
King's plates	2,310
Stud bills	546
Hunt bills	5,000
	£38,734
Deduct proceeds of useless horses sold	529
	£38,205

MASTER OF THE ROBES DEPT., 1836, £1,880

TOTAL EXPENSES:

Lord Chamberlain's Dept	41,898

Lord Steward's Dept	92,065
Master of the Horse Dept	38,205
Master of the Robes Dept	1,880
	£174,048

These figures were examined thoroughly, and Her Majesty's estimated expenses were based upon them, and the figure of £385,000, made up as follows, was fixed as the nation's contribution to the upkeep of the royal household:

	£
H.M. Privy Purse	60,000
Household salaries	131,260
Tradesmen's bills	172,500
Royal bounty, alms and charity	13,200
Unappropriated money	8,040

TOTAL . £385,000

Bruce Graeme, *The Story of Buckingham Palace* (1928)

The accession of Queen Victoria at Kensington Palace

When all was over, the Archbishop and the Lord Chamberlain ordered a carriage, and drove post-haste from Windsor to Kensington. They arrived at the Palace at five o'clock, and it was only with considerable difficulty that they gained admittance. At six the Duchess woke up her daughter, and told her that the Archbishop of Canterbury and Lord Conyngham were there, and wished to see her. She got out of bed, put on her dressing-gown, and went, alone, into the room where the messengers were standing. Lord Conyngham, fell on his knees, and officially announced the death of the King; the Archbishop added some personal details. Looking at the bending, murmuring dignitaries before her, she knew that she was Queen of England. 'Since it has pleased Providence,' she wrote that day in her journal, 'to place me in this station, I shall do my utmost to fulfil my duty towards my country; I am very young, and perhaps in many, though not in all things, inexperienced, but I am sure, that very few have more real good will and more real desire to do what is fit and right than I have.' But there was scant time for resolutions and reflections. At once, affairs were thick upon her. Stockmar came to breakfast, and gave some good advice. She wrote a letter to her uncle Leopold, and a hurried note to her sister Feodora. A letter came from the Prime Minister, Lord Melbourne, announcing his approaching arrival. He came at nine, in full court dress, and kissed her hand. She saw him alone, and repeated to him the lesson which, no doubt, the faithful Stockmar had taught her at breakfast. 'It has long been my intention to retain your Lordship and the rest of the present Ministry at the head of affairs'; whereupon Lord Melbourne again kissed her hand and shortly after left her. She then wrote a letter of condolence to Queen Adelaide. At eleven, Lord Melbourne came again; and at half past eleven she went downstairs into the red saloon to hold her first Council. The great assembly of lords and notables, bishops, generals, and Ministers of State, saw the doors thrown open and a very short, very slim girl in deep plain mourning come into the room alone and move forward to her seat with extraordinary dignity and grace; they saw a countenance, not beautiful, but prepossessing – fair hair, blue prominent eyes, a small curved nose, an open mouth revealing the upper teeth, a tiny chin, a clear complexion, and, over all, the strangely mingled signs of innocence, of gravity, of youth, and of composure; they heard a high unwavering voice reading aloud with perfect clarity; and then, the ceremony over, they saw the small figure rise and, with the same consummate grace, the same amazing dignity, pass out from among them, as she had come in, alone.

Lytton Strachey, *Queen Victoria* (1921)

The Great Exhibition

The glass house or, as Ruskin rudely called it, 'the cucumber frame between two chimneys', was not conceived by the Prince but his enthusiastic support for the design made its adoption certain.

Baulked of their main grievance the enemies of the Exhibition sought more fantastic objections. Foreign trash was to flood the country. The chastity of agricultural labourers was to be debauched by the temptations of London. Socialists and 'men of the Red Colour', as Brougham called them, would congregate in subversive masses round Hyde Park.

The Prince battled manfully with these absurd criticisms, meeting them with firmness and humour. The King of Prussia grew so alarmed at these imaginary dangers that he wished to stop his relations from coming to the Exhibition. To him Prince Albert wrote:

> Mathematicians have calculated that the Crystal Palace will blow down in the first strong gale, Engineers that the galleries would crash in and destroy the visitors; Political Economists have prophecied a scarcity of food in London owing to the vast concourse of people; Doctors that owing to so many races coming into contact with each other the Black Death of the Middle Ages would make its appearance as it did after the Crusades; Moralists that England would be infected by all the scourges of the civilized and uncivilized world; Theologians that this second Tower of Babel would draw upon it the vengeance of an offended God.
>
> I can give no guarantee against these perils, nor am I in a position to assume responsibility for the possibly menaced lives of your Royal relatives.

Inevitable fears that the Roman Catholics would use the Exhibition for their own nefarious propaganda purposes were forthcoming. The Prime Minister wrote to the Prince that complaints had been expressed that Pugin, the distinguished architect, who was a Roman Catholic, had turned his Mediaeval Court into a kind of advertising booth for Popery. The Prince replied that he had successfully prevented the Belgians from sending over a positive Madame Tussaud's Exhibition of the Pope and twelve cardinals (including Cardinal Wiseman) as an excuse for setting off the splendid intricacies of Brussels lace. He added, 'but I cannot prevent crucifixes, *rosiers*, altar plate etc. etc. which form legitimate articles of trade. Those who object to their idolatrous character must be relieved to find Indian Pagodas and Chinese Idols in other parts of the Exhibition.'

But on May Day 1851 all the anxious preparations, the tribulations and the sneering were forgotten in the gorgeous and spectacular triumph of the opening ceremony. 'Quite satisfactory' was the Prince's terse description of that day which the Queen, in her flamboyant style said, 'made my heart swell with pride and glory and thankfulness'. The Prince, in the full-dress uniform of a Field-Marshal, and the Queen in a dress of pink watered silk, with their two eldest children, drove out from Buckingham Palace soon after half-past eleven. It was estimated by the police that there were 700,000 people between Buckingham Palace and the glass house, while inside the latter were over 30,000 people. The opening ceremony took place in the main transept, which was largely filled with rich hangings, statuary and coloured porcelain. The size of the building was emphasized by the large elm beneath whose ample shade the Royal Party was grouped. After the Prince, as Chairman of the Commissioners, had welcomed the Queen, the Royal Family processed round the building, though they noticed that in most of the bays the foreign exhibits were not unpacked. With the music of Handel and the voices of a vast choir ringing in their ears the Queen and Prince were deeply and strangely moved. Back at the Palace they came out on the balcony, which would appear to be the first occasion on which this was done by an English sovereign.

Against a solid background of machinery and raw materials were the inevitable oddities of every exhibition, the garden-seat for Osborne made out of coal, champagne made from rhubarb, the safety swimming swan for shipwrecks, the 'char-volant' – a carriage drawn by kites, – a pulpit connec-ted by gutta-percha tubes to the pews of the deaf, a doctor's walking-stick which contained an enema, a knife with 300 blades, Lord Eldon and his brother, in their judicial robes, carved from a single block of 20 tons of marble, a statue of Queen Victoria in zinc and a group of stuffed frogs, one holding up an umbrella, from Wurtemberg.

Roger Fulford, *The Prince Consort* (1949)

The funeral of Queen Victoria

I think you will like to hear of my going down to Southampton to see the passing of our dear Queen from Osborne to Portsmouth.

I went on the *Scot*, where both Houses were embarked. We steamed out, and took up our position between the last British ship and the first foreign ships of war, on the south side of the double line down which the procession was to pass. The day was one of glorious sunshine, with the smoothest and bluest of seas. After a while a black torpedo destroyer came dashing down the line signalling that the *Alberta* was leaving Osborne and from every ship, both British and foreign, boomed out the minute guns for close on an hour before the procession reached us. The sun was now (3 p.m.) beginning to sink, and a wonderful golden pink appeared in the sky and as the smoke slowly rose from the guns it settled in one long festoon behind them, over Haslar, a purple festoon like the purple hangings ordered by the King.

Then slowly down the long line of battleships came eight Torpedo destroyers, dark gliding forms, and after them the white *Alberta* looking very small and frail next the towering battleships. We could see the motionless figures standing round the white pall which, with the crown and orb and sceptre, lay upon the coffin. Solemnly and slowly, it glided over the calm blue water, followed by the other three vessels, giving one a strange choke, and a catch in one's heart as memory flew back to her triumphal passage down her fleet in the last Jubilee review. As slowly and as silently as it came the cortège passed away into the haze: with the solemn booming of the guns continuing every minute till Portsmouth was reached. A wonderful scene and marvellously impressive, leaving behind it a memory of peace and beauty and sadness which it is impossible to forget.

Then on Saturday, Feb. 2nd, came the wonderful procession through London, which you will see fully described in the papers.

Molly, Dorothie, Lady Denbigh and I saw it from the Household Stand at Buckingham Palace, and had a very good view. The behaviour of the crowd was wonderful in its silence and reverence as the procession passed. And this was the same everywhere, the K. of P. [King of Portugal], told Denbigh that the crowd in Hyde Park was quite half a mile deep. The only thing which jarred was the harnessing of the celebrated creams, with their gold and crimson trappings to a gun carriage. The demeanour of our new King in his dignified sadness was very striking, and of course the coffin in its white pall and regalia, he and the Kaiser were the most observed. The slow solemn march of the naval men with their arms reversed, moved me much for I could not help comparing the then with the now as I thought of last year in Dublin when the naval contingent went past the Queen with heads erect and their wonderful brisk step.

Not a sound was heard from the crowd during the procession and a great hush fell upon it when the coffin came in sight.

When all was over we waited awhile for the crowd to move away and then tried unsuccessfully to get up Constitution Hill and St James, so went up Grosvenor Place only to find a line of cavalry across it near St George's Hospital, so made for Albert Gate via Belgrave Sq. only to meet such a dense crowd streaming out that we had to retreat up the steps of the French Embassy, where we waited for an hour, and then with difficulty made our way into the park, and so home. . . .

You should have seen the park on Sunday, it was strewn with paper as tho' an army had been encamped there, the small railings of the flower-beds were trampled flat.

The Countess of Denbigh, *The Fielding Album* (1902)

King George V's London routine

In the heart of London, the King established the clockwork routine of a ship's captain. First thing in the morning and last thing at night he consulted the barometer; between those two fixed points his daily progress was as predictable as the course of a planet. By the time he sat down to breakfast on the stroke of nine he had been up for two hours: working on his boxes of State papers, writing up his diary, reading *The Times* newspaper. The rest of the morning was devoted to his secretaries and other officials, to receiving ministers and ambassadors, perhaps to an investiture or similar ceremony. Before lunching with the Queen at half past one he took a sharp walk round the garden: a mechanical, somewhat joyless exercise over a measured mile. At the end of luncheon he would sleep in an armchair for exactly fifteen minutes, waking, his eldest son observed, as if an alarm clock had gone off in his head. In the afternoon there might be engagements outside the palace, a game of tennis with his household or an hour with his stamp collection. The day's flow of red despatch boxes would claim his early evening. Once court mourning was at an end, he would sometimes dine out with the Queen at one of the remaining patrician houses in London or watch a not too demanding play. But he preferred to dine quietly with his family, albeit in white tie and Garter star. The equerry-in-waiting could safely set his watch at 11.10 when he heard the King making his way to bed.

Kenneth Rose, *King George V* (1983)

Buckingham Palace

They're changing guard at Buckingham Palace –
Christopher Robin went down with Alice.
Alice is marrying one of the guard.
'A soldier's life is terrible hard,'
                    Says Alice.

They're changing guard at Buckingham Palace –
Christopher Robin went down with Alice.

We saw a guard in a sentry-box.
'One of the sergeants looks after their socks,'
Says Alice.

They're changing guard at Buckingham Palace –
Christopher Robin went down with Alice.
We looked for the King, but he never came.
'Well, God take care of him, all the same,'
Says Alice.

They're changing guard at Buckingham Palace –
Christopher Robin went down with Alice.
They've great big parties inside the grounds.
'I wouldn't be King for a hundred pounds,'
Says Alice.

They're changing guard at Buckingham Palace –
Christopher Robin went down with Alice.
A face looked out, but it wasn't the King's.
'He's much too busy a-signing things,'
Says Alice.

They're changing guard at Buckingham Palace –
Christopher Robin went down with Alice.
'Do you think the King knows all about *me*?'
'Sure to, dear, but it's time for tea,'
Says Alice.

A. A. Milne, *When We Were Very Young* (1924)

'How are the boys?'

[George] told a story of [W. H.] Auden when young: 'I gave a party,' he said, 'all the fucking queers for miles flocked in. I believe we even invited the Bishop of fucking London but he had the piles and couldn't come. Well, Auden who'd been had when he was fourteen* (that was a year before this party – ah, this party was, let me see now, 1936) – Auden was receiving

* W. H. Auden was born in 1907.

the King's gold medal for poetry or some shit so he said he might be late. "Come when you like," I said, "and we'll go round the Hammersmith Bridge afterwards looking for a bit of young trade," I said. Well, in spite of the absence of the fucking Bishop and her piles, we had a hell of a time, and Auden finally turned up. When I opened the door he said, "Ah, I've just come from one George to another!" ' George said, 'The whole thing was a bit of a fiasco really. I mean George V at the best of times wasn't fucking all there, and he'd been given this bit of paper by [John] Masefield, who's just kicked it, and about fucking time – he's been a disgrace to poetry for ninety bleeding years. However, the King had read this bit of paper and he said, "Now, Mr Auden, I very much admired that poem you wrote in 1826." Auden thought, "Oh Christ, he's really done it now" – "Ah, I mean 1926," the King said. After a bit of a natter the King said, "And how are the boys?" Auden thought he's tumbled, d'you see – he thought he's tumbled the trade he'd had under Hammersmith Bridge. So Auden turned and muttered something about the King. Turns out that on the piece of paper Masefield had presented the King with, it turned out that it said Auden had been a prep school teacher. It really gave W.H. the shits for a minute or two, I can tell you.'

Joe Orton, Diaries (1967)

The abdication crisis

4 December 1936

This evening Baldwin drove again to Fort Belvedere to see the King.

London is now properly divided and the King's faction grows; people process the streets singing 'God Save the King', and assemble outside Buckingham Palace, they parade all night. After the first shock the country is now reacting, and demands that their King be left in peace.

We had people to dine, all Cavaliers, except Duff Cooper who is revolted by the King's selfish stupidity. The King cannot understand that Wallis is still legally the wife of Ernest Simpson, and that the Courts are not disposed to hasten up the decree. Apparently the King talks of her as a free woman already, which is both untrue and in bad taste.

I rang Beaverbrook late for news and he said, 'Our cock would be all

right if only he would fight, but at the moment he will not even crow.'
'Cocks crow better in the morning,' I suggested. 'Not this one,' he laughed.

So the appalling drama goes on. . . .

6th. The crucial day. I woke late with a heaviness of heart, feeling all
was over unless something very drastic was done – the God from the
Machine. . . .

I have felt all day today that the tide is turning against the Government,
and is more pro-King. Indeed that a definite reaction has set in. Will it last?
I fear not, as the King is so badly advised, he seems destined to rush to his
fate and no human agency, nor divine, can save him unless the country rises
in his defence, which it will not. Oh why did Baldwin slam the door against
a morganatic marriage so firmly and irrevocably? What about Queen Mary's
uncle the Duke of Cambridge who married an actress, and lived happily
ever after, and the Duke of Sussex? He delivered a blow to the Monarchy on
Friday almost as great as the King's.

We must keep our King, until now the most popular man the Empire has
ever known; but I wonder whether his selfishness and stupidity over this
muddle do not really make him unfit to govern?

7th. The world is now divided into Cavaliers and Roundheads. Belisha is
a secret Cavalier, and there are many in the Cabinet: Duff Cooper is one,
Sam Hoare is another, and the newspapers this morning are tamer; other
news is beginning to creep back on to the front page.

People are weary of the crisis, and public opinion is hardening on both
sides. What meanwhile is in the Monarch's mind?

I walked to the House of Commons where I found much excitement and
a full House and one could hardly bear to listen to questions and answers, as
every one watched the clock and every brain thought only of one thing.
Only the supplementary question 'Where is the Spanish Government now?'
aroused any interest, when Maxton shouted 'Where is our own?'

Henry Channon, *Diaries* (1967)

Queen Mary all over again

When the time came for Queen Mary to leave Badminton House* for London – a day to which theoretically she had been looking forward for years – the Queen had tears in her eyes. She had come to love the life of Gloucestershire, and she had been loved in return. Never since her youth as Princess May of Teck had she enjoyed such freedom as at Badminton. Before leaving, Queen Mary gave separate audiences to the nine Heads of Departments on the Duke of Beaufort's estate. Tears streaming down her face, she handed to each a valuable and carefully chosen present. 'Oh, I *have* been happy here!' she said to one of them. 'Here I've been anybody to everybody, and back in London I shall have to begin being Queen Mary all over again.'

James Pope-Hennessy, *Queen Mary* (1959)

Larkin's gong

I duly got my CBE at the beginning of this month: Monica & I came up & visited the Palace with a crowd of nice ordinary-looking people who were on a similar errand. We got there at ten (for ten-thirty), and I had to wait for about $1\frac{1}{2}$ hours (in a large 'Dutch' room, to judge from the pictures – Rembrandt, Rubens, but no Van Hogspeuw) before the CBEs were formed up and marched off into another anteroom, from wch we were fed singly into the Ballroom and the royal presence. I bowed & she lassoed me with a pink silk ribbon from wch depended a gold (gold-coloured, anyway) cross with some enamelling. Then she asked if I was 'still writing' and I said I was still trying, so she grinned very nicely and shook hands, & I thankfully retreated. The chap in front of me, when I rejoined him, asked if the Queen knew I wrote. I said yes, she seemed to. He said rather thoughtfully that she'd asked him what he did! Well, *I* shouldn't have known, but he turned out to be one of your Trustees: Philip King. (Better not spread this yarn, I suppose.) So I felt one up, a feeble one, perhaps half one.

Philip Larkin, *Letters* (1992)

* She had been evacuated there during the Second World War.

HRH Queen Elizabeth the Queen Mother

A most loyal and devoted friend!

In 1989, Arnold accompanied the Queen Mother on her visit to the East End. In public, he tends to play down his deep friendships with many senior members of the Royal Family, but here puts his understandable reticence to one side in order to pay tribute to an old lady in whose heart he holds a most precious place.

W.A.

There has always been a special nook in the Queen Mother's heart for the cheery inhabitants of London's East End. When she last visited Rother-hithe in 1941, she was so overcome with affection for the cheery folk that she vowed there and then that she would definitely return within the next 48 years.

True to her word, the nation's favourite great-gran made that onerous trip to Rotherhithe last week. Together with Sir Roy Strong and Mr Kenneth Rose, I enjoyed the immense privilege of being in attendance. It was an experience I am never likely to forget.

'Now I can look the East End in the face,' she had said, all those years ago, after one of her corgis, too, had narrowly missed suffering a not inconsiderable hurt from flying shrapnel, and those cheery, salt-of-the-earth types never forgot it, gor' bless 'em. For they realize, as few people do, quite how tough life has been for this lovely, lovely lady, 88 years young. Early on in life, she received a severe blow when her husband suffered the grave misfortune of acceding to the throne of Britain. Now carrying the burden of Queenship, she had to move her possessions lock, stock and barrel to the agoraphobic conditions of Buckingham Palace, and she is still unable to go anywhere without a full retinue of servants. But this noble lady, never more radiant, has triumphed over all the setbacks life has dealt her, and is always willing to pass on a word of encouragement to the ordinary, common, cheery folk who so idolize her.

The wit of the lady is, of course, legendary. Every page of Robert Lacey's superb critical biography, *The Queen of All Our Hearts*, and its follow-up, *God Bless You Ma'am*, sparkles with a shining gem. And last week in Rotherhithe that comic tongue was once again on top form. 'Raining isn't it, Wallace?' she said to me as we motored along, adding, as quick as a flash, 'I hope we've brought the umbrella!'

I was honoured to be personally deputed to muster as many cheery Eastenders as possible to greet Her Majesty. Marvellous folk all, they are forever popping in and out of each other's two-up, two-downs bearing stews concocted from nutritious scraps, tap-dancing, playing 'spoons', indulging in a little good old-fashioned 'pick-pocketing' and talking to one another in rhyme. Alas, I was informed that most of 'em now live in Harlow New Town, but a large, jubilant crowd of roughly six gathered to pay homage to their own dear Queen Mum. 'Gissa kiss,' yelled one – possibly a 'Pearly King' in civvies. 'Everyone is so very natural here,' quipped back Her Majesty, to universal delight.

Able to speak to all classes, she retains a fondness for the British Pub, and, recognizing one – The Old Service Station – she insisted upon an unscheduled stop. 'Half of your very best,' she asked the pump attendant, and before long she was sipping a jar of Duckham's to her heart's content. A magical day spent with a magical, magical lady.

Craig Brown (ed.), The Agreeable World of Wallace Arnold (1990)

9

London at War

*One of the most powerful icons of the Second World War is the famous photo-
graph of St Paul's Cathedral in the Blitz. It is almost painterly. The chaos of
flames, smoke and destruction is as indistinct as if it had been described in a few
brush-strokes; Sir Christopher Wren's cathedral dome, by contrast, is clearly
delineated, solid and beautiful, against the night sky. The value of the picture as
propaganda is obvious: the force of Christian civilization stands firm in spite of
all the self-destructive malice of the enemy; Great Britain will not be sunk in a
Wagnerian Götterdämmerung. As Churchill remarked, the motto of the British
is 'Business as usual'.*

*Noël Coward's wartime song 'London Pride' is unashamedly sentimental, and
perhaps it needs to heard rather than read for its qualities to be best appreciated.
(The gay, brisk tune and Coward's own voice mitigate what might, for some
readers, cloy when merely seen as words on the page.) I still thought it was worth
the risk of including it here, because I am moved by it, even when I read it.*

> *Grey City*
> *Stubbornly implanted,*
> *Taken so for granted*
> *For a thousand years.*

*Evidently, the life of London during the Second World War was unforgettable
for those who lived through it – the need to evacuate families and young children,
the nightly raids, the sleeping figures, captured so poignantly in the drawings of
Henry Moore, huddled in the Underground stations with their bedding and
belongings, while, above ground, the Luftwaffe showered down explosives; the
tedium, fear and erotic excitement of the Black-out; the sense, stronger even than*

in peace-time, that London was made up of a floating population 'just passing through'; the perkiness, the jokes, the songs, the immediate and garish presence of violent death.

It was necessary to remind myself, and the reader, that London had lived through other wars; that Milton had been afraid of the 'captain or colonel or knight in arms' who might invade his peace in October 1642, when the Royalist forces marched on London; that Pepys had lived through the crisis of Dutch warships on the Thames; that even the Napoleonic Wars had their indirect effects on London and that the First World War saw the haunting departure of the troops from many of the London railway termini, and endured long enough to experience a few enemy bombs on the civilian population; but there was never any conflict in the city's history to match the drama of the Second World War.

London Pride

I

London Pride has been handed down to us.
London Pride is a flower that's free.
London Pride means our own dear town to us,
And our pride it for ever will be.
Woa, Liza,
See the coster barrows,
Vegetable marrows
And the fruit piled high.
Woa, Liza,
Little London sparrows,
Covent Garden Market where the costers cry.
Cockney feet
Mark the beat of history.
Every street
Pins a memory down.
Nothing ever can quite replace
The grace of London Town.

Interlude

There's a little city flower every spring unfailing
Growing in the crevices by some London railing,
Though it has a Latin name, in town and countryside
We in England call it London Pride.

2

London Pride has been handed down to us.
London Pride is a flower that's free.
London Pride means our own dear town to us,
And our pride it for ever will be.
Hey, lady,
When the day is dawning
See the policeman yawning
On his lonely beat.
Gay lady,
Mayfair in the morning,
Hear your footsteps echo in the empty street.
Early rain
And the pavement's glistening.
All Park Lane
In a shimmering gown.
Nothing ever could break or harm
The charm of London Town.

Interlude

In our city darkened now, street and square and crescent,
We can feel our living past in our shadowed present,
Ghosts beside our starlit Thames
Who lived and loved and died
Keep throughout the ages London Pride.

3

London Pride has been handed down to us.
London Pride is a flower that's free.
London Pride means our own dear town to us,
And our pride it for ever will be.
Grey city
Stubbornly implanted,
Taken so for granted

For a thousand years.
Stay, city,
Smokily enchanted,
Cradle of our memories and hopes and fears.
Every Blitz
Your resistance
Toughening,
From the Ritz
To the Anchor and Crown,
Nothing ever could override
The pride of London Town.

Noël Coward, *Lyrics* (1965)

Civil war

It was not long after the March of *Fairfax* and *Cromwel* through the City of *London* with the whole Army, to quell the Insurrections *Brown* and *Massy*, now Malecontents also, were endeavouring to raise in the City against the Armies proceedings, ere he left his great House in *Barbican*, and betook himself to a smaller in *High Holbourn*, among those that open backward into *Lincolns-Inn* Fields. Here he liv'd a private and quiet Life, still prosecuting his Studies and curious Search into Knowledge, the grand Affair perpetually of his Life; till such time as, the War being now at an end, with compleat Victory to the Parliament's side, as the Parliament then stood purg'd of all it's Dissenting Members, and the King after some Treaties with the Army, *re Infecta*, brought to his Tryal; the form of Government being now chang'd into a Free State, he was hereupon oblig'd to Write a Treatise, call'd the *Tenure of Kings and Magistrates*.

Edward Phillips, *The Life of Mr John Milton* (1694)

The Dutch in the Medway

12 June 1667

Up very betimes to our business at the office, there hiring of more fire-ships; and at it close all the morning. Ill newes is come to Court of the Dutch breaking the Chaine at Chatham, which struck me to the heart. And to White Hall to hear the truth of it; and there, going up the back-stairs, I did hear some lacquies speaking of sad newes come to Court, saying that hardly anybody in the Court but do look as if he cried. So home, where all our hearts do now ake; for the newes is true that the Dutch have broken the chaine and burned our ships, and particularly 'The Royal Charles': other particulars I know not, but most sad to be sure. And the truth is I do fear so much that the whole kingdom is undone that I do this night resolve to study with my father and wife what to do with the little that I have in money by me, for I give all the rest that I have in the King's hands for Tangier, for lost. So God help us!

13th. No sooner up but hear the sad newes confirmed of the Royall Charles being taken by them, and now in fitting by them (which Pett should have carried up higher by our several orders, and deserves therefore to be hanged for not doing it), and turning several others; and that another fleete is come up into the Hope. Upon which newes the King and Duke of York have been below* since four o'clock in the morning to command the sinking of ships at Barking-Creeke and other places, to stop their coming up higher: which put me into such a fear that I presently resolved of my father's and wife's going into the country; and at two hours' warning they did go by the coach this day, with about £1,300 in gold in their night-bag. Pray God give them good passage, and good care to hide it when they come home! but my heart is full of fear. They gone, I continued in fright and fear what to do with the rest. W. Hewer hath been at the banker's and hath got £500 out of Blackewell's hands of his own money; but they are so called upon that they will be all broke, hundreds coming to them for money: and their answer is, 'It is payable at twenty days: when the days are out we will pay you'; and those that are not so they make tell over their money, and make their bags false on purpose to give cause to retell it, and so spend time.

* I.e. below London Bridge.

Every minute some one or other calls for this or that order; and so I forced to be at the office most of the day.

Samuel Pepys, Diary

London in the Napoleonic War

When the eagles of Napoleon Bonaparte, the Corsican upstart, were flying from Provence, where they had perched after a brief sojourn in Elba, and from steeple to steeple until they reached the towers of Notre Dame, I wonder whether the Imperial birds had any eye for a little corner of the parish of Bloomsbury, London, which you might have thought so quiet, that even the whirring and flapping of those mighty wings would pass unobserved there?

'Napoleon has landed at Cannes.' Such news might create a panic at Vienna, and cause Russia to drop his cards, and take Prussia into a corner, and Talleyrand and Metternich to wag their heads together, while Prince Hardenberg, and even the present Marquis of Londonderry, were puzzled; but how was this intelligence to affect a young lady in Russell Square, before whose door the watchman sang the hours when she was asleep; who, if she strolled in the square, was guarded there by the railings and the beadle; who, if she walked ever so short a distance to buy a ribbon in Southampton Row, was followed by black Sambo with an enormous cane; who was always cared for, dressed, put to bed, and watched over by ever so many guardian angels, with and without wages? *Bon Dieu*, I say, is it not hard that the fateful rush of the great Imperial struggle can't take place without affecting a poor little harmless girl of eighteen, who is occupied in billing and cooing, or working muslin collars in Russell Square? You, too, kindly, homely flower! – is the great roaring war tempest coming to sweep you down, here, although cowering under the shelter of Holborn? Yes, Napoleon is flinging his last stake, and poor little Emmy Sedley's happiness forms, somehow, part of it.

In the first place, her father's fortune was swept down with that fatal news. All his speculations had of late gone wrong with the luckless old gentleman. Ventures had failed; merchants had broken; funds had risen when he calculated they would fall. What need to particularize? If success is rare and slow, everybody knows how quick and easy ruin is. Old Sedley had kept his own sad counsel. Everything seemed to go on as usual in the quiet, opulent house; the good-natured mistress pursuing, quite unsuspiciously, her bustling idleness, and daily easy avocations; the daughter absorbed still in one selfish, tender thought, and quite regardless of all the world besides, when that final crash came, under which the worthy family fell.

William Makepeace Thackeray, *Vanity Fair* (1848)

Piccadilly, 1916

They ate, they drank, and through the dark
    The wedding torches flared:
While gloomy Noah built his ark
    The people stood and stared,

A motley gathering, squire and dame,
    With laughter and with play,
Until the wild flood-waters came
    And swept them all away.

The dark creeps up across the Park,
    The searchlights wheel and flare:
O gloomy Noah, build your ark,
    And let us young ones stare.

A little life, a little light,
    A dinner and a play:
For these go back to-morrow night,
    And I go back to-day,

To hear the bugle and the drum,
    The cannon's roundelay –
Until the cold flood-waters come
    And sweep us all away.

John Meade Falkner, *Poems* (n.d.)

London in the First World War

Saturday, 29 September 1917

Letter to Beb and diary *before* getting up is my present morning technique. Michael walked to Selfridges with me and there I took the great step of buying a bicycle, having decided on that as my method of transport in London. I rode it home in triumph and found it delightful, and much less alarming than I anticipated. Of course, there is only about a third of the traffic there used to be and one can always dismount to cross Oxford Street or to meet any crisis.

I rode it to Audley Square, and Claud and I lunched at the Curzon Hotel. We talked of Johnson and wondered whether a really assiduous Boswell couldn't collect quite a good show of sayings from almost any of us. He turned up again at about seven and suggested our dining at Canuto's in Baker Street. There had been an air-raid warning, but the 'all clear' signal had come through. However, as we were finishing our dinner, a terrific row began. A nervous waiter was infuriated by our nonchalance. I was *delighted* at last to come in for a war perquisite. It is very difficult to restrain one's sight-seeing instincts. I couldn't help standing in the doorway. We saw shells bursting like stars and heard them whistling through the air, and all round the 'cold, fruitless moon' there was a wreath of white puffs of undissipated smoke. I couldn't hear anything that sounded like a bomb anywhere near. What made the terrific row was a huge gun in Regent's Park which coughed and coughed – I do find it a strangely exhilarating sound. The streets were quite empty, and most of the people in the restaurant bundled down into the cellar. There was a very comic middle-class dinner party anxious to show their coolness by facetiousness and cracking joke after joke: 'Let's have all-clear soup' was their happiest effort.

Lady Cynthia Asquith, *Diaries, 1915–1918* (1971)

The Victory March

I was in London for the Victory March [1919]. I had a place on a stand outside Buckingham Palace not far from the King's saluting point where the war correspondents and other newspaper men were assembled.

It was a magnificent pageant of the fighting men of all branches in the Army, and of naval men from the Grand Fleet, and airmen and merchant seamen, and women from the services. One forgot for a little while the troubled state of Europe, the low-grade morality of European statesmen, the land-grabbing already happening, the failure to make 'homes for heroes', or to redeem any of the promises held out to the nation. This was our Victory Day, and a tribute by vast crowds to those who had saved us in time of war. There were many men in the crowd who still wore hospital blue, and many – given front places – who had wheeled themselves here in chairs for cripples. One watched the passing of this pageant with emotion. These men marching by were those whom I had seen covered with the clay of Flanders and the white chalk of the Somme. Now for an hour or two they had their reward. They were the heroes. They deserved the roaring cheers of the crowd, rising louder, as I was glad to hear, when our merchant seamen – neglected before the war and forgotten afterwards – went by with unmartial step. We owed our victory, our liberty, our lives, to all of these. The old, old Past walked with them – all our history and all our ghosts.

That night London went mad, but the most part of it was a decent joyous madness without vice in it. I was caught up in the surging crowds who linked arms and were cheering and singing. Outside Buckingham Palace they called for the King time and time again, and he had come out to his balcony, with the Queen and his family, smiling down on this vast multitude, raising his hand to them. At night I found myself in Pall Mall, with sore feet which had been trodden on many times. A soldier, just a little drunk, was on the pedestal of Florence Nightingale's statue, with his arm round the figure of that lady. He was making a speech to which no one listened except myself. Over and over again he assured the crowds that the bloody war wouldn't have been won without the help of women like good old Florence. 'It's the women of England who won the war', he shouted, 'and that's the bloody truth of it!' No one challenged this statement.

No one listened except me, curious to know what he was saying with such fervour and passion. I never pass the statue of Florence Nightingale now without thinking of that champion of womanhood who was a little drunk.

Philip Gibbs, *The Pageant of the Years* (1946)

We Lose Our Religion

On the evening of 28 February 1944, Lionel Bradley was out reviewing a ballet at Sadler's Wells, and Harold Nicolson described the air raid later that night as 'amazingly beautiful'. During it, a stick of five-hundred-pound high-explosive bombs was released somewhere over Bloomsbury. The first hit the London Library, the last exploded in the road outside St James's Palace, blowing out all the ancient glass, and destroying the windows of the Chapel Royal.

Early next morning Joan Bailey arrived at the corner of Duke of York Street, on the north side of St James's Square, and found it cordoned off by air-raid wardens. A fireman asked her where she was going. She said the London Library, and he shook his head. The library had had a direct hit.

Her first thought was not for the books but for 'poor Mr Purnell'. Allowed through the cordon, she was at first reassured. The façade was still intact, and apart from broken glass and rubble lying on the pavement outside there did not seem to be any very extensive damage. When she walked up the steps through the broken glass and felt the grey dust hanging in the air, she saw that above the entrance hall the library was open to the sky.

Christopher Purnell's daughter Ruth reached the square a few moments later, on her way to work at the Clerical, Medical and General. The first thing she saw was her mother, waving to her from behind a broken window.

The Purnells had been in the basement, and 'a large bit of the ceiling' had fallen on them, but they and the fire-watchers had somehow escaped injury. If it had been released a split second earlier, the bomb would have entirely destroyed the library: a split second later and it would have missed. It had caught the roof at the back of the 1898 stacks and exploded, leaving a tangle of Osborne Smith's steel girders. They stuck out, bare and bent, some of them still supporting bookcases that hung in space above floors littered with plaster, rubble and torn books. The grey dust was everywhere.

Everyone who saw it that morning remembered the twisted steel – one poet imagined the moment of impact, 'books flying like bats past the bent

219

daffodil-stalk of a girder' – and almost immediately everyone began to work. Rain could ruin more books even than had been damaged by the bomb.

Staff and members climbed up and down through the grey dust, stacking books in those parts of the building that still had a roof. Joan Bailey worked with James Lees-Milne and Rose Macaulay, climbing as high as they dared, lifting books out of the hanging shelves and bringing them down. Rose Macaulay was bravest, telling them to hang on to her legs as she leant out into space. One member organized a chain of passers-by, including American servicemen, to hand books down to safety.

Harold Nicolson got there soon afterwards and describes the entrance hall with books dumped everywhere, the counters filled with dust. Purnell took him up to the Reading Room and showed him the hole in the roof, part of a wall hanging sideways and steel bookshelves jagged against the sky. 'All the books in the top store were flung out of their shelves and it will take months to sort them again.'

Then Mr Cox arrived from Wimbledon, wearing a soft black hat and a white silk scarf, looking, as someone said, 'as if he were going to the opera'. The girls found him an armchair and made him a cup of tea. According to one story he went upstairs, and a member met him coming down from the burned-out stacks at the top saying, 'We've lost our Religion!' Another, repeated by more than one witness, was that he sat flabbergasted in his chair, dust everywhere, the grey daylight coming in through the roof, and said, 'It's not what we're used to, you see!'

Something like 16,000 books were destroyed, either in the explosion, by fire, or by the water used to put it out. Purnell showed visitors a memento of 'the most exciting night of his life': a copy of George Adam Smith's *Modern System and Preaching of the Old Testament* with a piece of shrapnel embedded in it.

Harry Yates Thompson's Aldine *Theocritus* with the Dürer bookplate, given to celebrate peace in 1918, had been evacuated with Hagberg's other treasures at the beginning of the war. Purnell was delighted to find that 'the *Gentleman's Magazine* with Mitford's famous and eloquent review of Nyrene's *Cricketers of my Time* is more or less intact'.

Most of the Biography department had been destroyed, and *The Sunday Times* was particularly distressed about the damage to Theology. 'The contemporary bindings of many of the religious works of the Reformation are spoilt beyond recovery, and some German editions of the early fathers will hardly be used again.'

A notice appeared in *The Times:* 'The London Library – Members are Requested not to ask for Books or Return them until Further Notice.' A printed notice to the same effect was hung on the front door of the library.

Elizabeth Ray remembers two unexpected benefits of the bombing: one was the sudden warmth and friendliness of many of the members who had until then seemed rather cold and stand-offish; the second was that a copy of *Fanny Hill*, entirely undamaged and with charming coloured engravings, was blown from the seclusion of the librarian's cupboard. The girls fell on it, hiding it behind the radiator in the ladies' staff room, and taking turns to read it throughout the lunch hour.

John Wells, Rude Words (1991)

An air-raid

20 August 1944

A lovely morning. They raided London yesterday, and we raided Berlin. I work at my broadcast talk. At noon I hear aeroplanes and shortly afterwards the wail of the siren. People are becoming quite used to these interruptions. I find one practises a sort of suspension of the imagination. I do not think that that drone in the sky means death to many people at any moment. It seems so incredible as I sit here at my window, looking out on the fuchsias and the zinneas with yellow butterflies playing round each other, that in a few seconds above the trees I may see other butterflies circling in the air intent on murdering each other. One lives in the present. The past is too sad a recollection and the future too sad a despair.

I go up to London. After dinner I walk back to the Temple. It is a strange experience. London is as dark as the stage at Vicenza after all the lights have been put out. Vague gleamings of architecture. It is warm and the stars straddle the sky like grains of rice. Then the searchlights come on, each terminating in a swab of cotton-wool which is its own mist area. Suburban guns thump and boom. In the centre there are no guns, only a drone of aeroplanes, which may be enemy or not. A few lonely footsteps hurry along the Strand. A little nervous man catches up with me and starts a conversation. I embarrass him by asking him to have a cigarette and pausing lengthily while I light it. His hand trembles. Mine does not.

When I get into my rooms, I turn the lights off and sit at the window. There is still a drone of 'planes, and from time to time a dull thump in the distance. I turn on my lights and write this, but I hear more 'planes coming and must darken everything and listen in the night. I have no sense of fear whatsoever. Is this fatalism or what? It is very beautiful. I wait and listen. There are more drones and then the searchlights switch out and the all-clear goes. I shut my shutters, turn on my lights and finish this. The clocks of London strike midnight. I go to bed.

Harold Nicolson, *Diaries and Letters 1939–45* (1967)

A boating trip

H.N. TO V.S-W.

11 September 1941

4 King's Bench Walk, EC4

I did not tell you about my boating trip.* I picked my way down Westminster steps rather gingerly and climbed across a patrol-boat to the *Water Gipsy*. It is a long torpedo-shaped motor-boat with three cabins and an engine-room. There was only A. P. Herbert on board and Ed the engineman. We cast off and went under the dark bridges. Our job was to inspect the several posts down the river which are on the look-out for parachute mines. Herbert knows the river blindfold and hits off each post with miraculous ease. 'Post Number 31!' he shouts. 'O.K., sir,' comes the answer. 'Anything to report?' and then off we chug to another dim post among the docks and wharves. It was quite warm and there was a moon driving behind scudding clouds. The sides of the river loomed dark against the luminous waters. The Tower of London glimmered white and Greenwich also. One could not see how damaged it all was since the cranes all seemed to be intact and stood out from the wharves against the night. The black-out was complete and there was not a light to be seen anywhere. Herbert was in his best mood. He talked of the London River which he knows better than most men, and of Old Wapping stairs, and how well Dickens understood the river and its tides. When we got to Woolwich we tied up to a barge and had

* With A. P. Herbert down the Thames at night. He was MP for Oxford University and a Petty Officer in the Naval Auxiliary Patrol.

some coffee and fish-cakes. Then back again through the dark sides of the great river.

He tried to land me at the Temple steps, but it was too dark to see safely. Thus I landed at Westminster Bridge and walked home, reaching the Temple at 4 a.m. "Alt,' shouted a voice. 'Oo goes there?' 'Friend,' I answered – and why not? 'Advance friend, and be recognized.' I advanced cautiously towards the torch and saw the nose of a rifle aiming at me. I got out my pass. 'Thank you, sir,' he said, and the rifle was lowered.

Ibid.

A fighting sermon

Tuesday, 3 September

Went to a service at Westminster Abbey to commemorate the first anniversary of the war. The King and Queen were to have gone, but an air-raid warning sounded just before the service began. However the P.M. and a good many Ministers attended. I rescued Eden and Dill from a garden where they had been isolated by an over-zealous verger and where they would otherwise have been left and forgotten.

Bishop Hensley Henson, the new Canon, preached an eloquent fighting sermon, containing much alliteration, many fiery denunciations, a good deal of politics and no Christianity – which was what Winston had come to hear.

John Colville, *The Fringes of Power* (1985)

A wartime prisoner in Holloway

One night a bomb fell hard by the prison. It broke the water mains. In the dark early morning there was the sound of lavatory plugs being pulled in vain. The lavatories, always foul, became frightful. Floors awash with urine, everything choked, an appalling smell. We were all grey with grime because the bomb had shaken the old prison and a thick layer of dust and soot covered everything. We were given half a pint of water each, I drank a sip and tried to wash in the remainder but it only streaked the dirt. It so happened that I was to see Mr Hickson that day. When he came I said that the prison had become uninhabitable and unless something was done about the lavatories the Home Office would have hundreds of sick women on its hands. Mr Hickson made sympathetic noises.

'Don't you know anyone in the government I could appeal to for you?' he said.

'*Know* anyone in the government? I know *all* the Tories beginning with Churchill,' I cried.

This was an exaggeration, but I did know several of them and heartily despised them for their hypocrisy; always mouthing platitudes about freedom, free speech and the rule of law. 'The whole lot deserve to be shot,' I added.

Unlike murderers or burglars we were never allowed to see our lawyer alone; the little wardress in the corner must have reported my intemperate words, for 'Cousin Winston' knew what I had said, as I discovered years later.

When we were taken to the yard for exercise that day there was a rush for the row of outdoor lavatories. Mine was fairly clean, but when I emerged I was surrounded by horrified cries of, 'You *shouldn't* have gone in there!'

'Why not?'

'Didn't you see the V on the door?'

I had noticed that a red V was painted on the door, and thought it was for Victory. The papers were full of tales about Vs which apparently were to be seen here, there and everywhere; the prison was unlikely to be behindhand in this patriotic demonstration.

'That lavatory is only for women with venereal disease,' I was told.

Diana Mosley, A Life of Contrasts (1977)

Miss Anstruther's Letters

'Everyone out of the building!' shouted the police. 'Everyone out!'

Miss Anstruther asked why.

The police said there were to be no bloody whys, everyone out, the bloody gas pipe's burst and they're throwing down fire, the whole thing may go up in a bonfire before you can turn round.

A bonfire! Miss Anstruther thought, if that's so I must go up and save some things. She rushed up the stairs, while the rescue men were in Mrs Cavendish's flat. Inside her own blasted and twisted door, her flat lay waiting for death. God, muttered Miss Anstruther, what shall I save? She caught up a suitcase, and furiously piled books into it – Herodotus, *Mathematical Magick*, some of the twenty volumes of *Purchas his Pilgrimes*, the eight little volumes of Walpole's letters, *Trivia, Curiosities of Literature*, the six volumes of Boswell, then, as the suitcase would not shut, she turned out Boswell and substituted a china cow, a tiny walnut shell with tiny Mexicans behind glass, a box with a mechanical bird that jumped out and sang, and a fountain pen. No use bothering with the big books or the pictures. Slinging the suitcase across her back, she caught up her portable wireless set and her typewriter, loped down stairs, placed her salvage on the piled wreckage at what had been the street door, and started up the stairs again. As she reached the first floor, there was a burst and a hissing, a huge *pst-pst*, and a rush of flame leaped over Mortimer House as the burst gas caught and sprang to heaven, another fiery rose bursting into bloom to join that pandemonic red garden of night. Two rescue men, carrying Mrs Cavendish downstairs, met Miss Anstruther and pushed her back.

'Clear out. Can't get up there again, it'll go up any minute.'

It was at this moment that Miss Anstruther remembered the thing she wanted most, the thing she had forgotten while she gathered up things she wanted less.

She cried, 'I must go up again. I must get something out. There's time.'

'Not a bloody second,' one of them shouted at her, and pushed her back.

She fought him. 'Let me go, oh let me go. I tell you I'm going up once more.'

On the landing above, a wall of flame leaped crackling to the ceiling.

'Go up be damned. Want to go through that?'

They pulled her down with them to the ground floor. She ran out into the street, shouting for a ladder. Oh God, where are the fire engines? A hundred fires, the water given out in some places, engines helpless. Everywhere buildings burning, museums, churches, hospitals, great shops, houses, blocks of flats, north, south, east, west and centre. Such a raid never was. Miss Anstruther heeded none of it: with hell blazing and crashing round her, all she thought was, I must get my letters. Oh, dear God, my letters. She pushed again into the inferno, but again she was dragged back.

'No one to go in there,' said the police, for all human life was by now extricated. No one to go in, and Miss Anstruther's flat left to be consumed in the spreading storm of fire, which was to leave no wrack behind. Everything was doomed – furniture, books, pictures, china, clothes, manuscripts, silver, everything: all she thought of was the desk crammed with letters that should have been the first thing she saved. What had she saved instead? Her wireless, her typewriter, a suitcase full of books; looking round, she saw that all three had gone from where she had put them down. Perhaps they were in the safe keeping of the police, more likely in the wholly unsafe keeping of some rescue-squad man or private looter. Miss Anstruther cared little. She sat down on the wreckage of the road, sick and shaking, wholly bereft.

The bombers departed, their job well done. Dawn came, dim and ashy, in a pall of smoke. The little burial garden was like a garden in a Vesuvian village, grey in its ash coat. The air choked with fine drifts of cinders, Mortimer House still burned, for no one had put it out. A grimy warden with a note-book asked Miss Anstruther, have you anywhere to go?

'No,' she said, 'I shall stay here.'

'Better go to a rest centre,' said the warden, wearily doing his job, not caring where any one went, wondering what had happened in North Ealing, where he lived.

Miss Anstruther stayed, watching the red ruin smouldering low. Some time, she thought, it will be cool enough to go into.

There followed the haunted, desperate days of search which found nothing. Since silver and furniture had been wholly consumed, what hope for letters? There was no charred sliver of the old locked rosewood desk which had held them. The burning words were burnt, the lines, running small and close and neat down the page, difficult to decipher, with the o's and a's never closed at the top, had run into a flaming void and would never be deciphered more. Miss Anstruther tried to recall them, as she sat in the alien room; shutting her eyes, she tried to see again the phrases that, once you had made them out, lit the page like stars. There had been many hundreds of letters, spread over twenty-two years. Last year their writer had died; the letters were all that Miss Anstruther had left of him; she had not yet re-read them; she had been waiting till she could do so without the devastation of unendurable weeping. They had lain there, a solace waiting for her when she could take it. Had she taken it, she could have recalled them better now. As it was, her memory held disjointed phrases, could not piece them together. Light of my eyes. You are the sun and the moon and the stars to me. When I think of you life becomes music, poetry, beauty,

and I am more than myself. It is what lovers have found in all the ages, and
no one has ever found before. The sun flickering through the beeches on
your hair. And so on. As each phrase came back to her, it jabbed at her heart
like a twisting bayonet. He would run over a list of places they had seen
together, in the secret stolen travels of twenty years. The balcony where
they dined at the Foix inn, leaning over the green river, eating trout just
caught in it. The little wild strawberries at Andorra le Vieja, the mountain
pass that ran down to it from Ax, the winding road down into Seo d'Urgel
and Spain. Lerida, Zaragoza, little mountain towns in the Pyrenees, Jaca,
Saint Jean Pied-du-Port, the little harbour at Collioure, with its painted
boats, morning coffee out of red cups at Villefranche, tramping about
France in a hot July; truffles in the *place* at Perigueux, the stream that
rushed steeply down the village street at Florac, the frogs croaking in the
hills about it, the gorges of the Tarn, Rodez with its spacious *place* and
plane trees, the little walled town of Cordes with the inn courtyard a jumble
of sculptures, altar-pieces from churches, and ornaments from chateaux;
Lisieux, with ancient crazy- floored inn, huge four-poster, and preposterous little saint (before the grandiose white temple in her honour had arisen
on the hill outside the town), villages in the Haute-Savoie, jumbled among
mountain rocks over brawling streams, the motor bus over the Alps down
into Susa and Italy. Walking over the Amberley downs, along the Dorset
coast from Corfe to Lyme on two hot May days, with a night at Chideock
between, sauntering in Buckinghamshire beech-woods, boating off Buck-
lers Hard, climbing Dunkery Beacon to Porlock, driving on a June afternoon over Kirkdale pass . . . Baedeker starred places because we ought to
see them, he wrote, I star them because we saw them together, and those
stars light them up for ever . . . Of this kind had been many of the letters
that had been for the last year all Miss Anstruther had left, except memory,
of two-and-twenty years. There had been other letters about books, books
he was reading, books she was writing; others about plans, politics, health,
the weather, himself, herself, anything. I could have saved them, she kept
thinking; I had the chance; but I saved a typewriter and a wireless set and
some books and a walnut shell and a china cow, and even they are gone. So
she would cry and cry, till tears blunted at last for the time the sharp edge of
grief, leaving only a dull lassitude, an end of being. Sometimes she would
take out and look at the charred corner of paper which was now all she had
of her lover; all that was legible of it was a line and a half of close small
writing, the o's and the a's open at the top. It had been written twenty-one
years ago, and it said, 'leave it at that. I know now that you don't care

twopence; if you did you would' . . . The words, each time she looked at them, seemed to darken and obliterate a little more of the twenty years that had followed them, the years of the letters and the starred places and all they had had together. You don't care twopence, he seemed to say still; if you had cared twopence, you would have saved my letters, not your wireless and your typewriter and your china cow, least of all those little walnut Mexicans, which you know I never liked. Leave it at that.

Rose Macaulay (1972)

Smoking on duty

The last German plane had long since come and gone when I was present at my first fire. Every previous call had been a false alarm; but that evening, as I clung to the flanks of the engine, my helmet awry, my rubber boots, which I had not had time to secure, hanging in elephantine folds, my tunic half-unbuttoned and my belt undone, I thought we were bound upon some serious mission. Our objective was a Victorian office-building, next to the Law Courts, opposite St Mary-le-Strand, which showed not the slightest signs of the blaze we expected. We were told, however, that a fire had broken out somewhere in a central courtyard, and that our business was to gain the roof and subdue it from above. Carrying weighty rolls of hose, we climbed a dark and narrow staircase, reached a vantage-point and peered down five or six storeys into a many-windowed court. Behind some windows, or so we imagined, shone a faintly threatening gleam. As no officer had followed us up the stairs, we rankers used our own discretion and, aiming the nozzles of our hoses at various sheets of plate glass, immediately demolished them. It was a delightful exercise. As the windows crashed in and puissant jets of water shot through, we heard the sound of a miniature tidal wave surging round an empty office.

Our fun was too good to continue; a messenger soon arrived, who informed us that, far from extinguishing the fire, we had nearly drowned our colleagues on a lower level, and must instantly desist. We, therefore, rolled up our hoses – a long, back-breaking job – and prepared to join our friends. A roll of wet hose makes an awkward burden; I had one beneath each arm; and an unusually good-natured acquaintance lighted a cigarette,

which he shoved into my mouth, remarking 'Have a fag, Quenn!' When, at
length, I had cleared the ground floor, I was unlucky enough to come face
to face with an exasperated officer. A sharp little man, bearing gloves and
stick, he fiercely reprimanded me. 'To smoke on a fire', I learned, was
among the most atrocious offences in the British fireman's code. Since it
was difficult to eject the smouldering stub, I was temporarily speechless;
but, once I had recovered my voice, I was moved to shout back, and told
him what he could do with his fire and with the Fire-Service in general. He
then ordered me to report at the fire-station; and there I gave up my
uniform, helmet, belt and boots, and was summarily cashiered. I also heard
that, as a result of my recent behaviour, I need not expect a Fire-Force
medal. That was the severest penalty I paid. Three months later, peace
returned to Europe.

Peter Quennell, *The Wanton Chase* (1980)

In Westminster Abbey

Let me take this other glove off
  As the *vox humana* swells,
And the beauteous fields of Eden
  Bask beneath the Abbey bells.
Here, where England's statesmen lie,
Listen to a lady's cry.

Gracious Lord, oh bomb the Germans.
  Spare their women for Thy Sake,
And if that is not too easy
  We will pardon Thy Mistake.
But, gracious Lord, whate'er shall be,
Don't let anyone bomb me.

Keep our Empire undismembered
  Guide our Forces by Thy Hand,
Gallant blacks from far Jamaica,
  Honduras and Togoland;
Protect them Lord in all their fights,
And, even more, protect the whites.

Think of what our Nation stands for,
  Books from Boots' and country lanes,
Free speech, free passes, class distinction,
  Democracy and proper drains.
Lord, put beneath Thy special care
One-eighty-nine Cadogan Square.

Although dear Lord I am a sinner,
  I have done no major crime;
Now I'll come to Evening Service
  Whensoever I have the time.
So, Lord, reserve for me a crown,
And do not let my shares go down.

I will labour for Thy Kingdom,
  Help our lads to win the war,
Send white feathers to the cowards
  Join the Women's Army Corps,
Then wash the Steps around Thy Throne
In the Eternal Safety Zone.

Now I feel a little better,
  What a treat to hear Thy Word,
Where the bones of leading statesmen,
  Have so often been interr'd.
And now, dear Lord, I cannot wait
Because I have a luncheon date.

John Betjeman, *Collected Poems* (1970)

Dylan Thomas in the Home Guard

Meantime we were still stuck with the Home Guard, and Dylan wanted to
incorporate the Free Japanese who made lampshades below our office. He
said he had heard of Free French, Free Poles, Free Dutch, Free Italians and
if not actually Free Germans at any rate Free German-speaking people, but
never, no never Free Japanese; and he tried very hard to have them in the
script, while I objected on the grounds that their kimonos might lead to

their being lynched in a typical English village and which of us would write their bloody dialogue?

These questions were debated often in the office and occasionally, when we'd done a good morning's work, in an afternoon drinking place called the Horseshoe Club, which now no longer exists in Wardour Street. This was approached by the most sordid staircase that I've ever seen, on either side were leprous walls, and it was down these worn stone steps that Philip Lindsay most frequently fell. The club also had a Judas window in the door. Dylan led me proudly up to this, a panel slid aside and the eye of the proprietor appeared at an aperture which had previously seemed to be a knothole in the wood.

'You see?' Dylan hissed. 'Like a speakeasy or an opium den,' but behind the spyhole nothing much went on: bookies' touts or ageing Lesbians sitting on leather settees and sometimes some elderly character such as an art critic famous when President of the Union for subtle deadpan wit, of whom Dylan was particularly fond. I personally found this man a thumping bore, with his strange furry cap of hair, round staring eyes, and thread-like lips from which issued at long intervals a tiny insect voice; one strained one's ears in vain to catch some smart crack that never came, but then of course his Oxford days lay far behind. Dylan liked elderly men as a whole, he spoke often of his old mentor, the senior reporter so affectionately described in *Portrait of the Artist as a Young Dog*, and seemed generally to equate age with sage; in the early days he'd drag me off to Tidal Basin pubs to meet decaying ship's doctors or potato-nosed skippers who must have sailed with Bully Hayes; sometimes these were also present in the Horse-shoe, and in the end I largely cried off the club.

Julian Maclaren Ross, *Memoirs of the Forties* (1965)

A battered warhorse

30 April 1941   *London*

I walked a bit in London and was horrified . . . the capital looks like a battered old war horse. St James's Palace is the worst and the most poignant. . . . All the big houses overlooking the park . . . Spencer House, Bridgewater House, Mrs Macquire's, Stornoway House, Esmond

Rothermere's – all badly battered. The Press Lords seem almost to have been singled out for attack.

Henry Channon, *Diaries* (1967)

A dinner during the Blitz

14 October 1940

Geoffrey Lloyd, Alan and the Butlers dined, and it was a memorable evening . . . Sydney Butler's first evening in London since the blitz. Dinner proceeded, and suddenly Lambert, the butler, ushered in what appeared to be a Harlem nigger: it was Harold Balfour, black from head to foot. He had been standing in the smoking room of the Carlton Club with David Margesson and Victor Warrender drinking sherry before going into dinner: suddenly, with a blinding flash, the ceiling had fallen, and the club collapsed on them. A direct hit. Harold swam, as he put it, through the rubble, surprised to be alive, but soon realized that his limbs were all intact; he called out to his companions to see if they were still alive, and fortunately, all answered. Somehow he got to the front door . . . to find it jammed. At that moment he saw Lord Hailsham being half led, half carried out by his son, Quinton Hogg. A few other individuals, headed by Harold, put their shoulders to the door, and it crashed into the street, and only just in time as by then a fire had started. Harold remembered that he had left his car, an Air Force one, nearby, and went to it, and found only a battered heap of tin; but the chauffeur, an RAF man, was luckily untouched, as he had gone into the building. Harold came here for a bath, champagne, and succour, and we gave him all three.

Ibid.

Bomb damage in Bloomsbury

Tuesday, 10 September

Back from half a day in London – perhaps our strangest visit. When we got
to Gower St a barrier with Diversion on it. No sign of damage. But,
coming to Doughty St a crowd. Then Miss Perkins at the window. Meck S.
roped off. Wardens there, not allowed in. The house about 30 yards from
ours struck at one this morning by a bomb. Completely ruined. Another
bomb in the square still unexploded. We walked round the back. Stood by
Jane Harrison's house. The house was still smouldering. That is a great pile
of bricks. Underneath all the people who had gone down to their shelter.
Scraps of cloth hanging to the bare walls at the side still standing. A looking
glass I think swinging. Like a tooth knocked out – a clean cut. Our house
undamaged. No windows yet broken – perhaps the bomb has now broken
them. We saw Sage Bernal with an arm band jumping on top of the bricks –
who lived there?* I suppose the casual young men & women I used to see,
from my window; the flat dwellers who used to have flower pots & sit on the
balcony. All now blown to bits – The garage man at the back – blear eyed &
jerky told us he had been blown out of his bed by the explosion; made to
take shelter in a church – a hard cold seat, he said, & a small boy lying in my
arms. 'I cheered when the all clear sounded. I'm aching all over.' He said
the Jerrys had been over for 3 nights trying to bomb Kings X. They had
destroyed half Argyll Street, also shops in Grays Inn Road. Then Mr
Pritchard ambled up. Took the news as calm as a grig. 'They actually have
the impertinence to say this will make us accept peace – !' he said: he
watches raids from his flat roof & sleeps like a hog. So, after talking to Miss
Perkins & Mrs Jackson (a bloodless sand hopper), but both serene – Miss P.
had slept on a camp bed in her shelter – we went on to Grays Inn. Left the
car & saw Holborn. A vast gap at the top of Chancery Lane. Smoking still.
Some great shop entirely destroyed: the hotel opposite like a shell. In a wine
shop there were no windows left. People standing at the tables – I think
drink being served. Heaps of blue green glass in the road at Chancery Lane.
Men breaking off fragments left in the frames. Glass falling. Then into

---

* Jane Harrison (1850–1928), classical scholar and anthropologist; her house, where V. W. had
visited her just before she died, was at 11 Mecklenburgh Street, leading off the Square. J. D.
('Sage') Bernal (1901–71), Professor of Physics at Birkbeck College, London, and Scientific
Adviser to the Research and Experimental Department of the Ministry of Home Security.

Lincolns Inn. To the N.S. office: windows broken, but house untouched. We went over it. Deserted. Wet passages. Glass on stairs. Doors locked. So back to the car. A great block of traffic. The Cinema behind Mme Tussaud's torn open: the stage visible; some decoration swinging. All the R[egent's]. Park houses with broken windows, but undamaged. And then miles & miles of orderly ordinary streets – all Bayswater, & Sussex Sqre as usual. Streets empty. Faces set & eyes bleared. In Chancery Lane I saw a man with a barrow of music books. My typists office destroyed. Then at Wimbledon a Siren – people began running. We drove, through almost empty streets, as fast as possible. Horses taken out of the shafts. Cars pulled up. Then the all clear. The people I think of now are the very grimy lodging house keepers, say in Heathcote Street; with another night to face: old wretched women standing at their doors; dirty, miserable. Well – as Nessa said on the phone, its coming very near. I had thought myself a coward for suggesting that we shd. not sleep 2 nights at 37. I was greatly relieved when Miss P. telephoned advising us not to stay, & L. agreed.

Virginia Woolf, Diary (1984)

Struggling on

Sunday, 20 October

The most – what? – impressive, no, thats not it – sight in London on Friday was the queue, mostly children with suitcases, outside Warren St tube. This was about 11.30. We thought they were evacuees, waiting for a bus. But there they were, in a much longer line, with women, men, more bags & blankets, sitting still at 3. Lining up for the shelter in the nights raid – which came of course. Thus, if they left the tube at 6 (a bad raid on Thursday) they were back again at 11. So to Tavistock Sq. With a sigh of relief saw a heap of ruins. Three houses, I shd. say gone. Basement all rubble. Only relics an old basket chair (bought in Fitzroy Sqre days) & Penmans board To Let. Otherwise bricks & wood splinters. One glass door in the next door house hanging. I cd just see a piece of my studio wall standing: otherwise rubble where I wrote so many books. Open air where we sat so many nights, gave so many parties. The hotel not touched. So to Meck. All again litter, glass, black soft dust, plaster powder. Miss Talbot &

Miss Edwards in trousers, overalls, & turbans, sweeping. I noted the flutter of Miss T.'s hands: the same as Miss Perkins. Of course friendly & hospitable in the extreme. Jaunty jerky talk. Repetitions. So sorry we hadn't had her card . . . to save you the shock. Its awful . . . Upstairs she propped a leaning bookcase for us. Books all over dining room floor. In my sitting room glass all over Mrs Hunter's cabinet – & so on. Only the drawing room with windows almost whole. A wind blowing through. I began to hunt out diaries. What cd we salvage in this little car? Darwin, & the Silver, & some glass & china. Then, I on my chair hunting, Mabel came. As discreet & matronly as ever. Rather finer & sadder. I arranged that she shd. come here for a fortnight. She too almost, in her very trained servant way, overcome. Our house, she said, like a monkeys house. Hadnt had her clothes off since she left. And going to the hospital – here she paused. 'You hear them whistling round you, you wonder is it our turn next?' The flats had fallen on top of her shelter. Anxious of course to sweep to recover my fur coat. I worked with her in the kitchen packing Duncan's glasses, Nessa's plates. Very friendly, devoted, her training as helper uppermost. Offered her fare. She refused. (And she hasnt come, greatly to our relief – Oh the pleasure of the empty house – of the ship in wh. we're the crew . . .) Then lunch off tongue, in the drawing room. John came. I forgot the Voyage of the Beagle. No raid the whole day. So about 2.30 drove home. L. says £10 wd cover our damage. Cheered on the whole by London. Damage in Bloomsbury considerable. 3 houses out in Caroline Place: but miles & miles of Hyde Park, Oxford & Cambridge Terrace, & Queens Gate untouched. Now we seem quit of London.

Ibid.

Fire Duty

Fire Duty was something that came round at regular intervals. It meant hanging about the building all night, fully dressed, prepared to go on the roof, if the Warning sounded, with the object of extinguishing incendiary bombs that might fall there. These were said to be easily dealt with by use of sand and an instrument like a garden hoe, both of which were provided as equipment. On previous occasions, up to now, no raid had occurred, the hours passing not too unpleasantly with a book. Feeling I needed a change from the seventeenth century and Proust, I had brought Saltykov-Schredin's *The Golovlyov Family* to read. A more trivial choice would have been humiliating, because Corporal Curtis turned out to be the accompanying NCO that night, and had *Adam Bede* under his arm. We made whatever mutual arrangements were required, then retired to our respective off-duty locations.

Towards midnight I was examining a collection of photographs taken on D-Day, which had not long before this replaced the two Isbister-like oil paintings. Why the pictures had been removed after being allowed to hang throughout the earlier years of the blitz was not apparent. Mime, now a captain, had just hurried past with his telegrams, when the Warning sounded. I found my way to the roof at the same moment as Corporal Curtis.

'I understand, sir, that we ascend into one of the cupolas as an action station.'

'We do.'

'I thought I had better await your arrival and instructions, sir.'

'Tell me the plot of *Adam Bede* as far as you've got. I've never read it.'

Like the muezzin going on duty, we climbed up a steep gangway of iron leading into one of the pepperpot domes constructed at each corner of the building. The particular dome allotted to us, the one nearest the river, was on the far side from that above our own room. The inside was on two floors, rather like an eccentric writer's den for undisturbed work. Curtis and I proceeded to the upper level. These Edwardian belvederes, elaborately pillared and corniced like Temples of Love in a rococo garden, were not in themselves of exceptional beauty, and, when first erected, must have seemed obscure in functional purpose. Now, however, the architect's design showed prophetic aptitude. The exigencies of war had transformed them into true gazebos, not, as it turned out, frequented to observe the 'pleasing prospects' with which such rotundas and follies were commonly associated, but at least to view their antithesis, 'horridly gothick' aspects of the heavens, lit up by fire and rent with thunder.

This extension of purpose was given effect a minute or two later. The moonlit night, now the melancholy strain of the sirens had died away, was surprisingly quiet. All Ack-Ack guns had been sent to the coast, for there was no point in shooting down V.1's over built-up areas. They would come down anyway. Around lay the darkened city, a few solid masses, like the Donners-Brebner Building, recognizable on the far side of the twisting strip of water. Then three rapidly moving lights appeared in the southern sky, two more or less side by side, the third following a short way behind, as if lacking acceleration or will power to keep up. They travelled with that curious shuddering jerky movement characteristic of such bodies, a style of locomotion that seemed to suggest the engine was not working properly, might break down at any moment, which indeed it would. This impression that something was badly wrong with the internal machinery was increased by a shower of sparks emitted from the tail. A more exciting possibility was that dragons were flying through the air in a fabulous tale, and climbing into the turret with Curtis had been done in a dream. The raucous buzz could now be plainly heard. In imagination one smelt brimstone.

'They appear to be heading a few degrees to our right, sir,' said Curtis.

The first two cut-out. It was almost simultaneous. The noisy ticking of the third continued briefly, then also stopped abruptly. This interval between cutting-out and exploding always seemed interminable. At last it came; again two almost at once, the third a few seconds later. All three swooped to the ground, their flaming tails pointing upwards, certainly dragons now, darting earthward to consume their prey of maidens chained to rocks.

'Southwark, do you think?'

'Lambeth, sir – having regard to the incurvations of the river.'

'Sweet Thames run softly . . .'

'I was thinking the same, sir.'

'I'm afraid they've caught it, whichever it was.'

'I'm afraid so, sir.'

The All Clear sounded. We climbed down the iron gangway.

'Do you think that will be all for tonight?'

'I hope so, sir. Just to carry the story on from where we were when we were interrupted: Hetty is then convicted of the murder of her child and transported.'

Anthony Powell, The Military Philosophers (1968)

10

They Came as Strangers

The old song advances the hypothesis, 'Maybe it's because I'm a Londoner, that I love London town.' We don't know about the singer, so all we can say in reply is, 'Well, maybe.' The likelihood is, however, that we love London because we are Lithuanians, Ghanaians, Hungarians or New Yorkers. The English, throughout their history, have been a strange mixture of xenophobia and accommodation in their attitude to immigrants. This probably stems from the fact that almost everyone in these islands started out, at one stage, from somewhere else. Those whose ancestors came over in Viking or Norman long-boats might consider ourselves more British than those who arrived, clutching a British passport, at Heathrow airport from Kenya or Bangladesh, but we know that such an attitude is indefensible, either logically or morally. In earlier generations, London enriched itself (both materially and culturally) by welcoming Huguenots, Spanish Jews, French royalists, Russians (first revolutionary, then counter-revolutionary), as well as the influx from Hitler's Reich. It seemed sad that this generous tradition was sometimes forgotten when the immigrations from the countries of the former British Empire began in the late 1950s.

This is a chapter less about immigrants, however, than about exiles and visitors. There are a few exceptions – most notably the passage from C. Russell and H. S. Lewis about East End Jews; but this was chosen to illustrate the attitude of newly arrived Orthodox Jews to the more easy-going synagogues of the naturalized English Jews. The emphasis of the chapter is 'to see ourselves as others see us'. Herzen, buying filthy cigars from a London tobacconist and observing that 'all trade, especially in England, is based now on quantity and cheapness, and not all on quality', is glimpsing a truth similar to the shock felt by Casanova at English materialism. Lenin, by contrast (an unlikely

church-goer in the East End), is disgusted by the impurity of this materialist
outlook, finding that socialist feelings in the proletariat of Bethnal Green are 'all
mixed up with conservatism, religion and prejudice'. Not much changes.

How much has he got?

I passed a night which seemed like a never-ending nightmare, and I got up
sad and savage, feeling as if I could kill a man on the smallest provocation.
It seemed as if the house, which I had hitherto thought so beautiful, was
like a millstone about my neck. I went out in my travelling clothes, and
walked into a coffee-house where I saw a score of people reading the
papers.

I sat down, and, not understanding English, passed my time in gazing at
the goers and comers. I had been there some time when my attention was
attracted by the voice of a man speaking as follows in French:

'*Tommy* has committed suicide, and he was right, for he was in such
a state that he could only expect unhappiness for the rest of his
life.'

'You are quite mistaken,' said the other, with the greatest composure. 'I
was one of his creditors myself, and on making an inventory of his effects
I feel satisfied that he has done a very foolish and a very childish thing;
he might have lived on comfortably, and not killed himself for fully six
months.'

At any other time this calculation would have made me laugh, and, as it
was, I felt as if the incident had done me good.

I left the coffee-house without having said a word or spent a penny, and I
went towards the *Exchange* to get some money. *Bosanquet* gave me what
I wanted directly, and as I walked out with him I noticed a curious-looking
individual, whose name I asked.

'He's worth a hundred thousand,' said the banker.

'And who is that other man over there?'

'He's not worth a ten-pound note.'

'But I don't want to hear what they are worth; it's their names I want.'

'I really don't know.'

'How can you tell how much they are worth, not knowing their names?'

'Names don't go for anything here. What we want to know about a man is *how much he has got?*'

Giovanni Casanova, *My Life and Adventures* (1932)

John Florio

John Florio was borne in London in the beginning of King Edward VI, his father and mother flying from the Valtolin ('tis about Piedmont or Savoy) to London for Religion: Waldenses. – The family is originally of Siena, where the name is to this day.

King Edward dying, upon the persecution of Queen Mary, they fled back again into their owne countrey, where he was educated.

Afterwards he came into England, and was by King James made Informator to Prince Henry for the Italian and French tongues, and clarke to the closet to Queen Anne.

Scripsit: First and Second Fruits, being two books of the Instruction to learne the Italian tongue: Dictionary; and translated Montagne's Essayes.

He dyed of the great plague at Fulham anno 1625.

John Aubrey, *Brief Lives* (1693)

A Chinaman in London

Such accounts as these, I must confess, were my first motives for seeing England. These induced me to undertake a journey of seven hundred painful days, in order to examine its opulence, buildings, sciences, arts and manufactures on the spot. Judge then how great is my disappointment on entering London, to see no signs of that opulence so much talk'd of abroad; wherever I turn, I am presented with a gloomy solemnity in the houses, the streets and the inhabitants; none of that beautiful gilding which makes a principal ornament in Chinese architecture. The streets of Nankin are sometimes strewed with gold leaf; very different are those of London: in the midst of their pavements a great lazy puddle moves muddily along; heavy laden machines with wheels of unweildy thickness crowd up every passage, so that a stranger instead of finding time for observation, is often happy if he has time to escape from being crushed to pieces. The houses borrow very few ornaments from architecture; their chief decoration seems to be a paltry piece of painting, hung out at their doors or windows, at once a proof of their indigence and vanity. Their vanity in each having one of those pictures exposed to public view, and their indigence in being unable to get them better painted. In this respect, the fancy of their painters is also deplorable. Could you believe it? I have seen five black lions and three blue boars in less than a circuit of half a mile; and yet you know that animals of these colours are no where to be found except in the wild imaginations of Europe. From these circumstances in their buildings, and from the dismal looks of the inhabitants, I am induced to conclude that the nation is actually poor; and that like the Persians, they make a splendid figure every where but at home.

The proverb of Xixofou is, that a man's riches may be seen in his eyes; if we judge of the English by this rule, there is not a poorer nation under the sun. I have been here but two days, so will not be hasty in my decisions; such letters as I shall write to Fipsihi in Moscow, I beg you'll endeavour to forward with all diligence; I shall send them open, in order that you may take copies or translations, as you are equally versed in the Dutch and Chinese languages. Dear friend, think of my absence with regret, as I sincerely regret yours; even while I write, I lament our separation. Farewell.

Oliver Goldsmith, The Citizen of the World (1762)

China Town

There has long been a Chinese influence in Soho. Shortly after the First World War a five-foot Chinese, Brilliant Chang, trafficked in women and drugs, and he was almost certainly the supplier of the drugs which led to two well-publicized deaths. After the Victory Ball held at the Albert Hall, Billie Carleton, a pretty young actress, collapsed and died. The inquest showed she had died of cocaine poisoning and was addicted to opium smoking. It was common knowledge Chang had been a close friend but although her companion of the night before, Reggie de Veuille, was charged with manslaughter, nothing was ever proved against Chang. Then in March 1922 Freda Kempton, a dancing instructress, was also found dead from an overdose of cocaine. This time Brilliant Chang did feature. He had been with Freda the night before and faced a hostile series of questions at her inquest. 'She was a friend of mine, but I know nothing about the cocaine,' he told the coroner. 'It is all a mystery to me.'

Chang, gap-toothed with dark hair swept back, was apparently the son of a well-to-do Chinese businessman, and was sent to England to pursue a commercial career. Instead he opened a restaurant in Regent Street and started drug trafficking on the side from his private suite. If he saw a woman he fancied – and he was seemingly irresistible to many – he would send a note with a waiter:

Dear Unknown

Please don't regard this as a liberty that I write to you. I am really unable to resist the temptation after having seen you so many times. I should extremely like to know you better and should be glad if you would do me the honour of meeting me one evening when we could have a little dinner or supper together. I do hope you will consent to this as it will give me great pleasure indeed, and in any case do not be cross with me for having written to you. Yours hopefully, Chang.

From there it was, in many cases, a short step to drugs and degradation.

James Morton, *Gangland* (1992)

We do all love the Spanish and hate the French

30 September 1661

This morning up by mooneshine; at 5 a-clock to Whitehall to meet Mr Moore at the Privy Seale; but he not being come as appointed, I went into King-Streete to the Red Lyon to drink my morning draught and there I heard of a fray between the two Embassadors of Spaine and France; and that this day being the day of the entrance of an Embassador from Sweden, they were entended to fight for the precedence.* Our King, I heard, hath ordered that no Englishman should meddle in the business, but let them do what they would; and to that end, all the Souldiers in the town were in arms all the day long, and some of the train-bands in the City and a great bustle through the City all the day. Then I to the Privy Seale; and there, Mr Moore and a gentleman being come with him, we took coach (which was the business I came for) to Chelsy to my Lord Privy Seale and there got him to seal that business. Here I saw by day-light two very fine pictures in the gallery, that a little while ago I saw by night. And did also go all over the house, and find it to be the prettiest contrived house that ever I saw in my life. So to coach back again. And at White-hall light and saw the soldiers and people running up and down the streets. So I went to the Spanish Embassadors and the French, and there saw great preparations on both sides; but the French made the most noise and vaunted most, the other made no stir almost at all; so that I was afeared the other would have had too great a conquest over them.

Then to the Wardrobe and dined there; and then abroad, and in Cheape-side hear that the Spaniard hath got the best of it and killed three of the French coach-horses and several men† and is gone through the City next to our King's coach. At which it is strange to see how all the City did rejoice. And endeed, we do naturally all love the Spanish and hate the French.

But I, as I am in all things curious, presently got to the waterside and there took oares to Westminster-palace, thinking to have seen them come in thither with all the coaches; but they being come and returned, I run after them with my boy after me, through all the dirt and the streets full of people; till at last at the mewes I saw the Spanish coach go, with 50 drawne swords at least to guard it and our soldiers shouting for joy. And so I

* The Great Powers were from time to time involved in such disputes, until in 1815 they adopted the rule that the order of precedence should be fixed at each capital according to the seniority (by appointment) of their ambassadors there. In this period it was based on the supposed seniority (by foundation) of the monarchies themselves. France and Spain contested for first place among the secular powers: their ambassadors had quarrelled over it at The Hague in 1657. The dispute which Pepys reports occurred on the occasion of the state entry of the new Swedish ambassador, Brahe. He was to travel this afternoon by water from Westminster to the Tower, where he would enter a coach provided by the King and, at the head of a procession, ride to the court. Later he would be given his first public audience. The French and Spanish ambassadors (d'Estrades and Vatteville) were both determined to get the place next after the King's coach. Pepys's story is in part an eye-witness account, and because of the diplomatic disputes that followed, of special value.

† There had been a running fight from Tower Wharf to Crutched Friars; and, according to the French ambassador, six Frenchmen had been killed and 33 wounded.

fallowed the coach, and then met it at Yorke-house, where the Embassador lies; and there it went in with great state.

So then I went to the French house, where I observe still that there is no men in the world of a more insolent spirit where they do well or before they begin a matter, and more abject if they do miscarry, then these people are. For they all look like dead men and not a word among them, but shake their heads.

The truth is, the Spaniards were observed not only to fight most desperately, but also they did outwitt them; first in lining their owne harnesse with chains of iron, that they could not be cut – then in setting their coach in the most advantageous place, and to appoint men to guard every one of their horses, and others for to guard the coach, and others the coachmen. And above all, in setting upon the French horses and killing them, for by that means the French were not able to stir.

There were several men slain of the French, and one or two of the Spaniards, and one Englishman by a bullett – which is very observable, the French were at least four to one in number. And had near 100 case of pistolls among them, and the Spaniards had not one gun among them; which is for their honour for ever, and the others disgrace.

So having been very much dawbed with dirt, I got a coach and home – where I vexed my wife in telling of her this story and pleading for the Spaniard against the French.

Samuel Pepys, *Diary*

A Japanese Artist in London

One morning I quite decided to commit suicide, if that day's task were fruitless again. Though I was such a quite worthless little man, and it would make no difference whatever to the world whether I died or lived, it was something for me to die. It could not be a joke to me, I was in such a serious mood. Even now I cannot forget that feeling. Let me write down all my impressions at that moment.

As I am a Japanese I could not believe that suicide was a crime. If there is crime in a suicide case, the crime does not belong to the one who commits suicide, but to those who so cruelly drived suicider into such decision. They deserve the name 'manslaughterer', if not 'murderer'. . . .

From Brixton Road to Ludgate Hill every step of my feet made my heart beat. Death or Life – that was my question on each step. The porter of Cassell's took me to a little reception room, where I waited a few minutes. The assistant editor of *The Magazine of Art* (I think it was Mr Fisher. I am such a bad one to remember English names) came to see me first. He was so polite, and so modest. I felt myself something more like a human at last. We say in Japan, 'If you want to see a house master's nature, look at his servants how they behave themselves.' It was quite true in this case. He said he would take my portfolio to show to Mr Spielmann. Perhaps Mr Spielmann would come out to see me himself if I waited there awhile.

Mr M. H. Spielmann? I knew his name before, because Yone Noguchi told me he was a great art critic. While I was waiting in the room I already began to feel some great comfort through Mr Fisher's kind treatment.

After some five minutes the great art critic came into the room with my portfolio in his arm. He promised me to buy some of them and publish all my sketches. I myself thought I was such a clever actor to conceal all my anxieties from him. He never told me anything what he saw in me. But after a few years, when he wrote the introduction chapter of 'The Colour of London', to my great surprise I found out these words in his writing: 'He looked tired and pale. . . . I promised to buy one or two: his eyes danced, &c. &c.'

Now I see I was not quite a successful actor. His eyes must be X-ray.

What a sharp observer he was! . . .

Ever since, for some seven years, Mr Spielmann has been always Dew to a dying Morning Glory. It will be quite a thick volume if I write out every kindness he has done for me. I have three names for him:

1. The rescuer of my life.

2. The father of my Art, because he has been doing all sorts of good for my Art from both points of view – study, as well as selling.

3. The Custom House for all my English friends, because it was he who introduced me to all my most valuable friends I have now.

Yoshio Markino, A Japanese Artist in London (1910)

Pretenders

In May 1839, there was an abrupt increase in the numbers of French in London; since 1830 such has been the case after every Paris uprising, whose eddies have always been felt in the monster city; moreover, a few Frenchmen, not many certainly, came over with Prince Napoleon-Louis Bonaparte. I mention it merely to show how ill-founded are the assertions by which *Le Capitole* would have its readers believe that its 'prince' plays an important part in London.

Londoners, accustomed since the French Revolution to the presence of august emigrés and illustrious personages, appear perfectly indifferent and seem to attach no political importance whatsoever to the two 'pretenders' currently residing in their city. The so-called Duke of Normandy who modestly takes the title of Louis XVII, can be seen walking (and for good reason) in Regent Street without causing the least stir; the unfortunate king consoles himself for the scorn of nations by ordering his domestics (two maidservants) to address his son as *Monseigneur le Dauphin* and his daughter as *Mademoiselle*. The other pretender is frequently seen in Regent's Park driving in a tilbury or riding horseback. Few people appear to know him. If you are with some fashionable Frenchman or Englishman, he will point him out to you, but the former will inform you: '*Tiens*, there is Prince Napoleon.' The latter will say: 'That gentleman over there is Napoleon's cousin.' I had one young Englishman tell me, with perfect indifference: 'That is Napoleon's son.' What, indeed, does the degree of relationship matter? It is the name Napoleon, itself, which lives in the memory of men; each one feels that he was the man of his age, and that neither his genius nor his power can have any successor.

Flora Tristran, *London Journal* (1840)

An egotist in London

One day when I was talking about work in England the little fop who acted as our courier claimed his national honour was offended.

– You are right, I told him, but we're unhappy: we haven't any agreeable acquaintances.

– Sir, I'll look after the business for you. I'll do the bargaining myself. Don't approach anyone else, you'd be robbed, etc., etc.

My friends laughed. So, for having made fun of the fop's honour, I found myself involved with harlots. Nothing could be more cheerless and repellent than the details of the transaction our fellow made us go through the next day in showing us round London.

In the first place, our girls lived in an out-of-the-way district, in Westminster Road, an admirable place for Frenchmen to be beaten up by three or four sailor pimps. When we mentioned it to an English friend he said:

– It's an ambush! Keep well away!

The fop added that he'd bargained for a long time to get us tea in the morning when we got up. The girls didn't want to accord us their good graces and their tea for twenty-one shillings. But finally they'd agreed. Two or three English people told us:

– You'd never find an Englishman falling into such a trap. Do you know you'll be taken more than two miles from London?

We were completely agreed we wouldn't go. But when evening came Barot gave me a look I understood.

– We're strong, I said, and we have weapons.

Lussinge didn't dare come.

Barot and I took a cab and went over Westminster Bridge. Then the cab went down streets without houses, between some gardens. Barot laughed.

– If you were so brilliant with Alexandrine in a charming house in the middle of Paris, what won't you be here!

I felt profoundly disgusted; without the boredom of the period after dinner in London when there's nothing on at the theatre, as was the case that day, and without the slight stimulus of danger, I should never have been seen in Westminster Road. I seem to remember that finally, after having been on the point of overturning two or three times in unpaved tracks masquerading as roads, the swearing cabman stopped in front of a three-storied house which must have been about twenty-five feet high. I've never seen anything so small in my life.

Without the thought of the danger involved, I should certainly never have gone in. I expected to see three horrible sluts. The three girls were small and slight with beautiful chestnut hair: a little shy, very anxious to please, very pale.

The furniture was quite ridiculously small. Barot is big and fat; I'm fat, so that we literally couldn't find anywhere to sit down: the furniture seemed to be made for dolls, we were frightened of smashing it. Our diminutive girls saw our embarrassment and their own increased. We had no idea what to say. Fortunately Barot thought of mentioning the garden.

'Oh! We have a garden,' they said, not with pride, but with some joy at having an object of luxury to show us. We went down to see the garden with candles: it was twenty-five feet long and ten feet wide. Barot and I burst out laughing. All the poor girls' domestic equipment was there: their little wash-tub, their little vat with an elliptical contraption for brewing their own beer.

I was touched and Barot disgusted. He said to me in French:

– Let's pay them and be off.
– They'll feel so humiliated, I said.
– Bah! Humiliated! You know them well enough! They'll send for other clients, if it's not too late, or their lovers if this is anything like France.

These truths made no impression on me. I found their poverty, all those very clean, very old pieces of furniture, touching. We hadn't finished drinking before I was sufficiently intimate with them to confess, in broken English, to our fear of being assassinated. This disconcerted them a great deal.

– But look, I added, the proof that we don't misjudge you is that I'm telling you all this.

We sent the fop away. Then it seemed as if I was with dear friends whom I was seeing again after a year's absence.

There wasn't a door which shut – another subject for suspicion when we went to bed. But what good would doors and strong locks have been? The thin brick partitions could everywhere be knocked in with a blow of the fist. You could hear everything in this house. Barot, who had gone up to the second floor in the room above mine, cried out:

– If they come to murder you, call me!

I wanted to keep the light burning but the modesty of my new friend, who was otherwise so docile and obliging, would never permit it. She made a movement of obvious terror when she saw me laying out pistols and a dagger on the little table by the side of the bed opposite the door. She was charming: small, pale and with a good figure.

No one assassinated us. The next day we let them off providing tea and sent the courier for Lussinge, suggesting he come with cold meats and wine. He appeared very quickly, together with an excellent breakfast, thoroughly surprised by our enthusiasm.

The two sisters sent for one of their friends. We left them wine and some cold meat whose appetizing appearance seemed to surprise these poor girls.

They thought we were making fun of them when we told them we'd come back. Miss ——, my friend, said to me privately:

– I wouldn't go out if I could hope you'd come back this evening. But our house is too poor for people like you.

All day I thought only of the nice, quiet, calm evening ('full of snugness'), which was waiting for me. I found the play long. Barot and Lussinge wanted to see all the brazen young women who filled the foyer at Covent Garden. Finally Barot and I arrived at our little house. When the girls saw bottles of claret and champagne unpacked, the poor things were wide-eyed. I rather think they'd never before found themselves in front of an unopened bottle of 'real champaign'.

Fortunately our cork popped; they were completely happy; but in a quiet and seemly way. Nothing could be more seemly than their behaviour in general. We already knew that.

Stendhal, *Memoirs of an Egotist* (1832)

Garibaldi in London

There was a special train provided to take Garibaldi to London on Monday, the 11th April, and he walked to it at Southampton station through an avenue of women clothed for the most part in scarlet. The dressmakers had been busy; Garibaldi hats and Garibaldi blouses had suddenly become the fashion; and a biscuit maker, introducing a new line to the public, had seized upon the prevailing craze to christen his product after the General.

The journey to London took a long time. At Winchester, the Mayor insisted on haranguing the General at the door of his compartment and the band that struck up 'The Conquering Hero' was drowned by the roars of applause. As the train approached Vauxhall, the line was encumbered by hundreds of thousands of spectators crowded on railway waggons and locomotives, and on the roofs of houses, who howled their heads off as it passed. At its destination at Nine Elms Station, a large portrait of the hero decorated the platform and there was a vast concourse. There were innumerable speeches of welcome and it was long before the General could escape to the Duke of Sutherland's carriage which awaited him.

But the reception was nothing to what followed as the carriage, with its four horses, struggled along the Wandsworth Road towards the West End. It was estimated that more than half a million people packed the streets. Every working men's society was out with banners and bands, but they were swept aside by the exhilarated crowds, climbing on the carriage, all seeking to shake the hand of the General, all shouting and cheering and waving emblems.

It took so long to reach Westminster Bridge that the sun was setting as the cortège passed over with bells clanging and cheers resounding and when, at last, the carriage reached the quiet square outside Stafford House, there were scenes never before witnessed by that almost regal precinct. When the carriage was eventually taken into the stables it fell to pieces. That night, the Duke's lackeys were busy selling bottles of soapsuds alleged to have come from Garibaldi's washbasin.

The next day it was midday before Garibaldi appeared to the waiting crowds and he was then driven off to lunch with the Prime Minister, Lord Palmerston. What passed between them is not known but it was thought by some that Garibaldi emerged with a rather red face, as if there had been some acrimonious dispute; at any rate, in the afternoon when he visited the Dowager Duchess of Sutherland at her house in Chiswick, and met a host of titled aristocrats, there was no such atmosphere, although the Earl of Malmesbury was shocked to see him commit the unpardonable sin of lighting up a cigar in the Duchess's drawing-room. But the Duchess does not seem to have been offended, for in the next few days he was seen with her so often on his arm at receptions that it was widely rumoured that the fifty-seven-year-old sailor's son was going to marry the fifty-eight-year-old Duchess.

That week he was fêted by all the town as if he were royalty. Receptions were crowded for him; there were scenes of ecstasy at the opera; he was taken to Bedford to inspect the railworks; he dined with Gladstone, the Chancellor of the Exchequer, and with Lord John Russell, the Foreign Secretary; he was taken, of course, to see Barclays and Perkins brewery at Southwark and received a very different reception from that afforded an Austrian dignitary a few years earlier; at a great gala at the Crystal Palace he was presented with a sword of honour, all the Garibaldi hymns were sung and the whole house rose to its feet as Arditi's *La Garibaldina* was reached with its refrain:

> O Garibaldi, nostro salvator,
> Te seguiremo al campo del'onor,
> Risorga Italia,
> Il sol di liberta,
> All'armi, all'armi, andiamo.
>
> *Garibaldi, oh! our saviour,*
> *Thee we'll follow to the field of honour,*
> *To raise Italy,*
> *Sun of liberty,*
> *To arms! To arms! Let us go!*

He dined at Panizzi's house in a small circle of influential men, and Gladstone again sat next to him and they had an intimate conversation. He was escorted to Eton by the Duchess of Sutherland and received there with greater enthusiasm than if he had been royalty. And on the 25th April, there was conferred on him the honour of the freedom of the City of London. The banquet given to him the next day by the Fishmongers' Company was marred only by the fact that Menotti and Ricciotti – with their father – were under the impression that it was to be an assembly of tradesmen who dealt in fish; whereas, of course, that august body's closest acquaintance with the commodity was the *truites de Spey à l'Italienne* which appeared on the menu in honour of their guest. Consequently, they did not attend in evening-dress and were excluded. Their father, in his red shirt and grey trousers, led a glittering assembly in to dinner with the Dowager Duchess of Sutherland on his arm.

John Parris, *The Lion of Caprera* (1962)

Mazzini in London

I have previously recorded the rise of my feelings towards Mazzini, and the letters that had passed between us. I now come to the time when we met face to face.

The first time was on 30th January 1864. It was about four months after my marriage, and the first day available for me. I went from the Manor House, Chigwell, to meet my husband at 65 Cornhill, and he accompanied me (it was a Saturday) to Mazzini's lodgings at Brompton. We returned home the same evening. It was a fatiguing expedition, but all my days were full of fatigue. Mazzini lived then, and during all the years I knew him, in a house called 18 Fulham Road. It was one of a row of small, three-storied houses, standing a little way back from the road, with, in front, a little iron gate and a small grass plot. I believe the whole place has long been demolished. He occupied the first floor of two rooms, and his landlady's name was Mrs France. He went by the name of Signor Ernesti, and his letters were so addressed. This was a quite transparent disguise, as he was perfectly well known to the police; but it was probably convenient. I do not remember if we had previously announced our visit; but we found him at home. He was in the small front sitting-room, so filled with books and papers there was hardly room to move, and with his little canaries and greenfinches fluttering about the room. He had been smoking, but had put away his cigar. At last we stood face to face. I had a photograph of him, but a small and poor one, and it was with an indescribable emotion that I saw before me the slender emaciated form, the noble face and brow, and the great dark, liquid velvet eyes, with their wonderful fire and depth, and heard the gentle, caressing voice. He was dressed, as always, in the deep mourning, the black velvet waistcoat buttoned up to the throat, which was his distinctive costume. I have no recollection of what was said. I could only utter a few words of devotion and thankfulness: and though Mazzini himself was a fluent and eager talker, I do not remember that he said much, nor anything that he said. It was my husband who principally sustained the conversation. He had a peculiar gift, not the affectation of one, of being able to talk fluently about anything and to any one without having the slightest acquaintance with either. I do not think he had ever read anything of Mazzini's, nor had any but a vague idea about him, but he had accepted him wholly as my friend, and as a man of distinction: he met him with the greatest cordiality, and being himself a great speaker, he mainly did the talking. Mazzini and I gazed at one another. In spite of my emotion, the events of the past months had been for me so new, so amazing, and so bewildering, that I could no longer feel what I had felt a year before: I had entered into a new world, into new ties; and I felt sadly that something was lost in me. I felt disappointed, not in Mazzini, but in myself. He never took his large wonderful eyes from my face; and in them there was the expression of the deepest melancholy.

Mrs Hamilton King, *Letters and Recollections of Mazzini* (1912)

Talleyrand

It was a very different country that this lover of England was revisiting in 1830 from that which he had left in 1794. Never perhaps have thirty-six years effected so complete a change in the outward aspect and in the inward mind of a whole nation. It is hardly too much to say that the complete process of alteration from the eighteenth to the nineteenth century had taken place in that period. He had known the London of Horace Walpole and he came back to the London of Charles Greville. When he was last there Pitt and Fox had been at the height of their powers; now the young Disraeli was already older than Pitt had been when he became Prime Minister, and the young Gladstone was coming of age. He had left the London of knee-breeches and powdered hair, he returned to the London of frock-coats and top-hats. White's Club, down the steps of which he would have been kicked as a rascally Jacobin in 1794, elected him an honorary member. The famous bow window had been built over those steps in the interval and had already seen its greatest days, for the brief reign of Brummel was over, and the dandies of the Regency were no more. Boswell had been alive when he was last in London. The whole life-work of Keats, Shelley, and Byron had taken place during his absence and in this, the year of his return, the first publication of Tennyson saw the light. Those who were alive at his first visit could remember the reign of Queen Anne, those who were alive at his second could live into the reign of George V.

It is interesting to find him describing London as 'much more beautiful' than he had left it, an opinion corroborated by an American who, returning to London in this same year after an absence of nineteen years, said that it had become 'a thousand times more beautiful' than it was. Talleyrand was surprised that the sun should be shining in September and that all the members of the Government should be out of town – phenomena which would have caused less astonishment, then and now, in one better acquainted with the climate and the customs of the country.

The new Ambassador was well received by the Duke of Wellington and by Lord Aberdeen, who was Foreign Secretary. With the former he had for long been on friendly terms, for the two men understood one another. They were both great gentlemen of the old school. They were both intensely practical and they both hated any kind of humbug or cant. Aberdeen had been brought up in the tradition of Pitt and under the wing of Castlereagh. No Government, it was said, could be too liberal for him, provided it did not abandon its conservative character. He belonged to the European as opposed to the nationalist line of British Foreign Ministers and it had been mainly due to his advice that Wellington had overcome his scruples about recognizing the Government of Louis-Philippe.

Duff Cooper, *Talleyrand* (1938)

Esquimaux

He did not give me full credit when I mentioned that I had carried on a short conversation by signs with some Esquimaux who were then in London, particularly with one of them who was a priest. He thought I could not make them understand me. No man was more incredulous as to particular facts, which were at all extraordinary; and therefore no man was more scrupulously inquisitive, in order to discover the truth.

James Boswell, *Life of Johnson* (1791)

Lenin and Trotsky in the East End

Sometimes Trotsky would be permitted to accompany Lenin to socialist meetings in London. It was the time when socialism in England was being advanced with religious fervor and enthusiasm; at Sunday services in the East End of London sermons on socialist brotherhood would alternate with hymns. The hymns sometimes wore a republican character, and Trotsky says he heard them singing, 'Lord Almighty, let there be no more kings or rich men!' Lenin was puzzled by the English propensity for mixing the most diverse elements in their culture. When they left the church he said, 'There are many revolutionary and socialist elements among the English proletariat, but they are all mixed up with conservatism, religion and prejudice, and somehow the socialist and revolutionary elements never break through the surface and unite.'

To the end of his life Lenin was puzzled by the English, and contemptuous of them: what particularly disturbed him was their lack of socialist unity. He preferred the Germans, who obeyed rules and regulations and liked to see themselves as a unified mass. As Trotsky said, 'British Marxism was not interesting.' It lacked drama, tension, war between powerful personalities. It was in fact essentially parochial, and the Russians were incapable of thinking in parochial terms. For them the revolution was always meaningless unless it embraced the whole world, and if possible the entire universe.

Robert Payne, *The Life and Death of Lenin* (1963)

Royal Exchange

There is no place in the town which I so much love to frequent as the Royal Exchange. It gives me a secret satisfaction, and in some measure gratifies my vanity, as I am an Englishman, to see so rich an assembly of countrymen and foreigners, consulting together upon the private business of mankind, and making this metropolis a kind of *emporium* for the whole earth. I must confess I look upon high-change to be a great council, in which all considerable nations have their representatives. Factors in the trading world are what ambassadors are in the politic world; they negotiate affairs, conclude treaties, and maintain a good correspondence between those wealthy societies of men that are divided from one another by seas and oceans, or live on the different extremities of a continent. I have often been pleased to hear disputes adjusted between an inhabitant of Japan and an alderman of London; or to see a subject of the Great Mogul entering into a league with one of the Czar of Muscovy. I am infinitely delighted in mixing with these several ministers of commerce, as they are distinguished by their different walks and different languages. Sometimes I am jostled among a body of Armenians; sometimes I am lost in a crowd of Jews; and sometimes make one in a group of Dutchmen. I am a Dane, Swede, or Frenchman, at different times; or rather fancy myself like the old philosopher, who upon being asked what countryman he was, replied, that he was a citizen of the world.

Though I very frequently visit this busy multitude of people, I am known to nobody there but my friend Sir Andrew, who often smiles upon me as he sees me bustling in the crowd, but at the same time connives at my presence without taking farther notice of me. There is indeed a merchant of Egypt, who just knows me by sight, having formerly remitted me some money to Grand Cairo; but as I am not versed in modern Coptic, our conferences go no farther than a bow and a grimace.

This grand scene of business gives me an infinite variety of solid and substantial entertainments. As I am a great lover of mankind, my heart naturally overflows with pleasure at the sight of a prosperous and happy multitude, insomuch that at many public solemnities I cannot forbear expressing my joy with tears that have stolen down my cheeks. For this reason I am wonderfully delighted to see such a body of men thriving in their own private fortunes, and at the same time promoting the public stock; or, in other words, raising estates for their own families, by bringing into their country whatever is wanting and carrying out of it whatever is superfluous.

Nature seems to have taken particular care to disseminate her blessings among the different regions of the world, with an eye to this mutual intercourse and traffic among mankind, that the natives of the several parts of the globe might have a kind of dependence upon one another, and be united together by their common interest. Almost every degree produces something peculiar to it. The food often grows in one country, and the sauce in another. The fruits of Portugal are corrected by the produce of Barbadoes, and the infusion of a China plant is sweetened by the pith of an

Indian cane. The Philippic Islands give a flavour to our European bowls. The single dress of a woman of quality is often the product of a hundred climates. The muff and the fan come together from different ends of the earth. The scarf is sent from the torrid zone, and the tippet from beneath the pole. The brocade petticoat rises out of the mines of Peru, and the diamond necklace out of the bowels of Indostan.

If we consider our own country in its natural prospect, without any of the benefits and advantages of commerce, what a barren, uncomfortable spot of earth falls to our share! Natural historians tell us, that no fruit grows originally among us, besides hips and haws, acorns and pig-nuts, with other delicacies of the like nature; that our climate of itself, and without the assistance of art, can make no farther advances towards a plum than to a sloe, and carries an apple to no greater perfection than a crab: that our melons, our peaches, our figs, our apricots, and cherries, are strangers among us, imported in different ages, and naturalized in our English gardens; and that they would all degenerate and fall away into the trash of our own country, if they were wholly neglected by the planter, and left to the mercy of our sun and soil. Nor has traffic more enriched our vegetable world, than it has improved the whole face of nature among us. Our ships are laden with the harvest of every climate. Our tables are stored with spices, and oils, and wines. Our rooms are filled with pyramids of China, and adorned with the workmanship of Japan. Our morning's draught comes to us from the remotest corners of the earth. We repair our bodies by the drugs of America, and repose ourselves under Indian canopies. My friend, Sir Andrew, calls the vineyards of France our gardens; the spice-islands our hot-beds; the Persians our silk-weavers, and the Chinese our potters. Nature, indeed, furnishes us with the bare necessaries of life, but traffic gives us a great variety of what is useful, and at the same time supplies us with every thing that is convenient and ornamental. Nor is it the least part of this our happiness, that whilst we enjoy the remotest products of the north and south, we are free from those extremities of weather which give them birth; that our eyes are refreshed with the green fields of Britain, and at the same time that our palates are feasted with fruits that rise between the tropics.

For these reasons there are not more useful members in a commonwealth than merchants. They knit mankind together in a mutual intercourse of good offices, distribute the gifts of nature, find work for the poor, add wealth to the rich, and magnificence to the great. Our English merchant converts the tin of his own country into gold, and exchanges its wool for rubies. The Mahometans are clothed in our British manufacture, and the inhabitants of the frozen zone warmed with the fleeces of our sheep.

When I have been upon the 'Change, I have often fancied one of our old kings standing in person, where he is represented in effigy, and looking down upon the wealthy concourse of people with which that place is every day filled. In this case, how would he be surprised to hear all the languages of Europe spoken in this little spot of his former dominions, and to see so many private men, who in his time would have been the vassals of some powerful baron, negotiating like princes for greater sums of money than were formerly to be met with in the royal treasury! Trade, without enlarging the British territories, has given us a kind of additional empire. It has multiplied the number of the rich, made our landed estates infinitely more valuable than they were formerly, and added to them an accession of other estates as valuable as the lands themselves.

Joseph Addison, The Spectator, 19 May 1711

Disputes among the Jews

In the East End itself, the division between English and foreign Jews is roughly a division into the lax and the orthodox; and within the ranks of the latter there are numerous gradations of orthodoxy, which (also very roughly) correspond to the degree of Anglicization and length of residence in England. . . . Among the strictest sect of the new arrivals it is denied that there is such a thing as orthodoxy at all among the English Jews; they are all regarded as 'reformers', and the Chief Rabbi himself has been declared to be the 'Chief Reformer'. And to the ears of the devoutly orthodox such phrases perhaps carry a weight of sarcasm that a Gentile can scarcely appreciate.

A striking manifestation of the depth and extent of this hostile piety was recently evoked by a discussion of the *chedarim*, which took place at a West End conference on Jewish education. The *cheder* system was there rather sharply, but not unsympathetically, criticized; but the result was an astonishing outburst of indignation in the East End. A meeting was held at the Jewish Working Men's Club, at which the bitterest speeches were delivered; and a resolution was carried 'amidst a scene of tumultuous enthusiasm' to the effect, –

'That we East End Jews protest against the discussion upon the *chedarim* and *Talmud Torah* at the Elementary Education Conference.

'We further do not recognize the West End Jews as authorities upon Hebrew and religious education.'

In the course of his speech, the mover of this resolution, the Rev. H. Orleansky (according to the report in the *Jewish Chronicle*) 'made a violent attack upon English Jews, especially the clergy who,' he said, 'were ignorant of the Torah and the Talmud, and who did nothing for the East Enders. They had no right to find fault. Let them mind their own business. The Chief Rabbi was their *Rav*, to decide upon questions of ritual law, but not to interfere beyond. Whatever the English Jews had done had been wrong. They had pulled down a synagogue before building another. They had a free dispensary which was not free. The East End desired to be left alone. He protested against "reformers" dictating to those who were orthodox upon religious matters.'

C. Russell and H. S. Lewis, The Jew in London (1899)

Spanish Exiles

In those years a visible section of the London population, and conspicuous out of all proportion to its size or value, was a small knot of Spaniards, who had sought shelter here as Political Refugees. 'Political Refugees': a tragic succession of that class is one of the possessions of England in our time. Six-and-twenty years ago, when I first saw London, I remember those unfortunate Spaniards among the new phenomena. Daily in the cold spring air, under skies so unlike their own, you could see a group of fifty or a hundred stately tragic figures, in proud threadbare cloaks; perambulating, mostly with closed lips, the broad pavements of Euston Square and the regions about St Pancras new Church. Their lodging was chiefly in Somers Town, as I understood; and those open pavements about St Pancras Church were the general place of rendezvous. They spoke little or no English; knew nobody, could employ themselves on nothing, in this new scene. Old steel-grey heads, many of them; the shaggy, thick, blue-black hair of others struck you; their brown complexion, dusky look of suppressed fire, in general their tragic condition as of caged Numidian lions.

That particular Flight of Unfortunates has long since fled again, and vanished; and new have come and fled. In this convulsed revolutionary epoch, which already lasts above sixty years, what tragic flights of such have we not seen arrive on the one safe coast which is open to them, as they get successively vanquished, and chased into exile to avoid worse! Swarm after swarm, of ever new complexion, from Spain as from other countries, is thrown off, in those ever-recurring paroxysms; and will continue to be thrown off. As there could be (suggests Linnaeus) a 'flower-clock', measuring the hours of the day, and the months of the year, by the kinds of flowers that go to sleep and awaken, that blow into beauty and fade into dust: so in the great Revolutionary Horologe, one might mark the years and epochs by the successive kinds of exiles that walk London streets, and, in grim silent manner, demand pity from us and reflections from us.

Thomas Carlyle, *The Life of John Sterling* (1851)

An Italian prince

The Prince had always liked his London, when it had come to him; he was one of the Modern Romans who find by the Thames a more convincing image of the truth of the ancient state than any they have left by the Tiber. Brought up on the legend of the City to which the world paid tribute, he recognized in the present London much more than in contemporary Rome the real dimensions of such a case. If it was a question of an *Imperium*, he said to himself, and if one wished, as a Roman, to recover a little the sense of that, the place to do so was on London Bridge, or even, on a fine afternoon in May, at Hyde Park Corner. It was not indeed to either of those places that these grounds of his predilection, after all sufficiently vague, had, at the moment we are concerned with him, guided his steps; he had strayed simply enough into Bond Street, where his imagination, working at comparatively short range, caused him now and then to stop before a window in which objects massive and lumpish, in silver and gold, in the forms to which precious stones contribute, or in leather, steel, brass, applied to a hundred uses and abuses, were as tumbled together as if, in the insolence of the Empire, they had been the loot of far-off victories.

Henry James, *The Golden Bowl* (1904)

Dostoyevsky in the Haymarket

In London the masses can be seen on a scale and in conditions not to be seen anywhere else in the world.

I have been told, for example, that on Saturday nights half a million working men and women and their children spread like the ocean all over town, clustering particularly in certain districts, and celebrate their sabbath all night long until five o'clock in the morning, in other words guzzle and drink like beasts to make up for a whole week. They bring with them their weekly savings, all that was earned by hard work and with many a curse. Great jets of gas burn in meat and food shops, brightly lighting up the streets. It is as if a grand reception were being held for those white negroes. Crowds throng the open taverns and the streets. There they eat and drink. The beer houses are decorated like palaces. Everyone is drunk, but drunk joylessly, gloomily and heavily, and everyone is somehow strangely silent. Only curses and bloody brawls occasionally break that suspicious and oppressively sad silence. . . . Everyone is in a hurry to drink himself into insensibility . . . wives in no way lag behind their husbands and all get drunk together, while children crawl and run about among them.

One such night – it was getting on for two o'clock in the morning – I lost my way and for a long time trudged the streets in the midst of a vast crowd of gloomy people, asking my way almost by gestures, because I do not know a word of English. I found my way, but the impression of what I had seen tormented me for three days afterwards. The populace is much the same anywhere, but there all was so vast, so vivid that you almost physically felt things which up till then you had only imagined. In London you no longer see the populace. Instead, you see a loss of sensibility, systematic, resigned and encouraged. And you feel, as you look at all those social pariahs, that it will be a long time before the prophecy is fulfilled for them, a long time before they are given palm branches and white robes, and that for a long time yet they will continue to appeal to the Throne of the Almighty, crying: 'How long, oh Lord?' And they know it themselves and in the meantime take their revenge on society by producing all kinds of underground mormons, shakers, tramps . . . We are surprised at the stupidity which leads people to become shakers and tramps, and fail to understand that what we have here is a repudiation of our social formula, an obstinate and unconscious repudiation; an instinctive repudiation at any cost, in order to achieve salvation, a horrified and disgusted repudiation of the rest of us. Those millions of people, abandoned and driven away from the feast of humanity, push and crush each other in the underground darkness into which they have been cast by their elder brethren, they grope around seeking a door at which to knock and look for an exit lest they be smothered to death in that dark cellar. This is the last desperate attempt to huddle together and form one's own heap, one's own mass and to repudiate everything, the very image of man if need be, only to be oneself, only not to be with us . . .

I saw in London another and similar 'mass', such as you would never see on a like scale anywhere else. An unusual spectacle it certainly was. Anyone who has ever visited London must have been at least once in the Haymarket at night. It is a district in certain streets of which prostitutes swarm by night in their thousands. Streets are lit by jets of gas – something completely unknown in our own country. At every step you come across magnificent public houses, all mirrors and gilt. They serve as meeting places as well as shelters. It is a terrifying experience to find oneself in that crowd. And, what an odd amalgam it is. You will find old women there and beautiful women at the sight of whom you stop in amazement. There are no women in the world as beautiful as the English.

The streets can hardly accommodate the dense, seething crowd. The mob has not enough room on the pavements and swamps the whole street. All this mass of humanity craves for booty and hurls itself at the first comer with shameless cynicism. Glistening, expensive clothes and semi-rags and sharp differences in age – they are all there. A drunken tramp shuffling along in this terrible crowd is jostled by the rich and titled. You hear curses, quarrels, solicitations and the quiet, whispered invitation of some still bashful beauty. And how beautiful they sometimes are with their keepsake faces! I remember once I went into a 'casino'. The music was blaring, people were dancing, a huge crowd was milling round. The place was magnificently decorated. But gloom never forsakes the English even in the midst of gaiety; even when they dance they look serious, not to say sullen, making hardly any steps and then only as if in execution of some duty. Upstairs, in the gallery I saw a girl and stopped in amazement. She was sitting at a little table together with an apparently rich and respectable young man who, by all the signs, was an unaccustomed visitor to the casino. Perhaps he had been looking for her and they had at last found each other and arranged to meet there. He spoke to her little and only in short, jerky phrases as if he was not talking about what really interested him. Their conversation was punctuated by long and frequent silences. She, too, looked sad. Her face was delicate and fine, and there was something deep-hidden and sad, something thoughtful and melancholy in the proud expression of her eyes. I should say she had consumption. Mentally and morally she was, she could not fail to be, above the whole crowd of those wretched women; otherwise, what meaning would there be in a human face? All the same, however, she was then and there drinking gin, paid for by the young man. At last he got up, shook hands with her and went away. He left the casino, while she, her pale cheeks now flushed deep with drink, was soon lost in the crowd of women trading in their bodies.

In the Haymarket I noticed mothers who brought their little daughters to make them ply that same trade. Little girls, aged about twelve, seize you by the arm and beg you to come with them. I remember once amidst the crowd of people in the street I saw a little girl, not older than six, all in rags, dirty, bare-foot and hollow-cheeked; she had been severely beaten, and her body, which showed through the rags, was covered with bruises. She was walking along, as if oblivious of everybody and everything, in no hurry to get anywhere, and Heaven knows why loafing about in that crowd; perhaps she was hungry. Nobody was paying any attention to her. But what struck me most was the look of such distress, such hopeless despair on her face that to see that tiny bit of humanity already bearing the imprint of all that evil and despair was somehow unnatural and terribly painful. She kept on shaking her tousled head as if arguing about something, gesticulated and spread her little hands and then suddenly clasped them together and pressed them to her little bare breast. I went back and gave her sixpence. She took the small silver coin, gave me a wild look full of frightened surprise, and suddenly ran off as fast as her legs could carry her, as if afraid that I should take the money away from her. Jolly scenes, altogether. . . .

And then one night in the midst of a crowd of loose women and debauchees I was stopped by a woman making her way hurriedly through it. She was dressed all in black and her hat almost concealed her face; in fact I had hardly time to make it out, I only remember the steady gaze of her eyes. She said something in broken French which I failed to understand, thrust a piece of paper into my hand and hurried on. I examined the paper at the light of a café window: it was a small square slip. One side bore the words 'Crois-tu cela?' printed on it. The other, also in French: 'I am the Resurrection and the Life' . . ., etc. – the well-known text. This too, you must admit, is rather bizarre. It was explained to me afterwards that that was Catholic propaganda ferreting round everywhere, persistent and tireless. Sometimes they distribute these bits of paper in the streets, sometimes booklets containing extracts from the New Testament and the Bible. They distribute them free, thrust them into people's hands, press them on people. It is ingenious and cunning propaganda. A Catholic priest would search out and insinuate himself into a poor workman's family. He would find, for example, a sick man lying in his rags on a damp floor, surrounded by children crazy from cold and hunger, with a wife famished and often drunk. He would feed them all, provide clothes and warmth for them, give treatment to the sick man, buy medicine for him, become the friend of the family and finally convert them all to the Catholic faith. Sometimes, however, after the sick man has been restored to health, the priest is driven out with curses and kicks. He does not despair and goes off to someone else. He is chucked out again, but puts up with everything and catches someone in the end.

But an Anglican minister would never visit a poor man. The poor are not even allowed inside a church because they have not the money to pay for a seat.

Fyodor Dostoyevsky, *Winter Notes on Summer Impressions* (1985)

Walking in London

London life was very favourable for such a break. There is no town in the world which is more adapted for training one away from people and training one into solitude than London. The manner of life, the distances, the climate, the very multitude of the population in which personality vanishes, all this together with the absence of Continental diversions conduces to the same effect. One who knows how to live alone has nothing to fear from the tedium of London. The life here, like the air here, is bad for the weak, for the frail, for one who seeks a prop outside himself, for one who seeks welcome, sympathy, attention; the moral lungs here must be as strong as the physical lungs, whose task it is to separate oxygen from the smoky fog. The masses are saved by battling for their daily bread, the commercial classes by their absorption in heaping up wealth, and all by the bustle of business; but nervous and romantic temperaments, fond of living among people, fond of intellectual sloth and of idly luxuriating in emotion, are bored to death here and fall into despair.

Wandering lonely about London, through its stony lanes and stifling passages, sometimes not seeing a step before me for the thick, opaline fog, and colliding with shadows running – I lived through a great deal.

Alexander Herzen, *My Past and Thoughts* (1968)

Everything is within the reach of almost everyone

London is crowded . . . A hundred railway carriages coupled on are insufficient; there are forty theatres and not a seat free; a play has to be running for three months for the London public to be able to see it.

'Why are your cigars so bad?' I asked one of the leading London tobacconists.

'It is hard to get them, and, indeed, it is not worth taking trouble; there are few connoisseurs and still fewer well-to-do ones.'

'Not worth while? You charge eightpence each for them.'

'That hardly brings us out even. While you and a dozen like you will buy them, is there much profit in that? In one day I sell more twopenny and threepenny cigars than I do of these in a year. I am not going to order any more of them.'

Here was a man who had grasped the spirit of the age. All trade, especially in England, is based now on quantity and cheapness, and not at all on quality, as old-fashioned Russians imagine when they reverently buy Tula pen-knives with an English trademark on them. Everything receives wholesale, herd-like, rank-and-file consideration; everything is within the reach of almost everyone, but does not allow of aesthetic finish or personal taste. Everywhere the hundred-thousand-headed hydra waits expectantly close at hand round a corner, ready to listen to everything, to look at everything indiscriminately, to be dressed in anything, to gorge itself on anything – this is the autocratic crowd of 'conglomerated mediocrity' (to use Stuart Mill's expression) which purchases everything, and therefore owns everything. The crowd is without ignorance, but also without education. To please it art shouts, gesticulates, lies and exaggerates, or in despair turns away from human beings and paints dramatic scenes of animals and portraits of cattle, like Landseer and Rosa Bonheur.

Ibid.

On Descartes and Newton

A Frenchman arriving in London finds things very different, in natural science as in everything else. He has left the world full, he finds it empty. In Paris they see the universe as composed of vortices of subtle matter, in London they see nothing of the kind. For us it is the pressure of the moon that causes the tides of the sea; for the English it is the sea that gravitates towards the moon, so that when you think that the moon should give us a high tide, these gentlemen think you should have a low one. Unfortunately this cannot be verified, for to check this it would have been necessary to examine the moon and the tides at the first moment of creation.

Furthermore, you will note that the sun, which in France doesn't come into the picture at all, here plays its fair share. For your Cartesians everything is moved by an impulsion you don't really understand, for Mr Newton it is by gravitation, the cause of which is hardly better known. In Paris you see the earth shaped like a melon, in London it is flattened on two sides. For a Cartesian light exists in the air, for a Newtonian it comes from the sun in six and a half minutes. Your chemistry performs all its operations with acids, alkalis and subtle matter; gravitation dominates even English chemistry.

The very essence of things has totally changed. You fail to agree both on the definition of the soul and on that of matter. Descartes affirms that the soul is the same thing as thought, and Locke proves to him fairly satisfactorily the opposite.

Descartes also affirms that volume alone makes matter, Newton adds solidity. There you have some appalling clashes.

Non nostrum inter vos tantas componere lites

This Newton, destroyer of the Cartesian system, died in March last year, 1727. He lived honoured by his compatriots and was buried like a king who had done well by his subjects.

People here have eagerly read and translated into English the *Eulogy of Newton* that M. de Fontenelle delivered in the Académie des Sciences. In England it was expected that the verdict of M. de Fontenelle would be a solemn declaration of the superiority of English natural science. But when it was realized that he compared Descartes with Newton the whole Royal Society in London rose up in arms. Far from agreeing with this judgement they criticized the discourse. Several even (not the most scientific) were shocked by the comparison simply because Descartes was a Frenchman.

It must be admitted that these two great men were very different in their behaviour, their fortune and their philosophy.

Descartes was born with a lively, strong imagination, which made him a remarkable man in his private life as well as in his manner of reasoning. This imagination could not be concealed even in his philosophical writings, where ingenious and brilliant illustrations occur at every moment. Nature had made him almost a poet, and indeed he composed for the Queen of Sweden an entertainment in verse which for the honour of his memory has not been printed.

For a time he tried the career of arms, and having later become the complete philosopher he did not think it unworthy of him to make love. His mistress gave him a daughter named Francine, who died young and whose loss grieved him deeply. Thus he experienced everything pertaining to mankind.

For a long time he believed it necessary to avoid the company of men, and especially his own country, so as to meditate in freedom. He was right; the men of his time did not know enough to enlighten him, and could scarcely do anything but harm him.

He left France because he sought the truth, which was being persecuted there by the wretched philosophy of the School, but he found no more reason in the universities of Holland, to which he retreated. For at the time when in France they condemned the only propositions in his philosophy that were true, he was also persecuted by the self-styled philosophers of Holland, who understood him no better and who, seeing his glory nearer at hand, hated his person the more. He was obliged to leave Utrecht. He was accused of atheism, and this man who had devoted all the penetration of his mind to seeking new proofs of the existence of a God, was suspected of not recognizing any.

So much persecution suggested very great merit and a brilliant reputation, and he had both. Reason did pierce a little into the world through the darkness of the School and the prejudices of popular superstition. At length his name became so well known that they tried to lure him back to France by bribes. He was offered a pension of 1,000 écus, he came on that understanding, paid the fee for a patent which was for sale at that time, did not receive the pension and returned to work in his solitude in North Holland at the time when the great Galileo, aged eighty, was languishing in the prisons of the Inquisition for having demonstrated the movement of the earth. Finally he died in Stockholm – a premature death caused by faulty diet – amid a few hostile scientists and tended by a doctor who hated him.

The career of Sir Isaac Newton was quite different. He lived to be eighty-five, always tranquil, happy and honoured in his own country.

His great good fortune was not only to be born in a free country, but at a time when, scholastic extravagances being banished, reason alone was cultivated and society could only be his pupil and not his enemy.

A remarkable contrast between him and Descartes is that in the course of such a long life he had neither passion nor weakness; he never went near any woman. I have heard that confirmed by the doctor and the surgeon who were with him when he died. One can admire Newton for that, but must not blame Descartes.

In England, public opinion of the two of them is that the first was a dreamer and the other a sage.

Very few people in London read Descartes, whose works, practically speaking, have become out of date. Very few read Newton either, because much knowledge is necessary to understand him. However, everybody talks about them, conceding nothing to the Frenchman and everything to the Englishman. There are people who think that if we are no longer content with the abhorrence of a vacuum, if we know that the air has weight, if we use a telescope, it is all due to Newton. Here he is the Hercules of the fable, to whom the ignorant attributed all the deeds of the other heroes.

In a criticism made in London of the discourse of M. de Fontenelle, people have dared to assert that Descartes was not a great mathematician. People who talk like that can be reproached for beating their own nurse. Descartes covered as much ground from the point where he found mathematics to where he took it as Newton after him. He is the first to have found the way of expressing curves by algebraical equations. His mathematics, now common knowledge thanks to him, was in his time so profound that no professor dared undertake to explain it, and only Schooten in Holland and Fermat in France understood it.

He carried this spirit of mathematics and invention into dioptrics, which became in his hands quite a new art, and if he committed some errors it is because a man who discovers new territories cannot suddenly grasp every detail of them: those who come after him and make these lands fertile do at least owe their discovery to him. I will not deny that all the other works of Descartes are full of errors.

Mathematics was a guide that he himself had to some extent formed, and which would certainly have led him in his physical researches, but he finally abandoned this guide and gave himself up to a fixed system. Thereafter his philosophy was nothing more than an ingenious novel, at the best only plausible to ignoramuses. He was wrong about the nature of the soul, proofs of the existence of God, matter, the laws of dynamics, the nature of light; he accepted innate ideas, invented new elements, created a world and made man to his own specification, and it is said, rightly, that Descartes' man is only Descartes' man and far removed from true man.

He carried his metaphysical errors to the point of maintaining that two and two only make four because God has willed it so. But it is not too much to say that he was admirable even in his errors. He was wrong, but at least methodically and with a logical mind; he destroyed the absurd fancies with which youth had been beguiled for two thousand years, he taught the men of his time to reason and to use his own weapons against himself. He did not pay in good money, but it is no small thing to have denounced the counterfeit.

I don't think we really dare compare in any way his philosophy with that of Newton: the first is a sketch, the second is a masterpiece. But the man who set us on the road to the truth is perhaps as noteworthy as the one who since then has been to the end of the road.

Descartes gave sight to the blind; they saw the shortcomings of antiquity and his own. The path he opened has since become measureless. The little book by Rohaut was for a time a complete manual of physics; today all the collected writings of the Academies of Europe put together don't even make a beginning of a system. As one has gone deeper into this abyss it has revealed its infinity. We are about to see what Newton has quarried out of this chasm.

Voltaire, *Letters on England* (1734)

Jamaican meets Gambian, 1957

'You're Gambian, they tell me. Bathurst?'

He nodded at me and said, 'My friend was telling me of your interest in my greenhouse.'

'I saw you grew charge out there . . .'

'You want to smoke some?'

'Well, I don't mind. I used up all I had on the trip over. . . .'

269

'I'll roll you a stick,' this Billy Whispers said.

I sat on the bed, feeling pleased at the chance of blowing hay once more. For much as I care for alcoholic drinks of many kinds, my greatest enjoyment, ever since when a boy, is in charging with weed. Because without it, however good I feel, I'm never really on the top of my inspiration.

Meanwhile this Billy took out two cigarette-papers, and joined them together by the tongue. He peeled and broke down a piece of the ordinary fag he held between his lips, and then, from a brown-paper pack in a jar above the fireplace (a large pack, I noticed), he sprinkled a generous dose of the weed in the papers and began rolling and licking, easing the two ends of the stick into position with a match.

'But tell me,' I said, 'if it's not enquiring. You didn't grow all that hemp you have from outside in your greenhouse?'

'No, no. Is an experiment I'm making, to grow it myself from seed.'

'Otherwise you buy it?'

He nodded.

'You can get that stuff easy here?'

'It can be got. . . . Most things can be got in London when you know your way around.'

He gave the weed a final tender lick and roll, and handed it me by the thin inhaling end.

'And the Law,' I said. 'What do they have to say about consuming weed?'

'What they say is fifteen- or twenty-pound fine if you're caught. Jail on the second occasion.'

'Man! Why, these Jumbles have no pity!'

At which I lit up, took a deep drag, well down past the throat, holding the smoke in my lungs with little sharp sniffs to stop the valuable gust escaping. When I blew out, after a heavy interval, I said to him, 'Good stuff. And what do they make you pay for a stick here?'

'Retail, in small sticks, half a crown.'

'And wholesale?'

'Wholesale? For that you have to find your own supplier and make your personal arrangement.'

I took one more deep drag.

'You know such a supplier?' I enquired.

'Of course. . . . I know of several. . . .'

'You don't deal in this stuff personal, by any possible chance?'

Here Billy Whispers joined his two hands, wearing on each one a big coloured jewel.

'Mister,' he said, 'I think these are questions that you don't ask on so early an acquaintance.'

Which was true, so I smiled at him and handed him over the weed for his turn to take his drag on it.

He did this, and after some time in silence he blew on the smouldering end of the weed and said to me, 'And what is it, Fortune, I can do for you here?'

'I'm Dorothy's half-half-brother.'

'What say?'

'Arthur, her brother, is my brother too.' And I explained.

'But Dorothy she not know you,' he said to me. 'Never she's spoken to me about you.'

Then I explained some more.

'If that old lady or her sister's worried about Dorothy,' he said at last, 'just tell them to stop worrying because she's happy here with me, and will do just what I tell her.'

'Could I speak with her, perhaps?'

'No, man. You could not.'

At this stage of our interview, the door was opened and into the room came a short little fattish boy, all smiles and gesticulation, of a type that beats my time: that is, the Spade who's always acting Spadish, so as to make the Jumbles think we're more cool crazy than we are, but usually for some darker purpose to deceive them. But why play this game of his with me?

'Hullo, hullo, man,' he cried to me, grasping at both my hands. 'I ain't seen you around before. . . . Shake hands with me, my name is Mr Ronson Lighter.' And he let off his silly sambo laugh.

I said, 'What say?' unsmilingly, and freed my hands. 'What say, Mr Ronson Lighter. Did your own mother give you that peculiar name?'

He giggled like a crazy girl.

'No, no, no, mister, is my London name, on account of my well-known strong desire to own these things.'

And out of each side coat pocket he took a lighter, and sparkled the pair of them underneath my eyes.

Still not smiling, I got up on my feet.

And as I did – smack! Up in my head I got a very powerful kick from that hot weed which I'd been smoking. A kick like you get from superior Congo stuff, that takes your brain and wraps it up and throws it all away, and yet leaves your thoughts inside it sharp and clear: that makes all your legs and arms and body seem like if jet propelled without any tiring effort whatsoever.

But I watched these two, Billy Whispers and this Mr Ronson Lighter, as they talked in their barbarian Gambian language. I didn't understand no word, but sometimes I heard the name of 'Dorothy'.

Colin Macinnes, *City of Spades* (1957)

11

Mobs, Marches, Riots and Affrays

London is a battle-field. The major outbreaks of mass violence in my lifetime (born 1950) (such as the Brixton Riots of 1981, or the anti-Vietnamese War demonstrations in Grosvenor Square in 1968) seem like the most minor skirmishes when compared with some of the engagements of the past. One thinks of the Peasant's Revolt of 1381, when mob rule and anarchy temporarily possessed the City of London, or the even more sinister and frightening Gordon Riots of May 1780. These disturbances were the equivalent of a Kristallnacht *for the small Catholic population of London, most of whom were of European extraction, the indigenous Catholic population having been reduced to negligible numbers by the penal laws, and the Irish immigrations of the nineteenth century remaining in the future. Samuel Johnson, who was aged seventy-one and was still living in Fleet Street when the riots took place, gave a succinct account of them to his friend Mrs Thrale. Dickens dramatized the riots in* Barnaby Rudge. *Although perhaps the ugliest riots of the late eighteenth century, they were by no means the only ones. Indeed, Lord North, the Prime Minister at the time of the American War of Independence, was unable to set out in the streets of London for fear of being attacked by the mob, and lived almost permanently barricaded in his house surrounded by guards.*

Social historians have attempted to explain the conditions which are conducive to mob violence. By paradox, no one has ever written a completely convincing explanation of it, however, for if such an argument convinced completely it would not convince. One reason for mob tension might be urban overcrowding, and certainly, since the expansion of Elizabethan London in the sixteenth century, there have always been, arguably, too many people in too small a space in the metropolis. This does not explain why in some generations –

as poor, lice-infested and criminally-minded as the last – there will be periods of calm, and in others there will be a perpetual underlying violence beneath the surface of life. In one generation, Lord North is in hiding and the King (admittedly because he was a lunatic!) is locked up as a prisoner in his own castle at Windsor, and in the next William IV strolled about London, talking to people in parks with comparatively small danger to his person.

The Burdett Riots, 1810

As a result of these proceedings, Sir Francis* became a popular hero, and public indignation on his behalf ran very high. Some hundreds of people had already assembled outside his house by midday Friday, and these had increased by evening to several thousands; while yet more had gathered outside the Tower, and lined the streets through which he might be expected to pass on his way thither. The seriousness of the situation is reflected in the Lord Mayor's request, made as early as Friday, that Sir Francis should not be brought to the Tower through the City. The same night the crowds in Piccadilly and the adjoining streets stopped all vehicles and compelled the occupants to signify their adherence to the cause of Sir Francis. The Earl of Westmoreland, for delaying to comply with this request, was pelted with mud. In addition to these activities, they broke the windows of a Mr Raikes's house in Berkeley Square, thinking that it belonged to Mr Lethbridge; those of Lord Castlereagh's house in King Street, St James's, of Lord Dartmouth's in Berkeley Square, of Mr Yorke's, Mr Percival's, and Mr Anstruther's; and an attempt on Lord Chatham's in Hill Street was only frustrated by the appearance of a party of Life Guards. The mob demanded that all houses should be brightly lighted as a sign of sympathy, and, in self-defence, the whole West End was a blaze of illumination. Three hundred and fifty Foot Guards were posted to protect the magazine in Hyde Park.

By Saturday twenty-five thousand regular troops and a brigade of artillery were in London, and the Tower Hamlet's Militia had been summoned to hold themselves in readiness. The crowd outside Sir Francis's house

---

* Sir Francis Burdett defended the right of strangers to attend debates in the House of Commons.

stretched from Berkeley Street to beyond Clarges Street, and behaved in the same manner as on the previous day. A troop of Foot Guards were posted on the pavement outside the house with Horse Guards on the opposite side of the street. Troops were also stationed at various points throughout the town, and continued to patrol the streets during the whole week-end. Field guns were placed in St James's Park and Lincoln's Inn, and a howitzer and a six-pounder in Soho Square. The Life Guards were compelled to clear the streets, in the course of which operation several persons were wounded. But the mob, who gave Sir Francis a vociferous reception when he returned from his ride, and when from time to time he appeared at the window, were not seriously discouraged, and Mr Read had to be summoned to read the Riot Act. In the evening Lord Castlereagh's house was again attacked, and Mr Read was compelled to read the Riot Act and the troops to fire several times. The Government showed its determination to prevent any recurrence of disorder on the same scale as in 1780 by bringing up yet more artillery, and the situation was kept tolerably well in hand. The police offices remained open all night.

James Read, *The Bow Street Runners*

Wellington on the eve of the Reform Bill, 1832

His wife and the old order were slipping away together. When he heard that more and more country gentlemen were becoming alarmed at the Reform Bill, he felt no surprise. 'They are right. Their order will be annihilated even sooner than any of them expect.' It was the same when they told him that people were cutting down their establishments in preparation for 'the expected Storm'.

'They are very right. If the Bill passes we shall have it.'

In the ground-floor room Kitty clung to a hand that was no longer iron. Once she ran her fingers up inside his sleeve to feel if by chance he was still wearing an armlet she had given him long ago.

'She found it,' said the Duke to a friend, 'as she would have found it any time these twenty years, had she cared to look for it.' How strange it was, he reflected sadly, that two people could live together for half a lifetime 'and only understand one another at the end'.

The end came on 24 April, two days after King William dissolved

Parliament. The Duke and his sons immediately went down to the country, black edgings were ordered for his writing-paper, Apsley House was shut up and nothing remained but for the small coffin to make its journey to Stratfield Saye for burial in the family vault. Before the hearse was ready 'the expected Storm' broke.

The Lord Mayor of London ordered illuminations on 27 April in honour of the dissolution. From Westminster to Piccadilly there were sparkling pyramids of candles in the fine sash-windows of the wealthy. But not in all. A roistering reform mob marched up Piccadilly, breaking the windows of those who showed by their dark fronts that they regarded the dissolution as a black day for Britain.

Aspley House was in darkness because of the Duchess's passing rather than Parliament's. But the Duke would certainly not have illuminated for reform even if he had been at home. Stones smashed immense quantities of his new plate-glass on the ground floor. When the crowd pulled up the railings on the Piccadilly side the Duke's servant fired two blunderbusses over their heads (though loaded with gunpowder only). At once the crowd, who were out for a lark rather than a riot, turned their attention to fresh windows and pastures new in Grosvenor Square.

> I think my Servant John saved my House [wrote the Duke] or the lives of the Mob – possibly both – by firing as he did. They certainly intended to destroy the House, and did not care one Pin for the poor Duchess being dead in the House . . .

Having consulted his lawyers about compensation from the Hundred in which Apsley House stood, he found there was 'No Redress'. (These words were blazoned on the cover of his legal file, followed by twelve exclamation marks.) Compensation could be paid only if he proved felonious intent to demolish, pull down or destroy. Two days running he trumpeted forth his indignation to Mrs Arbuthnot. 'The people are rotten to the Core.' 'The people are gone Mad.'

Elizabeth Longford, Wellington, Pillar of State (1972)

The Peasants' Revolt

The last hope of real understanding and peace between the classes, if ever there had been any, was now extinguished by a tragic event. The rebels broke into the Tower. Authorities differ as to the exact moment, some place it during and some after the conference at Mile End. But it is unfortunately certain that no resistance was made by the very formidable body of well-armed soldiers, who might have defended such a stronghold for many days even against a picked army. These troops were ordered, or at least permitted, by the King to let in the mob. It appears that part of the agreement with the rebels was that the Tower and the refugees it contained were to be delivered over to their wrath. The dark passages and inmost chambers of that ancient fortress were choked with the throng of ruffians, while the soldiers stood back along the walls to let them pass, and looked on helplessly at the outrages that followed. Murderers broke into strong room and bower; even the King's bed was torn up, lest some one should be lurking in it. The unfortunate Leg, the farmer of the poll-tax, paid with his life-blood for that unprofitable speculation. A learned friar, the friend and adviser of John of Gaunt, was torn to pieces as a substitute for his patron. Though the hunt roared through every chamber, it was in the chapel that the noblest hart lay harboured. Archbishop Sudbury had realized that he was to be sacrificed. He had been engaged, since the King started for Mile End, in preparing the Treasurer and himself for death. He had confessed Hales, and both had taken the Sacrament. He was still performing the service of the Mass, when the mob burst into the chapel, seized him at the altar, and hurried him across the moat to Tower Hill, where a vast multitude of those who had been unable to press into the fortress greeted his appearance with a savage yell. His head was struck off on the spot where so many famous men have since perished with more seemly circumstance. The Treasurer Hales suffered with him, and their two heads, mounted over London Bridge, grinned down on the bands of peasants who were still flocking into the capital from far distant parts.

The Archbishop's death was greeted with shouts of acclamation by a vast concourse of people. Such a scene demonstrates the hopeless failure of the governing classes in Church and State to keep in touch with their subjects. When brought face to face, these were the real relations between them. The mob slew Sudbury, not so much because he was Archbishop, though that did not deter them, as because he was the Chancellor who had misgoverned the country and introduced the poll-tax. The one exercise of his episcopal authority, which counted against him, had been his imprisonment of John Ball. He had exerted his power against that disturber of society only in a half-hearted manner, but it had been better for him that day if he had burned John Wycliffe alive; for Ball had created the spirit of the rebellion, and an insult to the preacher was an insult to the thousands who hung on his lips. Everything we know of Sudbury's life is to his credit as a kind and good man, and in his last hour he showed a fearless dignity, which rivals Becket's determination to be struck down at his post. He won less respect from the Church than his manner of life and death deserved, for he had shown himself cool in defending overgrown ecclesiastical privilege, and had neglected or refused to persecute heretics. If he had lived, the gentle Sudbury would have had the will, though not the strength, to keep the Church off the fatal course of pride and persecution into which she was hurrying.

After these horrors the Tower was no fit place for the royal residence. The Queen-mother had been treated with insolence and vulgarity by the mob that burst into her apartments, but had been suffered to escape by boat. She was rowed up the river to Barnard Castle ward, where she landed and took up her residence at the Garde Robe, in Carter Lane, near St Paul's. Here she was joined by her son on his return from Mile End. The rest of the day was a busy one. The manumissions and pardons were being copied out, and distributed to the rebels with advice to return home as fast as possible. The bulk of the insurgents left London with the charters in their hands, on Friday evening and Saturday morning, but to the horror of the authorities a large body remained. Meanwhile murder went on faster than ever. The apprentices and men of London were engaged in slaughtering the Flemings, who lived in a quarter of their own by the river-side, and were, like most foreigners who had settled down in England for purposes of trade and industry, hateful to the native born. Men from the Kentish villages joined their city friends in the work, and the cries of slayers and slain went on long after sunset, making night hideous. Before morning several hundreds of these unfortunate foreigners had been massacred. As so often happens in popular uprisings, the worse elements rose to the top and took the lead as the revolt continued. The opening of the gaols had not improved the personnel of the crowd. While many an honest peasant was trudging home with his charter of liberty which he had won at the risk of his neck, the vilest of mankind were murdering, burning and robbing, not only in London, but in all parts of the country. But the massacre of the Flemings stands marked out by its peculiar atrocity. There is but one reference to the Rising in Chaucer's 'Canterbury Tales'. In the 'Nun's Priest's' tale he describes the farm servants chasing a fox:

> Certés Jack Straw and his meinie
> Ne maden never shoutés half so shrille
> Whan that they wolden any Fleming kille,
> As thilké day was made upon the fox.

For one victim of the mob we can feel little pity. John Lyons, who had on the Duke's return to power escaped all the forfeitures inflicted by the Good Parliament, at last paid the penalty of his frauds and public robberies. He was dragged from his own house and beheaded. The other great London citizens, who were not notorious for inflicting injuries on the community at large, were spared. One of them, the ex-mayor Brembre, was riding by the King's side on Friday, when his bridle was seized by a brewer called William Trueman, to whom he had done some injury during his period of office three years back. The fellow upbraided him in the King's presence, and no one dared reply. Later on the brewer came to Brembre's house in the city, 'with a captain of the mob, and by the power of the said captain frightened him and much disquieted all his family'. Trueman was finally appeased by a present of 3*l*. 10*s*. The power of the mob was on several similar occasions used by intriguers to settle private disputes.

Night closed down on scenes such as these, and on Saturday morning it was too clear that the authorities had succeeded in appeasing only a part of the rebels. Many thousands were leaving London, but many thousands still remained. Some of these were only waiting to receive their charters of liberty, which had not all been drawn up on Friday. But a large section, especially the men of Kent, declared that they were not yet satisfied. Many of them were wise enough to perceive that there would be no security for what had been gained, unless the King and government were kept under the pressure which had extorted the concessions. It is hard to say what form of political settlement they contemplated. They had probably many different views on the question, all more or less confused. The absurd accusations of intending to kill the King and restore the Heptarchy were sufficiently refuted by the action of the mob at Smithfield, where their patient loyalty to Richard was even pathetic. It is possible that the leader who was now at the head of the rebels remaining in London, had some design of securing for himself a permanent share in the government of the

279

country, probably by directing the counsels of the King. But even Wat Tyler's designs met with only half support from his followers, if we may judge from the acquiescent manner in which they accepted his death at the hands of Walworth. There were some social grievances which they wished to redress. The men of Kent, it is said, wanted the game laws abolished. No doubt, too, Froissart is right in saying that many of those who stayed on in London only stayed to loot. The last hours of the occupation were worse than the first. The rule professed by the destroyers of the Savoy had long given way to the desire for pillage and the instinct of murder.

G. M. Trevelyan, England in the Age of Wycliffe (1899)

The Gordon Riots, 1780

While Johnson was thus engaged in preparing a delightful literary entertainment for the world, the tranquillity of the metropolis of Great-Britain was unexpectedly disturbed, by the most horrid series of outrage that ever disgraced a civilized country. A relaxation of some of the severe penal provisions against our fellow-subjects of the Catholick communion had been granted by the legislature, with an opposition so inconsiderable that the genuine mildness of Christianity, united with liberal policy, seemed to have become general in this island. But a dark and malignant spirit of persecution soon shewed itself, in an unworthy petition for the repeal of the wise and humane statute. That petition was brought forward by a mob, with the evident purpose of intimidation, and was justly rejected. But the attempt was accompanied and followed by such daring violence as is unexampled in history. Of this extraordinary tumult, Dr Johnson has given the following concise, lively, and just account in his *Letters to Mrs Thrale*:

> On Friday, the good Protestants met in Saint George's-Fields, at the summons of Lord George Gordon, and marching to Westminster, insulted the Lords and Commons, who all bore it with great tameness. At night the outrages began by the demolition of the mass-house by Lincoln's-Inn.
>
> An exact journal of a week's defiance of government I cannot give you. On Monday, Mr Strahan, who had been insulted, spoke to Lord Mansfield, who had I think been insulted too, of the licentiousness of

the populace; and his Lordship treated it as a very slight irregularity. On Tuesday night they pulled down Fielding's house, and burnt his goods in the street. They had gutted on Monday Sir George Savile's house, but the building was saved. On Tuesday evening, leaving Fielding's ruins, they went to Newgate to demand their companions who had been seized demolishing the chapel. The keeper could not release them but by the Mayor's permission, which he went to ask; at his return he found all the prisoners released, and Newgate in a blaze. They then went to Bloomsbury, and fastened upon Lord Mansfield's house, which they pulled down; and as for his goods, they totally burnt them. They have since gone to Caen-wood, but a guard was there before them. They plundered some Papists, I think, and burnt a mass-house in Moorfields the same night.

On Wednesday I walked with Dr Scot to look at Newgate, and found it in ruins, with the fire yet glowing. As I went by, the Protestants were plundering the Sessions-house at the Old-Bailey. There were not, I believe, a hundred; but they did their work at leisure, in full security, without sentinels, without trepidation, as men lawfully employed, in full day. Such is the cowardice of a commercial place. On Wednesday they broke open the Fleet, and the King's-Bench, and the Marshalsea, and Wood-street Compter, and Clerkenwell Bridewell, and released all the prisoners.

At night they set fire to the Fleet, and to the King's Bench, and I know not how many other places; and one might see the glare of conflagration fill the sky from many parts. The sight was dreadful. Some people were threatened: Mr Strahan advised me to take care of myself. Such a time of terrour you have been happy in not seeing.

The King said in Council, 'That the magistrates had not done their duty, but that he would do his own'; and a proclamation was published, directing us to keep our servants within doors, as the peace was now to be preserved by force. The soldiers were sent out to different parts, and the town is now [*June* 9] at quiet.

The soldiers are stationed so as to be every where within call: there is no longer any body of rioters, and the individuals are hunted to their holes, and led to prison; Lord George was last night sent to the Tower. Mr John Wilkes was this day in my neighbourhood, to seize the publisher of a seditious paper.

Several chapels have been destroyed, and several inoffensive Papists have been plundered; but the high sport was to burn the gaols.

This was a good rabble trick. The debtors and the criminals were all set at liberty; but of the criminals, as has always happened, many are already retaken; and two pirates have surrendered themselves, and it is expected that they will be pardoned.

Government now acts again with its proper force; and we are all under the protection of the King and the law. I thought that it would be agreeable to you and my master to have my testimony to the publick security; and that you would sleep more quietly when I told you that you are safe.

There has, indeed, been an universal panick, from which the King was the first that recovered. Without the concurrence of his ministers, or the assistance of the civil magistrate, he put the soldiers in motion, and saved the town from calamities, such as a rabble's government must naturally produce.

The publick has escaped a very heavy calamity. The rioters attempted the Bank on Wednesday night, but in no great number; and like other thieves, with no great resolution. Jack Wilkes headed the party that drove them away. It is agreed, that if they had seized the Bank on Tuesday, at the height of the panick, when no resistance had been prepared, they might have carried irrecoverably away whatever they had found. Jack, who was always zealous for order and decency, declares that if he be trusted with power, he will not leave a rioter alive. There is, however, now no longer any need of heroism or bloodshed; no blue ribband is any longer worn.

Such was the end of this miserable sedition, from which London was delivered by the magnanimity of the Sovereign himself. Whatever some may maintain, I am satisfied that there was no combination or plan, either domestick or foreign; but that the mischief spread by a gradual contagion of frenzy, augmented by the quantities of fermented liquors, of which the deluded populace possessed themselves in the course of their depredations.

James Boswell, *Life of Johnson* (1791)

The Gordon Riots, 1780

The vintner's house, with half-a-dozen others near at hand, was one great, glowing blaze. All night, no one had essayed to quench the flames, or stop their progress; but now a body of soldiers were actively engaged in pulling down two old wooden houses, which were every moment in danger of taking fire, and which could scarcely fail, if they were left to burn, to extend the conflagration immensely. The tumbling down of nodding walls and heavy blocks of wood, the hooting and the execrations of the crowd, the distant firing of other military detachments, the distracted looks and cries of those whose habitations were in danger, the hurrying to and fro of frightened people with their goods; the reflections in every quarter of the sky of deep, red, soaring flames, as though the last day had come and the whole universe were burning; the dust, and smoke, and drift of fiery particles, scorching and kindling all it fell upon: the hot unwholesome vapour, the blight on everything; the stars, and moon, and very sky, obliterated: – made up such a sum of dreariness and ruin, that it seemed as if the face of Heaven were blotted out, and night, in its rest and quiet, and softened light, never could look upon the earth again.

But there was a worse spectacle than this – worse by far than fire and smoke, or even the rabble's unappeasable and maniac rage. The gutters of the street, and every crack and fissure in the stones, ran with scorching spirit, which being dammed up by busy hands, overflowed the road and pavement, and formed a great pool, into which the people dropped down dead by dozens. They lay in heaps all round this fearful pond, husbands and wives, fathers and sons, mothers and daughters, women with children in their arms and babies at their breasts, and drank until they died. While some stooped with their lips to the brink and never raised their heads again, others sprang up from their fiery draught, and danced, half in a mad triumph, and half in the agony of suffocation, until they fell, and steeped their corpses in the liquor that had killed them. Nor was even this the worst or most appalling kind of death that happened on this fatal night. From the burning cellars, where they drank out of hats, pails, buckets, tubs, and shoes, some men were drawn alive, but all alight from head to foot; who, in their unendurable anguish and suffering, making for anything that had the look of water, rolled, hissing, in this hideous lake, and splashed up liquid fire which lapped in all it met with as it ran along the surface, and neither spared the living nor the dead. On this last night of the great riots – for the last night it was – the wretched victims of a senseless outcry became themselves the dust and ashes of the flames they had kindled, and strewed the public streets of London.

Charles Dickens, Barnaby Rudge (1841)

Coldbath Fields, 1833

In May 1833 the National Political Union organized a public meeting at Coldbath Fields – a piece of ground very close to the site on which now stands Mount Pleasant Sorting Office. Deputations from the Union's branches in Camberwell, Whitechapel, Hoxton and other 'low districts' of London were to march through the streets to the meeting-ground, and so that all the world should know of their high aims they were to carry banners proclaiming 'HOLY ALLIANCE OF THE WORKING CLASSES' – 'LIBERTY OR DEATH' – and other appropriate sentiments.

At one side of Coldbath Fields stood a prison. Possibly that fact conjured up ideas, in the minds of the Government, of awful developments not dissimilar to the storming of the Bastille in the French Revolution. Or perhaps the mere threat of such a meeting of 'revolutionaries and anarchists' was enough to call for stern measures. In any case, the announcement of the meeting was taken very seriously and Lord Melbourne, as Home Secretary, decided that it must be prohibited. He issued posters to that effect. By some oversight those posters, although headed with the royal arms, did not bear any signature, ending only with the words 'On the Authority of the Secretary of State' . . . a fact which caused their legality to be later called in question.

The proclamation, however, was quite definite and clear in what it said. . . .

'Whereas a public meeting for such a purpose is dangerous to the public peace and illegal, all classes of His Majesty's subjects are hereby warned not to attend such meeting, nor to take any part in the proceedings thereof. And notice is hereby given that the Civil Authorities have strict orders to maintain and secure the public peace and to apprehend any persons offending therein, that they may be dealt with according to the Law.'

It was to be pointed out afterwards that the chief effect of that proclamation was to give wide publicity to 'a silly, ridiculous meeting which was not worth the attention of the magistrates'. It was also said afterwards that if no proclamation had been issued the meeting would only have been attended by those few members of the National Political Union who were willing to walk in procession for several miles – and that they could easily have been turned off by a mere handful of police. But as it was, a great many sightseers, apart from the much smaller number of 'revolutionaries', went to Coldbath Fields on the afternoon of May 12th, 1833, and by three o'clock the crowd gathered there was estimated to number between 4,000 and 6,000 people.

The instructions issued by the Home Secretary to the Commissioners of Police were that as soon as 'revolutionary' speeches had been delivered the meeting was to be broken up and dispersed, banners being seized and the ringleaders arrested.

To Lieut.-Col. Charles Rowan, who had been second-in-command of the 52nd Regiment at Waterloo and was now the elder of the two Commissioners of Police, that suggested a military operation and – except for the unusual *terrain* – the sort of thing to which he was well accustomed. He made his plans accordingly.

The 'enemy' was first to be surrounded and then to be attacked. There must therefore be containing troops, a striking force and a reserve contingent, all skilfully placed in the right strategic positions. From a well-sited headquarters he himself must be able to watch the progress of the operation – much as Wellington had watched the field of Waterloo from a hilltop. With his men in position, he must have scouts to bring him early news of enemy action . . . the delivery of revolutionary speeches . . . and aides-de-camp to take his orders to junior commanders. And finally, just in case of unanticipated difficulties – for had he not appreciated the value of Blücher's army at Waterloo? – there must be a fresh army which could march in and turn the scale at any critical moment.

When his plans were thus made, Colonel Rowan collected his forces.

His striking force consisted of 78 men from A Division under the command of Mr Superintendent John May, who until four years before had been a sergeant-major in the Grenadier Guards. His reserve contingent numbered 200 men, all from C Division under Mr Superintendent Thomas Baker, a former warrant-officer in the Royal Artillery. The containing troops came from various other divisions with their superintendents. The scouts were picked men, in plain clothes. For his last reserve – though of course Colonel Rowan did not believe it would be required, since his force of police upon the spot numbered nearly 800 men – it had been arranged for His Majesty's Foot Guards to be in waiting at their barracks, two of their officers being at the Colonel's headquarters in a livery stable and ready to send the necessary orders.

Colonel Rowan knew very well that even troops who were kept under discipline by the threat of the lash, as had been the case in Wellington's armies, could only be relied upon to keep their courage in the face of the enemy when they stood closely shoulder to shoulder, as in the famous hollow squares. He knew of no other military formation, so that was how his striking force was to advance, in solid ranks stretched across the road.

But as it was recognized that some of the crowd at Coldbath Fields might be innocent people without revolutionary intentions and brought there by curiosity rather than anarchy, Mr May had orders that his men were to keep on the roadway and leave the pavements open; so that anyone who wished to keep out of trouble could get away, while those that thought of showing fight could be properly dealt with.

After all, closely as this resembled a battle, the 'enemy' were subjects of His Majesty, even if not very loyal ones, and one did not wish to harm innocent people. Colonel Rowan therefore himself addressed the men of the striking force, telling them to be 'firm but temperate – to strike nobody and hurt nobody unless they were resisted'.

At a conference between Lord Melbourne and the Commissioners it had been decided that the Riot Act need not be read as long as the affair remained a police operation – although of course that must be done if the troops were called in and fire was to be opened on the crowd. Colonel Rowan, on taking up his post as Commissioner, had been sworn as a magistrate, so the final decision on that point – and indeed the whole conduct of the operation – could safely be left to him.

When the deputations had arrived with their banners, a cart was used as a platform for the meeting – though after a minute the driver took fright at the sight of so many policemen and drove off, leaving the speakers to do the best they could on ground level.

The leading speaker – unconsciously imitating Colonel Rowan – made an appeal to the crowd to be peaceful . . . but he did it in a way which implied that they had been given great provocation, by the presence of the police, to be violent, and peaceful behaviour was rather more than anyone could reasonably expect of them. The Government, he declared, had sent its own army to threaten the men of the working classes of London, so that their feelings might be excited and they might be brought to act offensively and thus give a pretext for their being 'led to the slaughter'.

At that, according to the newspapers, 'a most fearful shout burst from the lips of the crowd and showed that the people had been roused almost to a pitch of madness by the revolutionary doctrine which had been inculcated in them'.

Other speakers followed, one of them making a somewhat piteous appeal to the people to support his wife and children if he should 'fall a martyr to the cause'. He was answered by loud cheers.

By that time, the plain-clothes policemen who had mixed with the crowd had slipped away to report to Headquarters that 'most revolutionary speeches' were being delivered and that violence against the police was being threatened.

Colonel Rowan accordingly issued orders for his striking force to advance.

Grasping their truncheons, and with their gallant superintendent leading them, the 78 men of A Division began their attack.

The crowd 'hissed, groaned and hooted', but of course that was only the kind of reception to which the new police were well accustomed. Disregarding it, they advanced 'very slowly', in order that innocent people should be warned and have time to escape. With the same good intention, they halted two or three yards from the edge of the crowd. That was being 'firm but temperate' and giving every opportunity for the mob to disperse in the face of so determined a threat.

But both the situation as a whole and the temper of the constables changed completely when stones were thrown at them as they stood in close ranks across the street.

Hissings and groans and hooting could be ignored. Stone-throwing was a different matter altogether. From that moment, the police got out of hand. They went forward again, 'some of them with their staves raised above their heads, and rushed upon the people, whom they knocked down one by one as they came within their reach'.

In most cases, the rule that the pavement was to be left as 'a safe area' was still followed, but there was little mercy for people on the roadway. Men, women and children – the old and the young alike – were hit indiscriminately by the truncheons of the police.

One reliable witness, who was there only as a spectator and not as a revolutionary, said: 'I was knocked down by a blow on the temple, and while I was down I was beaten without mercy by several policemen for about five minutes, until their attention was called to a man and woman whom they then attacked and knocked down. . . . I saw at one time upwards of 50 persons wounded and bleeding.'

The reporter of the *Morning Advertiser* 'saw the police attack the people indiscriminately in a most ferocious manner. . . . The attack by the police was most brutal.'

And the editor of an evening paper called the *True Sun* 'saw several instances of persons prostrate on the ground being beaten with great violence'.

Belton Cobb, Murdered on Duty (1961)

Wilkes and Liberty, 1770

Wilkes was able to keep his people fairly quiet as he and Proctor sat together on the hustings. (The third candidate, George Cooke, was ill.) At least the rivals could from time to time hear themselves speak and, pointing to his excited supporters, Wilkes coolly observed, 'I wonder, sir, if there are more knaves or fools down there.'

Proctor said, 'I will tell them what you say, and they will put an end to you.'

'It is yourself,' Wilkes replied, 'who would be put an end to: for I would tell them it is a falsehood and they would destroy you in the twinkling of an eye.'

The count was postponed until next morning, but it was obvious who had won; and the mob streamed back to town in delirious excitement, stopping all coaches to scrawl 45 on their sides, bidding the occupants huzza for *Wilkes and Liberty*. Lady Mary Coke drove safely through Piccadilly by ordering her coachman to shout whatever they desired; but the Duchess of Bedford was pelted with dirt, and Horace Walpole had a window shattered because his passenger, a foreigner unaccustomed to freedom of expression, was not alert to pull it down quickly.

They smashed the glass of Mansion House and hurled two large flints into Lord Bute's bedroom. The Duke of Northumberland saved his windows only by the distasteful expedient of supplying men with beer and drinking to *Wilkes and Liberty*. Some defiant Scots, refusing to light up, had all their windows broken and spent the next two nights in total darkness. The Duchess of Hamilton stood a siege while the mob tore up paving-stones to batter at her gate.

Lord Weymouth, Under-Secretary of State, sent for more constables, but these were all at Brentford. The City-trained bands were called out by the Lady Mayoress (His Lordship being out of town), but were too few, too late and too Wilkite. Regular troops were marched through the streets, but the drummers drummed for *Wilkes and Liberty*. The Lord Chancellor departed to Bath, and the Prime Minister to Newmarket. The King, however, showed more sense of duty, informing the Secretary at War, 'I shall not stir from home, so you may send to me if anything arises that requires my immediate attention.'

Next day it was announced that Wilkes headed the poll with 1,292 votes. (Cooke had 827, Proctor 807.) That night Lady Mary Coke found London, 'a fine sight: every house was lighted up as I do not remember to have seen but on the greatest occasion'. Even Princess Amelia and the Duke of Cumberland, the King's aunt and his brother, had to illuminate their houses. The lanes and back streets were ablaze with lights; after two in the morning exhausted householders were roused and made to relight candles which had gone out. Benjamin Franklin, with a transatlantic passion for meaningless statistics, estimated that two nights had cost London £50,000 in candles alone, to say nothing of broken windows. Glaziers were believed to be ardent Wilkites.

Lady Mary Coke met with a woman in Piccadilly 'that was rather uncivil. She was crying out, "*Wilkes and Liberty*" and my servants making no answer, she gave such a blow to my chair that she very near overset it, and then said, "Why do you not say who you was for?" ' But Lady Mary fared better than the Austrian Ambassador, the most stately and ceremonious of men, 'So stiff and upright that you would think all his mistress's diamonds were on his head and that he was afraid of them dropping off.' This portentous diplomat was hauled from his coach and positively up-ended, so that 45 might be more conveniently chalked on the soles of his shoes. When next day he made formal complaint of this unparalleled outrage, the Ministers found it as difficult to keep straight faces as to give him redress.

Charles Chevenix Trench, *Portrait of a Patriot* (1962)

The Camden Town Riots, 1846

The Irish started the Camden Town battle; an injured policeman's credible evidence given at the Marylebone magistrates' court next day proves it; but why they started it, why their leaders – John Duggan and Joseph Glory – were bold enough to fight this policeman at the building-site gates, how much provocation they had had from the English before that afternoon, or whether they intended to force their way in to ask the contractor's ganger for work can never be known because the Marylebone magistrate, having decided to commit them for trial by jury, would not allow any extenuation pleas to be made in his court. They were all charged with starting a riot with felonious intent.

John Cooper said, 'How can they make it a felony? I have not stole anything; the fact is, your worship, the English have been abusing us for a long time past and have continually called us Irish ——. They have used other bad language which I can't recollect.'

No one knows how he wanted to go on because the magistrate cut him short and told him and others, who had spoken earlier, that 'when before the jury at the Old Bailey you can make whatever defence you think proper'. Long before the Old Bailey trial the police, in their usual way, had persuaded all but one of the twenty accused to plead guilty. It saves the police time and bother. No detailed evidence was printed at that time of not-guilty pleas, and I cannot find a manuscript record.

Anyone passing along that half-mile of the old Hampstead Road which is now called Chalk Farm Road can see the scene of the riot. It is a gloomy place to this day and frightening to walk on alone. If you keep to the left all the way from the canal you are overshadowed by a thick and sombre wall which was built before the Round House to protect the railway company's property. It seems to me higher and blacker than the wall of Manchester's gaol and, whichever way the sun is shining, it makes the pavement dark and damp. Few people choose to walk below it; you cross instinctively to the bright side of the road which is lined with small houses whose windows open to the south. These too were built by the railway company, for their skilled workmen – engine drivers, superior linesmen and such. The black brick wall soon blocked their view of Primrose Hill beyond the railway.

There are two wide gaps in the wall. One, near the canal, led to warehouses and stables and still has heavy gates, now seldom closed. The other was, in 1846, the entrance to the Round House building site and could be closed by a bar let down by the policeman on guard.

On Monday, 9 August, at about two o'clock in the afternoon Railway Constable No. 175 saw a large assembly of Irish navvies across the road by the houses. There were three or four others beside him, a little way off, near the wall. 'Inside the gate' were hundreds of English engaged on bricklaying and carrying, and a long way off towards the station hundreds of Irish at work. (The contractors, Messrs Bransom and Gwyther, employed equal numbers of each nationality.) Constable Carter was aware of the danger because small controllable affrays had happened now and then for months. When Thomas Duggan, one of the three or four, came up to him and asked to go through the gateway, Carter said he had orders not to admit anyone into the ground except those who were working on it. Duggan went back a little way, and afterwards again attempted to come in, at the same time beckoning to 'some of his companions to do so too'. Joseph Glory, the boldest of them, tried to force his way in alone. The constable, seizing hold of him, was immediately knocked down and kicked on the head and body by a dozen of Glory's friends. He cried out for help. A few English labourers, at work inside the gate, ran to see what was the matter. They were felled to the ground by the Irish who had by then in large numbers crossed the road. They were beaten with shovels and pickstaffs. But Carter managed to get on his feet, took hold of Glory again and dragged him away, upon which John Cumming and four others came up with brickbats threatening to knock his brains out if he did not let Glory go. No help from other policemen came and Carter, surrounded by a hostile crowd, in fear of his life, let Glory go. He was badly injured, but went back on duty at the gate. He remembered Glory's face and name.

By then the fighting between the English inside and the Irish who had broken in while he lay on the ground had become impossible to control. Carter went off to summon forces from his section at Holmes Road, Kentish Town, but by the time they reached the Round House the Irish who had been working near the station had come up to attack the English from the rear. The English were now surrounded. They defended themselves and were assaulted not only with the usual weapons – navvies' tools – but with bricks, of which there were stacks on the site, and, worse, with brickbats: portions of bricks, which were handier to throw. The English fought bravely but were outnumbered.

Mary Randall, hearing clamour through her open window across the road, looked out and saw men lying in their blood. She heard screams and people shouting 'Murder!', and ran downstairs and over to the Round House, afraid that something might have happened to her husband who was working there; could not find him but saw another Englishman 'lying upon the ground, while five other men were kicking him most brutally crying with an oath, "Kill the —— Protestant." ' She knew the man. He was Charles Keen who had merely gone, like many other local people, to see what the disturbance was. Ellis, her husband's foreman, lay dead nearby, she thought. Next day's newspapers said he was dead. He and one other who was thought to be dead and several of the seriously injured Englishmen were carried one by one on litters to the North London Hospital in Gower Street, a mile and a bit away. Meanwhile the battle spread all over the Camden Town railway land.

After fighting both English and Irish for an hour, the Kentish Town section of police, many of whom were wounded, withdrew and sent an express – a man on a horse – to the headquarters in Albany Street from which a larger force of constables, with inspectors, came in vans at the gallop and others on foot at quick march. The streets were blocked by spectators. Oval Road, on one side of which Regent's Park Terrace was half-built, and the entrance to Camden Town station at the end of it were completely blocked. The approach to the Round House was crowded. The railway ground was wide and open. Groups of men scattered before the police and joined again to fight far off. A thousand police could not have contained them. The headquarters force acknowledged their defeat and sent an express to their Somers Town section. The express rode back to tell the superintendent that the whole of the Somers Town force had gone to the funeral of a comrade who had died two days before. He was sent off at once to fetch them from the funeral and the man was buried without a guard of honour, with only a few friends and relatives at his graveside. But even this large reinforcement, the whole of the Somers Town force, was ineffectual. The police were utterly defeated. The battle ended only when everybody was exhausted. And as so often happens in such confusion arrests were made haphazardly. During a riot police have to grab the nearest offenders. No Englishmen were arrested.

Twenty Irishmen were carried to Albany Street police station that night, but 'so desperately did they fight that it took seven constables to carry one of them, who, it was stated, had struck an antagonist on the head with a pick-axe, to the Albany Street station house'.

Next day, the main entrance to the magistrates' court in Paradise Street, St Marylebone, where the case was to be heard, was surrounded by Irish navvies. Police had to drive them back to make way for the prisoners and witnesses. The court itself was crowded with reporters, spectators, and amateur ushers who had been summoned to help Mr Franklin, the court usher, who foresaw trouble. There was room at the bar for only five of the twenty accused. The others stood around it with constables to guard them.

The prosecution hurriedly dropped their first charge when Ellis, the foreman supposed to be dead, appeared as a witness to his own murder. His face was shockingly damaged but his voice showed volubly that he was alive. The other murder charge was dropped when news came from the hospital that its subject was recovering from his wounds. Four of his ribs were broken.

The newspapers did not mention even a black eye on any of the prisoners, but all the male witnesses, except a surgeon who had cared for some of the wounded on both sides of the fight, had visible cuts and bruises. Railway Constable Carter, the first of them, was 'much cut and bruised about the face'. Charles Keen had difficulty in standing up to give evidence; 'he was shockingly bruised and his eyes were much swollen'.

The Times said that 'from some cause at present unexplained an ill-feeling had been generated among the navvies', but neither Mr Rawlinson, the magistrate, nor any newspaper sought out the cause. Two of the accused were discharged because Mr Rawlinson did not believe they had been properly identified. The others were locked up, after being offered bail at the impossible sum of £50, the equivalent nowadays of nearly £1,000.

The witnesses who had been booed and jostled on their way in now found the way out blocked by a greater crowd of Irishmen who stoned them and set about them with their fists. The police drew their truncheons, cleared Paradise Street and hustled two more Irishmen into the court where one was ordered to find bail and the other fined ten shillings.

No police force in Great Britain had been able to defeat a mass of navvies united by anger, and it was only by a trick that the Metropolitan force stopped the Irish from rescuing the eighteen prisoners after the second hearing.

David Thomson, *In Camden Town* (1983)

The Angered Spirit

I took Mary to Notting Hill Gate so she could get a bus home to Hammersmith and as we walked up the posh residential section of Portobello Road we saw hundreds of people still heading down the hill, most of them drunken white continental youths presumably hoping to take part in any fighting still available. One group ran after a pair of constables until they saw a whole mob of police emerge from a nearby mews.

To reassure Mary I would not get into any trouble I told her of my instinct for avoiding really bad violence even though I had been beaten up by the police here and abroad several times merely for accidentally wandering into their path. But as I strolled home, keeping to the more salubrious side of Ladbroke Grove with its big houses and crowded flowery gardens, I heard pounding boots behind me; a fresh detachment of riot police had been released from a bus parked in Arundel Gardens and was running down into Ladbroke Grove towards the intersection at Elgin Crescent where the buses turn. The remains of a parade, two floats with torn coverings and ripped bunting, had stalled and a bus was stuck behind them. A few West Indians were standing around the floats and explaining what was happening but when they saw the column of visored men pouring down the hill several of them simply broke and ran and others got hastily back into the trucks. I recognized one of the people still on the float, there with his lovely buxom wife Alice who had been very kind to me during one of my bad depressions. The man I'd always called the Black Captain was looking vaguely around as if wondering if he should try to get away. His wife had nicknamed him the Captain because he had been a sailor when they married. The Black Captain was in fact so small he was often mistaken for a child, though he was at least fifty-five. I think I understood the danger more clearly than he did and found that I too was running towards the floats, with the idea of asking them back to Colville Terrace, a few minutes away, but the police reached the flatbed trucks first and struck them with massive force, instantly surrounding them. I saw them drag a driver from his cab, saw the Captain put his arm round his wife and try to push through the circle of police but I think this action spurred them to further terror, for it was not the first time I had observed police become murderous upon realizing a black man had a white woman friend. By no means a brave person, I am proud of whatever instinct made me force my way through the heavy serge uniforms shouting 'Press' at the top of my lungs and waving my expired NUJ card. Whether the press card or my authoritative middle-class tone, to which the police are conditioned to respond, worked I don't know but I managed to gain the float at the moment a mob of visored men hauled themselves up over the edge and fell upon my friend to Alice's outraged screams. Pulling myself onto the truck I cried: 'Stop that. You men! I say, stop that at once!'

They heard me. They paused. They looked from me to their inspector. 'What's going on, chaps?' He had seen my press card. 'Was the lady being attacked?'

'This gentleman is Sir Mombazhi Faysha, the Bardonese Ambassador,' I said, 'and the lady happens to be his wife.'

The inspector directed a look of fury at his brightly polished shoes. 'I'm very sorry, sir. You understand my men are under considerable pressure. Fall back, chaps, while we sort this out.' And he offered the Black Captain a reluctant salute. I helped Mombazhi Faysha and Alice down. Everyone else had drifted off and the floats were empty. They appeared to have released the driver of the float but now the bus driver began to blow his horn and half his passengers were in the street shouting angrily at the police, in no doubt about the cause of the obstruction. Mombazhi was holding his cut head. 'You bastards!' Alice was still uncontrollably angry. 'You bastards. You terrible bastards. My husband defended this country in the War. He saved people in the Blitz. You are wicked, horrible men!'

'It was an honest mistake, madam.' The inspector barely disguised his hatred for her. She looked at them all, trying to read the numbers deliberately hidden under capes.

'You cowards!' said Alice.

'They never change.' One of the women from the bus sniffed with hearty contempt. 'I'll sing you a song and it won't take long. All coppers are bastards.'

Michael Moorcock, Mother London (1988)

The Battle of Cable Street, 1936

In October 1936 when Mosley returned from the holiday at Sorrento there was planned for his re-appearance in the East End the biggest demonstration yet: a march would start by the Royal Mint near the Tower of London and would proceed through Shoreditch, Limehouse, Bow and Bethnal Green: in each district there would be a halt and a speech by Mosley. This was an occasion such as that of the meeting at Olympia two years earlier when the opposition also decided to make their biggest demonstration yet: as before, the technique would be to try to discredit British Union by making out that they were simply trouble-makers and thugs.

The march had been well-publicized: both fascists and anti-fascists rallied their forces. The anti-fascists (this was shortly after the outbreak of the Spanish Civil War) coined for their slogan that of the defenders of Madrid – 'They Shall Not Pass'. On the day itself, October 4th, bus-loads of communist and left-wing militants arrived in the area from outside: the local leader was Jack Spot; he had armed himself (so he told a newspaper reporter) with a 'type of cosh shaped like the leg of a sofa but filled with lead at the end which had been made for him by a cabinet-maker in Aldgate'. Before Mosley's arrival there was chanting and stone-throwing by the anti-fascists; the fascists were in orderly ranks; there were 6,000 police to keep the protagonists apart. When Mosley arrived – with a motor-cycle escort and standing up in the open Bentley doing the fascist salute in his new uniform (Jack Spot called this 'the rummiest sight I've ever seen in the East End') – he walked up and down the columns of blackshirts inspecting them while the crowd, beyond the lines of police, tried to charge, were pushed back, but here and there broke through. There were some arrests. The Police Commissioner Sir Philip Game told Mosley not to start his march before the police had set about clearing the streets across which barricades had been erected. The largest barricade had been built across Cable Street, on the route of the intended march going east from the Mint towards Limehouse. A lorry had been used to construct a formidable defence work.

Sir Philip Game saw the whole occasion as primarily one concerning the police: he seemed determined to show that the streets would be controlled by his men and not by rival gangs. The police tried to push their way through Cable Street; they failed; they charged the barricade and captured it only after a battle with the defenders in which stones, bricks, truncheons and iron bars were used. The defenders, however, withdrew to further barricades, scattering broken glass in their wake to discourage the police on horses. After two hours of this sort of fighting during which 83 anti-fascists were arrested and there were over 100 injuries including those to police – and during which time the fascists remained out of the action lined up by the Royal Mint – Sir Philip Game telephoned to the Home Secretary, Sir John Simon, who was in the country for the weekend, and asked for his permission to give orders for the march to be called off. Sir John Simon agreed. Sir Philip Game came to Mosley and said, 'As you can see for yourself, if you fellows go ahead there will be a shambles.' Oswald Mosley asked (this was according to newspaper reports), 'Is that an order?' Sir Philip Game said, 'Yes.' Then Mosley gave orders for his men to turn and to march the other way – back down Great Tower Street and Queen Victoria Street towards the Embankment. Newspapers reported that amongst his ranks there were 'cries of disappointment'. Before Mosley dismissed his men near Charing Cross Bridge he made a short speech:

> The Government surrenders to Red violence and Jewish corruption. We never surrender. We shall triumph over the parties of corruption because our faith is greater than their faith, our will is stronger than their will, and within us is the flame that shall light this country and shall later light this world.

The London District Committee of the Communist Party announced: 'This is the most humiliating defeat ever suffered by any figure in English politics.'

Nicholas Mosley, Beyond the Pale (1983)

The Chartist Uprising, 10 April 1848

At last the 10th dawned upon the waiting world. Prodigious preparations had been made by the authorities. Four thousand policemen guarded the bridges, Palace Yard, and Trafalgar Square; 1,500 Chelsea pensioners had been fetched out from their retirement and entrusted with the defence of Battersea and Vauxhall. Eight thousand soldiers were distributed over various strategic points along the Embankment between the Tower and Millbank. Twelve guns were in readiness at the Royal Mews. Three steamboats had been procured in order to move soldiers about from point to point should occasion arise for their services. The clerks at the General Post Office had been equipped with rifles. And, finally, over one hundred and fifty thousand special constables had been sworn in to protect property behind the firing line. Among these was Louis Napoleon, who paced a beat in the West End in the company of the cook of the Athenaeum Club, meditating the while, one likes to imagine, on the theory and practice of *coups d'état*. It is certainly one of the minor humours of history that while the last King of the French was painfully adapting himself to life in a London suburb, the future (and also the last) Emperor of the French, with a white band on his arm and a stave in his pocket, was acting as an amateur London policeman. . . . The papers published bulletins from hour to hour, by staffs of correspondents distributed all over London. At eight o'clock the Convention met, principally in order to hear O'Connor deny that he had ever intended not to be present, and to read aloud anonymous messages he had received from friends, to the effect that his life would be certainly ended by a bullet, should he insist on marching. At ten o'clock a car drawn by six horses arrived, decorated with flags and mottoes, and the delegates mounted and were driven to Kennington Common, *via* Holborn, where the Petition was fetched out of the offices of the N.C.A. and loaded into another car, and Blackfriars Bridge. At eleven o'clock they arrived, almost at the same time as a small procession of trade unionists. Within the next hour a number of other processions from various parts of London had congregated. What was the total number of Chartists present? According to the *Evening Sun*, 'at least 150,000'; according to the next day's *Times*, about 20,000, only about half of whom were Chartists. According to *The Northern Star*, 250,000. There is no reason to doubt the correctness of the official estimate of '15,000 to 20,000'. Before the speeches began a police officer approached the car and said that Mr Richard Mayne, one of the Commissioners of Police, wished to speak to O'Connor. The latter immediately left the car and spoke to Mayne. The crowd showed a hostile attitude towards the messenger, who was saved by O'Connor's declaration that Mayne was his 'best friend'. Then the Duke's strategy was revealed. O'Connor was told that the meeting could be held, but that the bridges were closed by the police, and no procession would be allowed to cross. O'Connor at once promised to abandon the procession. He returned to the Common from the Horns Assembly Rooms, where the interview with

Mayne had taken place, and the speech-making began. Doyle was put in the chair, and started proceedings. Then O'Connor broke the news. In accordance with his usual tactics he first allowed his prestige full play, adding to it for the occasion. Posing as a revolutionary of the deepest dye, he told the astonished crowd that his father had been tried five or six times for high treason, and was in prison for seven years of his life, that his uncle 'is now in the fifteenth year of his banishment, and is about to be made the first President of the Republic in France. My brother is Prime Minister and Commander-in-Chief of a Republic in South America.' Having by these means sufficiently impressed his listeners with the sense that he, O'Connor, was a man whose advice was well worth taking, he explained the situation as regards the police, and urged those present to pin their faith to the moral force of the six million signatures to the Petition, and to do nothing rash. Ernest Jones followed, echoing his leader's exhortations. O'Connor left the Common on the conclusion of Jones' speech, and the last speakers, Clark and Reynolds, were not very well listened to. About 2 p.m. the meeting dispersed. The Petition was packed into three cabs and, accompanied by Doyle, Clark, and M'Grath, was driven off to the House of Commons. They were refused a safe-conduct across Westminster Bridge, and had ignominiously to reach Westminster through back streets and over Blackfriars Bridge. A few Chartists stayed behind to listen to an Irish meeting in a corner of the Common, which Harney, West and Reynolds were invited to address. The remaining Chartists slowly dispersed, wondering greatly. The demonstration was at an end. At 2 p.m. Lord John Russell wrote out a report, and sent it to the Queen. 'Lord John Russell presents his humble duty to your Majesty, and has the honour to state that the Kennington Common meeting has proved a complete failure.'

A History of the Chartist Movement

The Hunger Marchers, 1936

The favourite marching song of the Scottish contingent was. . . .

> From Scotland we are marching,
> From ship yard, mill and mine,
> Our scarlet banners raise on high,

> We toilers are in line. . . .
> Now comes the day of reckoning,
> No longer we'll endure
> Starvation – we will conquer now,
> Our victory is sure.
> We are a strong determined band
> Each with a weapon in his hand.

As the lines of the last verse were sung, the marchers would all raise their heavy walking sticks in the air, as a mark of defiance against the government. . . .

From town to town the various contingents closed in upon London. . . . Sunday, 24th February, came; this was the great day to which they had all looked forward. For weeks the London reception committee had been preparing for this day of days.

The marchers were early astir, smartening themselves up for their last march to Trafalgar Square, which was again to be the venue of a mighty demonstration. . . .

The marchers were due to arrive in Trafalgar Square at 3 p.m., but those London demonstrations that were not accompanying contingents of marchers were due in at 2.30. An hour before this a big crowd began to gather in the square. Red rosettes and red flags were everywhere, and with every minute that passed the crowd grew larger. . . . The marshals of the demonstration had extreme difficulty in holding the crowds back and keeping a gangway, and as the head of the marchers' column reached the outskirts of the square, the London workers in their enthusiasm, rushed upon them with cheers and greetings. . . . Thousands of cigarettes are pitched into the ranks of the marchers as they pass. Cinematograph machines and cameras are working furiously to get pictures of the march; tears of joy and excitement swell up in the eyes of the marchers as the London workers vociferously welcome them.

Across the plinth is stretched a great white streamer, amongst dozens of working-class banners. The streamer throws out the words in bold letters:

'WELCOME TO THE HUNGER MARCHERS'

It was turned six o'clock and dark before the way could be cleared for the marchers to proceed out of the Square.

Wal Hannington, Unemployed Struggle 1919–1936 (1936)

Breaking windows, 1910

We had planned a demonstration for March 4th, and this one we announced. We planned another demonstration for March 1st, but this one we did not announce. Late in the afternoon of Friday, March 1st, I drove in a taxicab, accompanied by the Hon. Secretary of the Union, Mrs Tuke and another of our members, to No. 10 Downing Street, the official residence of the Prime Minister. It was exactly half past five when we alighted from the cab and threw our stones, four of them, through the window panes. As we expected we were promptly arrested and taken to Cannon Row police station. The hour that followed will long be remembered in London. At intervals of fifteen minutes relays of women who had volunteered for the demonstration did their work. The first smashing of glass occurred in the Haymarket and Piccadilly, and greatly startled and alarmed both pedestrians and police. A large number of the women were arrested, and everybody thought that this ended the affair. But before the excited populace and the frustrated shop owners' first exclamation had died down, before the police had reached the station with their prisoners, the ominous crashing and splintering of plate glass began again, this time along both sides of Regent Street and the Strand. A furious rush of police and people towards the second scene of action ensued. While their attention was being taken up with occurrences in this quarter, the third relay of women began breaking the windows in Oxford Circus and Bond Street. The demonstration ended for the day at half past six with the breaking of many windows in the Strand.

Emmeline Pankhurst, *My Own Story* (1914)

A Newgate fire, 1780

I should think myself very much to blame, did I here neglect to do justice to my esteemed friend Mr Akerman, the keeper of Newgate, who long discharged a very important trust with an uniform intrepid firmness, and at the same time a tenderness and a liberal charity, which entitle him to be recorded with distinguished honour.

Upon this occasion, from the timidity and negligence of magistracy on the one hand, and the almost incredible exertions of the mob on the other, the first prison of this great country was laid open, and the prisoners set free; but that Mr Akerman, whose house was burnt, would have prevented all this, had proper aid been sent to him in due time, there can be no doubt.

Many years ago, a fire broke out in the brick part which was built as an addition to the old gaol of Newgate. The prisoners were in consternation and tumult, calling out, 'We shall be burnt – we shall be burnt! Down with the gate – down with the gate!' Mr Akerman hastened to them, shewed himself at the gate, and having, after some confused vociferation of 'Hear him – hear him!' obtained a silent attention, he then calmly told them, that the gate must not go down; that they were under his care, and that they should not be permitted to escape: but that he could assure them, they need not be afraid of being burnt, for that the fire was not in the prison, properly so called, which was strongly built with stone; and that if they would engage to be quiet, he himself would come in to them, and conduct them to the further end of the building, and would not go out till they gave him leave. To this proposal they agreed; upon which Mr Akerman, having first made them fall back from the gate, went in, and with a determined resolution, ordered the outer turnkey upon no account to open the gate, even though the prisoners (though he trusted they would not) should break their word, and by force bring himself to order it. 'Never mind me, (said he,) should that happen.' The prisoners peaceably followed him, while he conducted them through passages of which he had the keys, to the extremity of the gaol which was most distant from the fire. Having, by this very judicious conduct, fully satisfied them that there was no immediate risk, if any at all, he then addressed them thus: 'Gentlemen, you are now convinced that I told you true. I have no doubt that the engines will soon extinguish this fire; if they should not, a sufficient guard will come, and you shall all be taken out and lodged in the Compters. I assure you, upon my word and honour, that I have not a farthing insured. I have left my house, that I might take care of you. I will keep my promise, and stay with you, if you insist upon it; but if you will allow me to go out and look after my family and property, I shall be obliged to you.' Struck with his behaviour, they called out, 'Master Akerman, you have done bravely; it was very kind in you: by all means go and take care of your own concerns.' He did so accordingly, while they remained, and were all preserved.

James Boswell, *Life of Johnson* (1791)

The mob at the pillory

About 12 o'clock the City Marshalls arrived with more than a hundred constables mounted, armed with pistols, and a hundred on foot. This force was ordered to rendezvous in Old Bailey Yard where a caravan used occasionally for carrying prisoners from the jails of London to the hulks waited to receive the culprits. The caravan was drawn by two shaft-horses led by two men armed with a brace of pistols. The gates of the Old Bailey were shut and all strangers were turned out. The miscreants were then brought out and placed in the caravan; Amos began a laugh, which induced his vile companions to reprove him, and they all sat upright apparently in a composed state, but having cast their eyes upwards, the sight of the spectators on the tops of the houses operated strongly on their fears, and they soon appeared to feel terror and dismay. At the instant the Church clock went half-past twelve, the gates were thrown open. The mob at the same time attempted to force their way in but they were repulsed. A grand sortie of the police was then made. About 60 officers armed and mounted as before described went forward with the City Marshalls. The caravan went next followed by about 40 officers and the Sheriffs. The first salute received by the offenders was a volley of mud and a serenade of hisses, shouting and execration, which compelled them to fall flat on their faces in the caravan. The mob, and particularly the women, had piled up balls of mud to afford the objects of their indignation a warm reception. The depots in many places appeared like pyramids of shot in a gun-wharf. These were soon exhausted and when the prisoners passed the old house which once belonged to the notorious Jonathan Wild they resembled beasts dipped in a stagnant pool. The shower of mud continued during their passage to the Haymarket. Before they reached half-way to the scene of their exposure they were not discernible as human beings. If they had had much further to go the cart would have been absolutely filled over them. The one who sat rather aloof from the rest was the landlord of the house, a fellow of stout bulky figure who could not stow himself away as easily as the others who were slighter; he was therefore as well as on account of his being known attacked with double fury. Dead cats and dogs, offal, potatoes, turnips, etc., rebounded from him on every side, while his apparently manly appearance drew down peculiar execrations on him, and nothing but the motion of the cart prevented his being killed on the spot. At 1 o'clock four of them were exalted on the new pillory made purposely for their accommodation. The remaining two, Cook and Amos, were honoured by being allowed to enjoy a triumph in the pillory alone. They were accordingly taken back in the caravan to St Martin's watch-house. Before any of them reached the place of punishment their faces were completely disfigured by blows and mud; and before they mounted their persons appeared one heap of filth. Upwards of fifty women were permitted to stand in a ring who assailed them incessantly with mud, dead cats, rotten eggs, potatoes, and buckets of grub, offal and dung, which were brought by a number of butchers' men from St James's Market. These criminals were very roughly handled; but as there were four of them they did not suffer so much as a less number might. When the hour was expired they were again put in the cart and conveyed to Coldbath Fields prison through St Martin's Lane, Compton Street, and Holborn, and in their journey received similar salutes to what they had met with on their way from Newgate. When they were taken from the pillory the butchers' men and the women who had been so active were plentifully regaled with gin and beer procured from a subscription made on the spot. In a few minutes the remaining two, Cook (who had been the landlord) and Amos (alias Fox), were desired to mount. Cook held his hands to his head and complained of the blows he had already received; and Amos made much the same complaint and showed a large brickbat which had struck him in the face. The Under-Sheriff told them that the sentence must be executed and they reluctantly mounted. Cook said nothing, but Amos, seeing the preparations that were making, declared in the most solemn manner that he was innocent; but it was vouchsafed from all quarters that he had been convicted before and in one minute they appeared a complete heap of mud and their faces were much more battered than those of the former four. Cook received several hits in his face and had a lump raised upon his eyebrow as large as a egg. Amos's two eyes were completely closed up; and when they were untied Cook appeared almost insensible, and it was necessary to help them both down and into the cart when they were conveyed to Newgate by the same road they had come and in their passage they continued to receive the same salutations the spectators had given them on the way out. Cook continued to lie upon the seat in the cart but Amos lay down among the filth till their entrance into Newgate sheltered the wretches from the further indignation of the most enraged populace you ever saw. As they passed the end of Panton Street, Strand, on their return a coachman stood up in his box and gave Cook five or six cuts with his whip.'

Morning Herald, 28 September 1810

The Brixton Riots, 1981

During the week-end of 10–12 April (Friday, Saturday and Sunday) the British people watched with horror and incredulity an instant audio-visual presentation on their television sets of scenes of violence and disorder in their capital city, the like of which had not previously been seen in this century in Britain. In the centre of Brixton, a few hundred young people – most, but not all of them, black – attacked the police on the streets with stones, bricks, iron bars and petrol bombs, demonstrating to millions of their fellow citizens the fragile basis of the Queen's peace. The petrol bomb was now used for the first time on the streets of Britain (the idea, no doubt, copied from the disturbances in Northern Ireland). These young people, by their criminal behaviour – for such, whatever their grievances or frustrations, it was – brought about a temporary collapse of law and order in the centre of an inner suburb of London.

The disturbances were at their worst on the Saturday evening. For some hours the police could do no more than contain them. When the police, heavily reinforced, eventually restored order in the afflicted area, the toll of human injury and property damage was such that one observer described the scene as comparable with the aftermath of an air-raid. Fortunately no one was killed: but on that Saturday evening 279 policemen were injured, 45 members of the public are known to have been injured (the number is almost certainly greater), a large number of police and other vehicles were damaged or destroyed (some by fire), and 28 buildings were damaged or destroyed by fire. Further, the commitment of all available police to the task of quelling the riot and dispersing the rioters provided the opportunity, which many seized, of widespread looting in the shopping centre of Brixton.

Two views have been forcefully expressed in the course of the Inquiry as to the causation of the disorders. The first is: oppressive policing over a period of years, and in particular the harassment of young blacks on the streets of Brixton. On this view, it is said to be unnecessary to look more deeply for an explanation of the disorders. They were 'anti police'. The second is that the disorders, like so many riots in British history, were a protest against society by people, deeply frustrated and deprived, who saw in a violent attack upon the forces of law and order their one opportunity of compelling public attention to their grievances. I have no doubt that each view, even if correct, would be an over-simplification of a complex situation. If either view should be true, it would not be the whole truth.

Lord Scarman, *Report on the Brixton Disorders* (1981)

12

Seedy

Seediness is a quality easier to illustrate than to define. If you turn the next few pages, you might consider that there is little in common between the Karachi Hotel in Elizabeth Bowen's masterpiece The Death of the Heart *and the opium den patronized by Sherlock Holmes and the Man with the Twisted Lip. After all, the Karachi is on one level perfectly respectable, as are its clientele. What I have attempted to illustrate in this section is the ready way in which London goes to seed. An example of what I mean is dinginess of staircases in houses divided into flats, even when the flats themselves are quite smart; the same tattiness could be observed in the past if you left the well-decorated dining-room of some Italian restaurant and found your way (hideous carpet, peeling paint) to the lavatory. During the 'boom' years of the 1980s, it seemed, distressingly, as if London were losing this tendency towards shabbiness and something always on the edge of the sinister, which I have called seediness. Everywhere seemed smart – even the gents in Soho restaurants. With straiter financial times, London's essentially seedy character is starting to reassert itself. An astonishingly high proportion of pubs are still devoid of any aesthetic or olde worlde charm. When they were first 'done up', they must have looked smart, but dinginess kept breaking through. London is like the man of whom his friends said that he only had to wear a new suit for half an hour to make it look as though it was crumpled and old. Of nothing is this truer than the 'modern architecture' in the city.*

I do not know whether there is a sexual dimension in all this, or whether the corollary is truer, that London manages, with the massage parlours and porn shops to which allusion is made in the following pages, to make even sex seem dingy. It is this world, where sex itself seems to have gone yellow and curly at the

edges like a stale sandwich, which is captured with such cruel faithfulness in
Joseph Conrad's The Secret Agent.

Mr Verloc's shop

The shop was small, and so was the house. It was one of those grimy brick houses which existed in large quantities before the era of reconstruction dawned upon London. The shop was a square box of a place, with the front glazed in small panes. In the daytime the door remained closed; in the evening it stood discreetly but suspiciously ajar.

The window contained photographs of more or less undressed dancing girls; nondescript packages in wrappers like patent medicines; closed yellow paper envelopes, very flimsy, and marked two and six in heavy black figures; a few numbers of ancient French comic publications hung across a string as if to dry; a dingy blue china bowl, a casket of black wood, bottles of marking ink, and rubber stamps; a few books with titles hinting at impropriety; a few apparently old copies of obscure newspapers, badly printed, with titles like the *Torch*,* the *Gong* – rousing titles. And the two gas-jets inside the panes were always turned low, either for economy's sake or for the sake of the customers.

These customers were either very young men, who hung about the window for a time before slipping in suddenly; or men of a more mature age, but looking generally as if they were not in funds. Some of that last kind had the collars of their overcoats turned right up to their moustaches, and traces of mud on the bottom of their nether garments, which had the appearance of being much worn and not very valuable. And the legs inside them did not, as a general rule, seem of much account either. With their hands plunged deep in the side pockets of their coats, they dodged in sideways, one shoulder first, as if afraid to start the bell going.

The bell, hung on the door by means of a curved ribbon of steel, was difficult to circumvent. It was hopelessly cracked; but of an evening, at the slightest provocation, it clattered behind the customer with impudent virulence.

It clattered; and at that signal, through the dusty glass door behind the

* An anarchist journal published by the precocious children of William Michael Rossetti.

painted deal counter, Mr Verloc would issue hastily from the parlour at the back. His eyes were naturally heavy; he had an air of having wallowed, fully dressed, all day on an unmade bed. Another man would have felt such an appearance a distinct disadvantage. In a commercial transaction of the retail order much depends on the seller's engaging and amiable aspect. But Mr Verloc knew his business, and remained undisturbed by any sort of aesthetic doubt about his appearance. With a firm, steady-eyed impudence, which seemed to hold back the threat of some abominable menace, he would proceed to sell over the counter some object looking obviously and scandalously not worth the money which passed in the transaction: a small cardboard box with apparently nothing inside, for instance, or one of those carefully closed yellow flimsy envelopes, or a soiled volume in paper covers with a promising title. Now and then it happened that one of the faded, yellow dancing girls would get sold to an amateur, as though she had been alive and young.

Sometimes it was Mrs Verloc who would appear at the call of the cracked bell. Winnie Verloc was a young woman with a full bust, in a tight bodice, and with broad hips. Her hair was very tidy. Steady-eyed like her husband, she preserved an air of unfathomable indifference behind the rampart of the counter. Then the customer of comparatively tender years would get suddenly disconcerted at having to deal with a woman, and with rage in his heart would proffer a request for a bottle of marking ink, retail value sixpence (price in Verloc's shop one and sixpence), which, once outside, he would drop stealthily into the gutter.

The evening visitors – the men with collars turned up and soft hats rammed down – nodded familiarly to Mrs Verloc, and with a muttered greeting, lifted up the flap at the end of the counter in order to pass into the back parlour, which gave access to a passage and to a steep flight of stairs. The door of the shop was the only means of entrance to the house in which Mr Verloc carried on his business of a seller of shady wares, exercised his vocation of a protector of society, and cultivated his domestic virtues.

Joseph Conrad, *The Secret Agent* (1907)

Rose of Soho

Soho Rosa lived over a grocer;
    Her telephone went 'Wee wee wee,
This little piggy comes to market.' But her clients
    Dwindled, were reduced to just three.

The first was a sad, tired businessman,
    And the second was a sailor from the sea,
And the third was a little, blind piano-tuner
    (And it might have been you or me).

The businessman called at lunchtime –
    He had a specialized taste:
She just had to sit there, stark naked in a mackintosh
    With a Union Jack coiled round her waist.

He stared for an hour at this pretty picture
    Till his dying embers were fired,
Then paid her ten guineas, and departed silently,
    If anything still more tired.

The sailor asked her merely to lie down:
    Her Sympleglades opened wide,
While he schoonered to the sweet Isles of Elsewhere,
    And dreamed of the boys in Port Said.

The piano-tuner called once a month
    To tune up her pianola:
It functioned informally, and entirely normally,
    On a gin and a stiff coca cola.

She was reclining on her 'contemporary' sofa
    When the piano-tuner, in the buff,
Cried 'God has created me with four senses,
    And they are not enough.'

She was not listening. He went across
    To the vase on the window-sill;
And selected (with which he thereupon strangled her)
    The stalk of a daffodil –

A plastic flower (three mouthfuls of rice
    For a poor widow in Hong Kong –
Confucian communicant of the Methodist Church,
    She had intended no wrong).

The businessman was drowned in the ocean;
    The sailor died of fatigue
In a pub he had opened down in Somerset,
    While they played piped music by Grieg.

The businessman fell from a plane that crashed
    On an important mission,
Selling coffee to Brazil, curry-powder to the Indians
    (There were rumours of nuclear fission).

The sailor and the businessman rest in the elements
    Enjoying their infinite leisure;
But they bundled the little piano-tuner off to Broadmoor
    During Her Majesty's pleasure.

A madrepore grows from the businessman's heart,
    The sailor's in church-mould is lain,
But the Devil is striking augmented fourths
    In the tuner's untuned brain.

Come Judgement Day, with a face of wrath
    God will dance over their graves;
But Christ knows, Jesus in His mercy knows
    Which of all four He saves.

John Heath-Stubbs, *Collected Poems* (1988)

Opium den

Upper Swandam Lane is a vile alley lurking behind the high wharves which
line the north side of the river to the east of London Bridge. Between a slop
shop and a gin shop, approached by a steep flight of steps leading down to a
black gap like the mouth of a cave, I found the den of which I was in search.
Ordering my cab to wait, I passed down the steps, worn hollow in the centre

by the ceaseless tread of drunken feet, and by the light of a flickering oil lamp above the door I found the latch and made my way into a long, low room, thick and heavy with the brown opium smoke, and terraced with wooden berths, like the forecastle of an emigrant ship.

Through the gloom one could dimly catch a glimpse of bodies lying in strange fantastic poses, bowed shoulders, bent knees, heads thrown back and chins pointing upwards, with here and there a dark, lack-lustre eye turned upon the new-comer. Out of the black shadows there glimmered little red circles of light, now bright, now faint, as the burning poison waxed or waned in the bowls of the metal pipes. The most lay silent, but some muttered to themselves, and others talked together in a strange, low, monotonous voice, their conversation coming in gushes, and then suddenly tailing off into silence, each mumbling out his own thoughts, and paying little heed to the words of his neighbour. At the further end was a small brazier of burning charcoal, beside which on a three-legged wooden stool there sat a tall, thin old man, with his jaw resting upon his two fists, and his elbows upon his knees, staring into the fire.

As I entered, a sallow Malay attendant had hurried up with a pipe for me and a supply of the drug, beckoning me to an empty berth.

'Thank you, I have not come to stay,' said I. 'There is a friend of mine here, Mr Isa Whitney, and I wish to speak with him.'

There was a movement and an exclamation from my right, and, peering through the gloom, I saw Whitney, pale, haggard, and unkempt, staring out at me.

'My God! It's Watson,' said he. He was in a pitiable state of reaction, with every nerve in a twitter. 'I say, Watson, what o'clock is it?'

'Nearly eleven.'

'Of what day?'

'Of Friday, June 19.'

'Good heavens! I thought it was Wednesday. It *is* Wednesday. What d'you want to frighten a chap for?' He sank his face on to his arms, and began to sob in a high treble key.

Arthur Conan Doyle, *The Adventures of Sherlock Holmes* (1892)

Profiles in String

Trapnel was like a child who suddenly decides to be fretful no longer. Now he was even full of gratitude. We reached Edgware Road with him still in this mood. There was a small stretch of the main highway to negotiate before turning off by the Canal. The evening was warm, stuffy, full of strange smells. For once Trapnel seemed suitably dressed in his tropical suit. We turned down the south side of the Canal, walking on the pavement away from the houses. Railings shut off a grass bank that sloped down to the tow-path. Trapnel had now moved into a pastoral dream.

'I love this waterway. I'd like to have a private barge, and float down it waving to the tarts.'

'Do you get a lot down here?' asked Bagshaw, interested.

'You see the odd one. They live round about, but tend to work other streets. What a mess the place is in.'

Most of London was pretty grubby at this period, the Canal no exception. On the surface of the water concentric circles of oil, undulating in the colours of the spectrum, were illuminated by moonlight. Through these luminous prisms floated anonymous off-scourings of every kind, tin cans, petrol drums, soggy cardboard boxes. Watery litter increased as the bridge was approached. Bagshaw pointed to a peculiarly obnoxious deposit bobbing up and down by the bank.

'Looks as if someone's dumped their unit's paper salvage. I used to have to deal with that at one stage of the war. Obsolete forms waiting to be pulped and made into other forms. An internal reincarnation. Fitted the scene in India.'

Trapnel stopped, and leant against the railings.

'Let's pause for a moment. Contemplate life. It's a shade untidy here, but romantic too. Do you know what all that mess of paper looks like? A manuscript. Probably someone's first novel. Authors always talk of burning their first novel. I believe this one's drowned his.'

'Or hers.'

'Some beautiful girl who wrote about her seduction, and couldn't get it published.'

'When lovely woman stoops to authorship?'

'I think I'll go and have a look. Might give me some ideas.'

'Trappy, don't be silly.'

Trapnel, laughing rather dementedly, began to climb the railings. Bag-shaw attempted to stop this. Before he could be persuaded otherwise, Trapnel had lifted himself up, and was halfway across. The railings pre-sented no very serious obstacle even to a man in a somewhat deranged state, who carried a stick in one hand. He dropped to the other side without difficulty. The bank sloped fairly steeply to the lower level of the tow-path and the water. Trapnel reached the footway. He paused for a moment, looking up and down the length of the Canal. Then he went to the water's edge, and began to poke with the swordstick at the sheets of paper floating about all over the surface.

'Come back, Trappy. You're not the dustman.'

Trapnel took no notice of Bagshaw. He continued to strain forward with the stick, until it looked ominously as if he would fall in. The pieces of paper, scattered broadcast, were all just out of reach.

'We shall have to get over,' said Bagshaw. 'He'll be in at any moment.'

Then Trapnel caught one of the sheets with the end of the stick. He guided it to the bank. For a second it escaped, but was recaptured. He bent down to pick it up, shook off the water and straightened out the page. The soaked paper seemed to fascinate him. He looked at it for a long time. Bagshaw, relieved that the railings would not now have to be climbed, for a minute or two did not intervene. At last he became tired of waiting.

'Is it a work of genius? Do decide one way or the other. We can't bear more delay to know whether it ought to be published or not.'

Trapnel gave a kind of shudder. He swayed. Either drink had once more overcome him with the suddenness with which it had struck outside the pub, or he was acting out a scene of feigned horror at what he read. Whichever it were, he really did look again as if about to fall into the Canal. Abruptly he stopped playing the part, or recovered his nerve. I suppose these antics, like the literary ramblings in the pub, also designed to delay discovery that Pamela had abandoned him; alternatively, to put off some frightful confrontation with her.

'Do come back, Trappy.'

Then an extraordinary thing happened. Trapnel was still standing by the edge of the water holding the dripping sheet of foolscap. Now he crushed it in his hand, and threw the ball of paper back into the Canal. He lifted the swordstick behind his head, and, putting all his force into the throw, cast it as far as this would carry, high into the air. The stick turned and descended, death's-head first. A mystic arm should certainly have risen from the dark waters of the mere to receive it. That did not happen. Trapnel's Excalibur struck the flood a long way from the bank, disappeared for a moment, surfaced, and began to float downstream.

'Now he really has become unmoored,' said Bagshaw.

Trapnel came slowly up the bank.

'You'll never get your stick back, Trappy. What ever made you do it? We'll hurry on to the bridge right away. It might have got caught up on something. There's not much hope.'

Trapnel climbed back on to the pavement.

'You were quite wrong, Books.'

'What about?'

'It was a work of genius.'

'What was?'

'The manuscript in the water – it was *Profiles in String*.'

I now agreed with Bagshaw in supposing Trapnel to have gone completely off his head. He stood looking at us. His smile was one of the consciously dramatic ones.

'She brought the MS along, and chucked it into the Canal. She knew I should be almost bound to pass this way, and it would be well on the cards I should notice it. We quite often used to stroll down here at night and talk about the muck floating down, french letters and such like. She must have climbed over the railings to get to the water. I'd like to have watched her doing that. I'd thought of a lot of things she might be up to – doctoring my pills, arranging for me to find her being had by the milkman, giving the bailiffs our address. I never thought of this. I never thought she'd destroy my book.'

He stood there, still smiling slightly, almost as if he were embarrassed by what had happened.

'You really mean that's your manuscript over there in the water?'

Trapnel nodded.

'The whole of it?'

'It wasn't quite finished. The end was what we had the row about.'

'You must have a copy?'

'Of course I haven't a copy. Why should I? I told you, it wasn't finished yet.'

Even Bagshaw was appalled. He began to speak, then stopped, something I had never seen happen before. There was certainly nothing to say. Trapnel just stood there.

'Come and look for the stick, Trappy.'

Trapnel was not at all disposed to move. Now the act had taken place, he wanted to reflect on it. Perhaps he feared still worse damage when the flat was reached, though that was hard to conceive.

'In a way I'm not surprised. Even though this particular dish never struck me as likely to appear on the menu, it all fits in with the cuisine. Christ, two years' work, and I'll never feel the same as when I was writing it. She may be correct in what she thinks about it, but I'll never be able to write it again – either her way or my own.'

Bagshaw, in spite of his feelings about the manuscript, could not forget the stick. The girl did not interest him at all.

'You'll never find a swordstick like that again. It was a great mistake to throw it away.'

Trapnel was not listening. He stood there musing. Then all at once he revealed something that had always been a mystery. Being Trapnel, an egotist of the first rank, he supposed this disclosure as of interest only in his own case, but a far wider field of vision was at the same time opened up by what was unveiled. In a sense it was of most interest where Trapnel was concerned, because he seems to have reacted in a somewhat different fashion to the rest of Pamela's lovers, but, applicable to all of them, what was divulged offered clarification of her relations with men. Drink, pills, the strain of living with her, the destruction of *Profiles in String*, combination of all those, brought about a confession hardly conceivable from Trapnel in other circumstances. He now spoke in a low, confidential tone.

'You may have wondered why a girl like that ever came to live with me?'

'Not so much as why she ever married that husband of hers,' said Bagshaw. 'I can understand all the rest.'

'I doubt if you can. Not every man can stand what's entailed.'

'I don't contradict that.'

'You don't know what I mean.'

'What do you mean?'

Trapnel did not answer for a moment. It was as if he were thinking how to phrase whatever he intended to say. Then he spoke with great intensity.

'It's when you have her. She wants it all the time, yet doesn't want it. She goes rigid like a corpse. Every grind's a nightmare. It's all the time, and always the same.'

Anthony Powell, *Books Do Furnish a Room* (1971)

Daughters of hospitality

Every evening as I return home from my usual solitary excursions, I am met by several of those well disposed daughters of hospitality, at different times and in different streets, richly dressed, and with minds not less noble than their appearance. You know that nature has indulged me with a person by no means agreeable, yet are they too generous to object to my homely appearance; they feel no repugnance at my broad face and flat nose; they perceive me to be a stranger, and that alone is a sufficient recommendation. They even seem to think it their duty to do the honours of the country by every act of complaisance in their power. One takes me under the arm, and in a manner forces me along; another catches me round the neck, and desires to partake in this office of hospitality; while a third kinder still, invites me to refresh my spirits with wine. Wine is in England reserved only for the rich, yet here even wine is given away to the stranger.

A few nights ago, one of those generous creatures, dressed all in white, and flaunting like a meteor by my side, forcibly attended me home to my own apartment. She seemed charmed with the elegance of the furniture, and the convenience of my situation. And well indeed she might, for I have hired an apartment for not less than two shillings of their money every week. But her civility did not rest here; for at parting, being desirous to know the hour, and perceiving my watch out of order, she kindly took it to be repaired by a relation of her own, which you may imagine will save some expense, and she assures me that it will cost her nothing. I shall have it back in a few days when mended, and am preparing a proper speech expressive of my gratitude on the occasion: Celestial excellence, I intend to say, happy I am in having found out, after many painful adventures, a land of innocence, and a people of humanity; I may rove into other climes, and converse with nations yet unknown, but where shall I meet a soul of such purity as that which resides in thy breast! sure thou hast been nurtured by the bill of the Shin Shin, or suck'd the breasts of the provident Gin Hiung. The melody of thy voice could rob the Chong Fou of her whelps, or inveigle the Boh that lives in the midst of the waters. Thy servant shall ever retain a sense of thy favours; and one day boast of thy virtue, sincerity, and truth among the daughters of China. Adieu.

Oliver Goldsmith, *The Citizen of the World* (1762)

Mr Quilp's summer-house

'There's a little summer-house overlooking the river, where we might take a glass of this delicious liquor with a whiff of the best tobacco – it's in this case, and of the rarest quality, to my certain knowledge – and be perfectly snug and happy, could we possibly contrive it; or is there any very particular engagement that peremptorily takes you another way, Mr Swiveller, eh?'

As the dwarf spoke, Dick's face relaxed into a compliant smile, and his brows slowly unbent. By the time he had finished, Dick was looking down at Quilp in the same sly manner as Quilp was looking up at him, and there remained nothing more to be done but to set out for the house in question. This they did, straightway. The moment their backs were turned, little Jacob thawed, and resumed his crying from the point where Quilp had frozen him.

The summer-house of which Mr Quilp had spoken was a rugged wooden box, rotten and bare to see, which overhung the river's mud, and threatened to slide down into it. The tavern to which it belonged was a crazy building, sapped and undermined by the rats, and only upheld by great bars of wood which were reared against its walls, and had propped it up so long that even they were decaying and yielding with their load, and of a windy night might be heard to creak and crack as if the whole fabric were about to come toppling down. The house stood – if anything so old and feeble could be said to stand – on a piece of waste ground, blighted with the unwholesome smoke of factory chimneys, and echoing the clank of iron wheels and rush of troubled water. Its internal accommodations amply fulfilled the promise of the outside. The rooms were low and damp, the clammy walls were pierced with chinks and holes, the rotten floors had sunk from their level, the very beams started from their places and warned the timid stranger from their neighbourhood.

To this inviting spot, entreating him to observe its beauties as they passed along, Mr Quilp led Richard Swiveller, and on the table of the summer-house, scored deep with many a gallows and initial letter, there soon appeared a wooden keg, full of the vaunted liquor. Drawing it off into the glasses with the skill of a practised hand, and mixing it with about a third part of water, Mr Quilp assigned to Richard Swiveller his portion, and lighting his pipe from an end of a candle in a very old and battered lantern, drew himself together upon a seat and puffed away.

'Is it good?' said Quilp, as Richard Swiveller smacked his lips, 'is it strong and fiery? Does it make you wink, and choke, and your eyes water, and your breath come short – does it?'

'Does it?' cried Dick, throwing away part of the contents of his glass, and filling it up with water, 'why, man, you don't mean to tell me that you drink such fire as this?'

'No?' rejoined Quilp. 'Not drink it? Look here. And here. And here again. Not drink it?'

As he spoke, Daniel Quilp drew off and drank three small glassfuls of the raw spirit, and then with a horrible grimace took a great many pulls at his pipe, and swallowing the smoke, discharged it in a heavy cloud from his nose. This feat accomplished he drew himself together in his former position, and laughed excessively.

Charles Dickens, *The Old Curiosity Shop* (1841)

Underground Man

After leaving the office I would travel either to Sloane Square or to Liverpool Street to have a drink in the station buffet. In the whole extension of the Underground system those two stations are, as far as I've been able to discover, the only ones which have bars actually upon the platform. The concept of the tube station platform bar excited me. In fact the whole Underground region moved me, I felt as if it were in some sense my natural home. These two bars were not just a cosy after-the-office treat, they were the source of a dark excitement, places of profound communication with London, with the sources of life, with the caverns of resignation to grief and to mortality. Drinking there between six and seven in the shifting crowd of rush-hour travellers, one could feel on one's shoulders as a curiously soothing yoke the weariness of toiling London, that blank released tiredness after work which can somehow console even the bored, even the frenzied. The coming and departing rattle of the trains, the drifting movement of the travellers, their arrival, their waiting, their vanishing forever presented a mesmeric and indeed symbolic fresco: so many little moments of decision, so many little finalities, the constant wrenching of texture, the constant destruction of cells which shifts and ages the lives of men and of universes. The uncertainty of the order of the trains. The dangerousness of the platforms. (Trains as lethal weapons.) The resolution of a given moment (but which?) to lay down your glass and mount the next train. (But why? There will be another in two minutes.) *Ah qu'ils sont beaux les trains manqués!* as I especially had cause to know. Then once upon the train that sense of its thrusting life, its intent and purposive turning which conveys itself so subtly to the traveller's body, its leanings and veerings to points of irrevocable change and partings of the ways. The train of consciousness, the present moment, the little lighted tube moving in the long dark tunnel. The inevitability of it all and yet its endless variety: the awful daylight glimpses, the blessed plunges back into the dark; the stations, each unique, the sinister brightness of Charing Cross, the mysterious gloom of Regent's Park, the dereliction of Mornington Crescent, the futuristic melancholy of Moorgate, the monumental ironwork of Liverpool Street, the twining *art nouveau* of Gloucester Road, the Barbican sunk in a baroque hole, fit subject for Piranesi. And in summer, like an excursion into the country, the flowering banks of the Westbound District Line. I preferred the dark however. Emergence was like a worm pulled from its hole. I loved the Inner Circle best. Twenty-seven stations for fivepence. Indeed, for fivepence as many stations as you cared to achieve. Sometimes I rode the whole Circle (just under an hour) before deciding whether to have my evening drink at Liverpool Street or at Sloane Square. I was not the only Circle rider. There were others, especially in winter. Homeless people, lonely people, alcoholics, people on drugs, people in despair. We recognized each other. It was a fit place for me, I was indeed an Undergrounder. (I thought of calling this story *The Memoirs of an Underground Man* or just simply *The Inner Circle*.)

Iris Murdoch, A Word Child (1975)

This dreadful hole

I was informed with vast glee by these wild young men that, during my secession, they had discovered two new houses of infinite merit, with which they were sure I should be wonderfully pleased, and to both of which they would introduce me before we parted. At the customary hour, being brimful of wine, we sallied forth, went the old Bow Street rounds, from whence I was led into an absolute hell upon earth. The first impression on my mind upon entering those diabolical regions never will be effaced from my memory. This den was distinguished by the name of Wetherby's, situate in the narrowest part of Little Russell Street, Drury Lane. Upon ringing at a door, strongly secured with knobs of iron, a cut-throat-looking rascal opened a small wicket, which was also secured with narrow iron bars, who in a hoarse and ferocious voice asked, 'Who's there?' Being answered 'Friends,' we were cautiously admitted one at a time, and when the last had entered, the door was instantly closed and secured, not only by an immense lock and key, but a massy iron bolt and chain.

I had then never been within the walls of a prison; yet this struck me like entering one of the most horrible kind. My companions conducted me into a room where such a scene was exhibiting that I involuntarily shrunk back with disgust and dismay, and would have retreated from the apartment, but that I found my surprise and alarm were so visible in my countenance as to have attracted the attention of several persons who came up, and good-naturedly enough encouraged me, observing that I was a young hand but should soon be familiarized and enjoy the fun. At this time the whole room was in an uproar, men and women promiscuously mounted upon chairs, tables, and benches, in order to see a sort of general conflict carrying on upon the floor. Two she-devils, for they scarce had a human appearance, were engaged in a scratching and boxing match, their faces entirely covered with blood, bosoms bare, and the clothes nearly torn from their bodies. For several minutes not a creature interfered between them, or seemed to care a straw what mischief they might do each other, and the contest went on with unabated fury.

In another corner of the same room, an uncommonly athletic young man of about twenty-five seemed to be the object of universal attack. No less than three Amazonian tigresses were pummelling him with all their might, and it appeared to me that some of the males at times dealt him blows with their sticks. He, however, made a capital defence, not sparing the women a bit more than the men, but knocking each down as opportunity occurred. As fresh hands continued pouring in upon him, he must at last have been miserably beaten, had not two of the gentlemen who went with me, (both very stout fellows) offended at the shameful odds used against a single person, interfered, and after a few knock-me-down arguments, succeeded in putting an end to the unequal conflict. This, to me, unusual riot, had a similar effect with Othello's sudden and unexpected appearance before his inebriated officer, Michael Cassio, for it produced an immediate restoration of my senses, the effect of which was an eager wish to get away; for which purpose I, in the confusion, slunk out of the room into the passage, and had just began fumbling at the street door, hoping to be able to liberate myself, when the same fierce and brutal Cerberus that had admitted my party coming up, roughly seized me by the collar exclaiming: 'Hulloa, what the devil have you been about here?'

To which I answered meekly: 'Nothing, but not being well I am desirous of going home.'

'Oh you are, are you! I think you came in not long since, and with a party. What! Do you want to tip us a bilk? Have you paid your reckoning, eh? No, no, youngster, no tricks upon travellers. No exit here until you have passed muster, my chick.'

More shocked than ever, I was compelled to return to the infuriate monsters, the ferocious door-keeper following me and addressing one of my companions whom he knew, said:

'So the young'un there wanted to be off, but I said as how I knew a trick worth two of that, too much experience to be taken in by such a sucker, told him not to expect to catch old birds with chaff, didn't I, young'un, hey?'

In this dreadful hole I was therefore obliged to stay until my friends chose to depart; and truly rejoiced did I feel at once more finding myself safe in the street.

William Hickey, Memoirs, 1749–1809 (1960)

Porn shops

TO ROBERT CONQUEST

7 February 1980
105 Newland Park,
Hull HU5 2DT

Dear Bob,

Many thanks for your letter. Hope you're settled into matrimony – are you still where I last visited you? Ah, London, London. I nip up from time to time, but the train journey, while faster, grows more tiresome. The porn shops aren't what they were, though I see Newport Court has branched off into Dominant Females and Fladge. Non nobis, domine, well, not much. I expect you've put all that behind you, haw haw.

Philip Larkin, Letters (1992)

A terrible clap

He writt a Play or Playes, and verses, which he did with so much sweetnesse and grace, that by it he got the love and friendship of his two Mecaenasses, Mr Endymion Porter and Mr Henry Jermyn (since Earl of St Albans) to whom he has dedicated his Poeme called *Madegascar*. Sir John Suckling was also his great and intimate friend.

After the death of Ben Johnson he was made in his place Poet Laureat.

He gott a terrible clap of a Black handsome wench that lay in Axe-yard, Westminster, whom he thought on when he speakes of Datga in *Gondibert*, which cost him his Nose, with which unlucky mischance many witts were too cruelly bold: e.g. Sir John Menis, Sir John Denham, etc.

John Aubrey, *Brief Lives* (1693)

The Karachi

The Karachi Hotel consists of two Kensington houses, of great height, of a style at once portentous and brittle, knocked into one – or, rather, not knocked, the structure might hardly stand it, but connected by arches at key points. Of the two giant front doors under the portico, one has been glazed and sealed up; the other up to midnight, yields to pressure on a round brass knob. The hotel's name, in tarnished gilt capitals, is wired out from the top of the portico. One former dining-room has been exposed to the hall and provides the hotel lounge; the other is still the dining-room, it is large enough. One of the first-floor drawing-rooms is a drawing-room still. The public rooms are lofty and large in a diluted way: inside them there is extensive vacuity, nothing so nobly positive as space. The fireplaces with their flights of brackets, the doors with their poor mouldings, the nude-looking windows exist in deserts of wall: after dark the high-up electric lights die high in the air above unsmiling armchairs. If these houses give little by becoming hotels, they lose little; even when they were homes, no intimate life can have flowered inside these walls or become endeared to them. They were the homes of a class doomed from the start, without natural privilege, without grace. Their builders must have built to enclose fog, which having seeped in never quite goes away. Dyspepsia, uneasy wishes, ostentation, and chilblains can, only, have governed the lives of families here.

In the Karachi Hotel, all upstairs rooms except the drawing-room, have been partitioned up to make two or three more: the place is a warren. The thinness of these bedroom partitions makes love or talk indiscreet. The floors creak, the beds creak; drawers only pull out of chests with violent convulsions; mirrors swing round and hit you one in the eye. Most privacy, though least air, is to be had in the attics, which were too small to be divided up.

Elizabeth Bowen, *The Death of the Heart* (1938)

Massage Capital of the World

28 February 1977

The *Evening Standard* reveals that there are 13 officials in Westminster Council with the duty of inspecting massage and sauna parlours in what is becoming the Massage Capital of the World.

This is a job I might well apply for when *Private Eye* is closed down. Massage Inspectors have the power to enter any premises where they have reason to believe that massage may be occurring, or may have recently occurred, or be about to occur.

It is important to keep standards high in this vital field. Massage and escort agencies between them now account for 27.4 per cent of all foreign earnings from tourism, according to figures released by the Central Statistics Office.

The scandal is that no government assistance is available. All state subsidy in this field has been grabbed by the resident homosexual community for its own personal pleasures.

These are English diversions, and while I am not necessarily urging an end to all buggers' subsidies, I feel it is time we started to think of our foreign guests, not to mention the resident heterosexual minority.

Auberon Waugh, *Diaries, 1976–1985* (1985)

Business Girls

From the geyser ventilators
    Autumn winds are blowing down
On a thousand business women
    Having baths in Camden Town.

Waste pipes chuckle into runnels,
    Steam's escaping here and there,
Morning trains through Camden cutting
    Shake the Crescent and the Square.

Early nip of changeful autumn,
    Dahlias glimpsed through garden doors,
At the back precarious bathrooms
    Jutting out from upper floors,

And behind their frail partitions
    Business women lie and soak,
Seeing through the draughty skylight
    Flying clouds and railway smoke.

Rest you there, poor unbelov'd ones,
    Lap your loneliness in heat.
All too soon the tiny breakfast,
    Trolley-bus and windy street!

John Betjeman, *Collected Poems* (1970)

13

Love

Which is self-explanatory.

Prothalamion

Calme was the day, and through the trembling ayre,
Sweete breathing *Zephyrus* did softly play
A gentle spirit, that lightly did delay
Hot *Titans* beames, which then did glyster fayre:
When I whom sullein care,
Through discontent of my long fruitless stay
In princes Court, and expectation vayne
Of idle hopes, which still doe fly away,
Like empty shaddowes, did aflict my brayne,
Walkt forth to ease my payne
Along the shoare of silver streaming *Themmes*,
Whose rutty Bancke, the which his River hemmes,
Was paynted all with variable flowers,
And all the meades adorned with daintie gemmes,
Fit to decke maydens bowers,
And crowne their Paramours,
Against the Brydale day, which is not long:
   Sweet *Themmes* runne softly, till I end my Song.

326

There, in a Meadow, by the Rivers side,
A Flocke of *Nymphes* I chaunced to espy,
All lovely Daughters of the Flood thereby,
With goodly greenish locks all loose untyde,
As each had bene a Bryde,
And each one had a little wicker basket,
Made of fine twigs entrayled curiously,
In which they gathered flowers to fill their flasket:
And with fine Fingers, cropt full featously
The tender stalkes on hye.
Of every sort, which in that Meadow grew,
They gathered some; the Violet pallid blew,
The little Dazie, that at evening closes,
The virgin Lillie, and the Primrose trew,
With store of Vermeil Roses,
To decke their Bridegromes posies,
Against the Brydale day, which was not long:
   Sweet *Themmes* runne softly, till I end my Song.

With that, I saw two Swannes of goodly hewe,
Come softly swimming downe along the Lee;
Two fairer Birds I yet did never see:
The snow which doth the top of *Pindus* strew,
Did never whiter shew,
Nor *Jove* himself when he a Swan would be
For love of *Leda*, whiter did appeare:
Yet Leda was they say as white as he,
Yet not so white as these, nor nothing neare;
So purely white they were,
That even the gentle streame, the which them bare,
Seem'd foule to them, and bad his billowes spare
To wet their silken feathers, least they might
Soyle their fayre plumes with water not so fayre,
And marre their beauties bright,
That shone as heavens light,
Against their Brydale day, which was not long:
   Sweet *Themmes* runne softly, till I end my Song.

Eftsoones the *Nymphes*, which now had Flowers their fill,
Ran all in haste, to see that silver brood,

As they came floating on the Christal Flood.
Whom when they sawe, they stood amazed still,
Their wondring eyes to fill,
Them seem'd they never saw a sight so fayre,
Of Fowles so lovely, that they sure did deeme
Them heavenly borne, or to be that same payre
Which through the Skie draw *Venus* silver Teeme,
For sure they did not seeme
To be begot of any earthly Seede,
But rather Angels or of Angels breede:
Yet were they bred of *Somers-heat* they say,
In sweetest Season, which each Flower and weede
The earth did fresh aray,
So fresh they seem'd as day,
Even as their Brydale day, which was not long:
   Sweet *Themmes* runne softly, till I end my Song.

Then forth they all out of their baskets drew,
Great store of Flowers, the honour of the field,
That to the sense did fragrant odours yield,
All which upon those goodly Birds they threw,
And all the Waves did strew,
That like old *Peneus* Waters they did seeme,
When downe along by pleasant *Tempes* shore
Scattred with Flowres, through *Thessaly* they streeme,
That they appeare through Lillies plenteous store,
Like a Brydes Chamber flore:
Two of those *Nymphes*, meane while, two Garlands bound,
Of freshest Flowres which in that Mead they found,
The which presenting all in trim Array,
Their snowie Foreheads therewithall they crownd,
Whilst one did sing this Lay,
Prepar'd against that Day,
Against their Brydale day, which was not long:
   Sweete *Themmes* runne softly, till I end my Song.

Ye gentle Birdes, the worlds faire ornament,
And heavens glorie, whom this happie hower
Doth leade unto your lovers blisfull bower,
Joy may you have and gentle hearts content

Of your loves couplement:
And let faire *Venus*, that is Queene of love,
With her heart-quelling Sonne upon you smile,
Whose smile they say, hath vertue to remove
All Loves dislike, and friendships faultie guile
For ever to assoile.
Let endlesse Peace your steadfast hearts accord,
And blessed Plentie wait upon your bord,
And let your bed with pleasures chast abound,
That fruitfull issue may to you afford,
Which may your foes confound,
And make your joyes redound,
Upon your Brydale day, which is not long:
    Sweete *Themmes* run softly, till I end my Song.

So ended she: and all the rest around
To her redoubled that her undersong,
Which said, their bridale daye should not be long.
And gentle Eccho from the neighbour ground,
Their accents did resound.
So forth those joyous Birdes did passe along,
Adowne the Lee, that to them murmurde low,
As he would speake, but that he lackt a tong
Yet did by signes his glad affection show,
Making his streame run slow.
And all the foule which in his flood did dwell
Gan flock about these twaine, that did excell
The rest, so far, as *Cynthia* doth shend*
The lesser starres. So they enranged well,
Did on those two attend,
And their best service lend,
Against their wedding day, which was not long:
    Sweete *Themmes* run softly, till I end my song.

At length they all to mery *London* came,
To mery London, my most kyndly Nurse,
That to me gave this Lifes first native sourse:
Though from another place I take my name,

* Surpass.

An house of auncient fame.
There when they came, whereas those bricky towres,
The which on *Themmes* brode aged backe doe ryde,
Where now the studious Lawyers have their bowers
There whylome wont the Templer Knights to byde,
Till they decayd through pride:
Next whereunto there stands a stately place,
Where oft I gayned gifts and goodly grace
Of that great Lord, which therein wont to dwell,
Whose want too well now feeles my freendles case:
But Ah here fits not well
Olde woes but joyes to tell
Against the bridale daye, which is not long:
    Sweete *Themmes* runne softly, till I end my Song.

Yet therein now doth lodge a noble Peer,
Great *Englands* glory and the Worlds wide wonder,
Whose dreadfull name, late through all *Spaine* did thunder,
And *Hercules* two pillors standing neere,
Did make to quake and feare:
Faire branch of Honor, flower of Chevalrie,
That fillest *England* with thy triumphs fame,
Joy have thou of thy noble victorie,
And endlesse happinesse of thine owne name
That promiseth the same:
That through thy prowesse and victorious armes,
Thy country may be freed from forraine harmes:
And great *Elisaes* glorious name may ring
Through al the world, fil'd with thy wide Alarmes,
Which some brave muse may sing
To ages following,
Upon the Brydale day, which is not long:
    Sweete *Themmes* runne softly, till I end my Song.

From those high Towers, this noble Lord issuing
Like Radiant *Hesper* when his golden hayre
In th' *Ocean* billowes he hath Bathed fayre,
Descended to the Rivers open vewing,
With a great traine ensuing.
Above the rest were goodly to be seene

Two gentle Knights of lovely face and feature
Beseeming well the bower of anie Queene,
With gifts of wit and ornaments of nature,
Fit for so goodly stature:
That like the twins of *Jove* they seem'd in sight,
Which decke the Bauldrick* of the Heavens bright.
They two forth pacing to the Rivers side,
Received those two faire Brides, their Loves delight,
Which at th' appointed tyde,
Each one did make his Bryde.
Against their Brydale day, which is not long:
    Sweet *Themmes* runne softly, till I end my Song.

Edmund Spenser (1594)

A Nightingale Sang in Berkeley Square

That certain night,
The night we met,
There was magic abroad in the air.
There were angels dining at the Ritz,
And a nightingale sang in Berkeley Square.
I may be right,
I may be wrong,
But I'm perfectly willing to swear
That when you turned and smiled at me,
A nightingale sang in Berkeley Square.

The moon that lingered over London town,
Poor puzzled moon, he wore a frown.
How could he know we two were so in love,
The whole darn world seemed upside down?
The streets of town were paved with stars
It was such a romantic affair.
And as we kissed and said, 'Good night',
A nightingale sang in Berkeley Square.

* Belt, girdle.

How strange it was,
How sweet and strange,
There was never a dream to compare
With that hazy, crazy night we met,
When a nightingale sang in Berkeley Square.
This heart of mine beat loud and fast,
Like a merry-go-round in a fair –
For we were dancing cheek to cheek
And a nightingale sang in Berkeley Square.

When dawn came stealing up all gold and blue
To interrupt our rendezvous,
I still remember how you smiled and said,
'Was that a dream, or was it true?'
Our homeward step was just as light
As the tap-dancing feet of Astaire,
And like an echo far away
A nightingale sang in Berkeley Square.
I know 'cause I was there,
That night in Berkeley Square.

Eric Maschwitz

The Telephone

To-night in million-voicèd London I
Was lonely as the million-pointed sky
Until your single voice. Ah! So the sun
Peoples all heaven, although he be but one.

Hilaire Belloc, *Complete Verse* (1991)

Trivial Pursuit

Six years ago when my last wife sensibly left me I thought never again. Anyway, I'd run out of love and could only splutter from time to time as a car does when it runs out of petrol. So now what really annoys me is that I've been smitten again. The lady in question is a waitress in the Groucho club. How can I describe her? Her hair is very dark brown, almost black, and it looks like silk. Her eyes are like a summer sky and the whites of them are as clear as the sparkle of her teeth behind lips that beg kissing. Between those eyes and that mouth there is the incident of a nose. How God and genes can make perfection out of gristle is nothing short of a miracle. It is the prow of a beautiful ship. And, talking of things maritime, although it is difficult to estimate her body beneath the severe black and white costume obligatory to serve drinks in the Groucho, it would seem to be ample. Not too big, not too skinny. Somewhere half way between the *Sky Lark* and the *Titanic*. To me, she is delicious. But what on earth do you say? So far our conversation has consisted of, 'Good afternoon, sir, what would you like?' and, 'A large vodka, ice and soda, please.' I have explained that my name is Jeff and not sir and I now think that 'sir' is a way of kindly saying 'piss off '.

The whole business is steeped in paranoia. The more I look at her the more I become aware of my age, weight loss, pending hair loss, pallidness, scruffiness and general physical disintegration. How can I tell her that the inside of the top of my skull is like the ceiling of the Sistine Chapel? Or that my head rings with toccatas and fugues? I can't. All she can see is a twit who spends most of his afternoons dreaming, sometimes snoozing, sometimes arguing in a club. I need a PR badly. Perhaps infatuation like drunkenness is temporary insanity. But I am too old to shoot lines. One is like what one looks like. The *Marie Celeste*.

I know what these people want. Bettina, for that is her name, will end up with a film-maker aged about 30 who drives a Ferrari coupé, one bronzed arm nonchalantly over the driving door, and who lives in a riverside pent-house with a Burmese cat, several gold medallions, a bottle of after-shave, an extremely expensive hi-fi set and no self-doubt whatsoever. All that is so very achievable if you take yourself seriously when you're young – all you have to do is to work hard which any idiot can do – but is it worth it? For Bettina, possibly. Another odd thing is that when I've looked at her in recent days I have noticed that I get slightly short of breath. Of course, I could be having mild coronaries but I don't think so. I think it is because she is so enormously huggable. She has the majesty of an Infanta. . . . I have nothing to offer except love, a half share in my current account, some vitamin C tablets and a bottle of Veuve Cliquot for breakfast. That is how we start the day, my landlady and I. Perhaps I should apply for a job as a waiter at the Groucho. It would be a sort of marriage. Oh dear, how very, very much I want to save her from falling into the hands of a really *nice* man. I could give her blood, sweat and tears.

Jeffrey Bernard, Low Life (1992)

Life with Bosie

I remember, for instance, in September 1893, to select merely one instance out of many, taking a set of chambers, purely in order to work undisturbed, as I had broken my contract with John Hare for whom I had promised to write a play and who was pressing me on the subject. During the first week you kept away. We had, not unnaturally indeed, differed on the question of the artistic value of your translation of *Salomé*. So you contented yourself with sending me foolish letters on the subject. In that week I wrote and completed in every detail, as it was ultimately performed, the first act of *An Ideal Husband*. The second week you returned and my work practically had to be given up. I arrived at St James's Place every morning at 11.30 in order to have the opportunity of thinking and writing without the interruption inseparable from my own household, quiet and peaceful as that household was. But the attempt was vain. At 12 o'clock you drove up and stayed smoking cigarettes and chattering till 1.30, when I had to take you out to luncheon at the Café Royal or the Berkeley. Luncheon with its liqueurs lasted usually till 3.30. For an hour you retired to White's. At tea-time you appeared again and stayed till it was time to dress for dinner. You dined with me either at the Savoy or at Tite Street. We did not separate as a rule till after midnight, as supper at Willis's had to wind up the entrancing day. That was my life for those three months, every single day, except during the four days when you went abroad. I then, of course, had to go over to Calais to fetch you back. For one of my nature and temperament it was a position at once grotesque and tragic.

You surely must realize that now.

Oscar Wilde, De Profundis (1949)

Love on the Underground

The accident had been as natural as anything in London ever is: Kate had one afternoon found herself opposite Mr Densher on the Underground Railway. She had entered the train at Sloane Square to go to Queen's Road, and the carriage in which she had found a place was all but full. Densher was already in it – on the other bench and at the furthest angle; she was sure of him before they had again started. The day and the hour were darkness, there were six other persons, and she had been busy placing herself; but her consciousness had gone to him as straight as if they had come together in some bright level of the desert. They had on neither part a second's hesitation; they looked across the choked compartment exactly as if she had known he would be there and he had expected her to come in; so that, though in the conditions they could only exchange the greeting of movements, smiles, silence, it would have been quite in the key of these passages that they should have alighted for ease at the very next station. Kate was in fact sure that the very next station was the young man's true goal – which made it clear that he was going on only from the wish to speak to her. He had to go on, for this purpose, to High Street, Kensington, as it was not till then that the exit of a passenger gave him his chance.

His chance put him, however, in quick possession of the seat facing her, the alertness of his capture of which seemed to show her his impatience. It helped them, moreover, with strangers on either side, little to talk; though this very restriction perhaps made such a mark for them as nothing else could have done. If the fact that their opportunity had again come round for them could be so intensely expressed between them without a word, they might very well feel on the spot that it had not come round for nothing. The extraordinary part of the matter was that they were not in the least meeting where they had left off, but ever so much further on, and that these added links added still another between High Street and Notting Hill Gate, and then between the latter station and Queen's Road an extension really inordinate. At Notting Hill Gate, Kate's right-hand neighbour descended, whereupon Densher popped straight into that seat; only there was not much gained when a lady, the next instant, popped into Densher's. He could say almost nothing to her – she scarce knew, at least, what he said; she was so occupied with a certainty that one of the persons opposite, a young-ish man with a single eyeglass, which he kept constantly in position, had made her out from the first as visibly, as strangely affected. If such a person made her out, what then did Densher do? – a question in truth sufficiently answered when, on their reaching her station, he instantly followed her out of the train. That had been the real beginning – the beginning of everything else; the other time, the time at the party, had been but the beginning of *that*. Never in life before had she so let herself go; for always before – so far as small adventures could have been in question for her – there had been, by the vulgar measure, more to go upon. He had walked with her to Lancaster Gate, and then she had walked with him away from it – for all the world, she said to herself, like the housemaid giggling to the baker.

Henry James, The Wings of the Dove (1902)

I could hardly refuse

I went down to the Embankment, where also, when out of cash, I had slept on a bench for a night or two. Here hundreds of downs-and-outs used to hang about every night, their hopelessness and hunger only momentarily alleviated by free soup from stalls run by charitable ladies. Near one such stall I found a young man – perhaps twenty years old – with a face that was pale and thin and wistfully appealing, and wearing clothes that were indeed more than threadbare, for he was literally out-at-elbows. On his head was a shabby cap. As he was about my height, and I was then pretty slim, I reckoned that his clothes would fit me, more or less, and mine him. I propositioned him: would he come and sleep the night with me at a cheap hotel and then, very early in the morning, change clothes with me? My clothes, though not elegant – probably grey flannel trousers, a 'sports' shirt and jacket – were a good deal better than his. He thought me crazy, but accepted with alacrity.

We walked up Farringdon Street, towards Smithfield, where there was an hotel 'for gentlemen only' at which one could get a double bed for a few shillings. It was a warm night: we agreed to sleep naked, with only a sheet over us. He was reasonably clean (he had been to the public baths that day) and, to my relief, free of 'crabs' – the *Pediculi pubis* which were, and are, so often transmitted in such circumstances. Before getting into bed, we smoked a few cigarettes to drown the smell of his socks. No doubt as a result of prolonged under-feeding, his ribs were too prominent, but his body was well-proportioned, his skin delicate and fair. We spoke little; he smiled – again that wistful look which had first moved me. We turned to each other, and kissed: the alternate thrust and withdrawal of his tongue – soft but firm, warm, and slightly flavoured with peppermint chewing-gum – suggested experience. In view of his general condition, I had not expected a strong sexual response; but now, beating and throbbing against me, was a surprisingly thick, hard organ. Then, still without speaking, he showed what he really wanted, or thought that I did; for, after another kiss, he rolled over with his back towards me, his bottom pressing against my genitals. Sodomy does not happen to be my favourite sexual pastime; but I could hardly refuse so unassuming a charmer.

Tom Driberg, Ruling Passions (1977)

Two love letters

Monday, 13 September 1819   *Fleet Street*

My dear Girl,

I have been hurried to Town by a Letter from my brother George; it is not of the brightest intelligence. Am I mad or not? I came by the Friday night coach and have not yet been to Hampstead. Upon my soul it is not my fault. I cannot resolve to mix any pleasure with my days: they go one like another undistinguishable. If I were to see you to day it would destroy the half comfortable sullenness I enjoy at present into downright perplexities. I love you too much to venture to Hampstead, I feel it is not paying a visit, but venturing into a fire. Que feraije? as the french novel writers say in fun, and I in earnest: really what can I do? Knowing well that my life must be passed in fatigue and trouble, I have been endeavouring to wean myself from you: for to myself alone what can be much of a misery? As far as they regard myself I can despise all events: but I cannot cease to love you. This morning I scarcely know what I am doing. I am going to Walthamstow. I shall return to Winchester to-morrow; whence you shall hear from me in a few days. I am a Coward, I cannot bear the pain of being happy: 'tis out of the question: I must admit no thought of it.

Yours ever affectionately

John Keats

TO FANNY BRAWNE

August 1820(?)

My dearest Girl,

I wish you could invent some means to make me at all happy without you. Every hour I am more and more concentrated in you; every thing else tastes like chaff in my Mouth. I feel it almost impossible to go to Italy – the fact is I cannot leave you, and shall never taste one minute's content until it pleases chance to let me live with you for good. But I will not go on at this rate. A person in health as you are can have no conception of the horrors that nerves and temper like mine go through. What Island do your friends propose retiring to? I should he happy to go with you there alone, but in company I should object to it; the backbitings and jealousies of new colonists who have nothing else to amuse themselves, is unbearable. Mr Dilke came to see me yesterday, and gave me a very great deal more pain than pleasure. I shall never be able any more to endure the society of any of those who used to meet at Elm Cottage and Wentworth Place. The last two years taste like brass upon my Palate. If I cannot live with you I will live alone. I do not think my health will improve much while I am separated from you. For all this I am averse to seeing you – I cannot bear flashes of light and return into my glooms again. I am not so unhappy now as I should be if I had seen you yesterday. To be happy with you seems such an impossibility! it requires a luckier Star than mine! it will never be. I enclose a passage from one of your letters which I want you to alter a little – I want (if you will have it so) the matter express'd less coldly to me. If my health would bear it, I could write a Poem which I have in my head, which would be a consolation for people in such a situation as mine. I would show some one in Love as I am, with a person living in such Liberty as you do. Shakespeare always sums up matters in the most sovereign manner. Hamlet's heart was full of such Misery as mine is when he said to Ophelia 'Go to a Nunnery, go, go!' Indeed I should like to give up the matter at once – I should like to die. I am sickened at the brute world which you are smiling with.

John Keats, *Letters* (1958)

Love in Wimpole Street

And now I will tell you. It is nearly two years ago since I have known Mr Browning. Mr Kenyon wished to bring him to see me five years ago, as one of the lions of London who roared the gentlest and was best worth my knowing; but I refused then, in my blind dislike to seeing strangers. Immediately, however, after the publication of my last volumes, he wrote to me, and we had a correspondence which ended in my agreeing to receive him as I never had received any other man. I did not know why, but it was utterly impossible for me to refuse to receive him, though I consented against my will. He writes the most exquisite letters possible, and has a way of putting things which I have not, a way of putting aside – so he came. He came, and with our personal acquaintance began his attachment for me, a sort of *infatuation* call it, which resisted the various denials which were my plain duty at the beginning, and has persisted past them all. I began with a grave assurance that I was in an exceptional position and saw him just in consequence of it, and that if ever he recurred to that subject again I never could see him again while I lived; and he believed me and was silent. To my mind, indeed, it was a bare impulse – a generous man of quick sympathies taking up a sudden interest with both hands! So I thought; but in the meantime the letters and the visits rained down more and more, and in every one there was something which was too slight to analyse and notice, but too decided not to be understood; so that at last, when the 'proposed respect' of the silence gave way, it was rather less dangerous. So then I showed him how he was throwing into the ashes his best affections – how the common gifts of youth and cheerfulness were behind me – how I had not strength, even of *heart*, for the ordinary duties of life – everything I told him and showed him. 'Look at this – and this – and this,' throwing down all my disadvantages. To which he did not answer by a single compliment, but simply that he had not then to choose, and that I might be right or he might be right, he was not there to decide; but that he loved me and should to his last hour. . . . That I was *constrained* to act clandestinely, and did not *choose* to do so, God is witness, and will set it down as my heavy misfortune and not my fault. Also, up to the very last act we stood in the light of day for the whole world, if it pleased, to judge us. I never saw him out of the Wimpole Street house; he came twice a week to see me – or rather, three times in the fortnight, openly in the sight of all, and this for nearly two years, and neither more nor less. Some jests used to be passed upon us by my brothers, and I allowed them without a word, but it would have been infamous in me to have taken any into my confidence who would have suffered, as a direct consequence, a blighting of his own prospects. My secrecy towards them all was my simple duty towards them all, and what they call want of affection was an affectionate consideration for them. My sisters did indeed know the truth to a certain point. They knew of the attachment and engagement – I could not help that – but the whole of the event I kept from them with a strength and resolution which really I did not know to be in me, and of which nothing but a sense of the injury to be done to them by a fuller confidence, and my tender gratitude and attachment to them for all their love and goodness, could have rendered me capable. Their faith in me, and undeviating affection for me, I shall be grateful for to the end of my existence, and to the extent of my power of feeling gratitude. My dearest sisters! – especially, let me say, my own beloved Arabel, who, with no consolation except the exercise of a most generous tenderness, has looked only to what she considered my good – never doubting me, never swerving for one instant in her love for me. May God reward her as I cannot. Dearest Henrietta loves me too, but loses less in me, and has reasons for not misjudging me. But both my sisters have been faultless in their bearing towards me, and never did I love them so tenderly as I love them now.

The only time I met R.B. clandestinely was in the parish church, where we were married before two witnesses – it was the first and only time. I looked, he says, more dead than alive, and can well believe it, for I all but fainted on the way, and had to stop for sal volatile at a chemist's shop. The support through it all was *my trust in him*, for no woman who ever committed a like act of trust has had stronger motives to hold by. Now may I not tell you that his genius, and all but miraculous attainments, are the least things in him, the moral nature being of the very noblest, as all who ever knew him admit? Then he has had that wide experience of men which ends by throwing the mind back on itself and God; there is nothing incomplete in him, except as all humanity is incompleteness. The only wonder is how such a man, whom any woman could have loved, should have loved *me*; but men of genius, you know, are apt to love with their imagination. Then there is something in the sympathy, the strange straight sympathy which unites us on all subjects. If it were not that I look up to him, we should be too alike to be together perhaps, but I know my place better than he does, who is too humble. Oh, you cannot think how well we get on after six weeks of marriage.

Elizabeth Barrett Browning, *Letters* (1897)

The Cockney Amorist

Oh when my love, my darling,
   You've left me here alone,
I'll walk the streets of London
   Which once seemed all our own.

The vast suburban churches
   Together we have found:
The ones which smelt of gaslight
   The ones in incense drown'd;
I'll use them now for praying in
   And not for looking round.

No more the Hackney Empire
   Shall find us in its stalls
When on the limelit crooner
   The thankful curtain falls,
And soft electric lamplight
   Reveals the gilded walls.

I will not go to Finsbury Park
   The putting course to see
Nor cross the crowded High Road
   To Williamsons' to tea,
For these and all the other things
   Were part of you and me.

I love you, oh my darling,
   And what I can't make out
Is why since you have left me
   I'm somehow still about.

John Betjeman, *Collected Poems* (1970)

341

Disraeli's courtship

To continue on the present basis would incur the charge of being a rich middle-aged widow's paid lover. On February 7 he resolved to put matters to the test. He called at Grosvenor Gate and pressed her with the strongest words at his command to marry him. Their followed a furious row. She flung the loan in his face, called him 'a selfish bully' and ordered him never to return to her house. Disraeli went back to his lodgings in Park Street and wrote a letter of over 1,500 words – it must have taken him at least two hours – and dispatched it that night. The letter is a remarkable production which has never been printed in full.

He wrote, he said, 'as if it were the night before my execution'. Everyone was talking of their forthcoming union except her. A friend had even offered him 'one of his seats for our happy month. The affair was then approaching absurdity.' She must 'as a woman of the world which you are thoroughly' recognize the difference between their positions.

> The continuance of the present state of affairs cd only render you *disreputable*; me it wd render *infamous* . . .
>
> This reputation impends over me . . . ere a few weeks I must inevitably chuse between being ridiculous or being contemptible. I must be recognized as being jilted, or I must at once sink into what your friend Lady Morgan has already styled me '*Mrs Wyndham-Lewis's De Novo*'.

He admitted that he had not been influenced by love when he made his first advances. But his heart was touched when he found her in sorrow. He felt that she was 'one whom I cd look upon with pride as the partner of my life, who cd sympathize with all my projects & feelings, console me in the moments of depression, share my hour of triumph & work with me for our honor & happiness'. As for her fortune, it was far less than he or the world had believed. What use was a mere jointure to him? 'Was this an inducement to sacrifice my sweet liberty & that indefinite future which is one of the charms of existence?' In the course of time he would succeed to that financial independence which was needful. 'All that society can offer is at my command. . . . I wd not condescend to be the minion of a princess. . . . My nature demands that my life shd be perpetual love.' He ended on a note of sombre prophecy:

For a few years you may flutter in some frivolous circle. But the time will come when you will sigh for any heart that could be fond and despair of one that could be faithful. Then will be the penal hour of retribution; then you will recall to your memory the passionate heart that you have forfeited and the genius you have betrayed.

Most women on receiving such a letter would have broken off the affair at once. But Mary Anne, eccentric and unsophisticated as she was, saw that there was something behind this theatrical extravagance. She realized, perhaps for the first time, that even if his feelings for her could not be described as love in the ordinary sense, at least they were not purely mercenary. 'For God's sake come to me', she wrote. 'I never desired you to leave the house, or implied or thought a word about money ... I am devoted to you.' And so all was well at last. She accepted him, and they were married very quietly at St George's, Hanover Square, on August 28, the day after the parliamentary session ended.

Robert Blake, *Disraeli* (1966)

A. E. Housman in Talbot Road, Bayswater

Cheery, beery Saturday night:
Moses went up to his own bedroom,
Alfred to his, alone –
To lie wakeful, his spirit tossed
By the four winds of fatality.

A night-time traveller in the western upland
Paused, hearing that unquiet ghost
Whispering among the leaves.

St Stephen's Sunday morning bells
Called 'Come to church, good people!' –
But Housman, he would stay,
And cursed the breaking day.

John Heath-Stubbs, *Collected Poems* (1988)

343

The cad

'Now for God's sake, darling – you really *must not* cry here.'

'I only am because my feet do hurt.'

'Didn't I say they would? Round and round this hellish pavement. Look, shut up – you really *can't*, you know.'

'Lilian always thinks people are looking. Now you are just like Lilian.'

'I must get a taxi.'

On the crest of a sob, she said: 'I've only got sixpence. Have you got any money?'

Portia stood like a stone while Eddie went for a taxi, came back with one, gave the address of his flat. Once they were in the taxi, with Henrietta Street reeling jerking past, he miserably took her in his arms, pushing his face with cold and desperate persistence into the place where her hair fell away from her ear. 'Don't,' he said, 'please don't, darling: things are quite bad enough.'

'I can't, I can't, I can't.'

'Well, weep if it helps. Only don't reproach me so terribly.'

'You told her about our walk in the wood.'

'I was only talking, you know.'

'But that wood was where I kissed you.'

'I can't live up to those things. I'm not really fit to have things happen, darling. For you and me there ought to be a new world. Why should we be at the start of our two lives when everything round us is losing its virtue? How can we grow up when there's nothing left to inherit, when what we must feed on is so stale and corrupt? No, don't look up: just stay buried in me.'

'*You're* not buried; you're looking at things. Where are we?'

'Near Leicester Square Station. Just turning right.'

Turning round in his arms to look up jealously, Portia saw the cold daylight reflected in Eddie's dilated eyes. Fighting an arm free, she covered his eyes with one hand and said: 'But why can't we alter everything?'

'There are too few of us.'

'No, you don't really want to. You've always only been playing.'

Elizabeth Bowen, *The Death of the Heart* (1938)

Sick with love

Selection of a place to be sick in is always a matter of personal importance and can add an extra tormenting dimension to the graceless horror of vomiting. Not on the carpet, not on the table, not over your hostess's dress. I did not want to be sick within the precincts of the Royal Opera House, nor was I. I emerged into a deserted shabby street and a pungent spicy smell of early dusk. The pillars of the Opera House, blazing a pale gold behind me, seemed in that squalid place like the portico of a ruined or perhaps imagined or perhaps magically fabricated palace, the green and white arcades of the foreign fruit market, looking like something out of the Italian Renaissance, actually clinging to its side. I turned a corner and confronted an array of about a thousand peaches in tiers of boxes behind a lattice grille. I carefully took hold of the grille with one hand and leaned well forward and was sick.

Vomiting is a curious experience, entirely *sui generis*. It is involuntary in a peculiarly shocking way, the body suddenly doing something very unusual with great promptness and decision. One cannot argue. One is *seized*. And the fact that one's vomit moves with such a remarkable drive contrary to the force of gravity adds to the sense of being taken and shaken by some alien power. I am told that there are people who enjoy vomiting, and although I do not share their taste I can, I think, faintly imagine it. There is a certain sense of achievement. And if one does not fight against the stomach's decree there is perhaps some satisfaction in being its helpless vehicle. The relief of having vomited is of course another thing.

I leaned there for a moment, looking down at what I had done, and aware too of the tear-wetness of my face upon which a faint breeze was coolly blowing. I remembered that casket of agony, steel coated in sugar. The inevitable loss of the beloved. And I *experienced* Julian. I cannot explain this. I simply felt in a sort of exhausted defeated cornered utmost way that she *was*. There was no particular joy or relief in this, but a sort of absolute categorical quality of *grasp* of her being.

I became aware that someone was standing beside me. Julian said, 'How are you feeling now, Bradley?'

I began to walk away from her, fumbling for my handkerchief. I wiped my mouth carefully, trying to cleanse it within with saliva.

I was walking along a corridor composed entirely of cages. I was in a prison, I was in a concentration camp. There was a wall composed of transparent sacks full of fiery carrots. They looked at me like derisive faces, like monkeys' bottoms. I breathed carefully and regularly and interrogated my stomach, stroking it gently with my hands. I turned into a lighted arcade and tested my stomach against a smell of decaying lettuce. I walked onward occupied in breathing. Only now I felt so empty and so faint. I felt that I had reached the end of the world, I felt like a stag when it can run no further and turns and bows its head to the hounds, I felt like Actaeon condemned and cornered and devoured.

Julian was following me. I could hear the soft tap–tap of her shoes on the sticky pavement and my whole body apprehended her presence behind me.

'Bradley, would you like some coffee? There's a stall there.'

'No.'

'Let's sit down somewhere.'

'Nowhere to sit.'

We passed between two lorries loaded with milky white boxes of dark cherries and came out into the open. It was becoming dark, lights had come on revealing the sturdy elegant military outline of the vegetable market, resembling a magazine, a seedy eighteenth-century barracks, though quiet at this time and sombre as a cloister. Opposite to us the big derelict eastern portico of Inigo Jones's church was now in view, cluttered up with barrows and housing at the far end the coffee stall referred to by Julian. Some mean and casual lamp–light, itself seeming dirty, revealed the thick pillars, a few lounging market men, a large pile of vegetable refuse and disintegrating cardboard boxes. It was like a scene in some small battered Italian city, rendered by Hogarth.

Julian seated herself on the plinth of one of the pillars at the dark end of the portico, and I sat down next to her, or as near next to her as the bulge of the column would allow. I could feel the thick filth and muck of London under my feet, under my bottom, behind my back. I saw, in a diagonal of dim light, Julian's silk dress hitched up, her tights, smoky blue, coloured by the flesh within, her shoes, also blue, against which I had so cautiously placed my own.

'Poor Bradley,' said Julian.

Iris Murdoch, The Black Prince (1973)

A male fantasy figure

'Nicola, I'm worried about you, as usual. And in a peculiar way, as usual. I'm worried they're going to say you're a male fantasy figure.'

'I *am* a male fantasy figure. I've been one for fifteen years. It really takes it out of a girl.'

'But they don't know that.'

'I'm sorry, I just *am*. You should see me in bed. I do all the gimmicks men read up on in the magazines and the hot books.'

'Nico*la*.'

'So they'll think you're just a sick dreamer. Who cares? You won't be around for that.'

'You neither. I was thinking. You're hard to categorize, even in the male fantasy area. Maybe you're a mixture of genres. A mutant,' I went on (I love these typologies). 'You're not a Sexpot. Not dizzy enough. You're not a Hot Lay either, not quite. Too calculating. You're definitely something of a Sack Artist. And a Mata Hari too. And a Vamp. And a Ballbreaker. In the end, though, I'm fingering you for a Femme Fatale. I like it. Nice play on words. Semi-exotic. No, I like it. It's cute.'

'A Femme Fatale? I'm not a Femme Fatale. Listen, mister: Femmes Fatales are ten a penny compared to what I am.'

'What are you then?'

'Christ, you still don't get it, do you.'

I waited.

'I'm a Murderee.'

We went out walking. We can do this. *Oh* – what you see in London streets at three o'clock in the morning, with it trickling out to the eaves and flues, tousled water, ragged waste. Violence is near and inexhaustible. Even death is near. But none of it can touch Nicola and me. It knows better, and stays right out of our way. It can't touch us. It knows this. We're the dead.

Martin Amis, London Fields (1989)

Netta

By now he had crossed Cromwell Road, and her window was in sight. Every morning, after breakfast, wet or fine, cold or warm, he made this trip up the Earl's Court Road to look at the house in which she lived. After he had passed it he walked on for about fifty yards, and then he turned and looked at it again as he came back. He had never seen her at this time of the morning, and he had very little hope of doing so: but the habit was now formed, and it never occurred to him to try and break it. He was prompted, perhaps, by the same sort of obsessed motivation which might make a miser ever and anon go and look at the outside of the box which contained the gold which was the cause of all his unhappiness. Then there was the miserable pleasure of mere proximity. For that appalling halo around Netta, that field of intense influence emanating from her in a room to a distance of about two feet, was only the inner, the most concentrated halo. It, in its turn, gave forth another halo – one which came out of her room, and out of the house and into the open street to as far as fifty or even a hundred yards – as far as any point, in fact, from which the house in which she lived might be espied by her lover. This second halo was infinitely weaker, of course, than the inner one which gave it birth, if only because it was more spread-out and in the fresh air, but nevertheless it pervaded the whole, trembling atmosphere amidst the roar of passing traffic, and cast its enthralling, uncanny influence upon every fixed object or passing person in the neighbourhood.

Finally, in this daily walk after breakfast past her house, there yet remained the lurking hope that he might see her 'by accident', that she might be coming out of the house for a walk, or on her way to some appointment; that she might be in some sort of distress in which she could make use of him, that he might go in a taxi with her somewhere, or be allowed to be with her or near her. In such a way he might be enabled to discover, and enter, Columbus-like, that unknown world, that mysterious earthly paradise, whose existence he knew about only by logical inference and hearsay, and whose character he could only imagine – the world of Netta's early morning life, her world before eleven o'clock – eleven o'clock being the earliest time she permitted him to phone her, let alone see her.

Patrick Hamilton, *Hangover Square* (1941)

After the Lunch

On Waterloo Bridge, where we said our goodbyes,
The weather conditions bring tears to my eyes.
I wipe them away with a black woolly glove
And try not to notice I've fallen in love.

On Waterloo Bridge I am trying to think:
This is nothing. You're high on the charm and the drink.
But the juke-box inside me is playing a song
That says something different. And when was it wrong?

On Waterloo Bridge with the wind in my hair
I am tempted to skip. *You're a fool.* I don't care.
The head does its best but the heart is the boss –
I admit it before I am halfway across.

Wendy Cope, Serious Concerns (1992)

14

Clubs, Taverns, Coffee-Houses

A big city offers the double opportunity of avoiding loneliness while remaining anonymous. Social engineers lament the decline of 'community' – streets where all the neighbours knew one another's business. Doubtless they are right to do so. But neighbours, and families, are a mixed blessing, and large towns – none more than London – offer the chance to escape the domestic hearth without being thrown back on the tedium of Wordsworthian solitude. If one had to single out one thing which made metropolitan life more attractive than life in the provinces, it would perhaps be the multiplicity of places in which human beings can congregate without going home. From the coffee-house to the coffee-bar, from the Mermaid Tavern to the Coach and Horses, we read of places, most of them vile, where you can go and sit. You might think that the sole function of pubs or clubs or cafés is concourse. On the contrary, it is the fact that you can go to such places and not meet other people which sometimes makes them so attractive. Unlike organized 'social life', the life of people in clubs, pubs, coffee-houses, and so on, is determined entirely by the mood of individuals. Those who go to such places can be as familiar or as anonymous as they choose. There is the world of difference between a pub in a small town, where most of the people in the bar are 'regulars', and a London pub where you may sit at a table by the wall reading a newspaper, or talk to your friends as the mood takes you.

For the gregarious, by contrast, there can be no better place to live than in London. It is the sheer variety of people, and the numbers, which have made its taverns and pubs, its clubs and cafés so necessary for the happiness of true Londoners.

Children in pubs

The idea of allowing children in pubs appals me. I'd have thought that the Home Secretary might have contemplated the fact that there are good reasons for not allowing dogs in restaurants and theatres before taking this grave step, which many will see as a liberal act.

Pubs attract enough bores as it is and I have yet to meet a 12-year-old who could sustain a conversation for the length of time it takes to drink a couple of pints of beer or a few large vodkas. The little beasts won't be standing their rounds either. Baby talk will catch on and we shall be hearing barmen uttering such banalities as, 'Who's a pretty boy then?'

The Government is already saying that there will be stern measures to make sure that the little brutes don't drink alcohol. Don't bet on them being effective. They already drink at home when they are under such stresses as exams or missing a good railway engine number, and I wouldn't turn my back on a large drink with children in the vicinity.

Pubs were never intended to be places of family entertainment. Pubs are drinking shops for desperate and serious men searching for the meaning of life. Occasional flashes of wit from one or two regulars liven the proceedings from time to time, but whoever came across an intentionally funny child?

And they will bring their mothers with them, God help us. Most of those mothers bear witness to the fact that children can drive you mad. It is not surprising. Once a woman gives birth she is in effect locked up with an idiot for the next 16 years. And I am sceptical about the claim that an early introduction to the ways of drinkers may have a civilizing effect on children. If my mother had introduced me to the pubs of Soho when I was seven I would doubtless be in a lunatic asylum. To all intents and purposes I am for a large part of the day. I wouldn't wish life membership of the Coach and Horses on the most obnoxious of children.

We shall probably hear the slurred speech of passive drinkers and the coughs of passive smokers. The prospects are awful. I can hear myself ordering a drink with some sense of urgency only to hear the barman say, 'I'm sorry sir. I'm serving this child at the moment.' Woe betide the day.

Jeffrey Bernard, Sunday Telegraph, 21 March 1993

A coffee-table dialogue

I took Dempster with me to the City, and to Child's. He did not enter into the spirit of it and went away soon. It is quite a place to my mind; dusky, comfortable, and warm, with a society of citizens and physicians who talk politics very fully and are very sagacious and sometimes jocular. 'What is the reason,' said one, 'that a sole is not a good fish?' 'Why, it is a good fish,' said another, 'if you dress it with a plain butter sauce. But you must have something so dev'lish high-seasoned. You might as well have a sauce of fire and brimstone.' I shall hereafter for the sake of neatness throw our conversation into my journal in the form of a dialogue. So that every Saturday this my Journal shall be adorned with

A DIALOGUE AT CHILD'S

1 CITIZEN: Pray now, what do you really think of this Peace?

2 CITIZEN: That it is a damned bad one, to be sure!

PHYSICIAN: Damned bad one? Pray what would you be at? Have you not had all that you wanted? Did you not begin the war to settle your boundaries in North America? And have not you got that done, as Mr Pitt the great champion of the Opposition acknowledged in the House, better than could have been expected? Have not you got a large tract of country ceded to you? Is not the line of division plain and straight?

BOSWELL: Suppose, Sir, I went out a-hunting with intention to bring home a hare to dinner, and catch three hares. Don't you think that I may also bring home the other two? Now, Sir, I grant you that we began the war with intention only to settle our boundaries in America and would have been satisfied with that and nothing more. But, Sir, we have had uncommon success. We have not only got what we intended, but we have also picked up some other little things, such as the Havana, Guadeloupe, &c. I should be glad to know why we are to part with them?

PHYSICIAN: Because the French will not make peace except we do so. And we cannot carry on the war another year.

1 CITIZEN: But we can.

PHYSICIAN: From whence have you the money? Who will furnish that?

1 CITIZEN: The City of London.

PHYSICIAN: Where will you get the men?
BOSWELL: I own to you that is a difficulty.

James Boswell, *Life of Johnson* (1891)

Coffee-Houses

In London there are a great number of coffee-houses, most of which, to tell the truth, are not over clean or well furnished, owing to the quantity of people who resort to these places and because of the smoke, which would quickly destroy good furniture. Englishmen are great drinkers. In these coffee-houses you can partake of chocolate, tea, or coffee, and of all sorts of liquors, served hot; also in many places you can have wine, punch, or ale. . . . What attracts enormously in these coffee-houses are the gazettes and other public papers. All Englishmen are great newsmongers. Workmen habitually begin the day by going to coffee-rooms in order to read the latest news. I have often seen shoeblacks and other persons of that class club together to purchase a farthing paper. . . . Some coffee-houses are a resort for learned scholars and for wits; others are the resort of dandies or of politicians, or again of professional newsmongers.

Ferdinand de Saussure, *A Foreign View of England in the Reigns of George I and George II*

(1902)

Kate Meyrick at the 43 Club

Her most famous club, the 43, was patronized by artists and bohemians such as Augustus John, Joseph Conrad, Jacob Epstein and J. B. Priestley when it opened in 1923, but as its fame spread it became the most fashionable night-club in London, attracting a richer clientele as its regulars, and a stream of visiting celebrities – from Russian Bolsheviks and East European aristocrats to American gangsters and film stars. Mrs Meyrick, selling her twelve shilling and sixpence champagne at thirty shillings during licensing hours and at two pounds afterwards, welcomed them all.

At the 43 Club the underworld and the aristocracy met on equal terms, free-spending burglars like Ruby Sparks mingling with the owners of the jewels and furs from whom they stole. Kate's adopted daughter, Renée Meyrick, recalled nights 'when we would see the cream of Britain's aristocracy sitting at their tables, while practically rubbing shoulders with them would be the roughest and toughest of the underworld, including the Sabini gang, who at that time were up to all sorts of tricks on the race-courses all over England'. Mrs Meyrick complained that underworld characters, particularly the racing gangsters, were too rowdy and dangerous, but the police were much more of a problem.

When fines failed to deter her, more draconian punishment was dealt out. In 1924 she was sentenced to six months in Holloway – not the most salubrious environment for an ailing woman of fifty. Fortunately, her experience of dealing with the diverse, rowdy clientele of her clubs stood her in good stead and she won the affection of the 'hoisters' (shop-lifters) who constituted the prison aristocracy. These 'soberly dressed women who looked like churchwardens' wives and swore like troopers' admired her spirit and ensured that she was treated with respect by the other inmates. Outside, her Roedean- and Girton-educated daughters – soon to be married into the aristocracy – continued to run the clubs.

Robert Murphy, *Smash and Grab* (1993)

A visit to a gaming house

1 January 1668

By and by I met with Mr Brisband, and having it in my mind this Christmas to go to see the manner of the gaming at the Groome-Porter's,* I did tell Brisband of it, and he did lead me thither: where, after staying an hour, they begun to play at about eight at night, where to see how differently one man took his losing from another, one cursing and swearing, and another only muttering and grumbling to himself, a third without any apparent discontent at all; to see how the dice will run good luck in one hand for half an hour together, and another have no good luck at all; to see how easily here, where they play nothing but guinnys, a £100 is won or lost; to see two

---

* The Groom Porter was the Court official in charge of the gaming tables.

or three gentlemen come in there drunk, and putting their stock of gold together, one 22 pieces, the second 4, and the third 5 pieces, and these to play one with another, and forget how much each of them brought, but he that brought the 22 thinks that he brought no more than the rest; to see the different humours of gamesters to change their luck when it is bad, how ceremonious they are as to call for new dice, to shift their places, to alter their manner of throwing, and that with great industry, as if there was anything in it; to see how some old gamesters that have no money now to spend as formerly do come and sit and look on as among others, Sir Lewis Dives, who was here, and hath been a great gamester in his time; to hear their cursing and damning to no purpose, as one man being to throw a seven if he could, and failing to do it after a great many throws cried he would be damned if ever he flung seven more while he lived, his despair of throwing it being so great, while others did it as their luck served almost every throw; to see how persons of the best quality do here sit down and play with people of any, though meaner; and to see how people in ordinary clothes shall come hither and play away 100, or 2 or 300 guinnys, without any kind of difficulty; and lastly, to see the formality of the groome-porter, who is their judge of all disputes in play and all quarrels that may arise therein, and how his under-officers are there to observe true play at each table, and to give new dice, is a consideration I never could have thought had been in the world, had I not now seen it. And mighty glad I am that I did see it, and it may be will find another evening before Christmas be over to see it again, when I may stay later, for their heat of play begins not till about eleven or twelve o'clock; which did give me another pretty observation of a man, that did win mighty fast when I was there. I think he won £100 at single pieces in a little time. While all the rest envied him his good fortune he cursed it, saying, 'A pox on it, that it should come so early upon me, for this fortune two hours hence would be worth something to me, but then, God damn me, I shall have no such luck.' This kind of prophane, mad entertainment they give themselves. And so I, having enough for once, refusing to venture, though Brisband pressed me hard, and tempted me with saying that no man was ever known to lose the first time, the devil being too cunning to discourage a gamester; and he offered me also to lend me ten pieces to venture, but I did refuse, and so went away, and took coach and home about 9 or 10 at night.

Samuel Pepys, *Diary*

Has it not passed like a dream?

Wednesday, 3 August 1763

I should have mentioned that on Monday night, coming up the Strand, I was tapped on the shoulder by a fine fresh lass. I went home with her. She was an officer's daughter, and born at Gibraltar. I could not resist indulging myself with enjoyment of her. Surely, in such a situation, when the woman is already abandoned, the crime must be alleviated, though in strict morality, illicit love is always wrong.

I last night sat up again, but I shall do so no more, for I was very stupid today and had a kind of feverish headache. At night Mr Johnson and I supped at the Turk's Head. He talked much for restoring the Convocation of the Church of England to its full powers, and said that religion was much assisted and impressed on the mind by external pomp. My want of sleep sat heavy upon me, and made me like to nod, even in Mr Johnson's company. Such must be the case while we are united with flesh and blood.

Thursday, 4th. This is now my last day in London before I set out upon my travels, and makes a very important period in my journal. Let me recollect my life since this journal began. Has it not passed like a dream? Yes, but I have been attaining a knowledge of the world. I came to town to go into the Guards. How different is my scheme now! I am now upon a less pleasurable but a more rational and lasting plan. Let me pursue it with steadiness and I may be a man of dignity. My mind is strangely agitated. I am happy to think of going upon my travels and seeing the diversity of foreign parts; and yet my feeble mind shrinks somewhat at the idea of leaving Britain in so very short a time from the moment in which I now make this remark. How strange must I feel myself in foreign parts. My mind too is gloomy and dejected at the thoughts of leaving London, where I am so comfortably situated and where I have enjoyed most happiness. However, I shall be the happier for being abroad, as long as I live. Let me be manly. Let me commit myself to the care of my merciful Creator.

James Boswell, *London Journal* (1950)

The Intrepid Fox

Honest Sam House, who kept the public-house at the corner of Peter Street and Wardour Street, the 'Intrepid Fox', was an old resident of Soho and remarkable for his oddities and for his political zeal in behalf of the Whigs. During the celebrated Westminster election of 1784, he kept open house at his own expense, and was honoured with the company of many of the Whig aristocracy. An early caricature, by Gilray, entitled 'Returning from Brooks's', represents the Prince of Wales in a state of considerable inebriety, wearing the election cockade and supported by Fox and the patriotic publican. The wit of the ministerial papers was often expended on honest Sam. At the beginning of the election, when Fox seemed to be in a hopeless minority, one of them inserted a paragraph stating that the publican had committed suicide in despair. He is said to have been a very successful canvasser in the course of the election.

> See the brave Sammy House, he's as still as a mouse,
>   And does canvass with prudence so clever;
> See what shoals with him flock, to poll for brave Fox,
>   Give thanks to Sam House, for ever, for ever, for ever!
>   Give thanks to Sam House, boys, for ever!
>
> Brave bald-headed Sam, all must own is the man,
>   Who does canvass for brave Fox so clever;
> His aversion, I say, is to *small beer and Wray*!
>   May his bald head be honour'd for ever, for ever, for ever!
>   May his bald head be honour'd for ever!

But the most active and successful of Fox's canvassers was the beautiful and accomplished Georgiana Spencer, Duchess of Devonshire. Attended by several other of the beauties of the Whig aristocracy, she was almost daily present at the election, wearing Fox's cockade, and she went about personally soliciting votes, which she obtained in great numbers by the influence of her personal charms and by her affability. The Tories were greatly annoyed at her Ladyship's proceedings; they accused her of wholesale bribery, and it was currently reported that she had in one instance bought the vote of a butcher with a kiss, an incident which was immediately exhibited to the people's eyes in multitudes of pictures, with more or less of exaggeration. But nothing could be more disgraceful than the profusion of scandalous and indecent abuse which was heaped upon this noble lady by the ministerial press, especially by its two great organs, the *Morning Post* and the *Advertiser*. The insult in some cases was merely coarse, such as the following from the *Morning Post*: 'The Duchess of Devonshire yesterday canvassed the different alehouses of Westminster in favour of Mr Fox; about one o'clock she took her share of a pot of porter at Sam House's in Wardour Street.'

The same paper makes her write to the candidate: 'Yesterday I sent you three votes, but went through great fatigue to secure them; it cost me *ten kisses* for every *plumper*. I am much afraid *we are done up*. Will see you at the *porter-shop* and consult about ways and means.' All this is, of course, much exaggerated; but it is certain her Grace was a frequent visitor at the sign of the 'Intrepid Fox'.

The portrait of Sam House occurs in many caricatures of the time. He was remarkable for his clean and perfectly bald head, over which he never wore hat or wig. His unvaried dress consisted of nankeen jacket and breeches, brightly polished shoes and buckles, and he had his waistcoat open in all seasons, and wore remarkably white linen. His legs were generally bare; but, when clad, stockings of the finest quality of silk were worn.

E. F. Rimbault, *Soho and Its Associations* (1895)

The Mermaid Tavern

Souls of Poets dead and gone,
What Elysium have ye known,
Happy field or mossy cavern,
Choicer than the Mermaid Tavern?
Have ye tippled drink more fine
Than mine host's Canary wine?
Or are fruits of Paradise
Sweeter than those dainty pies
Of venison? O generous food!
Drest as though bold Robin Hood
Would, with his maid Marian,
Sup and bowse from horn and can.

I have heard that on a day
Mine host's sign-board flew away,
Nobody knew whither, till
An astrologer's old quill
To a sheep-skin gave the story, –
Said he saw you in your glory,
Underneath a new old-sign
Sipping beverage divine,
And pledging with contented smack
The Mermaid in the Zodiac.

Souls of Poets dead and gone,
What Elysium have ye known,
Happy field or mossy cavern,
Choicer than the Mermaid Tavern?

John Keats, Collected Poems (1818)

The Mitre, Cheapside

The Mitre was one of the taverns in Cheapside permitted to continue
their trade in 1554; and the Mitre and the Bull-Head are the two taverns
mentioned in Chepe in the curious list of the fifteen important London
taverns in a blackletter sheet of Queen Elizabeth's reign, entitled 'Newes
from Bartholomew Fayre'.

There hath been great sale and utterance of Wine,
Besides Beere, and Ale, and Ipocras fine,
In every country, region, and nation,
But chiefly in Billingsgate, at the Salutation;
And the Bore's Head, near London Stone;
The Swan at Dowgate, a tavern well knowne;
The Miter in Cheape, and the Bull Head,
And many like places that make noses red;
The Bore's Head in Old Fish Street; Three Cranes in the Vintry;
And now, of late, St Martin's in the Sentree;
The Windmill in Lothbury; the Ship at th' Exchange;
King's Head in New Fish-street, where roysterers do range;

The Mermaid in Cornhill; Red Lion in the Strand;
Three Tuns in Newgate Market; Old Fish-street at the Swan.

'Sentree' is a corruption of Sanctuary, and refers to St Martin-le-Grand;
Stow relates that the Church there was destroyed in 1548, and a large wine
tavern built on part of the site. Thomas Heywood, the dramatist, wrote a
rhymed list of taverns about 1608, purporting to give the type of frequenter
of each, but he obviously makes the people suit the particular sign. Here is
an extract from it:

> The Gentry to the King's Head,
> The Nobles to the Crown,
> The Knights unto the Golden Fleece,
> And to the Plough the Clown.
> The Churchman to the Mitre,
> The Shepherd to the Star,
> The gardener hies him to the Rose,
> To the Drum the man of war;
> To the Feathers, ladies you; the Globe
> The seaman doth not scorn;
> The usurer to the Devil, and
> The townsman to the Horn. . . .

I propose to give some quotations from the old dramatists referring to
the Mitre here, though I shall give reasons later for supposing that the
Bread Street tavern may have been meant, and in two instances was actually
named.

In one of his amusing Comedies, Ben Jonson mentions the Mitre, and
although he does not fix its locality, it was probably the Cheapside tavern.
Every Man out of His Humour (1599), Act III. Sc. 1:

CARLO. 'I'll design the other a place too, that we may see him.
PUNTARVOLO. No better place than the Mitre, that we may be
    spectators with you, Carlo.'
    Scene 1 is in 'the Middle Aisle of St Paul's' . . . the usual meeting
place for gallants and various idlers, including cutpurses, in the
morning before the midday dinner. The great Nave was known as
'Paul's Walk', and was a regular promenade, and business affairs were
also transacted there. Later in the scene Sogliardo says, 'Where shall
we go, Signior?' and Puntarvolo answers, 'Your Mitre is your best

house.' Sogliardo then questions Carlo about the Ordinaries . . . 'they say there resorts your most choice gallants'.

CARLO. 'True, and the fashion is, when any stranger comes in amongst 'em, they all stand up and stare at him, as he were some unknown beast, brought out of Africk; but that will be helped by a good adventurous face. You must be impudent enough, sit down, and use no respect; when anything's propounded above your capacity, smile at it, make two or three faces, and 'tis excellent; they'll think you have travelled.'

In Act V. Sc. 4, Macilente says: 'Our supper at the Mitre must of necessity hold tonight, if you love your reputations.'

Scene IV takes place in a Room at the Mitre.

CARLO. 'Holloa! where be these shot-sharks?

(*Enter Drawer.*)

DRAW. By and by; you are welcome, good Master Buffone.

CARLO. Where's George? call me George hither quickly.

DRAW. What wine please you have, sir? I'll draw you that's neat, Master Buffone.

CARLO. Away, neophite, do as I bid thee, bring my dear George to me.

(*Enter George.*)

GEORGE. Welcome, Master Carlo.

CARLO. What, is supper ready, George? . . . Draw me the biggest shaft you have out of the butt you wot of; away . . . George, quick!

(*Re-enter George, with two jugs of wine.*)

GEORGE. Here, Master Carlo.

CARLO. Is it right, boy?

GEORGE. Ay, sir, I assure you 'tis right.

(*Carlo gets rid of the drawers and drinks.*)

CARLO. Ay, marry, sir, here's purity; O George . . . I could bite off his nose for this now; sweet rogue, he has drawn nectar, the very soul of the grape! I'll wash my temples with some on't presently, and drink some half a score draughts; 'twill heat the brain, kindle my imagination; I shall talk nothing but crackers and fireworks tonight. So, Sir! please you to be here, Sir, and I here: so.

(*Carlo then sets the two cups asunder, drinks with the one and pledges with the other, speaking for each of the cups, and drinking alternately:*)

I CUP. Now, sir, here's to you; and I present you so much of my Love.

2 CUP. I take it kindly from you sir (*drinks*) and will return you the like proportion.'

It is impossible to quote more here, but the whole scene is amusing.

Scene 6 is also in 'A Room at the Mitre', and Scene 7 in the Counter. This was probably the Compter in the Poultry, close by – the other Compter or prison, was then in Wood Street. It is noteworthy that in Act V, Scene 5, when Macilente tells Deliro that his brother-in-law is left in pawn for the reckoning at a tavern – *Deliro* asks, 'What tavern is it? *Mac.* The Mitre, Sir. *Del.* O! why, Fido! my shoes.' – which suggests that 'the Mitre' was understood as a particular tavern, and probably the one in Cheapside?

George, the chief drawer at the Mitre, was evidently a well known character at this time, and a popular one. He is referred to in 'Westward Hoe', the play by Dekker and John Webster, 1607. Tenterhook, in Act IV, Scene 1, has blindfolded Lucy with his hands and she makes various guesses as to his identity: 'You are not Sir Gosling Glowworm for he wears no rings of his fingers; Master Freezeleather? . . . O, you are George the drawer at the Mitre . . . pray you, unblind me.'

Kenneth Rogers, The Mermaid and Mitre Taverns in Old London (1928)

East End Pubs in the Evening

My exploration of the East End led me, not unwillingly, to the pubs. Apart from those outside the dock gates, these were cavernously empty at lunchtime. I had made the mistake a few years earlier of taking a bus to a popular pub in Hackney one Saturday lunchtime, a journey that took so long, with a maze of wrong directions, that I arrived there shortly before it closed for the afternoon. There was the additional disappointment of finding it empty, apart from an ill-tempered barman who replied 'Evenings' with a terseness I deserved when I asked if I had come to the right place. Surprisingly, I was accompanied on this abortive venture by Francis Bacon, who was equally engrossed by the unfamiliar landscape, and equally unworldly in assuming that Saturday lunchtimes in the East End would prove as crowded as they were 'up West'. Expressing some impatience with my stupidity, he managed to find a taxi to take us back to the Colony Room in Soho where we could drink in the afternoon. We did not return.

Now I discovered the numerous East End pubs which pulsated with live entertainment in welcome contrast to the taped variety on television which had settled into a transatlantic rut.

Far from predictable, the entertainment ranged from modern jazz at Bermondsey (the south, and therefore the wrong side of the river), to stand-up comics and the female impersonators so beloved by the British.

I took Antony Armstrong-Jones and the actress Jacquie Chan to the Bridge House at Canning Town one Sunday lunchtime – Sundays were the festive exception – to join the crowd of dockers who cheered lustily a few minutes before closing time as the girl strippers removed every garment, and then staggered home to a late, traditional lunch. Armstrong-Jones wrote to me later that he had returned to the pub to find that the strip-tease had been replaced by elderly Indian fire-eaters: 'It was not the same.'

With pubs featuring their favourite turns, which attracted a following of regulars, it occurred to me that here was a form of music hall that had returned to its roots. There was the same challenge for the artist to establish himself immediately by sheer force of personality: also, a similar vulnerability, for though the pub performers had the armour of a microphone, they needed to rise above the clash and clatter of the crowd. Even more than with music hall, the audience was part of the fun. There was no courtesy towards an indifferent performer who was drowned by noise, but if the customers took to an artist they listened attentively, though applause was sparse due to the difficulty of clapping with a beer mug in one hand. At least this was not chained to the seat as it had been in the rougher halls where the orchestra was protected from a hail of trotter bones by a mesh screen.

When an artist triumphed, the atmosphere was warm and the comments generous. Unlike the southern English who dared to be amused, the East Enders set out for the night determined to enjoy themselves, a quality they shared with the north. After all, what was the point of sinking to the occasion?

For me, the constant delight was the 'local talent': members of the audience who needed little prompting to get up on stage and perform, like the taxi-driver who impersonated the Al Jolson numbers whose sentimentality made them perennially popular. If the performers lacked refinement, they possessed a raw vitality which was more exciting than the images on television. By comparison, the West End nightclubs looked stale.

Daniel Farson, *Limehouse Days* (1991)

Club Snobs

Bacchus is the divinity to whom Waggle devotes his especial worship. 'Give me wine, my boy,' says he to his friend Wiggle, who is prating about lovely woman; and holds up his glass full of the rosy fluid, and winks at it portentously, and sips it, and smacks his lips after it, and meditates on it, as if he were the greatest of connoisseurs.

I have remarked this excessive wine-amateurship especially in youth. Snoblings from college, Fledglings from the army, Goslings from the public schools, who ornament our Clubs, are frequently to be heard in great force upon wine questions. 'This bottle's corked,' says Snobling; and Mr Sly, the butler, taking it away, returns presently with the same wine in another jug, which the young amateur pronounces excellent. 'Hang champagne!' says Fledgling; 'it's only fit for gals and children. Give me pale sherry at dinner, and my twenty-three claret afterwards.' 'What's port now?' says Gosling; 'disgusting thick sweet stuff – where's the old dry wine one *used* to get?' Until the last twelvemonth, Fledgling drank small-beer at Doctor Swishtail's; and Gosling used to get his dry old port at a gin-shop in Westminster – till he quitted that seminary, in 1844.

Anybody who has looked at the caricatures of thirty years ago, must remember how frequently bottle-noses, pimpled faces, and other Bardolphian features are introduced by the designer. They are much more rare now (in nature, and in pictures, therefore) than in those good old times; but there are still to be found amongst the youth of our Clubs lads who glory in drinking-bouts, and whose faces, quite sickly and yellow, for the most part are decorated with those marks which Rowland's Kalydor is said to efface. 'I was *so* cut last night, old boy!' Hopkins says to Tomkins (with amiable confidence). 'I tell you what we did. We breakfasted with Jack Herring at twelve, and kept up with brandy and soda-water and weeds till four; then we toddled into the Park for an hour; then we dined and drank mulled port till half-price; then we looked in for an hour at the Haymarket; then we came back to the Club, and had grills and whisky-punch till all was blue. – Hullo, waiter! Get me a glass of cherry-brandy.' Club waiters, the civilest, the kindest, the patientest of men, die under the infliction of these cruel young topers. But if the reader wishes to see a perfect picture on the stage of this class of young fellows, I would recommend him to witness the ingenious comedy of *London Assurance* – the amiable heroes of which are represented, not only as drunkards and five-o'clock-in-the-morning men, but as showing a hundred other delightful traits of swindling, lying, and general debauchery, quite edifying to witness.

How different is the conduct of these outrageous youths to the decent behaviour of my friend, Mr Papworthy, who says to Poppins, the butler at the Club: –

Papworthy. – 'Poppins, I'm thinking of dining early; is there any cold game in the house?'

Poppins. – 'There's a game-pie, sir; there's cold grouse, sir; there's cold pheasant, sir; there's cold peacock, sir; cold swan, sir; cold ostrich, sir,' etc., etc. (as the case may be).

Papworthy. – 'Hem! What's your best claret now, Poppins? – in pints, I mean.'

Poppins. – 'There's Cooper and Magnum's Lafite, sir; there's Lath and Sawdust's St Julien, sir; Bung's Leoville is considered remarkably fine; and I think you'd like Jugger's Château-Margaux.'

Papworthy. – 'Hum! – hah! – well – give me a crust of bread and a glass of beer. I'll only *lunch*, Poppins.'

Captain Shindy is another sort of Club bore. He has been known to throw all the Club in an uproar about the quality of his mutton-chop.

'Look at it, sir! Is it cooked, sir? Smell it, sir! Is it meat fit for a gentleman?' he roars out to the steward, who stands trembling before him, and who in vain tells him that the Bishop of Bullocksmithy has just had three from the same loin. All the waiters in the Club are huddled round the captain's mutton-chop. He roars out the most horrible curses at John for not bringing the pickles; he utters the most dreadful oaths because Thomas has not arrived with the Harvey sauce; Peter comes tumbling with the water-jug over Jeames, who is bringing 'the glittering canisters with bread'. Whenever Shindy enters the room (such is the force of character), every table is deserted, every gentleman must dine as he best may, and all those big footmen are in terror.

He makes his account of it. He scolds, and is better waited upon in consequence. At the Club he has ten servants scudding about to do his bidding.

Poor Mrs Shindy and the children are, meanwhile, in dingy lodgings somewhere, waited upon by a charity-girl in pattens.

William Makepeace Thackeray, The Book of Snobs (1846–8)

The Diogenes Club

I had never heard of the institution, and my face must have proclaimed as much, for Sherlock Holmes pulled out his watch.

'The Diogenes Club is the queerest club in London, and Mycroft one of the queerest men. He's always there from a quarter to five till twenty to eight. It's six now, so if you care for a stroll this beautiful evening I shall be very happy to introduce you to two curiosities.'

Five minutes later we were in the street, walking towards Regent Circus.

'You wonder,' said my companion, 'why it is that Mycroft does not use his powers for detective work. He is incapable of it.'

'But I thought you said – !'

'I said that he was my superior in observation and deduction. If the art of the detective began and ended in reasoning from an arm-chair, my brother would be the greatest criminal agent that ever lived. But he has no ambition and no energy. He would not even go out of his way to verify his own solutions, and would rather be considered wrong than take the trouble to prove himself right. Again and again I have taken a problem to him and have received an explanation which has afterwards proved to be the correct one. And yet he was absolutely incapable of working out the practical points which must be gone into before a case could be laid before a judge or jury.'

'It is not his profession, then?'

'By no means. What is to me a means of livelihood is to him the merest hobby of a dilettante. He has an extraordinary faculty for figures, and audits the books in some of the Government departments. Mycroft lodges in Pall Mall, and he walks round the corner into Whitehall every morning and back every evening. From year's end to year's end he takes no other exercise, and is seen nowhere else, except only in the Diogenes Club, which is just opposite his rooms.'

'I cannot recall the name.'

'Very likely not. There are many men in London, you know, who, some from shyness, some from misanthropy have no wish for the company of their fellows. Yet they are not averse to comfortable chairs and the latest periodicals. It is for the convenience of these that the Diogenes Club was started, and it now contains the most unsociable and unclubbable men in town. No member is permitted to take the least notice of any other one. Save in the Strangers' Room, no talking is, under any circumstances, permitted, and three offences, if brought to the notice of the committee, render the talker liable to expulsion. My brother was one of the founders, and I have myself found it a very soothing atmosphere.'

We had reached Pall Mall as we talked, and were walking down it from the St James's end. Sherlock Holmes stopped at a door some little distance from the Carlton, and, cautioning me not to speak, he led the way into the hall. Through the glass panelling I caught a glimpse of a large and luxurious room in which a considerable number of men were sitting about and reading papers, each in his own little nook.

Arthur Conan Doyle, 'The Greek Interpreter' in *The Memoirs of Sherlock Holmes* (1893)

An old clubman

One fine morning in the full London season, Major Arthur Pendennis came over from his lodgings, according to his custom, to breakfast at a certain Club in Pall Mall, of which he was a chief ornament. As he was one of the finest judges of wine in England, and a man of active, dominating, and inquiring spirit, he had been very properly chosen to be a member of the Committee of this Club, and indeed was almost the manager of the institution, and the stewards and waiters bowed before him as reverentially as to a Duke or a Field-Marshal.

At a quarter past ten the Major invariably made his appearance in the best blacked boots in all London, with a checked morning cravat that never was rumpled until dinner-time, a buff waistcoat which bore the crown of his sovereign on the buttons, and linen so spotless that Mr Brummel himself asked the name of his laundress, and would probably have employed her had not misfortunes compelled that great man to fly the country. Pendennis's coat, his white gloves, his whiskers, his very cane, were perfect of their kind as specimens of the costume of a military man *en retraite*. At a distance, or seeing his back merely, you would have taken him to be not more than thirty years old: it was only by a nearer inspection that you saw the factitious nature of his rich brown hair, and that there were a few crows'-feet round about the somewhat faded eyes of his handsome mottled face. His nose was of the Wellington pattern. His hands and wristbands were beautifully long and white. On the latter he wore handsome gold buttons given to him by His Royal Highness the Duke of York, and on the others more than one elegant ring, the chief and largest of them being emblazoned with the famous arms of Pendennis.

He always took possession of the same table in the same corner of the room, from which nobody ever now thought of ousting him. One or two mad wags and wild fellows had, in former days, and in freak or bravado, endeavoured twice or thrice to deprive him of this place; but there was a quiet dignity in the Major's manner as he took his seat at the next table, and surveyed the interlopers, which rendered it impossible for any man to sit and breakfast under his eye; and that table – by the fire, and yet near the window – became his own. His letters were laid out there in expectation of his arrival, and many was the young fellow about town who looked with wonder at the number of those notes, and at the seals and franks which they bore. If there was any question about etiquette, society, who was married to whom, of what age such and such a duke was, Pendennis was the man to whom every one appealed. Marchionesses used to drive up to the Club, and leave notes for him, or fetch him out. He was perfectly affable. The young men liked to walk with him in the Park or down Pall Mall; for he touched his hat to everybody, and every other man he met was a lord.

The Major sate down at his accustomed table then, and while the waiters went to bring him his toast and his hot newspaper, he surveyed his letters through his gold double eyeglass. He carried it so gaily, you would hardly have known it was spectacles in disguise, and examined one pretty note after another, and laid them by in order. There were large solemn dinner cards, suggestive of three courses and heavy conversation; there were neat little confidential notes, conveying female entreaties; there was a note on thick official paper from the Marquis of Steyne, telling him to come to Richmond to a little party at the Star and Garter, and speak French, which language the Major possessed very perfectly; and another from the Bishop of Ealing and Mrs Traill, requesting the honour of Major Pendennis's company at Ealing House – all of which letters Pendennis read gracefully, and with the more satisfaction, because Glowry, the Scotch surgeon, break-fasting opposite to him, was looking on, and hating him for having so many invitations, which nobody ever sent to Glowry.

These perused, the Major took out his pocket-book to see on what days he was disengaged, and which of these many hospitable calls he could afford to accept or decline.

He threw over Cutler, the East India Director, in Baker Street, in order to dine with Lord Steyne and the little French party at the Star and Garter; the Bishop he accepted, because, though the dinner was slow, he liked to dine with bishops – and so went through his list and disposed of them according to his fancy or interest. Then he took his breakfast and looked over the paper, the gazette, the births and deaths, and the fashionable intelligence, to see that his name was down among the guests at my Lord So-and-so's *fête*, and in the intervals of these occupations carried on cheerful conversation with his acquaintances about the room.

Among the letters which formed Major Pendennis's budget for that morning there was only one unread, and which lay solitary and apart from all the fashionable London letters, with a country post-mark and a homely seal. The superscription was in a pretty delicate female hand, and though marked 'immediate' by the fair writer with a strong dash of anxiety under the word, yet the Major had, for reasons of his own, neglected up to the present moment his humble rural petitioner, who to be sure could hardly hope to get a hearing among so many grand folks who attended his levee. The fact was, this was a letter from a female relative of Pendennis, and while the grandees of her brother's acquaintance were received and got their interview, and drove off, as it were, the patient country letter remained for a long time waiting for an audience in the antechamber, under the slop-basin.

William Makepeace Thackeray, Pendennis (1848)

A gin shop

We will endeavour to sketch the bar of a large gin-shop, and its ordinary customers, for the edification of such of our readers as may not have had opportunities of observing such scenes; and on the chance of finding one well suited to our purpose, we will make for Drury Lane, through the narrow streets and dirty courts which divide it from Oxford Street, and that classical spot adjoining the brewery at the bottom of Tottenham Court Road, best known to the initiated as the 'Rookery'.

The filthy and miserable appearance of this part of London can hardly be imagined by those (and there are many such) who have not witnessed it. Wretched houses with broken windows patched with rags and paper: every room let out to a different family, and in many instances to two or even three – fruit and 'sweet-stuff' manufacturers in the cellars, barbers and red-herring vendors in the front parlours, cobblers in the back: a bird-fancier in the first floor, three families on the second, starvation in the attics. Irishmen in the passage, a 'musician' in the front kitchen, and a char-woman and five hungry children in the back one – filth everywhere – a gutter before the houses and a drain behind – clothes drying and slops emptying, from the windows; girls of fourteen or fifteen, with matted hair, walking about barefoot, and in white great-coats, almost their only cover-ing; boys of all ages, in coats of all sizes and no coats at all; men and women, in every variety of scanty and dirty apparel, lounging, scolding, drinking, smoking, squabbling, fighting, and swearing.

You turn the corner. What a change! All is light and brilliancy. The hum of many voices issues from that splendid gin-shop which forms the commencement of the two streets opposite; and the gay building with the fantastically ornamented parapet, the illuminated clock, the plate-glass windows surrounded by stucco rosettes, and its profusion of gas-lights in richly-gilt burners, is perfectly dazzling when contrasted with the darkness and dirt we have just left. The interior is even gayer than the exterior. A bar of French-polished mahogany, elegantly carved, extends the whole width of the place; and there are two side-aisles of great casks, painted green and gold, enclosed within a light brass rail, and bearing such inscriptions as 'Old Tom, 549'; 'Young Tom, 360'; 'Samson, 1421' – the figures agreeing, we presume, with 'gallons', understand. Beyond the bar is a lofty and spacious saloon, full of the same enticing vessels, with a gallery running round it, equally well furnished. On the counter, in addition to the usual spirit apparatus, are two or three little baskets of cakes and biscuits, which are carefully secured at the top with wicker-work, to prevent their contents being unlawfully abstracted. Behind it are two showily-dressed damsels with large necklaces, dispensing the spirits and 'compounds'. They are assisted by the ostensible proprietor of the concern, a stout coarse fellow in a fur cap, put on very much on one side to give him a knowing air, and to display his sandy whiskers to the best advantage.

The two old washerwomen, who are seated on the little bench to the left of the bar, are rather overcome by the head-dresses and haughty demeanour of the young ladies who officiate. They receive their half-quartern of gin and peppermint, with considerable deference, prefacing a request for 'one of them soft biscuits', with a 'Jist be good enough, ma'am.' They are quite astonished at the impudent air of the young fellow in a brown coat and bright buttons, who, ushering in his two companions, and walking up to the bar in as careless a manner as if he had been used to green and gold ornaments all his life, winks at one of the young ladies with singular coolness, and calls for a 'kervorten and a three-out-glass', just as if the place were his own. 'Gin for you, sir?' says the young lady when she has drawn it: carefully looking every way but the right one, to show that the wink had no effect upon her. 'For me, Mary, my dear,' replies the gentleman in brown. 'My name an't Mary as it happens,' says the young girl, rather relaxing as she delivers the change. 'Well, if it an't, it ought to be,' responds the irresistible one; 'all the Marys as ever *I* see, was handsome gals.' Here the young lady, not precisely remembering how blushes are managed in such cases, abruptly ends the flirtation by addressing the female in the faded feathers who has just entered, and who, after stating explicitly, to prevent any subsequent misunderstanding, that 'this gentleman pays', calls for 'a glass of port wine and a bit of sugar'.

Those two old men who came in 'just to have a drain', finished their third quartern a few seconds ago: they have made themselves crying drunk: and the fat comfortable-looking elderly women, who had 'a glass of rum-srub' each, having chimed in with their complaints on the hardness of the times, one of the women has agreed to stand a glass round, jocularly observing that 'grief never mended no broken bones, and as good people's wery scarce, what I says is, make the most on 'em, and that's all about it!' a sentiment which appears to afford unlimited satisfaction to those who have nothing to pay.

It is growing late, and the throng of men, women, and children, who have been constantly going in and out, dwindles down to two or three occasional stragglers – cold, wretched-looking creatures, in the last stage of emaciation and disease. The knot of Irish labourers at the lower end of the place, who have been alternately shaking hands with, and threatening the life of each other, for the last hour, become furious in their disputes, and finding it impossible to silence one man, who is particularly anxious to adjust the difference, they resort to the expedient of knocking him down and jumping on him afterwards. The man in the fur cap, and the potboy rush out; a scene of riot and confusion ensues; half the Irishmen get shut out, and the other half get shut in: the potboy is knocked among the tubs in no time: the landlord hits everybody, and everybody hits the landlord; the barmaids scream; the police come in; the rest is a confused mixture of arms, legs, staves, torn coats, shouting, and struggling. Some of the party are borne off to the station-house, and the remainder slink home to beat their wives for complaining, and kick the children for daring to be hungry.

Charles Dickens, *Sketches by Boz* (1836)

The Gargoyle Club

The Gargoyle, like so many other night clubs, holds its revels in 'Dark Soho', which you may reach from the roaring Charing Cross Road *via* the Palace, or north-by-east out of the fluff and glare and glitter of Piccadilly Circus. Turn into Dean Street and then – why then just fade away into that seemingly negligible and wholly unobtrusive alley, which is as shrinking as the primrose, indeterminable as air, and elusive as Will-o'-the-wisp. Do not go too early. The alley does not materialize before about 9.30 p.m. It just *happens* at about that hour and has no real existence before. It fades, like Hamlet's ghost, upon the 'crowing of the cock'. This alley will conduct you to the Lilliputian lift which will just hold four, if the visitors are thin and have not dined. Mount boldly, and step out into the Elizabethan kitchen; surprising, but London is full of surprises. The open fire of mellow red brick, oak tables, oak dresser, oak rafters – nothing lacks to complete the picture. . . .

The lighting of the Club premises displays an odd fantasy upon the part of the electrician, for a rosy glow filters *upwards* through the frosted glass of the tops of the tables. Electricians can be as mad as anybody if they really care to make the effort. I must admit, however, that the effect is the reverse of unpleasing. There is no glare. The light is adequate and very restful to the eyes. Excepting these table lights illumination is lacking save for the moon – a luminary justly associated by our ancestors with all kinds of sorcery and witchcraft. It is a superb glimpse which this roof of the Gargoyle affords of a lulled and moon-bathed London. The yellow twinkling of this city, extensive as a province, fills the soul with wonder at its immensity, and the soft canopy of the London night sky – if the moon be up and the threat of rain be absent – is no whit less lovely than that of Venice. 'The poor chimneys become campanili, and the whole city hangs in the heavens, and fairyland is before us.' Whistler looked upon London with the eyes of a lover, but he brought the world to acknowledge the beauty of his mistress.

Among the people of note whom you may happen upon at the Gargoyle are Noël Coward, Eugene Goossens, Hermione Baddeley, Molly Kerr, Elizabeth Pollard, George Belcher and Arnold Bennett. I once, when very young, found myself sitting next the last-named – or so I supposed – at the performance of one of his plays.

'Are you Mr Bennett?' I interjected, hoping by direct attack to surprise him into a confession.

'*Wish I wos*,' replied the individual whom I had addressed – but evasively, methought, and with counterfeit accent. And I have not to this day discovered whether this gentleman was Mr Arnold Bennett, or Mr Arnold Bennett's double, or some Scotland Yard detective disguised for some obscure purpose as Mr Arnold Bennett, or merely some hum-drum character designing to impersonate Mr Arnold Bennett at some fancy dress ball 'after the show'.

Kenneth Hare, London's Latin Quarter (1926)

Our club

Our club consisted of twenty, and was always well attended; any member who absented himself, no matter from what cause, on a club day forfeited half a crown, which was put through a hole made in the lid of a box, kept under lock and key, and opened only once a year, when the amount of forfeits was laid out in an extra dinner at the Red House, generally about 20th December, and consisting of venison and of all sorts of dainties, the liquors being claret and madeira, purchased for the occasion. Besides our regular days, some of the members met every evening during the summer months to have a little field tennis. It was just a mile from Buckingham Gate to the Chelsea waterworks, from whence Burt's boat immediately conveyed us across the water, being rowed by an extraordinary man, who, though born deaf and dumb, was the quickest and most intelligent creature, and could make us perfectly understand who were already arrived, having a particular sign by which he distinguished each member. This person went daily to Clare Market, where he would execute punctually every order, purchasing all that was wanted as correctly as if he had not been deprived of the faculties of speech and hearing. At the time I am now speaking of, he was a stout well-looking fellow of about two- or three-and-twenty, and as we all saw, a laborious and useful servant.

The annual dinner I have above alluded to, took place this year (1767) on 19th December, on which day I rowed myself up to the Red House, got abominably drunk, as did most of the party, and in spite of the remonstrances of Burt and his wife, backed by Sally too, I, at two o'clock in the morning, staggered to my boat, which I literally tumbled into, and, without recollecting one word of the matter, obstinately refused to let anyone accompany me, and pushed off. Whether, intoxicated as I was, it came into my head everybody would be in bed at Roberts's at Lambeth, where my boat was kept, or not, I cannot tell, or what guided my proceedings; but it seems I ran her ashore at Milbank, there got out, and endeavoured to walk home. Unfortunately for me they were then paving anew the lower parts of Westminster, and I in consequence encountered various holes, and various heaps of stone and rubbish, into and over which I tumbled and scrambled, God only knows how, or how I contrived to get so far on my way as Parliament Street; but a little after seven in the morning, a party who had supped, and afterwards played whist all night, at a Mr James's, were just sallying forth to get into a hackney coach, waiting to convey them to their respective homes. Mr Smith, one of the company, who was a riding master of His Majesty's, stepping to the rear of the coach to make water, descried a human figure laying in the kennel, whereupon he called to his companions, who, upon examination, found it was poor pilgarlic in woeful plight.

Being thus recognized, though I was utterly incapable of giving any account of myself, or of even articulating, they lifted me into their coach, Mr Smith and another attending to support me; and thus I was conveyed to my father's and there put to bed, having no more recollection of a single circumstance that had occurred for the preceding twelve hours, than if I had been dead. My boat, which was known to all the watermen above bridge, was found at daylight laying aground at Milbank, having only one scull in her. Upon enquiry, a watchman said he had observed a young gentleman, who appeared very tipsy, land from her, and seeing how incapable he was of walking, and that he fell every yard, offered to assist him, which was violently rejected; and he therefore went to his watch-house, it being near break of day.

I awoke the following day in my own bed, as from a horrible dream, unable to move hand or foot, being most miserably bruised, cut and maimed in every part of my body.

William Hickey, *Memoirs, 1749–1809* (1960)

The Cats' Run

After I left Kensington Palace I had a curious and rather difficult time to go through. I had a bed-sitting-room in a ladies' club, not really very comfortable, the food not very good, but I had a little Beatrice stove. Of course, the smell of paraffin in my bed-sitting-room was not exactly the *parfum de luxe* I should have chosen, but still that little stove was very useful because my faithful maid and I used to fry sausages, or poach and scramble eggs, to try to supplement the not very ample rations of downstairs. I called the club 'the Cats' Run', which was not really very complimentary as the inhabitants were not old cats and some of them were very charming. Madame Melba frequently resided at my club during the First World War, and we shared many funny experiences. She was a delightful and interesting companion.

One evening I had been out to a little dinner, and came home with my host and hostess and another guest to find the front door of the 'Cats' Run' locked and the night watchman not available; so we sat on the kerb. Eventually, my host climbed over the area railings to try to force his way through the basement. A policeman came by and asked what the unofficial burglars were doing. He also assisted, and after an hour we managed to wake up the night watchman and all was well. The result of being locked out of my 'Cats' Run' was that my hostess, dear Celia Noble, wrote to me the following day saying that she had some vacant rooms in her Knightsbridge home, beautiful Kent House, and could she put them at my disposal where I would be her honoured and very dear guest. Here I spent two years.

Princess Marie Louise, *My Memories of Six Reigns* (1946)

Sun and Fun

SONG OF A NIGHT-CLUB PROPRIETRESS

I walked into the night-club in the morning,
    There was kummel on the handle of the door,
The ashtrays were unemptied,

375

The cleaning unattempted,
    And a squashed tomato sandwich on the floor.

I pulled aside the thick magenta curtains
    – So Regency, so Regency, my dear –
And a host of little spiders
Ran a race across the ciders
    To a box of baby 'pollies by the beer.

Oh sun upon the summer-going by-pass
    Where ev'rything is speeding to the sea,
And wonder beyond wonder
That here where lorries thunder
    The sun should ever percolate to me.

When Boris used to call in his Sedanca,
    When Teddy took me down to his estate
When my nose excited passion,
When my clothes were in the fashion,
    When my beaux were never cross if I was late,

There was sun enough for lazing upon beaches,
    There was fun enough for far into the night.
But I'm dying now and done for,
What on earth was all the fun for?
    For I'm old and ill and terrified and tight.

                                John Betjeman, *Collected Poems* (1970)

The 'Unclubbables'

This chapter has already shown that in Bethnal Green the proportion of
'unclubbables' or 'unattached' is small. For this reason, our research can say
little about what sort of boys stay away.

Though statistical analysis could tell us little, we looked closely at the
boys who did not join clubs and others who, though they did join, did not
stay long. They seemed to fall into two main categories. Some were painfully shy. They could not bring themselves to go to clubs because it would
have faced them with the problem of mixing with others. A 16 year old said:

'People tell me I ought to join a youth club, because I would be able to mix with other people. I can't seem to bring myself to do it. I know I ought to, and perhaps I will some day, but the truth is that I do not get on well with other people.'

Rather more common seemed another type of misfit – the boy who was anti-club. An 18-year-old building labourer said:

'I've been to quite a few of these youth clubs. Most of them I left after a couple of months. If you ask me, mate, they're a load of crap.'

Among such boys there seemed a minority who saw each club and each leader as a challenge, an opportunity to 'have a giggle' – or in other words cause some trouble. According to Jimmy Grove, this was the attitude of himself and his friends.

'We go to quite a lot of the clubs round here, but we mostly go for a giggle. We got chucked out of the one along here only a fortnight ago and then we went back again. He said, "Oh, you're back again, are you? You got chucked out, didn't you?" He says, "Go on, you can go in, but don't muck about like that," so we all go in like. We're always getting into trouble with these clubs. I start saucing him and all that sort of thing, and he says, "You're being saucy. Go on, get out," like that. One night, when he chucked us out, to pay him back we went round and let the air out of his tyres. Another time we had a lark – he asked us to fit the gym gear up. We said O.K. We fitted up the box and the first one who went over, the lot collapsed. He went nutty, chased us out. When he got us in the gym he used to make us do a sort of course; we had to keep on running round and round. Running round sweating our guts out we were, so we packed it up. Then we went into the boxing and started throwing the gloves about and he chucked us out for that. When we go into these youth clubs it often seems to end up like that. We don't dislike the people there or anything like that. We just do it for fun, it's just that you go in and you mess about and you start getting told off and before long you're monkeying about and playing up.'

There were further examples from boys who had left clubs. The reason a few gave for leaving was that they had been expelled or suspended. 'I got chucked out for mucking about,' said one boy; 'Suspended for throwing bottles,' said another. Again, these boys were often among those who did not get on well at school or at work either.

Peter Wilmott, *Adolescent Boys of East London* (1969)

Chimes at midnight

FALSTAFF: Come, I will go drink with you, but I cannot tarry dinner. I am glad to see you, by my troth, Master Shallow.

SHALLOW: O, Sir John, do you remember since we lay all night in the windmill in Saint George's fields?

FALSTAFF: No more of that, good Master Shallow, no more of that.

SHALLOW: Ha! it was a merry night. And is Jane Nightwork alive?

FALSTAFF: She lives, Master Shallow.

SHALLOW: She never could away with me.

FALSTAFF: Never, never; she would always say she could not abide Master Shallow.

SHALLOW: By the mass, I could anger her to the heart. She was then a bona-roba. Doth she hold her own well?

FALSTAFF: Old, old, Master Shallow.

SHALLOW: Nay, she must be old; she cannot choose but be old; certain she's old; and had Robin Nightwork by old Nightwork before I came to Clement's Inn.

SILENCE: That's fifty-five year ago.

SHALLOW: Ha! cousin Silence, that thou hadst seen that that this knight and I have seen. Ha! Sir John, said I well?

FALSTAFF: We have heard the chimes at midnight, Master Shallow.

SHALLOW: That we have, that we have, that we have; in faith, Sir John, we have. Our watchword was, 'Hem, boys!' Come, let's to dinner; come, let's to dinner. Jesus, the days that we have seen! Come, come.

(*Exeunt Shallow and Silence.*)

. . .

FALSTAFF: Fare you well, gentle gentlemen. On, Bardolph; lead the men away. (*Exeunt Bardolph, Recruits, &c.*) As I return, I will fetch off these justices: I do see the bottom of Justice Shallow. Lord, Lord! how subject we old men are to this vice of lying. This same starved justice hath done nothing but prate to me of the wildness of his youth and the feats he hath done about Turnbull Street; and every third word a lie, duer paid to the hearer than the Turk's tribute. I do remember him at Clement's Inn like a man made after supper of a cheese-paring: when a' was naked he was for all the world like a forked radish, with a head fantastically carved upon it with a knife: a' was so forlorn that his dimensions to any thick sight were invincible: a' was the very genius of famine; yet lecherous as a monkey, and the whores called him mandrake: a' came ever in the rearward of the fashion and sung those tunes to the over-scutched huswives that he heard the carmen whistle, and sware they were his fancies or his good-nights. And now is this Vice's dagger become a squire, and talks as familiarly of John a Gaunt as if he had been sworn brother to him; and I'll be sworn a' never saw him but once in the Tilt-yard, and then he burst his head for crowding among the marshal's men. I saw it and told John a Gaunt he beat his own name; for you might have thrust him and all his apparel into an eel-skin; the case of a treble hautboy was a mansion for him, a court; and now has he land and beefs. Well, I will be acquainted with him, if I return; and it shall go hard but I will make him a philosopher's two stones to me. If the young dace be a bait for the old pike, I see no reason in the law of nature but I may snap at him. Let time shape, and there an end. (*Exit.*)

William Shakespeare, Henry IV Part 2, III.ii

15

Mrs Roebeck

If the last chapter dealt with human concourse of an unarranged character, this one deals with 'social life' which has come about as a result of the whim, or will, of someone or another. The Veneerings with their repeated dinner parties are archetypes. The modern-day Twemlow sits in bafflement at such tables, unable to decide whether he is Veneering's oldest friend, or newest friend. Belloc's Mrs Roebeck is an archetypal figure, too. She is ever to be seen at publishers' 'launch' parties, though she is usually too busy to have read the books which these parties supposedly celebrate. Her photograph frequently appears in the pages of 'Jennifer's Diary', and she gives plenty of nice little dinners of her own, as well as attending everyone else's, and being seen at all the 'first nights', private views, charity balls, weddings and memorial services with which the better-heeled Londoners beguile their time.

Ballade of Hell and of Mrs Roebeck

I

I'm going out to dine at Gray's
  With Bertie Morden, Charles and Kit,
And Manderly who never pays,
  And Jane who wins in spite of it,
  And Algernon who won't admit

The truth about his curious hair
    And teeth that very nearly fit: –
And Mrs Roebeck will be there.

II

And then to-morrow someone says
    That someone else has made a hit
In one of Mister Twister's plays.
    And off we go to yawn at it;
    And when it's petered out we quit
For number 20, Taunton Square,
    And smoke, and drink, and dance a bit: –
And Mrs Roebeck will be there.

III

And so through each declining phase
    Of emptied effort, jaded wit,
And day by day of London days
    Obscurely, more obscurely, lit;
    Until the uncertain shadows flit
Announcing to the shuddering air
    A Darkening, and the end of it: –
And Mrs Roebeck will be there.

Envoi

Prince, on their iron thrones they sit,
    Impassible to our despair,
The dreadful Guardians of the Pit: –
    And Mrs Roebeck will be there.

Hilaire Belloc, Complete Verse (1991)

For Patrick, aetat: LXX*

How glad I am that I was bound apprentice
To Patrick's London of the 1920s.

---

* Patrick Balfour, 3rd Baron Kinross, b.1904.

Estranged from parents (as we all were then),
Let into Oxford and let out again,
Kind fortune led me, how I do not know,
To that Venetian flat-cum-studio
Where Patrick wrought his craft in Yeoman's Row.

For Patrick wrote and wrote. He wrote to live:
What cash he had left over he would give
To many friends, and friends of friends he knew,
So that the 'Yeo' to one great almshouse grew –
Not a teetotal almshouse, for I hear
The clink of glasses in my memory's ear,
The spurt of soda as the whisky rose
Bringing its heady scent to memory's nose
Along with smells one otherwise forgets:
Hairwash from Delhez, Turkish cigarettes,
The reek of Ronuk on a parquet floor
As parties came cascading through the door:
Elizabeth Ponsonby in leopard-skins
And Robert Byron and the Ruthven twins,
Ti Cholmondeley, Joan Eyres Monsell, Bridget Parsons,
And earls and baronets and squires and squarsons –
'Avis, it's *ages*! . . . Hamish, but it's *aeons* . . .'
(Once more that record, the Savoy Orpheans).

Leader in London's preservation lists
And least Wykehamical of Wykehamists:
Clan chief of Paddington's distinguished set,
Pray go on living to a hundred yet!

John Betjeman, A Nip in the Air (1974)

Balls

I will now try to describe what a ball was like in Victorian and Edwardian days. Your hostess and her daughter stood at the head of the staircase, each of these ladies holding a fan and a bouquet. The guests struggled up the stairs, as there was invariably a crush. No ball or entertainment was considered a success unless there were far more guests present than the ball-and-supper-rooms could accommodate with comfort. Your name, or names as the case might be, were announced, and after shaking hands with your hostess you drifted away to the ballroom, the young ladies in search of their partners and the mamas, dowagers, and chaperons proceeding to seat themselves on small gilt chairs along the wall. The daughters, unless they were dancing, stood by their side. The young girls who were not fortunate in finding partners were rather cruelly termed 'wallflowers'. I do not think that there are any 'wallflowers' nowadays!

If you were seen dancing more than once with the same young man, the latter ran the risk of being questioned as to what were 'his intentions', and I wonder how many budding romances came to nought owing to these very searching and rather tactless questions.

The following day, visiting-cards had to be left on one's hostess of the party, ball, or dinner of preceding evening. I believe the leaving of visiting-cards has gone out of fashion, and a little note of 'thank you', often accompanied by a few carefully chosen flowers, has taken their place.

Princess Marie Louise, *My Memories of Six Reigns* (1946)

Charlotte Brontë in 'Literary London'

At the end of November she went up to the 'big Babylon', and was immediately plunged into what appeared to her a whirl; for changes, and scenes, and stimulus which would have been a trifle to others, were much to her. As was always the case with strangers, she was a little afraid at first of the family into which she was now received, fancying that the ladies looked on her with a mixture of respect and alarm; but in a few days, if this state of feeling ever existed, her simple, shy, quiet manners, her dainty personal and household ways, had quite done away with it, and she says that she thinks they begin to like her, and that she likes them much, for 'kindness is a potent heart-winner'. She had stipulated that she should not be expected to see many people. The recluse life she had led was the cause of a nervous shrinking from meeting any fresh face, which lasted all her life long. Still, she longed to have an idea of the personal appearance and manners of some of those whose writings or letters had interested her. Mr Thackeray was accordingly invited to meet her, but it so happened that she had been out for the greater part of the morning, and, in consequence, missed the luncheon hour at her friend's house. This brought on a severe and depressing headache in one accustomed to the early, regular hours of a Yorkshire parsonage; besides the excitement of meeting, hearing, and sitting next a man to whom she looked up with such admiration as she did to the author of *Vanity Fair*, was of itself overpowering to her frail nerves. She writes about this dinner as follows:

> *Dec. 10th, 1849.*
> As to being happy, I am under scenes and circumstances of excitement; but I suffer acute pain sometimes – mental pain, I mean. At the moment Mr Thackeray presented himself I was thoroughly faint from inanition, having eaten nothing since a very slight breakfast, and it was then seven o'clock in the evening. Excitement and exhaustion made savage work of me that evening. What he thought of me I cannot tell.

She told me how difficult she found it, this first time of meeting Mr Thackeray, to decide whether he was speaking in jest or in earnest, and that she had (she believed) completely misunderstood an inquiry of his, made on the gentlemen's coming into the drawing-room. He asked her 'if she had perceived the scent of their cigars'; to which she replied literally, discovering in a minute afterwards, by the smile on several faces, that he was alluding to a passage in *Jane Eyre*. Her hosts took pleasure in showing her the sights of London. On one of the days which had been set apart for some of these pleasant excursions, a severe review of *Shirley* was published in the *Times*. She had heard that her book would be noticed by it, and guessed that there was some particular reason for the care with which her hosts mislaid it on that particular morning. She told them that she was aware why she might not see the paper. Mrs Smith at once admitted that her conjecture was right, and said that they had wished her to go to the day's engagement before reading it. But she quietly persisted in her request to be allowed to have the paper. Mrs Smith took her work, and tried not to observe the countenance, which the other tried to hide between the large sheets; but she could not help becoming aware of tears stealing down the face and dropping on the lap. The first remark Miss Brontë made was to express her fear lest so severe a notice should check the sale of the book, and injuriously affect her publishers. Wounded as she was, her first thought was for others. Later on (I think that very afternoon) Mr Thackeray called; she suspected (she said) that he came to see how she bore the attack on *Shirley*; but she had recovered her composure and conversed very quietly with him: he only learnt from the answer to his direct inquiry that she had read the *Times'* article. She acquiesced in the recognition of herself as the authoress of *Jane Eyre*, because she perceived that there were some advantages to be derived from dropping her pseudonym. One result was an acquaintance with Miss Martineau. She had sent her the novel just published, with a curious note, in which Currer Bell offered a copy of *Shirley* to Miss Martineau, as an acknowledgment of the gratification *he* had received from her works. From *Deerbrook he* had derived a new and keen pleasure, and experienced a genuine benefit. In *his* mind *Deerbrook*, etc.

Miss Martineau, in acknowledging this note and the copy of *Shirley*, dated her letter from a friend's house in the neighbourhood of Mr Smith's residence; and when, a week or two afterwards, Miss Brontë found how near she was to her correspondent, she wrote, in the name of Currer Bell, to propose a visit to her. Six o'clock, on a certain Sunday afternoon (10th December), was the time appointed. Miss Martineau's friends had invited the unknown Currer Bell to their early tea; they were ignorant whether the name was that of a man or a woman; and had had various conjectures as to sex, age, and appearance. Miss Martineau had, indeed, expressed her private opinion pretty distinctly by beginning her reply, to the professedly masculine note referred to above, with 'Dear Madam'; but she had addressed it to 'Currer Bell, Esq.' At every ring the eyes of the party turned towards the door. Some stranger (a gentleman, I think) came in; for an instant they fancied he was Currer Bell, and indeed an Esq.; he stayed some time – went away. Another ring; 'Miss Brontë' was announced; and in came a young-looking lady, almost child-like in stature, 'in a deep mourning dress, neat as a Quaker's, with her beautiful hair smooth and brown, her fine eyes blazing with meaning, and her sensible face indicating a habit of self-control'. She came, – hesitated one moment at finding four or five people assembled, – then went straight to Miss Martineau with intuitive recognition, and with the freemasonry of good feeling and gentle breeding she soon became as one of the family seated round the tea-table; and, before she left, she told them, in a simple, touching manner, of her sorrow and isolation, and a foundation was laid for her intimacy with Miss Martineau.

After some discussion on the subject, and a stipulation that she should not be specially introduced to anyone, some gentlemen were invited by Mr Smith to meet her at dinner the evening before she left town. Her natural place would have been at the bottom of the table by her host, and the places of those who were to be her neighbours were arranged accordingly; but, on entering the dining-room, she quickly passed up so as to sit next to the lady of the house, anxious to shelter herself near some one of her own sex. This slight action arose out of the same womanly seeking after protection on every occasion when there was no moral duty involved in asserting her independence, that made her about this time write as follows: 'Mrs —— watches me very narrowly when surrounded by strangers. She never takes her eye from me. I like the surveillance; it seems to keep guard over me.'

Respecting this particular dinner-party, she thus wrote to the Brussels schoolfellow of former days, whose friendship had been renewed during her present visit to London:

The evening after I left you passed better than I expected. Thanks to my substantial lunch and cheering cup of coffee, I was able to wait the eight o'clock dinner with complete resignation, and to endure its length quite courageously, nor was I too much exhausted to converse; and of this I was glad, for otherwise I know my kind host and hostess would have been much disappointed. There were only seven gentlemen at dinner besides Mr Smith, but of these five were critics – men more dreaded in the world of letters than you can conceive. I did not know how much their presence and conversation had excited me till they were gone and the reaction commenced. When I had retired for the night, I wished to sleep – the effort to do so was vain. I could not close my eyes. Night passed; morning came, and I rose without having known a moment's slumber. So utterly worn out was I when I got to Derby, that I was again obliged to stay there all night.

Elizabeth Gaskell, *The Life of Charlotte Brontë* (1857)

'I don't know half the people here'

A friend of mine in Portland Place has a wife who inflicts upon him every season two or three immense evening parties. At one of these parties he was standing in a very forlorn condition, leaning against the chimney-piece, when a gentleman, coming up to him, said, 'Sir, as neither of us is acquainted with any of the people here, I think we had best go home.'

Maria Edgeworth describes a similarly absurd situation at a party given at Duchess Street in 1813: 'I asked Mr Hope who someone was? "I really don't know; I don't know half the people here, nor do they know me or Mrs Hope even by sight. Just now I was behind a lady who was making her *speech*, as she thought to Mrs Hope, but she was addressing a stranger." '

David Watkin, *Thomas Hope and the Neoclassical Idea* (1968)

Good Night to the Season

Good night to the Season! 'Tis over!
    Gay dwellings no longer are gay;
The courtier, the gambler, the lover,
    Are scattered like swallows away:
There's nobody left to invite one
    Except my good uncle and spouse;
My mistress is bathing at Brighton,
    My patron is sailing at Cowes:
For want of a better employment,
    Till Ponto and Don can get out,
I'll cultivate rural enjoyment,
    And angle immensely for trout.

Good night to the Season! – the lobbies,
    Their changes, and rumours of change,
Which startled the rustic Sir Bobbies,
    And made all the Bishops look strange;
The breaches, and battles, and blunders,
    Performed by the Commons and Peers;
The Marquis's eloquent blunders,
    The Baronet's eloquent ears;
Denouncings of Papists and treasons,
    Of foreign dominion and oats;
Misrepresentations of reasons,
    And misunderstandings of notes.

Good night to the Season! – the buildings
    Enough to make Inigo sick;

The paintings, and plasterings, and gildings
   Of stucco, and marble, and brick;
The orders deliciously blended,
   From love of effect, into one;
The club-houses only intended,
   The palaces only begun;
The hell, where the fiend in his glory
   Sits staring at putty and stones,
And scrambles from story to story,
   To rattle at midnight his bones.

Good night to the Season! – the dances,
   The fillings of hot little rooms,
The glancings of rapturous glances,
   The fancyings of fancy costumes;
The pleasures which fashion makes duties,
   The praisings of fiddles and flutes,
The luxury of looking at Beauties,
   The tedium of talking to mutes;
The female diplomatists, planners
   Of matches for Laura and Jane;
The ice of her Ladyship's manners,
   The ice of his Lordship's champagne.

W. M. Praed, Poems (1864)

A dinner dance

As we covered the short distance to Belgrave Square, she dropped her bag on the floor, recovering it before anyone else could help, opened the clasp, and began to rummage in its depths. There she found whatever she had been seeking. Archie Gilbert was sitting next to the door by which we should descend, and now she made as if to offer him some object concealed in her hand, the thing, no doubt a coin, for which she had been searching in the bag. However, he strenuously denied acceptance of this.

'Please,' said Lady Walpole-Wilson. 'You must.'

'On the contrary.'

'I insist.'

'No, no, absurd.'

'Mr Gilbert!'

'Really.'

'I shall be very cross.'

'Not possibly.'

During the several seconds that elapsed before we finally drew up, delayed for a time by private cars and other taxis waiting in a queue in front of our own, the contest continued between them; so that by the moment when the taxi had at last stopped dead in front of the Huntercombes' house, and Archie Gilbert, flinging open the door, had reached the pavement, I was still doubtful whether or not he had capitulated. Certainly he had ejected himself with great rapidity, and unhesitatingly paid the taxi-driver, brushing aside a proferred contribution.

There seemed no reason to suppose, as Barbara had suggested, that we might have come too early. On the contrary, we went up the carpeted steps into a hall full of people, where Sir Gavin, whose taxi had arrived before our own, was already waiting impatiently for the rest of his party. His reason for personal attendance at a dance which he would not have normally frequented was presumably because the Huntercombes lived near the Walpole-Wilsons in the country. In fact there could be no doubt that a good many country neighbours had been asked, for, even on the way up the stairs, densely packed with girls and young men, some of them already rather hot and flushed, there was that faint though perceptible flavour of the hunt ball to be observed about some of the guests. While putting away our hats, curiosity had overcome me, and I asked Archie Gilbert whether he had, in fact, refused or accepted Lady Walpole-Wilson's money. At the coarseness of the question his smile had been once again somewhat reproving.

'Oh, I took it,' he said. 'Why not? It wasn't enough. It never is.'

These words made me wonder if, after all, some faint trace of dissatisfaction was concealed deep down under that armour of black-and-white steel that encased him; and, for a moment, the terrible suspicion even suggested itself that, night after night, he danced his life away through the ballrooms of London in the unshakable conviction that the whole thing was a sham. Was he merely stoical like the Spartan boy – clad this time in a white tie – with the fox of bitterness gnawing, through stiff shirt, at his vitals. It was a thought in its horror to be dismissed without further examination. Such cynicism could hardly be possible.

Anthony Powell, *A Buyer's Market* (1952)

In the swim

Saturday, 27 March 1926

Leonard came in & then we went off on a blowing night to dine at Rose M[acaulay]'s 'pothouse', as I so mistakenly called it. There were 10 second rate writers in second rate dress clothes, Lynds, Goulds, O'Donovan: no, I won't in any spasm of hypocritical humanity include Wolves. L. by the way was in his red brown tweed. Then the pitter patter began; the old yard was scratched over by these baldnecked chickens. The truth was that we had no interests private; literature was our common ground; & though I will talk literature with Desmond or Lytton by the hour, when it comes to pecking up grains with these active stringy fowls my gorge rises. What d'you think of the Hawthornden prize? Why isn't Masefield as good as Chaucer, or Gerhardi as good as Tchekov: how can I embark with Gerald Gould on such topics? He reads novels incessantly; got a holiday 3 years ago, & prided himself on reading nothing but Tchekhov; knows all about a novel in the first chapter. Sylvias & Geralds & Roberts & Roses chimed & tinkled round the table. A stout woman called Gould got steadily more & more mustard & tomato coloured. I said Holy Ghost? when Mr O'Donovan said the whole of the coast. Lodged on a low sofa in Rose's underground cheerful, sane, breezy room I talked to a young cultivated man, who turned out to be Hinks, Rogers, British Museum, mild aesthete, variety of Leigh Ashton; but thank God, not a second rate journalist. All the time I kept saying to myself Thank God to be out of that; out of the Nation; no longer brother in arms with Rose & Robert & Sylvia. It is a thinblooded set; so 'nice', 'kind', respectable, cleverish & in the swim.

Virginia Woolf, Diary (1980)

A story of Lord Curzon

Tuesday, 30 October 1917

Bicycled in oilskins to McEvoy. It was greasy and windy, and I made a long detour. I arrived a very windswept, rain-washed model. McEvoy was very rattled. He has been asked to paint for the Admiralty. He worked at an *utterly* pre-Raphaelite version of me, hands uplifted in the type of clasping a crystal, a pomegranate, or even a pigeon. It is a bore to be such an anachronism. His running, enraptured stream of dewdrops is a great change after John. 'Lovely hands! Oh! It's too wonderful, etc., etc.'

I bicycled to Grosvenor Gardens to lunch at the American Chancellery with Elizabeth. A man called Davis was our host. Seldom have I had so unpleasant a meal. The basement was stifling, the meat uneatably tough, and the twangs deafening. I had an impossibly ill-mannered American on one side – Lord Lytton the other. When Elizabeth sat down she announced that she had been treating a headache with brandy all the morning: she then proceeded to drink three glasses of red wine, followed by two of port and three cups of coffee. I like this story of Lord Curzon. The new Lady C. said, 'George works so hard and sits up so late. He often doesn't come to bed till 2.30, but stays down writing out the menus for the servants in his different country houses.'

Lady Cynthia Asquith, Diaries, 1915–1918 (1971)

Robert, Third Marquess of Salisbury

Since it was in this role that he has cut a figure in history, it seems an appropriate moment to stop and take a look at his mature personality. Mature is the word; profoundly changed from what he had been as a young man, he was already the venerable father-figure of my mother's reminiscences, bald, bearded and filled out to a majestic size. 'Put his Lordship in the carriage with the fresh horses,' my grandmother was once heard to say to her coachman. 'They cannot run away very far, with his weight to pull.'

His demeanour harmonized with his appearance. The nervous shyness of youth had softened to a benign aloofness, as of one who wished to be polite but was a little vague about whom he was talking to. He found it hard to recognize his fellow men, even his relations, if he met them in unexpected circumstances. Once, standing behind the throne at a Court ceremony, he noticed a young man smiling at him. 'Who is my young friend?' he whispered to a neighbour. 'Your eldest son,' the neighbour replied.

David Cecil, The Cecils of Hatfield House (1973)

The insoluble question

Mr and Mrs Veneering were bran-new people in a bran-new house in a bran-new quarter of London. Everything about the Veneerings was spick and span new. All their furniture was new, all their friends were new, all their servants were new, their plate was new, their carriage was new, their harness was new, their horses were new, their pictures were new, they themselves were new, they were as newly married as was lawfully compatible with their having a bran-new baby, and if they had set up a great-grandfather, he would have come home in matting from the Pantechnicon, without a scratch upon him, French-polished to the crown of his head.

For, in the Veneering establishment, from the hall-chairs with the new coat of arms, to the grand pianoforte with the new action, and up-stairs again to the new fire-escape, all things were in a state of high varnish and polish. And what was observable in the furniture, was observable in the Veneerings – the surface smelt a little too much of the workshop and was a trifle sticky.

There was an innocent piece of dinner-furniture that went upon easy castors and was kept over a livery stable-yard in Duke Street, Saint James's, when not in use, to whom the Veneerings were a source of blind confusion. The name of this article was Twemlow. Being first cousin to Lord Snigsworth, he was in frequent requisition, and at many houses might be said to represent the dining-table in its normal state. Mr and Mrs Veneering, for example, arranging a dinner, habitually started with Twemlow, and then put leaves in him, or added guests to him. Sometimes, the table consisted of Twemlow and half-a-dozen leaves; sometimes, of Twemlow and a dozen leaves; sometimes, Twemlow was pulled out to his utmost extent of twenty leaves. Mr and Mrs Veneering on occasions of ceremony faced each other in the centre of the board, and thus the parallel still held; for, it always happened that the more Twemlow was pulled out, the further he found himself from the centre, and the nearer to the sideboard at one end of the room, or the window-curtains at the other.

But, it was not this which steeped the feeble soul of Twemlow in confusion. This he was used to, and could take soundings of. The abyss to which he could find no bottom, and from which started forth the engrossing and ever-swelling difficulty of his life, was the insoluble question whether he was Veneering's oldest friend, or newest friend. To the excogitation of this problem, the harmless gentleman had devoted many anxious hours, both in his lodgings over the livery stable-yard, and in the cold gloom, favourable to meditation, of St James's Square. Thus, Twemlow had first known Veneering at his club, where Veneering then knew nobody but the man who made them known to one another, who seemed to be the most intimate friend he had in the world, and whom he had known two days – the bond of union between their souls, the nefarious conduct of the committee respecting the cookery of a fillet of veal, having been accidentally cemented at that date. Immediately upon this, Twemlow received an invitation to dine with Veneering, and dined: the man being of the party. Immediately upon that, Twemlow received an invitation to dine with the man, and dined: Veneering being of the party. At the man's were a Member, an Engineer, a Payer-off of the National Debt, a Poem on Shakespeare, a Grievance, and a Public Office, who all seemed to be utter strangers to Veneering. And yet immediately after that, Twemlow received an invitation to dine at Veneering's, expressly to meet the Member, the Engineer, the Payer-off of the National Debt, the Poem on Shakespeare, the Grievance, and the Public Office, and, dining, discovered that all of them were the most intimate friends Veneering had in the world, and that the wives of all of them (who were all there) were the objects of Mrs Veneering's most devoted affection and tender confidence.

Thus it had come about, that Mr Twemlow had said to himself in his lodgings, with his hand to his forehead: 'I must not think of this. This is enough to soften any man's brain,' – and yet was always thinking of it, and could never form a conclusion.

Charles Dickens, Our Mutual Friend (1865)

Social life for the sake of social life

Friday, 10 December 1762

I went to Northumberland House in the forenoon. The porter told me there was nobody at home; but looking at me, 'Sir,' said he, 'is your name Boswell?' Upon my answering, 'Yes,' 'My Lady is at home, Sir,' said he. Upon which I was shown up to her Ladyship, with whom I sat about twenty minutes in the most easy, agreeable way. She told me that she had a private party every Friday for particular friends, and that she would always be glad to see me there when I had nothing else to do. I exulted, and thanked her, and said that I could not think how I deserved all this, but that I hoped we should be better acquainted, and that I should run about the house like a tame spaniel. An old gentleman then came in. I sat a little longer and then withdrew, full of joy at being reckoned a particular friend of the heir of the great Percy and a woman of the first consequence in London. She mentioned my commission, and kindly desired me not to be impatient, and I would get it. If the Duke does not do it for me, she will be my next resource. But it is better to have but one patron at a time and stick close to him.

At night I went back to Northumberland House, about seven. We had tea and chatted for a while till the company (about twenty picked people) gathered. They then sat down to the card-tables. But I told my Lady that I never played, which she found no fault with. A few did not play besides. However, I felt not so easy as those who did, and began to tire. I stayed there till eleven, and then came home.

James Boswell, London Journal (1762)

A Letter to Ben Jonson

Mr Francis Beaumont's Letter to Ben Jonson, written before he and Mr Fletcher came to London, with two of the precedent Comedies then not finisht, which deferrd their merry meetings at the Mermaid.

> The Sun which doth the greatest comfort bring
> To absent friends, because the self-same thing
> They know they see however absent, is
> Here our best Hay-maker (forgive me this,
> It is our Country's style). In this warm shine,
> I lie and dream of your full Mermaid wine.
> Oh we have water mixt with Claret Lees,
> Drink apt to bring in drier heresies
> Than beer, good only for the Sonnet's strain,
> With fustian metaphors to stuff the brain,
> So mixt, that given to the thirstiest one,
> 'Twill not prove alms, unless he have the stone:
> I think with one draught man's invention fades,

Two Cups had quite spoil'd *Homer's Iliads*;
'Tis Liquor that will find out *Sutcliff*'s wit,
Lie where he will, and make him write worse yet;
Fill'd with such moisture in most grievous qualms,
Did *Robert Wisdome* write his singing Psalms;
And so must I do this, and yet I think
It is a potion sent us down to drink
By special Providence, keeps us from fights,
Makes us not laugh, when we make legs to Knights.
'Tis this that keeps our minds fit for our States,
A Medicine to obey our Magistrates:
For we do live more free than you, no hate,
No envy at one another's *happy* State
Moves us, we are all equal every whit:
Of Land that God gives men here is their wit,
If we consider fully: for our best
And gravest man will, with his main house jest,
Scarce please you; we want subtilty to do
The City tricks, lie, hate, and flatter too:
Here are none that can bear a painted show,
Strike when you winch, and then lament the blow:
Who like Mills set the right way for to grind,
Can make their gains alike with every wind:
Only some fellows with the subtil'st pate
Amongst us, may perchance equivocate
At selling of a Horse, and that's the most.
Methinks the little wit I had is lost
Since I saw you, for wit is like a rest
Held up at Tennis, which men do the best,
With the best gamesters: What things have we seen,
Done at the Mermaid! heard words that have been
So nimble, and so full of subtill flame,
As if that every one from whence they came,
Had meant to put his whole wit in a jest,
And had resolv'd to live a fool, the rest
Of his dull life; then when there hath been thrown
Wit able enough to justify the Town
For three days past, with that might warrant be
For the whole City to talk foolishly

Till that were cancel'd, and when that was gone,
We left an air behind us, which alone,
Was able to make the two next companies
Right witty; though but downright fools, more wise.
When I remember this, and see that now
The Country gentlemen begin to allow
My wit for dry bobs, then I needs must cry,
I see my days of ballating grow nigh;
I can already riddle, and can sing
Catches, sell bargains, and I fear shall bring
My self to speak the hardest words I find,
Over as oft as any, with one wind,
That takes no medicines: But one thought of thee
Makes me remember all these things to be
The wit of our young men, fellows that show
No part of good, yet utter all they know:
Who like trees of the Guard, have growing souls.
Only strong destiny, which all controls,
I hope hath left a better fate in store,
For me thy friend, than to live ever poor,
Banisht unto this home; fate once again
Bring me to thee, who can'st make smooth and plain
The way of Knowledge for me, and then I,
Who have no good but in thy company,
Protest it will my greatest comfort be
To acknowledge all I have to flow from thee.
Ben, when these Scenes are perfect, we'll taste wine;
I'll drink thy Muse's health, thou shalt quaff mine.

Francis Beaumont (c. 1610)

An Easter dinner

To my great surprize he asked me to dine with him on Easter-day [1773]. I
never supposed that he had a dinner at his house; for I had not then heard
of any one of his friends having been entertained at his table. He told me, 'I
generally have a meat pye on Sunday: it is baked at a publick oven, which is

very properly allowed, because one man can attend it; and thus the advantage is obtained of not keeping servants from church to dress dinners.'

James Boswell, Life of Johnson (1791)

Going out immensely

Sara S. tells me that you labor under the impression that I 'go out
immensely' in London, have a career etc. Disabuse yourself of this: I lead a
very quiet life. One must dine somewhere and I sometimes dine in company; that is all. I have been to several dinners the last fortnight [May
1877], two or three of which I can't for my life recall, though I have been
trying for the last ten minutes in order to enumerate them all. I can mention
however that I dined one day at Lady Rose's, a big sumptuous banquet
where I sat on one side, next to Lady Cunliffe. (Lady Rose is one of the
easiest, agreeablest women I have seen in London.) Then I dined at
the banquet of the Literary fund, invited nominally by Lord Derby, the
chairman, in reality by good Frederick Locker. I sat next to young Julian
Sturgis, and opposite his papa (Russell S.) but the thing was dull and the
speech-making bad to an incredible degree – dreary, didactic and witless.
As many Americans would certainly have done better. Then I feasted at
Mme Van de Weyer – a feast and nothing more, some unrememorable fine
folk. Then a pleasant dinner at Hamilton Aïdé's, whom Alice will remember as the author of novels which she used to read in the days of the 'Fanny
Perry intimacy'. He is an aesthetic bachelor of a certain age and a certain
fortune, moving apparently in the best society and living in sumptuous
apartments. The dinner was in particular to George Du Maurier of *Punch* a
delightful little fellow, with a tall handsome wife like his picture-women. I
sat on one side next Mrs Procter, widow of Barry Cornwall, (mother of
Adelaide P.) a most shrewd, witty and juvenile old lady – a regular London
diner-out. *H.J.* 'Tennyson's conversation seems very prosaic.' *Mrs P.* 'Oh
dear yes. You expect him never to go beyond the best way of roasting a
buttock of beef.' She has known everyone. On t'other side was a very
handsome and agreeable Mrs Tennant, an old friend and flame of Gustave
Flaubert. She was brought up in France. I dined a week ago at Lady
Goldsmid's – a very nice, kindly elderly childless Jewess, cultivated, friend
of George Eliot etc. who is of colossal fortune and gives banquets to match

397

in a sort of country house in the Regents' Park. *H.J. to a lady after dinner.* 'It's a very fine house.' *The lady.* 'Ow – it's like a goodish country house.' I sat at Lady G's next to Mlle de Peyronnet, a very nice English-French youthful spinster, whose mother with whom I afterwards talked (Mme de P.) is, though an English-woman, the Horace de Lagardie who used to write *causeries* in the *Journal des Débats*, and of whom there is a tattered volume somewhere in Quincy Street. I met the mother and daughter (there is another daughter, Lady Arthur Russell, whose husband I have been introduced to and talked with at the *Cosmopolitan*) again at an evening crush at Lord Houghton's, of which the Princess Louise (a charming face) was the heroine; and where also, much *entourée*, was the Miss Balch whom Alice will remember at Newport, red-faced and driving in a little pony-trap, and who now figures in England as a beauty, a fortune and a fast person. She *is*, strange to say, divinely fair, not at all red-faced, smothered in pearls and intimate with the Marchioness of Salisbury (with whom, that is, I saw her hob-nobbing and who looks as if she had just cooked the dinner). Such is life.

Henry James, Letters (1987)

The Pooters at the Mansion House

I felt as if we had been invited to the Mansion House by one who did not know the Lord Mayor himself. Crowds arrived, and I shall never forget the grand sight. My humble pen can never describe it. I was a little annoyed with Carrie, who kept saying: 'Isn't it a pity we don't know anybody?'

Once she quite lost her head. I saw someone who looked like Franching, from Peckham, and was moving towards him when she seized me by the coat-tails, and said quite loudly: 'Don't leave me,' which caused an elderly gentleman, in a court-suit, and a chain round him, and two ladies, to burst out laughing. There was an immense crowd in the supper-room, and, my stars! it was a splendid supper – any amount of champagne.

Carrie made a most hearty supper, for which I was pleased; for I sometimes think she is not strong. There was scarcely a dish she did not taste. I was so thirsty, I could not eat much. Receiving a sharp slap on the shoulder, I turned, and, to my amazement, saw Farmerson, our ironmonger. He said, in the most familiar way: 'This is better than Brickfield Terrace, eh?' I simply looked at him, and said coolly: 'I never expected to see you here.' He said, with a loud, coarse laugh: 'I like that – if *you*, why not *me*?' I replied: 'Certainly.' I wish I could have thought of something better to say. He said: 'Can I get your good lady anything?' Carrie said: 'No, I thank you,' for which I was pleased. I said, by way of reproof to him: 'You never sent to-day to paint the bath, as I requested.' Farmerson said: 'Pardon me, Mr Pooter, no shop when we're in company, please.'

Before I could think of a reply, one of the sheriffs, in full Court costume, slapped Farmerson on the back and hailed him as an old friend, and asked him to dine with him at his lodge. I was astonished. For full five minutes they stood roaring with laughter, and stood digging each other in the ribs. They kept telling each other they didn't look a day older. They began embracing each other and drinking champagne.

To think that a man who mends our scraper should know any member of our aristocracy! I was just moving with Carrie, when Farmerson seized me rather roughly by the collar, and addressing the sheriff, said: 'Let me introduce my neighbour, Pooter.' He did not even say 'Mister'. The sheriff handed me a glass of champagne. I felt, after all, it was a great honour to drink a glass of wine with him, and I told him so. We stood chatting for some time, and at last I said: 'You must excuse me now if I join Mrs Pooter.' When I approached her, she said: 'Don't let me take you away from friends. I am quite happy standing here alone in a crowd, knowing nobody!'

George and Weedon Grossmith, The Diary of a Nobody (1892)

Leaving London

By this time Gilbert and Frances had moved from Edwardes Square to a flat in Battersea. G. K. disliked flats, but the name Over-Strand Mansions appealed to him. It was a sizeable place and he was able to entertain his friends who came in droves. Frances also had her special following – Charles Masterman, Saxon Mills, Wynne Mathieson and his wife were often there. Our Fleet Street contingent behaved with great propriety, remaining in the drawing-room until, late in the evening, catching G. K.'s beckoning eye we followed him into the cosy little kitchen where mounds of sausages were eaten and pints of beer consumed and the talk grew better and better. Gilbert's symbol of hospitality was always sausages and beer.

The parents, occasionally among the guests, remained decorously with Frances, though I am sure that Marie Louise would have liked to join us in the kitchen. One evening, when there was a huge crush, a literary lion brought a young American devotee to Edward and his wife, and without preface or introduction, pointed them out as the great man's father and mother.

Marie Louise smiled sweetly, 'Yes,' she said, simply, 'we are his humble parents. . . . Who, may I ask, are you?'

There were all kinds of Fleet Street junketing – a Johnsonian dinner at the Cheshire Cheese, where Gilbert, in a costume of the period, enacted the great Doctor, and Cecil appeared as Liberty Wilkes. There were Pickwickian evenings, Gilbert as Turveydrop, and parties at Warwick Gardens. It was a happy time, and it was impossible to think that it could suddenly and tragically alter. But change was in the air. Frances, who rarely joined in these expeditions, withdrew even more distantly, and only rarely came to Warwick Gardens. Cecil sensed that things were not quite so rosy on the Battersea front, but none of us dreamed just what was going to materialize.

We heard the news on one of the best evenings I can remember. I was having dinner with Gilbert and Cecil, at the Gourmets Restaurant, famed for its cooking and its mascot, a great white rabbit that ate out of your hand. We sat late and drank red wine, and Gilbert smoked interminable cigars, his favourite small, black, strong cheroots, which he always carried in a paper packet. As the lights began to dim – it was after midnight – he looked up as though he'd suddenly come to a decision.

'Frances wants to leave London,' he said.

And there was silence.

Mrs Cecil Chesterton, The Chestertons (1941)

16

Low Life

One of the Kray twins, whose exploits are recorded in this chapter ('It was as though he wanted to be shot,' he said of George Cornell), has recently gone on record to express his anxiety about the spread of urban crime. The Krays are not the only ones to believe that life in London has become nastier, crueller and more frightening. Londoners seem to have been believing this since the Middle Ages. Certainly, any reader of English novels of the eighteenth century must realize that the problem of crime is not new to London. Henry Fielding, the author of Tom Jones, *also wrote an* Enquiry into the Causes of the late Increase of Robbers *in the city, and, like many modern observers, attributed the crime rate in large measure to the squalid and poverty-stricken conditions in which many of the population were constrained to live. Fielding's half-blind brother Sir John was the originator of the Bow Street Runners, the ancestors of the Metropolitan Police Force. In 1777, Sir John wrote a tract entitled* Thieving Detected: Being a True and Particular Description of the Various Methods and Artifices Used by Thieves and Sharpers to Take in and Deceive the Public; with Proper Cautions to Guard against Such Destructive Measures.

In the eighteenth century, as one can tell from reading such tracts, and from the letters and diaries of the period, every privately owned house was an armed stronghold. As in the Wild West, citizens slept with firearms beside the bed (indeed, beds of the period were constructed with a shelf for the blunderbuss under the pillows).

But this chapter is not solely devoted to crime, so much as to surviving the Low Life. Charles Lamb's essay lamenting the decline of beggars on the streets of London makes strange reading today, when Lincoln's Inn Fields, Waterloo Arches and the Embankments have once more filled up with mendicants and vagrants. Lamb trots out a version of the urban myth (there is a Sherlock Holmes story which repeats it, 'The Man With the Twisted Lip') of the rich beggar, the man who makes more money begging than from working as a bank clerk in the City. The sheer numbers of modern beggars, with their monotonous street cry of 'Gotney chinge, please! Gotney chinge, please!' encourages the resuscitation of the myth. I was confidently told by a rich young woman in Kensington recently that it was possible to make £100 per day merely by sitting outside the Underground Station in Kensington High Street with a ring through your nose and a thin dog on the end of an old rope. I noticed that she had not elected to accumulate her money in this way and preferred the doubtless more strenuous alternative of taking an allowance from her father, supplemented by a little job on a glossy magazine.

Little Dorrit Born in Prison

It was a hot summer day, and the prison rooms were baking between the high walls. In the debtor's confined chamber, Mrs Bangham, charwoman and messenger, who was not a prisoner (though she had been once), but was the popular medium of communication with the outer world, had volunteered her services as fly-catcher and general attendant. The walls and ceiling were blackened with flies. Mrs Bangham, expert in sudden device, with one hand fanned the patient with a cabbage leaf, and with the other set traps of vinegar and sugar in gallipots; at the same time enunciating sentiments of an encouraging and congratulatory nature, adapted to the occasion.

'The flies trouble you, don't they, my dear?' said Mrs Bangham. 'But p'raps they'll take your mind off it, and do you good. What between the buryin' ground, the grocer's, the waggon-stables, and the paunch trade, the Marshalsea flies gets very large. P'raps they're sent as a consolation, if we only know'd it. How are you now, my dear? No better? No, my dear, it ain't to be expected; you'll be worse before you're better, and you know it, don't you? Yes. That's right! And to think of a sweet little cherub being born inside the lock! Now ain't it pretty, ain't *that* something to carry you through it pleasant? Why, we ain't had such a thing happen here, my dear, not for I couldn't name the time when. And you a-crying too?' said Mrs Bangham, to rally the patient more and more. 'You! Making yourself so famous! With the flies a-falling into the gallipots by fifties! And everything a-going on so well! And here if there ain't,' said Mrs Bangham as the door opened, 'if there ain't your dear gentleman along with Dr Haggage! And now indeed we *are* complete, I *think*!'

The doctor was scarcely the kind of apparition to inspire a patient with a sense of absolute completeness, but as he presently delivered the opinion, 'We are as right as we can be, Mrs Bangham, and we shall come out of this like a house a-fire'; and as he and Mrs Bangham took possession of the poor helpless pair as everybody else and anybody else had always done; the means at hand were as good on the whole as better would have been. The special feature in Dr Haggage's treatment of the case, was his determination to keep Mrs Bangham up to the mark. As thus:

'Mrs Bangham,' said the doctor, before he had been there twenty minutes, 'go outside and fetch a little brandy, or we shall have you giving in.'

'Thank you, sir. But none on my accounts,' said Mrs Bangham.

'Mrs Bangham,' returned the doctor, 'I am in professional attendance on this lady, and don't choose to allow any discussion on your part. Go outside and fetch a little brandy, or I foresee that you'll break down.'

'You're to be obeyed, sir,' said Mrs Bangham, rising. 'If you was to put your own lips to it, I think you wouldn't be the worse, for you look but poorly, sir.'

'Mrs Bangham,' returned the doctor, 'I am not your business, thank you, but you are mine. Never you mind *me*, if you please. What you have got to do is, to do as you are told, and to go and get what I bid you.'

Mrs Bangham submitted; and the doctor, having administered her potion, took his own. He repeated the treatment every hour, being very determined with Mrs Bangham. Three or four hours passed; the flies fell into the traps by hundreds; and at length one little life, hardly stronger than theirs, appeared among the multitude of lesser deaths.

'A very nice little girl indeed,' said the doctor; 'little, but well-formed. Halloa, Mrs Bangham! You're looking queer. You be off, ma'am, this minute, and fetch a little more brandy, or we shall have you in hysterics.'

By this time, the rings had begun to fall from the debtor's irresolute hands, like leaves from a wintry tree. Not one was left upon them that night, when he put something that chinked into the doctor's greasy palm. In the meantime Mrs Bangham had been out on an errand to a neighbouring establishment decorated with three golden balls, where she was very well known.

'Thank you,' said the doctor, thank you. Your good lady is quite composed. Doing charmingly.'

'I am very happy and very thankful to know it,' said the debtor, 'though I little thought once, that – '

'That a child would be born to you in a place like this?' said the doctor. 'Bah, bah, sir, what does it signify? A little more elbow-room is all we want here. We are quiet here; we don't get badgered here; there's no knocker here, sir, to be hammered at by creditors and bring a man's heart into his mouth. Nobody comes here to ask if a man's at home, and to say he'll stand on the door-mat till he is. Nobody writes threatening letters about money to this place. It's freedom, sir, it's freedom! I have had to-day's practice at home and abroad, on a march, and aboard ship, and I'll tell you this: I don't know that I have ever pursued it under such quiet circumstances as here this day. Elsewhere, people are restless, worried, hurried about, anxious respecting one thing, anxious respecting another. Nothing of the kind here, sir. We have done all that – we know the worst of it; we have got to the bottom, we can't fall, and what have we found? Peace. That's the word for it. Peace.' With this profession of faith, the doctor, who was an old jail-bird, and was more sodden than usual, and had the additional and unusual stimulus of money in his pocket, returned to his associate and chum in hoarseness, puffiness, red-facedness, all-fours, tobacco, dirt, and brandy.

Charles Dickens, Little Dorrit (1857)

Richard Savage in Newgate

I now write to you from my confinement in Newgate, where I have been ever since Monday last was se'nnight, and where I enjoy myself with much more tranquillity than I have known for upwards of a twelvemonth past; having a room entirely to myself, and pursuing the amusement of my poetical studies, uninterrupted, and agreeable to my mind. I thank the Almighty, I am now all collected in myself; and, though my person is in confinement, my mind can expatiate on ample and useful subjects with all the freedom imaginable. I am now more conversant with the Nine than ever; and if instead of a Newgate-bird, I may be allowed to be a bird of the Muses, I assure you Sir, I sing very freely in my cage; sometimes indeed in the plaintive notes of the nightingale; but, at others, in the cheerful strains of the lark.

In another letter he observes, that he ranges from one subject to another, without confining himself to any particular task, and that he was employed one week upon one attempt, and the next upon another.

Surely the fortitude of this man deserves, at least, to be mentioned with applause; and, whatever faults may be imputed to him, the virtue of suffering well cannot be denied him. . . .

He was treated by Mr Dagg, the keeper of the prison, with great humanity; was supported by him at his own table without any certainty of recompence; had a room to himself, to which he could at any time retire from all disturbance; was allowed to stand at the door of the prison, and sometimes taken out into the fields; so that he suffered fewer hardships in prison than he had been accustomed to undergo in the greatest part of his life.

The keeper did not confine his benevolence to a gentle execution of his office, but made some overtures to the creditor for his release, though without effect; and continued, during the whole time of his imprisonment, to treat him with the utmost tenderness and civility.

Samuel Johnson, *The Lives of the English Poets* (1779–81)

Casuals

Morning after morning I am up early, watching the struggle for work at the dock gates; and observing the leisurely unloading of sailing vessels compared to the swift discharge of steamers.

This morning [I record early in May] I walked along Billingsgate to the London Docks. Crowded with loungers smoking villainous tobacco; coarse talk with the clash of the halfpenny on the pavement every now and again. Bestial content or hopeless discontent on their faces. The lowest form of leisure – the senseless curiosity about street rows, idle gazing at the street sellers, low jokes – this is 'the chance' the docks offer! I met Dartford, respectable tenant K[atherine] B[uildings], and he greeted me cordially. He is always in work, and

complains that he never gets a holiday – says that many of the unemployed do not want to work, and get sacked for not turning up. 'I
make a point of not mixing up with anyone. Women get thick
together, and then there is always a row. The curse is the daily payment; it is always a mistake not to give the woman the money once a
week instead of at odd times.' Said [that] the worse a man is, the more
work he will get at the docks. [MS. diary, May 1887.]

. . .

Among those I interview are the School Board Visitors for the district;
and here is an account of two interviews with Kerrigan, School Board
Visitor for the Stepney Division.

Describes his casuals, about 900, as hereditary casuals, London-born.
The worst scoundrel is the cockney-born Irishman. The woman is
the Chinaman of the place: drudges as the women of savage races: she
slaves all day and night. Describes the communism of this class. They
do not migrate out of the district, but they are constantly changing
their lodgings: 'They are like the circle of the suicides in Dante's
Inferno; they go round and round within a certain area.' They work
for each other: hence low ideal of work. They never see excellence in
work. They never leave the neighbourhood. From the dock-gate they
lounge back to the street: 'treating' and being 'treated', according to
as they have earned a few pence. Live chiefly on 'tobacco' which is a
compound of sugar, vinegar, brown paper and German nicotine. The
teapot is constantly going – bread and a supply of dried haddock
which goes through a domestic preparation: dried in the chimney and
acquiring a delicate flavour by lying between the mattresses of the
beds. They never read. Except the Catholics, they never go to church.
On the Bank Holiday the whole family goes to Victoria Park. 'Permanent' men live outside the neighbourhood – Forest Gate, Hackney,
Upton, some even at Walthamstow. Kerrigan does not think that
corruption and bribery goes on in the West India Dock, as it does at
the London and St Katherine's. 'Permanent' men might be classed
just above the artisan and skilled mechanics. They read Herbert
Spencer and Huxley, and are speculative of intelligent working men.
[MS. diary, May 1887.]

Beatrice Webb, *My Apprenticeship* (1926)

A Hit and Run Driver, 1337

On Thursday [February 13], about the hour of vespers, two carters taking two empty carts out of the city were urging their horses apace, when the wheels of one of the carts collapsed opposite the rent of the hospital of St Mary, Bishopsgate, so that the cart fell on Agnes de Cicestre, who immediately died. The carter thereupon left his cart and three horses and took flight in fear, although he was not suspected of malicious intent. The cart and its trappings were appraised by jurors of the ward of Bishopsgate at 6s. 8d.; the first horse, of a dun color, at 10s., the second, a gray, and blind of both eyes, at 4s., and the third, a black, at 6s.; also five old sacks and five pounds of candles of 'coton' which were in the cart at the time of the accident at 16½d. Total 28s. ½d., for which John de Northhalle, one of the sheriffs, will answer.

Calendar of the Coroners Rolls, quoted in Edith Rickert, *Chaucer's World* (1948)

Cock-Fighting

18 June 1710

In the afternoon we went to see the cock-fighting. This is a sport peculiar to the English, which, however great the pleasure this nation takes in it, seems very foolish to foreigners. A special building has been erected for it near 'Gray's Inn'. When there is to be a fight, printed bills are carried round and sometimes invitations to fanciers appear in the news-sheets as well as the amount of the wagers and the number and species of cocks that are to fight. The building is round like a tower and inside it is just like a 'theatrum anatomicum' as all round it there are benches in tiers, on which the spectators sit. In the middle is a round table covered with mats, on which the cocks have to fight. When it is time to begin the persons appointed to do so bring in the cocks hidden in two sacks and then, before they have seen the birds, everyone starts to shout their wagers. The people, gentlefolk as well as commoners (they all sit together), act like madmen and go on raising the odds to twenty guineas and more. As soon as one of the bidders calls 'done' . . . , the other is held to his bargain. Then the cocks are taken out of the sacks and fitted with silver spurs, . . . As soon as the cocks appear, the shouts grow even louder and the betting is continued. When they are put on to the table, some attack at once while others run away from the rest and, as we ourselves saw, try in their fright to jump down from the table among the crowd; they are then however thrown back with loud cries (especially from those who have put their money on the lively cocks which chase the others) and are thrust at each other until they get angry. Then one should just see how they peck at each other, and especially how they hack with their spurs. Their combs bleed quite horribly and they often slit each other's crop and abdomen with the spurs. There is nothing so amusing as when one cock seems quite exhausted and there are great shouts of joy and terrific bets and then, though he seemed quite done for, he suddenly recovers and masters the other. When one of the two is dead, the victor never fails to start crowing and jumping on the other and it often happens that they sing their song of triumph before victory is assured and the other wins after all. Sometimes when both are exhausted and neither will attack the other again, they are removed and others take their place; in this case the wagers are cancelled. But if one of them wins those who put their money on the loser have to pay immediately, so that an ostler in his apron often wins several guineas from a lord. If a man has made a bet and is unable to pay he is made, as a punishment, to sit in a basket tied to the ceiling and is drawn up in it amidst mighty laughter. The people become as heated about their wagers as the cocks themselves.

Karl von Uffenbach, *Merkwuerdige Reisen* (1710), quoted in F. M. Wilson, *Strange Island* (1955)

A public execution

Some time after my arrival in London I witnessed a spectacle which certainly was not as magnificent or as brilliant as the Lord Mayor's Show; it is true it was quite a different kind of entertainment. I saw thirteen criminals all hanged at the same time. It will interest you, no doubt, to know something about justice in England, how it is practised, how criminals are punished, in what manner they are executed, as here it is done in quite a different way to what it is in other countries.

The day before the execution those who desire it may receive the sacrament, provided the chaplain thinks that they have sincerely repented and are worthy of it. On the day of execution the condemned prisoners, wearing a sort of white linen shirt over their clothes and a cap on their heads, are tied two together and placed on carts with their backs to the horses' tails. These carts are guarded and surrounded by constables and other police officers on horseback, each armed with a sort of pike. In this way part of the town is crossed, and Tyburn, which is a good half-mile from the last suburb, is reached, and here stands the gibbet. One often sees criminals going to their death perfectly unconcerned, others so impenitent that they fill themselves full of liquor and mock at those who are repentant. When all the prisoners arrive at their destination they are made to mount on a very wide cart made expressly for the purpose, a cord is passed round their necks and the end fastened to the gibbet, which is not very high. The chaplain who accompanies the condemned men is also on the cart; he makes them pray and sing a few verses of the Psalms. The relatives are permitted to mount the cart and take fare-well. When the time is up – that is to say about a quarter of an hour – the chaplain and the relations get off the cart, which slips from under the condemned men's feet, and in this way they remain all hanging together. You often see friends and relations tugging at the hanging men's feet so that they should die quicker and not suffer. The bodies and clothes of the dead belong to the executioner; relatives must, if they wish for them, buy them from him, and unclaimed bodies are sold to surgeons to be dissected. You see most amusing scenes between the people who do not like the bodies to be cut up and the messengers the surgeons have sent for the bodies; blows are given and returned before they can be got away, and sometimes in the turmoil the bodies are quickly removed and buried. Again, the populace often come to blows as to who will carry the bought corpses to the parents who are waiting in coaches and cabs to receive them, for the carriers are well paid for their trouble. All these scenes are most diverting, the noise and confusion is unbelievable, and can be witnessed from a sort of amphitheatre erected for spectators near the gibbet.

Ferdinand de Saussure, *A Foreign View of England in the Reigns of George I and George II*

(1902)

Gang rivalry

A meeting was summoned at that gentlemen's club for villains, the Astor, for a discussion between the twins, Ian Barrie and Ron Hart, Charlie and Eddie Richardson, Frankie Fraser and George Cornell. The meeting became heated, with the Richardsons apparently claiming a substantial interest in the Kray–Mafia business arrangements. It was then that George Cornell, never lacking in courage, called Ronnie a big fat poof and told him to bugger off when he asked to be cut into the blue film racket. It was not an insult that could be accepted lightly. . . . The Firm was put on war alert. Donaghue recalls:

> We were each given a name. Ronnie Hart and I had to look after Brian Mottram if it came to it. We were all given the names and addresses of clubs, pubs, girlfriends, where our people could be found. Freddie Foreman had a spy in the Richardson scrapyard. If we went south to see Freddie it was like we were going into Indian country. We would go in a hired car with a gun so if we got a pull it wasn't our car and we could say we knew nothing about it. Going south of the river was like going abroad.

Still the Krays did not believe they were strong enough without help. To counter the ferocity of Frankie Fraser someone just as fearless was needed to be their own private man. The person they chose was Frank Mitchell. There was only one problem – he was serving a sentence in Dartmoor Prison.

In the meantime they began wearing bullet-proof vests and a member of the Firm was deputed to be their personal bodyguard, leaving any public house or club first to survey the street. Although they felt themselves in need of protection they did not carry weapons and were becoming increasingly reluctant to allow members of the Firm to do so either. Wednesday nights were when the Krays went visiting around the various local pubs and before these evening visits, members of the Firm would go to the pub or club and hide weapons in lavatory cisterns. They were right to be careful. Shots were fired at the windows of the Widows, the name for the Lion pub in Tapp Street where the Krays used to drink. A few days later a mini-cab owner who resembled Ronnie was knocked down by a car which mounted the pavement. . . .

George Cornell survived the Mr Smith's Club affray which had led to the arrest of the Richardsons, only to die on the next evening, 9 March 1966. Ronnie received word that Cornell was deep in the heart of Kray territory, sitting on a stool at the bar of the Blind Beggar public house near Whitechapel tube station in the Mile End Road. Around 8.30 the door opened and in walked Ronnie Kray and Ian Barrie. Had they been a few minutes earlier they would have met a local Detective Inspector having a drink and sandwich. The story is that Cornell looked up and said 'Look who's here.' If he did say that those were the last words he spoke. Ronnie shot him at point-blank range with a Luger pistol.

He justifies the shooting quite simply:

Richard Hart had to be avenged. No one could kill a member of the Kray gang and expect to get away with it. . . . Typical of the yobbo mentality of the man. Less than twenty-four hours after the Catford killing and here he was, drinking in a pub that was officially on our patch. It was as though he wanted to be shot.

James Morton, *Gangland* (1992)

The Tiger in the Smoke

KILLER ROAMING LONDON FOG

FAMOUS DOCTOR STRANGLED   THREE DEAD IN OFFICE

Police Cordon Thwarted as Convict Patient Escapes

As the Tiddington man stared at the announcement his face grew swollen and fiery under its translucent skin. Having identified himself with the first statement, the remainder appeared to him to be a fantastic lie, backed, most alarmingly, with the authority of the printed word. He snatched the paper and strode out under the light with it, using his elbows freely as the others dragged about him.

' "From our special correspondent, London." ' He read each word with equal emphasis, moving his head with the type. ' "At a late hour last night the picked men of London's crack Criminal Investigation Department had to confess that an escaped convict, who is possibly one of the most dangerous criminals this country has ever known, was still ranging the fog-bound streets of their city, possibly with a still crimson knife in his hand. Meanwhile, in a solicitor's office in the western area, three innocent people, one of them a Detective Officer, lay murdered, each, so say experts, butchered with professional skill with an identical weapon. Earlier in the evening, on the other side of the metropolis, in famous Guy's Hospital, the well-loved savant whom men called The Kind Healer, fought gallantly for life. . . ." '

The news story, battling magnificently with too much jam, the laws of libel and contempt of court, was a work of art of its kind, but to the Suffolk man in the cellar it failed in the first degree and was incomprehensible.

'Knifed?' he bellowed suddenly. ''Oo said Duds was knifed?'

'No, Tiddy. Look down 'ere. See the pictures.'

It was Bill who flipped the sheet from him with fingers delicate as a woman's and dirty as a monkey's, and turned it down to show the reproduction of two photographs from the police files. Hard lighting and coarse printing had done their worst with them and the result was wooden and meaningless to any but the initiated.

'If you see this man, dial 999 and – take cover' ran the legend above the panel, and underneath in smaller type, 'This is the man the police are seeking, Jack Havoc, aged 33.'

Tiddy Doll remained rigid and Roly began to chatter in his excitement.

'Tiddy don't know 'im. 'E ain't never seen 'im. That's 'im, Tiddy! 'E's changed 'is name like we said 'e would, but that's 'im, that's the Gaffer.'

Margery Allingham, *The Tiger in the Smoke* (1937)

City scandals

3 December 1667

Up by candlelight, the only time I think I have done so this winter, and a coach being got over night, I to Sir W. Coventry's, the first time I have seen him at his new house since he came to lodge there. At noon home to dinner, and busy all the afternoon, and at night home, and there met W. Batelier, who tells me the first great news that my Lord Chancellor is fled this day. By and by to Sir W. Pen's. But here I hear the whole; that my Lord

Chancellor is gone, and left a paper behind him for the House of Lords, telling them the reason of him retiring, complaining of a design for his ruin. But the paper I must get: only the thing at present is great, and will put the King and Commons to some new counsels certainly. So home to supper and to bed. Sir W. Pen I find in much trouble this evening, having been called to the Committee this afternoon about the business of prizes. Sir Richard Ford told us this evening an odd story of the basenesse of the late Lord Mayor, Sir W. Bolton, in cheating the poor of the City out of the collections made for the people that were burned, of £1,800; of which he can give no account, and in which he hath forsworn himself plainly, so as the Court of Aldermen have sequestered him from their Court till he do bring in an account; which is the greatest piece of roguery that they say was ever found in a Lord Mayor. He says also that this day hath been made appear to them that the Keeper of Newgate, at this day, hath made his house the only nursery of rogues and pickpockets and thieves in the world, where they were bred and entertained, and the whole society met: and that for the sake of the Sheriffes they durst not this day committ him for fear of making him let out the prisoners, but are fain to go by artifice to deal with him. He tells me also speaking of the new street that is to be made from Guild Hall down to Cheapside, that the ground is already most of it bought. And tells me of one particular, of a man that hath a piece of ground lieing in the very middle of the street that must be; which, when the street is cut out of it, there will remain ground enough, of each side, to build a house to front the street. He demanded £700 for the ground, and to be excused paying any thing for the melioration of the rest of his ground that he was to keep. The Court consented to give him £700, only not to abate him the consideration: which the man denied; but told them, and so they agreed, that he would excuse the City the £700 that he might have the benefit of the melioration without paying any thing for it. So much some will get by having the City burned! But he told me that in other cases ground by this means that was not 4d. a-foot before will now, when houses are built, be worth 15s. a-foot. But he tells me that the common standard now reckoned on between man and man, in places where there is no alteration of circumstances but only the houses burnt, there the ground which, with a house on it, did yield £100 a-year, is now reputed worth £33 6s. 8d.

Samuel Pepys, *Diary*

413

Shabby-Genteel People

There are certain descriptions of people who, oddly enough, appear to appertain exclusively to the metropolis. You meet them, every day, in the streets of London, but no one ever encounters them elsewhere; they seem indigenous to the soil, and to belong as exclusively to London as its own smoke, or the dingy bricks and mortar. We could illustrate the remark by a variety of examples, but, in our present sketch, we will only advert to one class as a specimen – that class which is so aptly and expressively designated as 'shabby-genteel'.

Now, shabby people, God knows, may be found anywhere, and genteel people are not articles of greater scarcity out of London than in it; but this compound of the two – this shabby-gentility – is as purely local as the statue at Charing Cross, or the pump at Aldgate. It is worthy of remark, too, that only men are shabby-genteel; a woman is always either dirty and slovenly in the extreme, or neat and respectable, however poverty-stricken in appearance. A very poor man, 'who has seen better days', as the phrase goes, is a strange compound of dirty-slovenliness and wretched attempts at faded smartness. . . .

We were once haunted by a shabby-genteel man: he was bodily present to our senses all day, and he was in our mind's eye all night. . . . He first attracted our notice, by sitting opposite to us in the reading-room at the British Museum: and what made the man more remarkable was, that he always had before him a couple of shabby-genteel books – two old dog's-eared folios, in mouldy worm-eaten covers, which had once been smart. He was in his chair every morning, just as the clock struck ten: he was always the last to leave the room in the afternoon; and when he did, he quitted it with the air of a man who knew not where else to go for warmth and quiet. There he used to sit all day, as close to the table as possible, in order to conceal the lack of buttons on his coat: with his old hat carefully deposited at his feet, where he evidently flattered himself it escaped observation.

About two o'clock, you would see him munching a French roll or a penny loaf; not taking it boldly out of his pocket at once, like a man who knew he was only making a lunch; but breaking off little bits in his pocket, and eating them by stealth. He knew too well it was his dinner.

When we first saw this poor object, we thought it quite impossible that his attire could ever become worse. We even went so far as to speculate on the possibility of his shortly appearing in a decent second-hand suit. We knew nothing about the matter; he grew more and more shabby-genteel every day. The buttons dropped off his waistcoat one by one: then, he buttoned his coat; and when one side of the coat was reduced to the same condition as the waistcoat, he buttoned it over on the other side. He looked somewhat better at the beginning of the week than at the conclusion, because the neckerchief, though yellow, was not quite so dingy; and, in the midst of all this wretched- ness, he never appeared without gloves and straps. He remained in this state for a week or two. At length, one of the buttons on the back of the coat fell off, and then the man himself disappeared, and we thought he was dead.

We were sitting at the same table about a week after his disappearance, and as our eyes rested on his vacant chair, we insensibly fell into a train of meditation on the subject of his retirement from public life. We were wondering whether he had hung himself, or thrown himself off a bridge – whether he really was dead or had only been arrested – when our conjec- tures were suddenly set at rest by the entry of the man himself. He had undergone some strange metamorphosis, and walked up the centre of the room with an air which showed he was fully conscious of the improvement in his appearance. It was very odd. His clothes were a fine, deep, glossy black; and yet they looked like the same suit; nay, there were the very darns with which old acquaintance had made us familiar. The hat, too – nobody could mistake the shape of that hat, with its high crown gradually increasing in circumference towards the top. Long service had imparted to it a reddish-brown tint; but now it was as black as the coat. The truth flashed suddenly upon us – they had been 'revived'. It is a deceitful liquid that black and blue reviver; we have watched its effects on many a shabby- genteel man. It betrays its victims into a temporary assumption of import- ance: possibly into the purchase of a new pair of gloves, or a cheap stock, or some other trifling article of dress. It elevates their spirits for a week, only to depress them, if possible, below their original level. It was so in this case; the transient dignity of the unhappy man decreased, in exact proportion as the 'reviver' wore off. The knees of the unmentionables, and the elbows of the coat, and the seams generally, soon began to get alarmingly white. The hat was once more deposited under the table, and its owner crept into his seat as quietly as ever.

There was a week of incessant small rain and mist. At its expiration the 'reviver' had entirely vanished, and the shabby-genteel man never after- wards attempted to effect any improvement in his outward appearance.

Charles Dickens, Sketches by Boz (1836)

Dead drunk for twopence

Archenholz, a German traveller, writing circa 1784, describes the streets of London as crowded with beggars. 'These idle people,' says this curious observer, 'receive in alms three, four, and even five shillings a day. They have their clubs in the parish of St Giles's, where they meet, drink, and feed well, read the papers, and talk politics. One of my friends put on one day a ragged coat, and promised a handsome reward to a beggar to introduce him to his club. He found the beggars gay and familiar, and poor only in their rags. One threw down his crutch, another untied a wooden leg, a third took off a grey wig or removed a plaister from a sound eye; then they related their adventures, and planned fresh schemes. The female beggars hire children for sixpence and sometimes even two shillings a day: a very deformed child is worth four shillings.'

In the same parish the pickpockets met to dine and exchange or sell snuff-boxes, handkerchiefs, and other stolen property.

About fifty years before, says Archenholz, there had been a pickpockets' club in St Giles's, where the knives and forks were chained to the table and the cloth was nailed on. Rules were, however, decorously observed, and chairmen chosen at their meetings. Not far from this house was a celebrated gin-shop, on the sign-post of which was written –

'Here you may get drunk for a penny, dead drunk for twopence, and straw for nothing.'

The cellars of this public-spirited man were never empty.

Walter Thornbury, *Haunted London* (1865)

Miserable creatures

The following account I have had from Mr Welch, the high-constable of Holborn; and none who know that gentleman, will want any confirmation of the truth of it.

That in the parish of St Giles's there are great numbers of houses set apart for the reception of idle persons and vagabonds, who have their lodgings there for two pence a night; that in the above parish, and in St George, Bloomsbury, one woman alone occupies seven of these houses, all properly accommodated with miserable beds from the cellar to the garret, for such two-penny lodgers: that in these beds, several of which are in the same room, men and women, often strangers to each other, lie promiscuously; the price of a double bed being no more than three-pence, as an encouragement to them to lie together; but as these places are thus adapted to whoredom, so are they no less provided for drunkenness, gin being sold in them all at a penny a quartern; so that the smallest sum of money serves for intoxication; that in the execution of search-warrants Mr Welch rarely finds less than twenty of these houses open for the receipt of all comers at the latest hours; that in one of these houses, and that not a large one, he hath numbered fifty-eight persons of both sexes, the stench of whom was so intolerable that it compelled him in a short time to quit the place.

Nay, I can add, what I myself once saw in the parish of Shoreditch, where two little houses were emptied of near seventy men and women; amongst whom was one of the prettiest girls I had ever seen, who had been carried off by an Irishman, to consummate her marriage on her wedding-night in a room where several others were in bed at the same time.

If one considers the destruction of all morality, decency, and modesty; the swearing, whoredom, and drunkenness, which is eternally carrying on in these houses, on the one hand, and the excessive poverty and misery of most of the inhabitants on the other, it seems doubtful whether they are more the objects of detestation or compassion; for such is the poverty of these wretches, that, upon searching all the above number, the money found upon all of them (except the bride, who, as I afterwards heard, had robbed her mistress) did not amount to one shilling; and I have been credibly informed, that a single loaf hath supplied a whole family with their provisions for a week. Lastly, if any of these miserable creatures fall sick (and it is almost a miracle that stench, vermin, and want, should ever suffer them to be well) they are turned out in the streets by their merciless host or hostess, where, unless some parish officer of extraordinary charity relieves them, they are sure miserably to perish, with the addition of hunger and cold to their disease.

Henry Fielding, *Enquiry into the Causes of the late Increase of Robbers* (1752)

A Squabble between Beggars, 1399

John Dray, beggar, had been attached to answer Ralph Goodson in a plea of assault and battery [etc.]. Goodson by his attorney stated that on Thursday before the Feast of SS. Tiburtius and Valerian, 22 Richard II [1399], in the parish of S. Faith, ward of Farringdon Within, Dray attacked him and caused him to suffer damage to the amount of £20.

John Dray in his own person denied the charge and said that on the day and in the place mentioned he and the said Ralph were sitting together and begging, when John Stowe, a monk of Westminster, came by and gave them a penny in common. Ralph received the penny, but would not give Dray his share. A quarrel arose and Ralph assaulted him with a stick. Any injury Ralph received was done in self-defense.

Ralph denied any grounds for John's assault; they put themselves on the country. Dray found mainpernors.

Coram Rege Roll, quoted in Edith Rickert, *Chaucer's World* (1948)

Beggars

I am pacing Pall Mall in a rapt reverie, –
I am thinking if Sophy is thinking of me,
When I'm roused by a ragged and shivering wretch,
Who appears to be well on his way to Jack Ketch.

He has got a bad face, and a shocking bad hat;
A comb in his fist, and he sees I'm a flat,
For he says, 'Buy a comb, it's a fine un to wear;
Only try it, my Lord, through your whiskers and 'air.'

He eyes my gold chain, as if anxious to crib it;
He looks just as if he'd been blown from a gibbet.
I pause . . . and pass on, and beside the club fire
I settle that Sophy is all I desire.

As I walk from the club, and am deep in a strophè
That rolls upon all that's delicious in Sophy,

I'm humbly address'd by an 'object' unnerving,
So tatter'd a wretch must be 'highly deserving'.

She begs, and I'm touch'd, but I've much circumspection:
I stifle remorse with the soothing reflection
That cases of vice are by no means a rarity –
The worst vice of all's indiscriminate charity.

Am I right? How I wish that my clerical guide
Would settle this question – and others beside!
For always one's heart to be hardening thus,
If wholesome for beggars, is hurtful for us.

A few minutes later (how pleasant for me!)
I'm seated by Sophy at five-o'clock for tea:
Her table is loaded, for when a girl marries,
What bushels of rubbish they send her from *Barry's*!

'There's a present for you, Sir!' Yes, thanks to her thrift,
My pet has been able to buy me a gift;
And she slips in my hand, the delightfully sly thing,
A paper-weight form'd of a bronze lizard writhing.

'What a charming *cadeau!* and so truthfully moulded;
But perhaps you don't know, or deserve to be scolded,
That in casting this metal a live, harmless lizard
Was cruelly tortured in ghost and in gizzard?'

'Po-oh!' – says my lady, (she always says 'Pooh'
When she's wilful, and does what she oughtn't to do!)
'Hopgarten protests they've no feeling, and so
It was only their *muscular movement*, you know!'

Thinks I (when I've said *au revoir*, and depart –
A Comb in my pocket, a Weight – at my heart),
And when wretched mendicants writhe, there's a notion
That begging is only their 'muscular motion'.

Frederick Locker Lampson, London Lyrics (1874)

The moderation of prostitutes

Throughout my adventures in the underworld, I did not meet a drunken woman. There is a fixed idea also that those poor little prostitutes, with their pitiful earnings of pence and shillings (it is an event if they should get a pound), spend a large proportion of their income in alcoholic refreshment. This is not so. The girls I met at Kennedy Court, like those I met at Camden Town, the Old Kent Road and all over London, are very moderate in their spirituous tastes. There is a freehanded dispensation of chocolate, and they are extravagant in the matter of fruitdrops and lemonade, but they rarely buy drink for themselves, and there is not much cigarette smoking. The causes for this abstinence may be economic, though, personally, I do not believe that shortage of money affects the manner in which that money is spent. If a woman wants drink, be she in the possession of fourpence, four shillings or four pounds, drink she will have. But, as I say, it is not a craving from which these pretty young prostitutes suffer.

Mrs Cecil Chesterton, *In Darkest London* (1926)

It won't do

As we walked along the Strand to-night, arm in arm, a woman of the town accosted us, in the usual enticing manner. 'No, no, my girl, (said Johnson) it won't do.' He, however, did not treat her with harshness, and we talked of the wretched life of such women; and agreed, that much more misery than happiness, upon the whole, is produced by illicit commerce between the sexes.

James Boswell, *Life of Johnson* (1791)

The state of the poor

We talked of the state of the poor in London. – JOHNSON. 'Saunders Welch, the Justice, who was once High-Constable of Holborn, and had the best opportunities of knowing the state of the poor, told me, that I under-rated the number, when I computed that twenty a week, that is, above a thousand a year, died of hunger; not absolutely of immediate hunger; but of the wasting and other diseases which are the consequences of hunger. This happens only in so large a place as London, where people are not known. What we are told about the great sums got by begging is not true: the trade is overstocked. And, you may depend upon it, there are many who cannot get work. A particular kind of manufacture fails: those who have been used to work at it, can, for some time, work at nothing else. You meet a man begging; you charge him with idleness: he says, "I am willing to labour. Will you give me work?" – "I cannot." – "Why, then you have no right to charge me with idleness." '

Ibid.

A death as glorious as his life

At length the morning came which Fortune at his birth had resolutely ordained for the consummation of our hero's GREATNESS: he had himself indeed modestly declined the public honour she intended him, and had taken a quantity of laudanum, in order to retire quietly off the stage; but we have already observed, in the course of our wonderful history, that to struggle against this lady's decrees is vain and impotent; and whether she hath determined you shall be hanged or be a prime minister, it is in either case lost labour to resist. Laudanum, therefore, being unable to stop the breath of our hero, which the fruit of hemp-seed, and not the spirit of poppy-seed, was to overcome, he was at the usual hour attended by the proper gentleman appointed for that purpose, and acquainted that the cart was ready. On this occasion he exerted that greatness of courage which hath been so much celebrated in other heroes; and, knowing it was impossible to resist, he gravely declared he would attend them. He then descended to that

421

room where the fetters of great men are knocked off in a most solemn and
ceremonious manner. Then shaking hands with his friends (to wit, those
who were conducting him to the tree), and drinking their healths in a
bumper of brandy, he ascended the cart, where he was no sooner seated
than he received the acclamations of the multitude, who were highly rav-
ished with his GREATNESS.

The cart now moved slowly on, being preceded by a troop of horse-
guards bearing javelins in their hands, through streets lined with crowds all
admiring the great behaviour of our hero, who rode on, sometimes sighing,
sometimes swearing, sometimes singing or whistling, as his humour varied.

When he came to the tree of glory, he was welcomed with an universal
shout of the people, who were there assembled in prodigious numbers to
behold a sight much more rare in populous cities than one would reasonably imagine it should be, viz. the proper catastrophe of a great man.

But though envy was, through fear, obliged to join the general voice in
applause on this occasion, there were not wanting some who maligned this
completion of glory, which was now about to be fulfilled to our hero, and
endeavoured to prevent it by knocking him on the head as he stood under
the tree, while the ordinary was performing his last office. They therefore
began to batter the cart with stones, brickbats, dirt, and all manner of
mischievous weapons, some of which, erroneously playing on the robes
of the ecclesiastic, made him so expeditious in his repetition, that with
wonderful alacrity he had ended almost in an instant, and conveyed himself
into a place of safety in a hackney-coach, where he waited the conclusion
with a temper of mind described in these verses:

> Suave mari magno, turbantibus aequord ventis,
> E terra alterius magnum spectare laborem.

We must not, however, omit one circumstance, as it serves to shew the
most admirable conversation of character in our hero to his last moment,
which was, that, whilst the ordinary was busy in his ejaculations, Wild, in
the midst of the shower of stones, etc., which played upon him, applied his
hands to the parson's pocket, and emptied it of his bottle-screw, which he
carried out of the world in his hand.

The ordinary being now descended from the cart, Wild had just opportunity to cast his eyes around the crowd, and to give them a hearty curse,
when immediately the horses moved on, and with universal applause our
hero swung out of this world.

Thus fell Jonathan Wild the GREAT, by a death as glorious as his life had been, and which was so truly agreeable to it, that the latter must have been deplorably maimed and imperfect without the former; a death which hath been alone wanting to complete the characters of several ancient and modern heroes, whose histories would then have been read with much greater pleasure by the wisest in all ages. Indeed we could almost wish that whenever Fortune seems wantonly to deviate from her purpose, and leaves her work imperfect in this particular, the historian would indulge himself in the licence of poetry and romance, and even do a violence to truth, to oblige his reader with a page which must be the most delightful in all his history, and which could never fail of producing an instructive moral.

Narrow minds may possibly have some reason to be ashamed of going this way out of the world, if their consciences can fly in their faces and assure them they have not merited such an honour; but he must be a fool who is ashamed of being hanged, who is not weak enough to be ashamed of having deserved it.

Henry Fielding, Jonathan Wild (1743)

Hopeless poverty in Bethnal Green

17 February 1832

The cholera has produced more alertness than alarm here; in fact, at present it is a mere trifle – in three days twenty-eight persons. Nothing like the disorders which rage unheeded every year and every day among the lower orders. It is its name, its suddenness, and its frightful symptoms that terrify. The investigations, however, into the condition of the different parishes have brought to light dreadful cases of poverty and misery. A man came yesterday from Bethnal Green with an account of that district. They are all weavers, forming a sort of separate community; there they are born, there they live and labour, and there they die. They neither migrate nor change their occupation; they can do nothing else. They have increased in a ratio at variance with any principles of population, having nearly tripled in twenty years, from 22,000 to 62,000. They are for the most part out of employment, and can get none. 1,100 are crammed into the poor-house, five or six in a bed; 6,000 receive parochial relief. The parish is in debt; every day adds to the number of paupers and diminishes that of ratepayers.

These are principally small shopkeepers, who are beggared by the rates. The district is in a complete state of insolvency and hopeless poverty, yet they multiply, and while the people look squalid and dejected, as if borne down by their wretchedness and destitution, the children thrive and are healthy. Government is ready to interpose with assistance, but what can Government do? We asked the man who came what could be done for them. He said 'employment', and employment is impossible.

Charles Cavendish Fulke Greville, Leaves from the Greville Diary (1929)

The spread of cholera

In the meantime the cholera has made its appearance in London, at Rotherhithe, Limehouse, and in a ship off Greenwich – in all seven cases. These are amongst the lowest and most wretched classes, chiefly Irish, and a more lamentable exhibition of human misery than that given by the medical men who called at the Council Office yesterday I never heard. They are in the most abject state of poverty, without beds to lie upon. The men live by casual labour, are employed by the hour, and often get no more than four or five hours' employment in the course of the week. They are huddled and crowded together by families in the same room, not as permanent lodgers, but procuring a temporary shelter; in short, in the most abject state of physical privation and moral degradation that can be imagined. We have sent down members of the Board of Health to make preparations and organize boards; but, if the disease really spreads, no human power can arrest its progress through such an Augean stable.

Ibid.

Fever-stricken

Shelton Street was just wide enough for a vehicle to pass either way, with room between curb-stone and houses for one foot-passenger to walk; but vehicles would pass seldom, and foot-passengers would prefer the roadway to the risk of tearing their clothes against projecting nails. The houses, about forty in number, contained cellars, parlours, and first, second, and third floors, mostly two rooms on a floor, and few of the 200 families who lived here occupied more than one room. In little rooms no more than 8 ft square would be found living father, mother and several children. Some of the rooms, from the peculiar build of the houses (shallow houses with double frontage) would be fairly large and have a recess 6 ft wide for the bed, which in rare instances would be curtained off. If there was no curtain, anyone lying on the bed would perhaps be covered up and hidden, head and all, when a visitor was admitted, or perhaps no shyness would be felt. . . . Drunkenness and dirt and bad language prevailed, and violence was common, reaching at times even to murder. Fifteen rooms out of twenty were filthy to the last degree, and the furniture in none of these would be worth 20*s.*, in some cases not 5*s.* Not a room would be free from vermin, and in many life at night was unbearable. Several occupants have said that in hot weather they don't go to bed, but sit in their clothes in the least infested part of the room. What good is it, they said, to go to bed when you can't get a wink of sleep for bugs and fleas? A visitor in these rooms was fortunate indeed if he carried nothing of the kind away with him. . . . The passage from the street to the back-door would be scarcely ever swept, to say nothing of being scrubbed. Most of the doors stood open all night as well as all day, and the passage and stairs gave shelter to many who were altogether homeless. Here the mother could stand with her baby, or sit with it on the stairs, or companions would huddle together in cold weather. The little yard at the back was only sufficient for dust-bin and closet and water-tap, serving for six or seven families. The water would be drawn from cisterns which were receptacles for refuse, and perhaps occasionally a dead cat. At one time the street was fever-stricken; the mortality was high, and the authorities interfered with good effect so that the sanitary condition of the street just before it was destroyed was better than it had been formerly. The houses looked ready to fall, many of them being out of the perpendicular. Gambling was the amusement of the street. Sentries would be posted, and if the police made a rush the offenders would slip into the open houses and hide until danger was past. Sunday afternoon and evening was the heyday time for this street. Every doorstep would be crowded by those who sat or stood with pipe and jug of beer, while lads lounged about, and the gutters would find amusement for not a few children with bare feet, their faces and hands besmeared, while the mud oozed through between their toes. Add to this a group of fifteen or twenty young men gambling in the middle of the street and you complete the general picture.

Charles Booth, *Life and Labour of the People of London* (1902–3)

The Decay of Beggars

If I were not the independent gentleman that I am, rather than I would be a retainer to the great, a led captain, or a poor relation, I would choose, out of the delicacy and true greatness of my mind, to be a Beggar.

Rags, which are the reproach of poverty, are the Beggar's robes, and graceful *insignia* of his profession, his tenure, his full dress, the suit in which he is expected to show himself in public. He is never out of the fashion, or limpeth awkwardly behind it. He is not required to put on court mourning. He weareth all colours, fearing none. His costume hath undergone less change than the Quaker's. He is the only man in the universe who is not obliged to study appearances. The ups and downs of the world concern him no longer. He alone continueth in one stay. The price of stock or land affecteth him not. The fluctuations of agricultural or commercial prosperity touch him not, or at worst but change his customers. He is not expected to become bail or surety for any one. No man troubleth him with questioning his religion or politics. He is the only free man in the universe.

The Mendicants of this great city were so many of her sights, her lions. I can no more spare them than I could the Cries of London. No corner of a street is complete without them. They are as indispensable as the Ballad Singer; and in their picturesque attire as ornamental as the Signs of old London. They were the standing morals, emblems, mementos, dial-mottos, the spital sermons, the books for children, the salutary checks and pauses to the high and rushing tide of greasy citizenry –

___ Look
Upon that poor and broken bankrupt there.

Above all, those old blind Tobits that used to line the wall of Lincoln's Inn Garden, before modern fastidiousness had expelled them, casting up their ruined orbs to catch a ray of pity, and (if possible) of light, with their faithful Dog Guide at their feet, – whither are they fled? or into what corners, blind as themselves, have they been driven, out of the wholesome air and sun-warmth? immersed between four walls, in what withering poor-house do they endure the penalty of double darkness, where the chink of the dropt half-penny no more consoles their forlorn bereavement, far from the sound

426

of the cheerful and hope-stirring tread of the passenger? Where hang their useless staves? and who will farm their dogs? . . .

These dim eyes have in vain explored for some months past a well-known figure, or part of the figure, of a man, who used to glide his comely upper half over the pavements of London, wheeling along with most ingenious celerity upon a machine of wood; a spectacle to natives, to foreigners, and to children. He was of a robust make, with a florid sailor-like complexion, and his head was bare to the storm and sunshine. He was a natural curiosity, a speculation to the scientific, a prodigy to the simple. The infant would stare at the mighty man brought down to his own level. The common cripple would despise his own pusillanimity, viewing the hale stoutness, and hearty heart, of this half-limbed giant. Few but must have noticed him; for the accident, which brought him low, took place during the riots of 1780, and he has been a groundling so long. He seemed earth-born, as Antaeus, and to suck in fresh vigour from the soil which he neighboured. He was a grand fragment; as good as an Elgin marble. The nature, which should have recruited his reft legs and thighs, was not lost, but only retired into his upper parts, and he was half a Hercules. I heard a tremendous voice thundering and growling, as before an earthquake, and casting down my eyes, it was this mandrake reviling a steed that had started at his portentous appearance. He seemed to want but his just stature to have rent the offending quadruped in shivers. He was as the man-part of a Centaur, from which the horse-half had been cloven in some dire Lapithan controversy. He moved on, as if he could have made shift with yet half of the body-portion which was left him. The *os sublime* was not wanting; and he threw out yet a jolly countenance upon the heavens. Forty-and-two years had he driven this out of door trade, and now that his hair is grizzled in the service, but his good spirits no way impaired, because he is not content to exchange his free air and exercise for the restraints of a poor-house, he is expiating his contumacy in one of those houses (ironically christened) of Correction.

Was a daily spectacle like this to be deemed a nuisance, which called for legal interference to remove? or not rather a salutary and a touching object, to the passers-by in a great city? Among her shows, her museums, and supplies for ever-gaping curiosity (and what else but an accumulation of sights – endless sights – *is* a great city; or for what else is it desirable?) was there not room for one *Lusus* (not *Naturae*, indeed, but) *Accidentium*? What if in forty-and-two years' going about, the man had scraped together enough to give a portion to his child (as the rumour ran) of a few hundreds – whom had he injured? – whom had he imposed upon? The contributors

427

had enjoyed their *sight* for their pennies. What if after being exposed all day to the heats, the rains, and the frosts of heaven – shuffling his ungainly trunk along in an elaborate and painful motion – he was enabled to retire at night to enjoy himself at a club of his fellow cripples over a dish of hot meat and vegetables, as the charge was gravely brought against him by a clergyman deposing before a House of Commons' Committee – was *this*, or was his truly paternal consideration, which (if a fact) deserved a statue rather than a whipping-post, and is inconsistent at least with the exaggeration of nocturnal orgies which he has been slandered with – a reason that he should be deprived of his chosen, harmless, nay edifying, way of life, and be committed in hoary age for a sturdy vagabond? –

There was a Yorick once, whom it would not have shamed to have sate down at the cripples' feast, and to have thrown in his benediction, ay, and his mite too, for a companionable symbol. 'Age, thou hast lost thy breed.'

Half of these stories about the prodigious fortunes made by begging are (I verily believe) misers' calumnies. One was much talked of in the public papers some time since, and the usual charitable inferences deduced. A clerk in the Bank was surprised with the announcement of a five hundred pound legacy left him by a person whose name he was a stranger to. It seems that in his daily morning walks from Peckham (or some village thereabouts) where he lived, to his office, it had been his practice for the last twenty years to drop his halfpenny duly into the hat of some blind Bartimeus, that sate begging alms by the wayside in the Borough. The good old beggar recognized his daily benefactor by the voice only; and, when he died, left all the amassings of his alms (that had been half a century perhaps in the accumulating) to his old Bank friend. Was this a story to purse up people's hearts, and pennies, against giving an alms to the blind? – or not rather a beautiful moral of well-directed charity on the one part, and noble gratitude upon the other?

I sometimes wish I had been that Bank clerk.

Charles Lamb, *Essays of Elia* (1823)

17

Hating It

For British people happily settled in what Londoners would call the provinces, the metropolis can seem a hateful place. I have sometimes sat on trains at the greater London termini, and watched the strain and anxiety on the faces of day-trippers as they clamber aboard. Whether they have come up to do a little shopping, or to take a child to a much-vaunted theatrical show, or to conduct some business, their journey has caused them nothing but anxiety. Clutching street maps, they have got lost twenty times in the day. The bus which said 'Knightsbridge' so clearly on the front of it had already been to Knightsbridge and so transported them, much against their will, to Piccadilly Circus. The underground railway, crammed to bursting with visitors and commuters, was claustrophobic and terrifying, not least because of that 'security alert' at Tottenham Court Road. The pub at lunch-time had been over-priced, and over-crowded. And the traffic! ('Thank goodness we did not drive!') Dark memories survive in the out-of-towner's mind of the time he thought he'd be adventurous and bring the car up to London: nowhere to park, the one-way systems incomprehensible, and murderous taxi-drivers, coming at them from the inside lane and shaking their fists in rage.

It is easy to see why anyone would hate London. And these out-of-towners whom I have observed may be seen to relax as the train begins to glide out of Euston or Paddington. By the time the train is rattling through Watford or Slough they have begun to feel human again. How anyone could choose to live in London must seem incomprehensible to them.

Those who do live in London, either by accident or choice, must have had many occasions to see its hateful aspect – some of which we have already surveyed in the chapter on 'Low Life', for example. And there must be many

429

children who would echo the young Auberon Waugh's belief that London – in spite of all the treats laid on by a parent anxious to please – is 'a bit dull'.

Dull London

It begins the moment you set foot ashore, the moment you step off the boat's gangway. The heart suddenly, yet vaguely, sinks. It is no lurch of fear. Quite the contrary. It is as if the life-urge failed, and the heart dimly sank. You trail past the benevolent policeman and the inoffensive passport officials, through the fussy and somehow foolish customs – we don't *really* think it matters if somebody smuggles in two pairs of false-silk stockings – and we get into the poky but inoffensive train, with poky but utterly inoffensive people, and we have a cup of inoffensive tea from a nice inoffensive boy, and we run through small, poky but nice and inoffensive country, till we are landed in the big but unexciting station of Victoria, when an inoffensive porter puts us into an inoffensive taxi and we are driven through the crowded yet strangely dull streets of London to the cosy yet strangely poky and dull place where we are going to stay. And the first half-hour in London, after some years abroad, is really a plunge of misery. The strange, the grey and uncanny, almost deathly sense of *dulness* is overwhelming. Of course, you get over it after a while, and admit that you exaggerated. You get into the rhythm of London again, and you tell yourself that it is *not* dull. And yet you are haunted, all the time, sleeping or waking, with the uncanny feeling: It is dull! It is all dull! This life here is one vast complex of dulness! I am dull! I am being dulled! My spirit is being dulled! My life is dulling down to London dulness.

This is the nightmare that haunts you the first few weeks of London. No doubt if you stay longer you get over it, and find London as thrilling as Paris or Rome or New York. But the climate is against me. I cannot stay long enough. With pinched and wondering gaze, the morning of departure, I look out of the taxi upon the strange dulness of London's arousing; a sort of death; and hope and life only return when I get my seat in the boat-train, and I hear all the Good-byes! Good-bye! Good-bye! Thank God to say Good-bye!

Now to feel like this about one's native land is terrible. I am sure I am an exceptional, or at least an exaggerated case. Yet it seems to me most of my fellow-countrymen have the pinched, slightly pathetic look in their faces, the vague, wondering realization: It is dull! It is always essentially dull! My life is dull!

Of course, England is the easiest country in the world, easy, easy and nice. Everybody is nice, and everybody is easy. The English people on the whole are surely the *nicest* people in the world, and everybody makes everything so easy for everybody else, that there is almost nothing to resist at all. But this very easiness and this very niceness become at last a nightmare. It is as if the whole air were impregnated with chloroform or some other pervasive anaesthetic, that makes everything easy and nice, and takes the edge off everything, whether nice or nasty. As you inhale the drug of easiness and niceness, your vitality begins to sink. Perhaps not your physical vitality, but something else: the vivid flame of your individual life. England can afford to be so free and individual because no individual flame of life is sharp and vivid. It is just mildly warm and safe. You couldn't burn your fingers at it. Nice, safe, easy: the whole ideal. And yet under all the easiness is a gnawing uneasiness, as in a drug-taker.

It used not to be so. Twenty years ago London was to me thrilling, thrilling, thrilling, the vast and roaring heart of all adventure. It was not only the heart of the world, it was the heart of the world's living adventure. How wonderful the Strand, the Bank, Charing Cross at night, Hyde Park in the morning!

True, I am now twenty years older. Yet I have not lost my sense of adventure. But now all the adventure seems to me crushed out of London. The traffic is too heavy! It used to be going somewhere, on an adventure. Now it only rolls massively and overwhelmingly, going nowhere, only dully and enormously *going*. There is no adventure at the end of the 'buses' journey. The 'bus lapses into an inertia of dulness, then dully starts again. The traffic of London used to roar with the mystery of man's adventure on the seas of life, like a vast sea-shell, murmuring a thrilling, half-comprehensible story. Now it booms like monotonous, far-off guns, in a monotony of crushing something, crushing the earth, crushing out life, crushing everything dead.

And what does one do, in London? I, not having a job to attend to, lounge round and gaze in bleak wonder on the ceaseless dulness. Or I have luncheons and dinners with friends, and talk. Now my deepest private dread of London is my dread of this talk. I spend most of my days abroad, saying little, or with a bit of chatter and a silence again. But in London I feel like a spider whose thread has been caught by somebody, and is being drawn out of him, so he must spin, spin, spin, and all to no purpose. He is not even spinning his own web, for his own reasons.

So it is in London, at luncheon, dinner or tea. I don't want to talk. I don't mean to talk. Yet the talk is drawn out of me, endlessly. And the others talk, endlessly so. It is ceaseless, it is intoxicating, it is the only real occupation of us who do not jazz. And it is purely futile. It is quite as bad as ever the Russians were: talk for talk's sake, without the very faintest intention of a result in action. Utter inaction and storms of talk. That again is London to me. And the sense of abject futility in it all only deepens the sense of abject dulness, so all there is to do is to go away.

D. H. Lawrence, *Assorted Articles* (1932)

In Partibus

The 'buses run to Battersea,
The 'buses run to Bow,
The 'buses run to Westbourne Grove,
And Notting Hill also;
But I am sick of London Town,
From Shepherd's Bush to Bow.

I see the smut upon my cuff,
And feel him on my nose;
I cannot leave my window wide
When gentle Zephyr blows,
Because he brings disgusting things,
And drops 'em on my 'clo'es'.

The sky, a greasy soup-tureen,
Shuts down atop my brow.
Yes, I have sighed for London Town
And I have got it now:
And half of it is fog and filth,
And half is fog and row.

And when I take my nightly prowl,
'Tis passing good to meet

The pious Briton lugging home
　　His wife and daughter sweet,
Through four packed miles of seething vice,
　　Thrust out upon the street.

Earth holds no horror like to this
　　In any land displayed,
From Suez unto Sandy Hook,
　　From Calais to Port Said;
And 'twas to hide their heathendom
　　The beastly fog was made.

I cannot tell when dawn is near,
　　Or when the day is done,
Because I always see the gas
　　And never see the sun,
And now, methinks, I do not care
　　A cuss for either one.

But stay, there was an orange, or
　　An aged egg its yolk;
It might have been a Pears' balloon
　　Or Barnum's latest joke:
I took it for the sun and wept
　　To watch it through the smoke.

It's Oh to see the morn ablaze
　　Above the mango-tope,
When homeward through the dewy cane
　　The little jackals lope,
And half Bengal heaves into view,
　　New-washed – with sunlight soap.

It's Oh for one deep whisky-peg
　　When Christmas winds are blowing,
When all the men you ever knew,
　　And all you've ceased from knowing,
Are 'entered for the Tournament,
　　And everything that's going'.

But I consort with long-haired things
　　In velvet collar-rolls,

Who talk about the Aims of Art,
　And 'theories' and 'goals',
And moo and coo with womenfolk
　About their blessed souls.

But that they call 'psychology'
　Is lack of liver-pill,
And all that blights their tender souls
　Is eating till they're ill,
And their chief way of winning goals
　Consists of sitting still.

It's Oh to meet an Army man,
　Set up, and trimmed and taut,
Who does not spout hashed libraries
　Or think the next man's thought,
And walks as though he owned himself,
　And hogs his bristles short.

Hear now a voice across the seas
　To kin beyond my ken,
If ye have ever filled an hour
　With stories from my pen,
For pity's sake send some one here
　To bring me news of men!

The 'buses run to Islington,
　To Highgate and Soho,
To Hammersmith and Kew therewith,
　And Camberwell also,
But I can only murmur 'Bus!'
　From Shepherd's Bush to Bow.

　　　　　Rudyard Kipling, *Rudyard Kipling's Verse* (1940)

London

I wander thro' each charter'd street,
Near where the charter'd Thames does flow,
And mark in every face I meet
Marks of weakness, marks of woe.

In every cry of every Man,
In every Infant's cry of fear,
In every voice, in every ban,
The mind-forg'd manacles I hear.

How the Chimney-sweeper's cry
Every black'ning Church appalls;
And the hapless Soldier's sigh
Runs in blood down Palace walls.

But most thro' midnight streets I hear
How the youthful Harlot's curse
Blasts the new born Infant's tear,
And blights with plagues the Marriage hearse.

William Blake, *Songs of Experience* (1794)

Fear of muggers

Monday, 9 February

About mugging, it never occurred to me till last Monday that a man could
be afraid of me in the street – women often are, as when I've tried to ask
them the way. But last Monday, as it was growing dark and the street lamps
were at the red-hot stage above the wide pavement of Maida Vale, I was
walking on the inside near one of the low walls that run beside the endless
blocks of flats when a person came towards me on the same track, almost
touching the wall as I was. I began to move out. I would have done so
anyway, but I thought it was a woman and wanted to let her keep her path.
It was a man. He must have started to move out at the same moment, but

435

the farther I stepped towards the road, the farther he stepped as though he was trying to stop me, to confront me. We came very close to each other and I could not understand him, he seemed determined not to let me pass on the outside of him, the road side of him. I was puzzled and only afraid at the very last moment when he could have grasped or hit me. I swerved quickly in again towards the wall and passed him and as I did so he stared into my face, turning his to keep me in sight as I passed.

So much passed between us during these seconds. Neither knew the other's feelings yet our minds were as close as strangers' can be.

I walked on without quickening my pace and without looking back. He had stared at me so tensely that I thought he might follow me. He did not. Soon I reached the bus stop where many people were.

It did not occur to me that he might have been afraid until I was telling M. about it days later.

David Thomson, *In Camden Town* (1983)

Home

It was a Sunday evening in London, gloomy, close and stale. Maddening church bells of all degrees of dissonance, sharp and flat, cracked and clear, fast and slow, made the brick-and-mortar echoes hideous. Melancholy streets in a penitential garb of soot, steeped the souls of the people who were condemned to look at them out of windows in dire despondency. In every thoroughfare, up almost every alley, and down almost every turning, some doleful bell was throbbing, jerking, tolling, as if the Plague were in the city and the dead-carts were going round. Everything was bolted and barred that could by possibility furnish relief to an over-worked people. No pictures, no unfamiliar animals, no rare plants or flowers, no natural or artificial wonders of the ancient world – all *taboo* with that enlightened strictness, that the ugly South Sea gods in the British Museum might have supposed themselves at home again. Nothing to see but streets, streets, streets. Nothing to breathe but streets, streets, streets. Nothing to change the brooding mind, or raise it up. Nothing for the spent toiler to do, but to compare the monotony of his seventh day with the monotony of his six days, think what a weary life he led, and make the best of it – or the worst, according to the probabilities.

At such a happy time, so propitious to the interests of religion and morality, Mr Arthur Clennam, newly arrived from Marseilles by way of Dover, and by Dover coach the Blue-eyed Maid, sat in the window of a coffee-house on Ludgate Hill. Ten thousand responsible houses surrounded him, frowning as heavily on the streets they composed, as if they were every one inhabited by the ten young men of the Calender's story, who blackened their faces and bemoaned their miseries every night. Fifty thousand lairs surrounded him where people lived so unwholesomely, that fair water put into their crowded rooms on Saturday night, would be corrupt on Sunday morning; albeit my lord, their county member, was amazed that they failed to sleep in company with their butcher's meat. Miles of close wells and pits of houses, where the inhabitants gasped for air, stretched far away towards every point of the compass. Through the heart of the town a deadly sewer ebbed and flowed, in the place of a fine fresh river. What secular want could the million or so of human beings whose daily labour, six days in the week, lay among these Arcadian objects, from the sweet sameness of which they had no escape between the cradle and the grave – what secular want could they possibly have upon their seventh day? Clearly they could want nothing but a stringent policeman.

Mr Arthur Clennam sat in the window of the coffee-house on Ludgate Hill, counting one of the neighbouring bells, making sentences and burdens of songs out of it in spite of himself, and wondering how many sick people it might be the death of in the course of the year. As the hour approached, its changes of measure made it more and more exasperating. At the quarter, it went off into a condition of deadly-lively importunity, urging the populace in a voluble manner to Come to church, Come to church, come to church! At the ten minutes, it became aware that the congregation would be scanty, and slowly hammered out in low spirits, They *won't* come, they *won't* come, they *won't* come! At the five minutes, it abandoned hope, and shook every house in the neighbourhood for three hundred seconds, with one dismal swing per second, as a groan of despair.

'Thank Heaven!' said Clennam, when the hour struck, and the bell stopped.

But its sound had revived a long train of miserable Sundays, and the procession would not stop with the bell, but continued to march on. 'Heaven forgive me,' said he, 'and those who trained me. How I have hated this day!'

There was the dreary Sunday of his childhood, when he sat with his hands before him, scared out of his senses by a horrible tract which commenced business with the poor child by asking him in its title, why he was going to Perdition? – a piece of curiosity that he really in a frock and drawers was not in a condition to satisfy – and which, for the further attraction of his infant mind, had a parenthesis in every other line with some such hiccupping reference as 2 Ep. Thess. c. iii. v. 6 & 7. There was the sleepy Sunday of his boyhood, when, like a military deserter, he was marched to chapel by a picquet of teachers three times a day, morally handcuffed to another boy; and when he would willingly have bartered two meals of indigestible sermon for another ounce or two of inferior mutton at his scanty dinner in the flesh. There was the interminable Sunday of his nonage; when his mother, stern of face and unrelenting of heart, would sit all day behind a Bible – bound, like her own construction of it, in the hardest, barest, and straitest boards, with one dinted ornament on the cover like the drag of a chain, and a wrathful sprinkling of red upon the edges of the leaves – as if it, of all books! were a fortification against sweetness of temper, natural affection, and gentle intercourse. There was the resentful Sunday of a little later, when he sat glowering and glooming through the tardy length of the day, with a sullen sense of injury in his heart, and no more real knowledge of the beneficent history of the New Testament, than if he had been bred among idolaters. There was a legion of Sundays, all days of unserviceable bitterness and mortification, slowly passing before him.

Charles Dickens, Little Dorrit (1857)

The Effects of Stock-Jobbing

The City is the Center of its Commerce and Wealth.

The Court of its Gallantry and Splendor.

The Out-parts of its Numbers and Mechanicks; and in all these, no City in the World can equal it.

Between the Court and the City, there is a constant Communication of Business to that degree, that nothing in the World can come up to it.

As the City is the Center of Business; there is the *Custom-house*, an Article, which, as it brings in an immense Revenue to the Publick, so it cannot be removed from its Place, all the vast Import and Export of Goods being, of Necessity, made there; nor can the Merchants be removed, the River not admitting the Ships to come any farther.

Here, also, is the *Excise* Office, the *Navy* Office, the *Bank*, and almost all the Offices where those vast Funds are fixed, in which so great a Part of the Nation are concerned, and on the Security of which so many Millions are advanced.

Here are the *South Sea* Company, the *East India* Company, the *Bank*, the *African* Company, *&c.* whose Stocks support that prodigious Paper Commerce, called *Stock-Jobbing*; a Trade, which once bewitched the Nation almost to its Ruin, and which, tho' reduced very much, and recover'd from that terrible Infatuation which once overspread the whole Body of the People, yet is still a Negotiation, which is so vast in its Extent, that almost all the Men of Substance in *England* are more or less concerned in it, and the Property of which is so very often alienated, that even the Tax upon the Transfers of Stock, tho' but Five Shillings for each Transfer, brings many Thousand Pounds a Year to the Government; and some have said, that there is not less than a Hundred Millions of Stock transferred forward or backward from one Hand to another every Year, and this is one thing which makes such a constant Daily Intercourse between the Court Part of the Town, and the City; and this is given as one of the principal Causes of the prodigious Conflux of the Nobility and Gentry from all Parts of *England* to *London*, more than ever was known in former Years, *viz.* That many Thousands of Families are so deeply concerned in those Stocks, and find it so absolutely necessary to be at Hand to take the Advantage of buying and selling, as the sudden Rise or Fall of the Price directs, and the Loss they often sustain by their Ignorance of Things when absent, and the Knavery of Brokers and others, whom, in their Absence, they are bound to trust, that they find themselves obliged to come up and live constantly here, or at least, most Part of the Year.

This is the Reason why, notwithstanding the Encrease of new Buildings, and the Addition of new Cities, as they may be called, every Year to the old, yet a House is no sooner built, but 'tis tenanted and inhabited, and every Part is crouded with People, and that not only in the Town, but in all the Towns and Villages round, as shall be taken Notice of in its Place.

But let the Citizens and Inhabitants of *London* know, and it may be worth the Reflection of some of the Landlords, and Builders especially, that if Peace continues, and the publick Affairs continue in honest and upright Management, there is a Time coming, at least the Nation hopes for it, when the publick Debts being reduced and paid off, the Funds or Taxes on which they are established, may cease, and so Fifty or Sixty Millions of the Stocks, which are now the solid Bottom of the *South-Sea Company, East-India Company, Bank, &c.* will cease, and be no more; by which the Reason of this Conflux of People being removed, they will of Course, and by the Nature of the Thing, return again to their Country Seats, to avoid the expensive living at *London*, as they did come up hither to share the extravagant Gain of their former Business here.

What will be the Condition of this overgrown City in such a Case, I must leave to Time; but all those who know the temporary Constitution of our Funds, know this, 1. That even, if they are to spin out their own Length, all those Funds which were given for Thirty-two Years, have already run out one Third, and some of them almost half the Time, and that the rest will soon be gone: 2. That as in Two Years more, the Government which receives Six *per Cent.* and pays but Five, and will then pay but Four *per Cent.* Interest, will be able every Year to be paying off and lessening the publick Debt, 'till, in Time, 'tis to be hoped, all our Taxes may cease, and the ordinary Revenue may, as it always used to do, again supply the ordinary Expence of the Government.

Then, I say, will be a Time to expect the vast Concourse of People to *London*, will separate again and disperse as naturally, as they have now crouded hither: What will be the Fate then of all the fine Buildings in the Out Parts, in such a Cafe, let any one judge.

Daniel Defoe, A Tour Through the Whole Island of Great Britain (1724–6)

A racking headache

With rapid decision they resolved that Charlotte and Anne should start for London that very day, in order to prove their separate identity to Messrs Smith, Elder & Co., and demand from the credulous publisher his reasons for a 'belief' so directly at variance with an assurance which had several times been given to him. Having arrived at this determination, they made their preparations with resolute promptness. There were many household duties to be performed that day; but they were all got through. The two sisters each packed up a change of dress in a small box, which they sent down to Keighley by an opportune cart; and after early tea they set off to walk thither – no doubt in some excitement; for independently of the cause of their going to London, it was Anne's first visit there. A great thunderstorm overtook them on their way that summer evening to the station; but they had no time to seek shelter. They only just caught the train at Keighley, arrived at Leeds, and were whirled up by the night train to London.

About eight o'clock on the Saturday morning they arrived at the Chapter Coffee House, Paternoster Row – a strange place, but they did not well know where else to go. They refreshed themselves by washing, and had some breakfast. Then they sat still for a few minutes to consider what next should be done.

When they had been discussing their project in the quiet of Haworth Parsonage the day before, and planning the mode of setting about the business on which they were going to London, they had resolved to take a cab, if they should find it desirable, from their inn to Cornhill; but amidst the bustle and 'queer state of inward excitement' in which they found themselves, as they sat and considered their position on the Saturday morning, they quite forgot even the possibility of hiring a conveyance; and when they set forth they became so dismayed by the crowded streets, and the impeded crossings, that they stood still repeatedly, in complete despair of making progress, and were nearly an hour in walking the half-mile they had to go. Neither Mr Smith nor Mr Williams knew that they were coming; they were entirely unknown to the publishers of *Jane Eyre*, who were not, in fact, aware whether the 'Bells' were men or women, but had always written to them as to men.

On reaching Mr Smith's, Charlotte put his own letter into his hands – the same letter which had excited so much disturbance at Haworth Parsonage only twenty-four hours before. 'Where did you get this?' said he, – as if he could not believe that the two young ladies dressed in black, of slight figures and diminutive stature, looking pleased yet agitated, could be the embodied Currer and Acton Bell, for whom curiosity had been hunting so eagerly in vain. An explanation ensued, and Mr Smith at once began to form plans for their amusement and pleasure during their stay in London. He urged them to meet a few literary friends at his house; and this was a strong temptation to Charlotte, as amongst them were one or two of the writers whom she particularly wished to see; but her resolution to remain unknown induced her firmly to put it aside.

The sisters were equally persevering in declining Mr Smith's invitation to stay at his house. They refused to leave their quarters, saying they were not prepared for a long stay.

When they returned back to their inn, poor Charlotte paid for the excitement of the interview, which had wound up the agitation and hurry of the last twenty-four hours, by a racking headache and harassing sickness. Towards evening, as she rather expected some of the ladies of Mr Smith's family to call, she prepared herself for the chance by taking a strong dose of sal volatile, which roused her a little, but still, as she says, she was 'in grievous bodily case' when their visitors were announced in full evening costume. The sisters had not understood that it had been settled that they were to go to the Opera, and therefore were not ready. Moreover, they had no fine, elegant dresses either with them or in the world. But Miss Brontë resolved to raise no objections in the acceptance of kindness. So, in spite of headache and weariness, they made haste to dress themselves in their plain high-made country garments.

Charlotte says, in an account which she gives to her friend of this visit to London, describing the entrance of her party into the Opera House:

Fine ladies and gentlemen glanced at us, as we stood by the box-door, which was not yet opened, with a slight, graceful superciliousness, quite warranted by the circumstances. Still I felt pleasurably excited in spite of headache, sickness, and conscious clownishness; and I saw Anne was calm and gentle, which she always is. The performance was Rossini's 'Barber of Seville', – very brilliant, though I fancy there are things I should like better. We got home after one o'clock. We had never been in bed the night before; had been in constant excitement for twenty-four hours; you may imagine we were tired. The next day, Sunday, Mr Williams came early to take us to church; and in the afternoon Mr Smith and his mother fetched us in a carriage, and took us to his house to dine.

On Monday we went to the Exhibition of the Royal Academy, the National Gallery, dined again at Mr Smith's, and then went home to tea with Mr Williams at his house.

On Tuesday morning we left London, laden with books Mr Smith had given us, and got safely home. A more jaded wretch than I looked it would be difficult to conceive. I was thin when I went, but I was meagre indeed when I returned, my face looking grey and very old, with strange deep lines ploughed in it – my eyes stared unnaturally. I was weak and yet restless. In a while, however, these bad effects of excitement went off, and I regained my normal condition.

Elizabeth Gaskell, *The Life of Charlotte Brontë* (1857)

The Great Stink

The climax came in June 1858, when an exceptionally hot summer and unusually low rainfall combined to produce what all London knew as 'The Great Stink'. Parliament was in a good position to appreciate the nuisance, for the windows at Westminster had to be draped with curtains soaked in chloride of lime so that members could breathe. To cross Westminster Bridge it was necessary to hold a handkerchief firmly over one's nose and mouth and those who travelled on the river steamers suffered greatly when the paddles churned the water into stinking eddies. No one could face the refreshments offered on board, and few dared to travel at all in this way, so that the owners of these pleasure-craft found they were running at a loss, and laid most of them up. There was talk of moving the Law Courts to Oxford or St Albans, and a Select Committee was set up to report on the Stink and to find means of its abatement. One ingenious witness, a Mr Gurney, wanted to seal the ends of the sewers – there were 369 of them between Putney and Blackwell – and to lead the gas by means of pipes to chosen high points and then fire it so that it would burn away – he said – harmlessly. Gurney was particularly anxious to carry a pipe from the huge new Victoria sewer through New Palace Yard to the Clock Tower; this he was allowed to do, although a more practical engineer was able to prevent the subsequent explosion from utterly destroying the Clock Tower (and perhaps completing Guy Fawkes's plan). A more conventional remedy, the use of slaked lime in large quantities, and the coming of the rain cured the Great Stink, but it had served its purpose in awakening Londoners to the realities of their position and had even ousted the Indian Mutiny as the chief topic of conversation.

R. J. Mitchell and M. R. D. Leys, *A History of London Life* (1958)

'Black Bull of Aldgate'

Black Bull of Aldgate, may thy horns rot from the sockets!
For, jingling threepence, porter's pay, in hungry pockets,
And thirty times at least beneath thy doorway stepping

I've waited for this lousy coach that runs to Epping.
Ill luck befall thee, that hast made me so splenetic,
Through all thy holes and closets up from tap to attic,
Through all thy boys and bootses, chambermaids, and waiters,
And yonder booking-office-clerk in fustian gaiters.
Black Bull of Aldgate! mayst thou more miscarry
Than ever hasty Clement's did with bloated Harry!

Alfred, Lord Tennyson (?1837)

Mr Dombey's house

Mr Dombey's house was a large one, on the shady side of a tall, dark, dreadfully genteel street in the region between Portland Place and Bryanstone Square. It was a corner house, with great wide areas containing cellars frowned upon by barred windows, and leered at by crooked-eyed doors leading to dustbins. It was a house of dismal state, with a circular back to it, containing a whole suit of drawing-rooms looking upon a gravelled yard, where two gaunt trees, with blackened trunks and branches, rattled rather than rustled, their leaves were so smoke-dried. The summer sun was never on the street, but in the morning about breakfast-time, when it came with the water-carts and the old-clothes men, and the people with geraniums, and the umbrella-mender, and the man who trilled the little bell of the Dutch clock as he went along. It was soon gone again to return no more that day: and the bands of music and the straggling Punch's shows going after it, left it a prey to the most dismal of organs, and white mice; with now and then a porcupine, to vary the entertainments; until the butlers whose families were dining out, began to stand at the house-doors in the twilight, and the lamplighter made his nightly failure in attempting to brighten up the street with gas.

It was as blank a house inside as outside. When the funeral was over, Mr Dombey ordered the furniture to be covered up – perhaps to preserve it for the son with whom his plans were all associated – and th. rooms to be ungarnished, saving such as he retained for himself on the ground floor. Accordingly, mysterious shapes were made of tables and chairs, heaped together in the middle of rooms, and covered over with great winding-sheets. Bell-handles, window-blinds, and looking-glasses, being papered up in journals, daily and weekly, obtruded fragmentary accounts of deaths and dreadful murders. Every chandelier or lustre, muffled in holland, looked like a monstrous tear depending from the ceiling's eye. Odours, as from vaults and damp places, came out of the chimneys. The dead and buried lady was awful in a picture-frame of ghastly bandages. Every gust of wind that rose, brought eddying round the corner from the neighbouring mews, some fragments of the straw that had been strewn before the house when she was ill, mildewed remains of which were still cleaving to the neighbourhood; and these, being always drawn by some invisible attraction to the threshold of the dirty house to let immediately opposite, addressed a dismal eloquence to Mr Dombey's windows.

Charles Dickens, *Dombey and Son* (1848)

The Food of Londoners

I am pent up in frowsy lodgings, where there is not room enough to swing a cat, and I breathe the steams of endless putrefaction; and these would, undoubtedly, produce a pestilence, if they were not qualified by the gross acid of sea-coal, which is itself a pernicious nuisance to lungs of any delicacy of texture. But even this boasted corrector cannot prevent those languid sallow looks that distinguish the inhabitants of London from those ruddy swains that lead a country life. I go to bed after midnight, jaded and restless from the dissipations of the day. I start every hour from my sleep, at the horrid noise of the watchmen bawling the hour through every street, and thundering at every door; a set of useless fellows, who serve no other purpose but that of disturbing the repose of the inhabitants; and, by five o'clock, I start out of bed, in consequence of the still more dreadful alarm made by the country carts, and noisy rustics bellowing green peas under my window. If I would drink water, I must quaff the mawkish contents of an open aqueduct, exposed to all manner of defilement, or swallow that which comes from the river Thames, impregnated with all the filth of London and Westminster. Human excrement is the least offensive part of the concrete, which is composed of all the drugs, minerals, and poisons used in mechanics and manufactures, enriched with the putrefying carcases of beasts and men, and mixed with the scourings of all the wash-tubs, kennels, and common sewers within the bills of mortality.

This is the agreeable potation extolled by the Londoners as the finest water in the universe. As to the intoxicating potion sold for wine, it is a vile, unpalatable, and pernicious sophistication, balderdashed with cider, corn spirit, and the juice of sloes. In an action at law, laid against a carman for having staved a cask of port, it appeared, from the evidence of the cooper, that there were not above five gallons of real wine in the whole pipe, which held above a hundred, and even that had been brewed and adulterated by the merchant at Oporto. The bread I eat in London is a deleterious paste, mixed up with chalk, alum, and bone-ashes, insipid to the taste, and destructive to the constitution. The good people are not ignorant of this adulteration; but they prefer it to wholesome bread, because it is whiter than the meal of corn. Thus they sacrifice their taste and their health, and the lives of their tender infants, to a most absurd gratification of a misjudging eye; and the miller or the baker is obliged to poison them and their families, in order to live by his profession. The same monstrous depravity appears in their veal, which is bleached by repeated bleedings, and other villanous arts, till there is not a drop of juice left in the body, and the poor animal is paralytic before it dies; so void of all taste, nourishment, and savour, that a man might dine as comfortably on a white fricassee of kidskin gloves, or chip hats from Leghorn.

Tobias Smollett, *Humphrey Clinker* (1771)

'A Bit dull'

TO LAURA WAUGH

25 August 1945   *White's*

Darling Laura,

I have regretfully come to the conclusion that the boy Auberon is not yet a suitable companion for me.

Yesterday was a day of supreme self-sacrifice. I fetched him from Highgate, took him up the dome of St Pauls, gave him a packet of triangular stamps, took him to luncheon at the Hyde Park Hotel, took him on the roof of the hotel, took him to Harrods & let him buy vast quantities of toys (down to your account) took him to tea with Maimie who gave him a pound and a box of matches, took him back to Highgate, in a state (myself not the boy) of extreme exhaustion. My mother said 'Have you had a lovely day?' He replied 'A bit dull.' So that is the last time for some years I inconvenience myself for my children. You might rub that in to him.

I had a very enjoyable evening getting drunk at the House of Commons with Hollis & Fraser and the widow Hartington (who is in love with me I think) & Driberg & Nigel Birch & Lord Morris and Anthony Head & my communist cousin Claud Cockburn.

Last night I dined with Maimie. Vsevolode kept going to bed and coming down again.

London is fuller & noisier than ever.

All my love
Evelyn

Evelyn Waugh, *Letters* (1980)

Driven out

10 April 1981

Twenty years ago when I lived in London, the place was full of women like Mrs Shirley Williams with bossy, fatuous opinions about education, redistribution of wealth and all that dreary rubbish.

In those days everybody drank filthy wine and served messed-up chickens with tomatoes in a sort of casserole. After a time, they succeeded in driving me out of London. But at least nobody thought their smug, half-witted opinions (which would require a gigantic police state apparatus to maintain) had anything to do with real politics.

Now this insufferably stupid woman is hailed everywhere as a great political moderate, the person who will save us from the deeper lunacies of Wedgwood Benn. But what on earth is one to do with these women?

The time is long past when one could thrash them soundly and lock them in their bedrooms. Perhaps some philanthropist will organize a Moderate Females' Mass Fun-Run down to the sea and over the cliffs at Beachy Head.

Auberon Waugh, *Diaries, 1976–1985* (1985)

London Renounced

For who wou'd leave, unbrib'd, Hibernia's land,
Or change the rocks of Scotland for the Strand?
There none are swept by sudden fate away,
But all whom hunger spares, with age decay:
Here malice, rapine, accident, conspire,
And now a rabble rages, now a fire;
Their ambush here relentless ruffians lay,
And here the fell attorney prowls for prey;
Here falling houses thunder on your head,
And here a female atheist talks you dead.

While Thales waits the wherry that contains
Of dissipated wealth the small remains,
On Thames's banks, in silent thought we stood,
Where Greenwich smiles upon the silver flood;
Struck with the feat that gave Eliza birth,
We kneel, and kiss the consecrated earth;
In pleasing dreams the blissful age renew,
And call Britannia's glories back to view;
Behold her cross triumphant on the main,
The guard of commerce, and the dread of Spain,
Ere masquerades debauch'd, excise oppress'd,
Or English honour grew a standing jest.

A transient calm the happy scenes bestow,
And for a moment lull the sense of woe.
At length awaking, with contemptuous frown,
Indignant Thales eyes the neighb'ring town.

Since worth, he cries, in these degen'rate days
Wants ev'n the cheap reward of empty praise;
In those curs'd walls, devote to vice and gain,
Since unrewarded science toils in vain;
Since hope but soothes to double my distress,
And ev'ry moment leaves my little less;
While yet my steady steps no staff sustains,
And life still vig'rous revels in my veins;
Grant me, kind Heaven, to find some happier place,

Where honesty and sense are no disgrace;
Some pleasing bank where verdant osiers play,
Some peaceful vale with nature's paintings gay;
Where once the harass'd Briton found repose,
And safe in poverty defi'd his foes:
Some secret cell, ye pow'rs indulgent, give,
Let — live here, for — has learn'd to live.
Here let those reign, whom pensions can incite
To vote a patriot black, a courtier white;
Explain their country's dear-bought rights away,
And plead for pirates in the face of day;
With slavish tenets taint our poison'd youth,
And lend a lie the confidence of truth.

. . .

Could'st thou resign the park and play content,
For the fair banks of Severn or of Trent;
There might'st thou find some elegant retreat,
Some hireling senator's deserted seat;
And stretch thy prospects o'er the smiling land,
For less than rent the dungeons of the Strand;
There prune thy walks, support thy drooping flow'rs,
Direct thy rivulets, and twine thy bow'rs;
And, while thy grounds a cheap repast afford,
Despise the dainties of a venal lord:
There ev'ry bush with Nature's music rings,
There ev'ry breeze bears health upon its wings;
On all thy hours security shall smile,
And bless thine evening walk and morning toil.
  Prepare for death if here at night you roam,
And sign your will before you sup from home.
Some fiery fop, with new commission vain,
Who sleeps on brambles till he kills his man;
Some frolic drunkard, reeling from a feast,
Provokes a broil, and stabs you for a jest.
Yet ev'n these heroes, mischievously gay,
Lords of the street, and terrors of the way,
Flush'd as they are with folly, youth, and wine,
Their prudent insults to the poor confine;
Afar they mark the flambeau's bright approach,

And shun the shining train and golden coach.
   In vain these dangers past, your doors you close,
And hope the balmy blessings of repose:
Cruel with guilt, and daring with despair,
The midnight murd'rer bursts the faithless bar;
Invades the sacred hour of silent rest,
And leaves unseen a dagger in your breast.
   Scarce can our fields, such crowds at Tyburn die,
With hemp the Gallows and the Fleet supply.
Propose your schemes, ye senatorian band,
Whose ways and means support the sinking land,
Lest ropes be wanting in the tempting spring,
To rig another convoy for the King.
   A single gaol in Alfred's golden reign
Could half the nation's criminals contain;
Fair Justice then, without constraint ador'd,
Held high the steady scale, but sheath'd the sword;
No spies were paid, no special juries known,
Blest age! but ah! how diff'rent from our own!
   Much could I add, – but see the boat at hand,
The tide retiring calls me from the land:
Farewell! – When youth, and health, and fortune spent,
Thou fli'st for refuge to the wilds of Kent;
And, tir'd like me with follies and with crimes,
In angry numbers warn'st succeeding times,
Then shall thy friend, nor thou refuse his aid,
Still foe to vice, forsake his Cambrian shade;
In virtue's cause once more exert his rage,
Thy satire point, and animate thy page.

Samuel Johnson, *London* (1738)

18

When a Man Is Tired of London . . .

Anyone who compiles an anthology must ask himself whether he should attempt to surprise the readers with items they had never read before, or to delight them with the old and the familiar. Surely a balance is needed between the two. A book of London, for example, which did not contain Wordsworth's sonnet on Westminster Bridge would strike me as eccentric.

Possibly the most famous saying about London – so famous that it has become an axiom, or a cliché – is Samuel Johnson's assertion that the man who is tired of London is tired of life. I have decided that these words could not be omitted, and that they should really stand as the conclusion to this book. They are the sentiments towards which all the other extracts in this book have been aspiring and gravitating. Poems like Dunbar's 'The Flour of Cities All' might seem competitive, or even chauvinistic in their love of London. This chapter is not concerned with competition, nor with the merits of London compared with those of other towns and cities. For all a Londoner knows, there might be grander churches in Rome, better football in Manchester, greater restaurants in Paris or New York. Such subjective assertions could never be tested or proved. What I have tried to convey in the final extracts here is the extraordinary capacity which London has to make people happy. Even those who have not seen William Blake's pillars of gold stretching to heaven from Marylebone or Islington will have known that lift to the spirits which cheered Mrs Dalloway, as she realized how much she loved 'life; London; this moment of June'.

The happiness of London

Talking of a London life, he said, 'The happiness of London is not to be conceived but by those who have been in it. I will venture to say, there is more learning and science within the circumference of ten miles from where we now sit, than in all the rest of the kingdom.' BOSWELL. 'The only disadvantage is the great distance at which people live from one another.' JOHNSON. 'Yes, Sir; but that is occasioned by the largeness of it, which is the cause of all the other advantages.' BOSWELL. 'Sometimes I have been in the humour of wishing to retire to a desart.' JOHNSON. 'Sir, you have desart enough in Scotland.'

James Boswell, *Life of Johnson* (1791)

Wonderful treats

Presently I began to take the children about. We started quietly, leaving Hamilton Gardens one day by the private gate and walking out into the park. No one paid any attention to us, so we went farther afield. There was the Serpentine in Hyde Park, with its ducks and friendly birds and rowing-boats and sea-gulls to be visited, and we even got as far as the Round Pond near Kensington Palace on more than one occasion and watched other children sailing toy yachts.

Other children always had an enormous fascination, like mystic beings from a different world, and the little girls used to smile shyly at those they liked the look of. They would so have loved to speak to them and make friends, but this was never encouraged. I often have thought it a pity. The Dutch and Belgian Royal children walked about the streets in their countries as a matter of course.

Only once were we beleaguered by the Press. A persuasive young man recognized the children and wanted to take a picture. I knew that if this happened it would be the end of our unofficial outings, so I drove him off mercilessly.

'Crawfie, you were savage,' Lilibet said, delighted. 'I am sure he thinks now that Crawfies bite!'

452

We explored Hyde Park and the gardens in this quite unofficial way. The little girls loved it. The Duke and Duchess apparently approved, for they made no comment whatever. Alah, I know, thoroughly disapproved, but I think even she was beginning to realize she could not keep her darlings safely cloistered for ever.

One day as we passed Hyde Park Corner people were streaming out of the Underground station and Lilibet said wistfully, 'Oh, dear, what fun it must be to ride in those trains.' I thought, *why not?* It seemed such a simple request. I asked the Duke about it that evening.

As long as we had someone with us, neither of the children's parents objected in the least. So it was arranged that the house detective should accompany us at a discreet distance, and that the Duchess's lady-in-waiting, Lady Helen Graham, should also be one of this exciting party.

Anyone would have thought we were going on an expedition to the stately pleasure domes of Kubla Khan rather than for a ride in an Underground train. The little girls bought their tickets out of their own purses. This was part of the fun. It always took them an immense time to get the money out and collect their change, and the whole business was solemn as an investiture.

Lilibet had a shilling a week pocket-money until she was fourteen or fifteen. Mostly she just saved this up for the Christmas or summer holidays. Margaret did not get any pocket-money at all at this time. She never seemed to be very interested in it. Even when they were quite grown up the King would pass a shilling along to them in church, when the time came to put it in the plate. A pound note for himself and one for the Queen, and a shilling for each Princess. I provided my own. From time to time, Alah would generously present Margaret with a half-crown. This lasted her an immensely long time. They each had a little embroidered purse they kept in their handkerchief drawer.

The escalator to the Underground seemed a perilous trip. Margaret's hand tightened on mine, and she swallowed apprehensively. Once safely on, down we sailed and caught our train. The little girls sat there very demurely, wide-eyed and enchanted, until suddenly at the far end of the same carriage we spotted our detective! He looked so very obviously a detective that people began to look round to try to discover what he was detecting. Mercifully, we arrived at Tottenham Court Road and got out before anyone had discovered the reason.

Our jaunt was to the YWCA. This had had to be planned ahead, but we still tried to keep it entirely unofficial, and few there knew who the children were. We collected our own tea on trays with the rest of the clientele. Lilibet left her teapot behind. The lady in charge bawled out to her, 'If you want it you must come and fetch it.' Tea out of thick cups, other people's bread and butter, tea you paid for with money, these were wonderful treats.

That afternoon our fun was rather spoiled because someone recognized them, word went round, and crowds began to gather. I sent a hasty message from the office for a car to be sent from the Duke's garage, and we had to drive home.

The next grand occasion was to be a ride on a bus. On *top* of a bus. Lilibet insisted. It seemed to her such a wonderful idea that when you were on top of a bus you would be able to see right into other people's gardens. Sad to tell, these pleasant jaunts came to a sudden end. The Irish Republican Army started about this time to put bombs in letter-boxes, and to commit other public nuisances to draw attention to their demand for Home Rule for Ireland. It was not quite certain in what even less desirable directions their efforts might not lead them if it were known that the two Princesses were often afoot in London, unprotected.

Marion Crawford, *The Little Princesses* (1950)

Hobbes the Londoner

Anno 1650 or 1651, he returned into England, and lived most part in Fetter-lane, where he writt, or finished, his booke *de Corpore*, in Latin and then in English.

He was much in London till the restauration of his Majesty, having here convenience not only of Bookes, but of learned Conversation. I have heard him say, that at his Lord's house in the Countrey there was a good Library, and bookes enough for him, and that his Lordship stored the Library with what bookes he thought fitt to be bought; but he sayd, the want of learned Conversation was a very great inconvenience, and that though he conceived he could order his thinking as well perhaps as another man, yet he found a great defect. Methinkes in the country, for want of good conversation, one's Witt growes mouldy.

John Aubrey, *Brief Lives* (1693)

Pillars of gold

The fields from Islington to Marybone,
To Primrose Hill and Saint John's Wood,
   Were builded over with pillars of gold,
And there Jerusalem's pillars stood.

   Her Little-ones ran on the fields,
The Lamb of God among them seen,
   And fair Jerusalem his Bride,
Among the little meadows green.

   Pancrass & Kentish-town repose
Among her golden pillars high,
   Among her golden arches which
Shine upon the starry sky.

   The Jew's-harp-house & the Green Man,
The Ponds where Boys to bathe delight,
   The fields of Cows by Willan's farm,
Shine in Jerusalem's pleasant sight.

   She walks upon our meadows green,
The Lamb of God walks by her side,
   And every English Child is seen
Children of Jesus & his Bride.

William Blake, Jerusalem (1803)

The Flour of Cities All

London, thou art of townes *A per se*.
   Soveraign of cities, semeliest in sight,
Of high renoun, riches, and royaltie;
   Of lordis, barons, and many goodly knyght;
   Of most delectable lusty ladies bright;
Of famous prelatis, in habitis clericall;

Of merchauntis full of substaunce and myght:
London, thou art the Flour of Cities all.

Gladdith anon thou lusty Troynovaunt,
  Citie that some tyme cleped was New Troy,
In all the erth, imperiall as thou stant,
  Pryncesse of townes, of pleasure and of joy,
  A richer restith under no Christen roy;
For manly power, with craftis naturall,
  Fourmeth none fairer sith the flode of Noy:
London, thou art the Flour of Cities all.

Gemme of all joy, jasper of jocunditie,
  Most myghty carbuncle of vertue and valour,
Strong Troy in vigour and strenuytie;
  Of royall cities rose and geraflour;
  Emperesse of townes, exalt in honour,
In beautie berying the crone imperiall;
  Swete paradise, precelling in pleasure;
London, thou art the Flour of Cities all.

Aboue all ryuers thy Ryuer hath renowne,
  Whose beryall stremys, pleasant and preclare,
Under thy lusty wallys renneth down,
  Where many a swanne doth swymme with wingis fare;
  Where many a barge doth saile, and row with are,
Where many a ship doth rest with toppe-royall.
  O! towne of townes, patrone and not compare:
London, thou art the Flour of Cities all.

Upon thy lusty Brigge of pylers white
  Been merchauntis full royall to behold;
Upon thy stretis goeth many a semely knyght
  (Arrayit) in velvet gownes and cheynes of gold.
  By Julyus Cesar thy Tour founded of old
May be the Hous of Mars victoryall,
  Whos artillary with tonge may not be told:
London, thou art the Flour of Cities all.

Strong be thy wallys that about thee standis;
  Wise be the people that within thee dwellis;

Fresh is thy ryuer with his lusty strandis;
  Blith be thy churches, wele sownyng thy bellis;
  Riche be thy merchauntis in substaunce that excellis;
Fair be their wives, right lovesom, white and small;
  Clere be thy virgyns, lusty under kellis:
London, thou art the Flour of Cities all.

Thy famous Maire, by pryncely governaunce,
  With swerd of justice the ruleth prudently.
No Lord of Paris, Venyce, or Floraunce
  In dygnitie or honoure goeth to hynm nye.
  He is exampler, loodë-ster, and guye,
Principall patrone and roose orygynalle,
  Above all Maires as maister moost worthy:
London, thou art the Flour of Cities all.

William Dunbar, Collected Poems (1501)

Life; London; this moment of June

For having lived in Westminster – how many years now? over twenty, – one feels even in the midst of the traffic, or waking at night, Clarissa was positive, a particular hush, or solemnity; an indescribable pause; a suspense (but that might be her heart, affected, they said, by influenza) before Big Ben strikes. There! Out it boomed. First a warning, musical; then the hour, irrevocable. The leaden circles dissolved in the air. Such fools we are, she thought, crossing Victoria Street. For Heaven only knows why one loves it so, how one sees it so, making it up, building it round one, tumbling it, creating it every moment afresh; but the veriest frumps, the most dejected of miseries sitting on doorsteps (drink their downfall) do the same; can't be dealt with, she felt positive, by Acts of Parliament for that very reason: they love life. In people's eyes, in the swing, tramp, and trudge; in the bellow and the uproar; the carriages, motor cars, omnibuses, vans, sandwich men shuffling and swinging; brass bands; barrel organs; in the triumph and the jingle and the strange high singing of some aeroplane overhead was what she loved; life; London; this moment of June.

Virginia Woolf, Mrs Dalloway (1925)

457

A little sun

Guy walked down Maida Vale. Having lost their leaves too early, the trees sunbathed, wrinkled and topless and ashamed. London birds croaked in pity or defiance. The sun was doing what it did and always had done, day and night, for fifteen billion years, which is burn. Why didn't more people worship the sun? The sun had so much going for it. It created life; it was profoundly mysterious; it was so powerful that no one on earth dared to look its way. Yet humans worshipped the human, the anthropomorphic. They worshipped promiscuously: anybody. An Indian keep-fit fanatic, an Ethiopian mass-murderer, a nineteenth-century American angel called *Moroni* – Guy's own Catholic God or Nobodaddy. Almost humorous in some lights, the down on her upper lip. The sun was a unit away: an astronomical unit. But today you felt that the sun was no higher than Everest. Not good to be out in it, really. Giver of all life, the sun was now taking life away, the lifetaker, the carcinogenic sun. A trick of perception, or is there a certain spacing in the join of her hips and legs, a curved triangle of free air between the thighs, just at the top? Guy walked on, down Elgin Avenue. He felt happy – in obedience, perhaps, to the weather (and if this sun were rendered in a children's book it would surely be smiling); happy anticipations, happy memories, an embarrassment of happiness. He remembered one morning over a year ago. Yes, he had just burped Marmaduke; in fact the child had been sick on his shoulder (the drycleaning man comes and scratches the corduroy with a doubtful fingernail and you say 'Baby sick', and everyone smiles, forgivingly, everyone understands). I was sitting on the bed with the baby, while she changed or bathed next door. I felt cold suddenly – his sick was cooling on my shoulder – and there was the baby's head, the hair slicked flat with womb-gloss, biospherical, like a world. Or a heavenly body. I felt its heat, the warmth of the baby's head, and I thought (oh these puns and their shameful mediocrity – but I meant it, I really meant it): I've got, I now have . . . I now have a little sun.

Martin Amis, London Fields (1989)

Rural Felicity

Well, the country's a pleasant place, sure enough, for people that's country
  born,
And useful, no doubt, in a natural way, for growing our grass and corn.
It was kindly meant of my cousin Giles, to write and invite me down,
Tho' as yet all I've seen of a pastoral life only makes one more partial to
  Town.

.   .   .

At first I thought I was really come down into all sorts of rural bliss;
For Porkington Place, with its cows and its pigs, and its poultry, looks not
  much amiss;
There's something about a dairy farm, with its different kinds of live
  stock,
That puts one in mind of Paradise, and Adam and his innocent flock;
But somehow the good old Elysium fields have not been well handed
  down,
And as yet I have found no fields to prefer to dear Leicester Fields up in
  town.

.   .   .

And after all, an't there new-laid eggs to be had upon Holborn Hill?
And dairy-fed pork in Broad St Giles's, and fresh butter wherever you
  will?
And a covered cart that brings cottage bread quite rustical-like and
  brown?
So one isn't so very uncountrified in the very heart of the town.

.   .   .

Howsomever my mind's made up, and although I'm sure cousin Giles will
  be vext,
I mean to book me an inside place up to town upon Saturday next,
And if nothing happens, soon after ten, I shall be at the old *Bell and
  Crown*,
And perhaps I may come to the country again, when London is all burnt
  down.

Thomas Hood, *Collected Poems* (1839)

Not equal to Fleet Street

We walked in the evening in Greenwich Park. He asked me, I suppose, by way of trying my disposition, 'Is not this very fine?' Having no exquisite relish of the beauties of Nature, and being more delighted with 'the busy hum of men', I answered, 'Yes, Sir; but not equal to Fleet-street.' JOHNSON. 'You are right, Sir.'

I am aware that many of my readers may censure my want of taste. Let me, however, shelter myself under the authority of a very fashionable Baronet in the brilliant world, who, on his attention being called to the fragrance of a May evening in the country, observed, 'This may be very well; but, for my part, I prefer the smell of a flambeau at the playhouse.'

We staid so long at Greenwich, that our sail up the river, in our return to London, was by no means so pleasant as in the morning; for the night air was so cold that it made me shiver. I was the more sensible of it from having sat up all the night before, recollecting and writing in my journal what I thought worthy of preservation; an exertion, which, during the first part of my acquaintance with Johnson, I frequently made. I remember having sat up four nights in one week, without being much incommoded in the day time.

Johnson, whose robust frame was not in the least affected by the cold, scolded me, as if my shivering had been a paltry effeminacy, saying, 'Why do you shiver?' Sir William Scott, of the Commons, told me, that when he complained of a head-ache in the post-chaise, as they were travelling together to Scotland, Johnson treated him in the same manner: 'At your age, Sir, I had no head-ache.' It is not easy to make allowance for sensations in others, which we ourselves have not at the time. We must all have experienced how very differently we are affected by the complaints of our neighbours, when we are well and when we are ill. In full health, we can scarcely believe that they suffer much; so faint is the image of pain upon our imagination: when softened by sickness, we readily sympathize with the sufferings of others.

We concluded the day at the Turk's Head coffee-house very socially.

James Boswell, *Life of Johnson* (1791)

Free pleasures

Guilford Street being only a short walk from the British Museum, which meant to me chiefly the Reading Room, I could get down to serious study and start trying to educate myself in earnest. Even in a capitalist society there is a degree of communism. In London the National Gallery and the Reading Room are good examples. On free days I could go to the National Gallery where all the schools of painting from the earliest Italians are so finely represented – and at that time I had two volumes of a catalogue with a whole page of commentary devoted to each picture, written by Ruskin! As for music, the radio came in, and for a tiny fee, literally worth thousands of pounds, one can hear all the great composers of the world over and over again, a communal gift of such priceless value to me personally that no words can express my gratitude.

The British Museum Reading Room is a unique institution. Provided you can justify a claim to receive a ticket of admission you can spend the whole of every week-day in the Reading Room for the rest of your life. And the wonderful thing about it is that you can get out any book that has been published (at least in the English language) – even R. Zon's brochure on 'Forests and Water in the Light of Scientific Investigation', published by the Washington Government Printing Office. No doubt this policy will lead to disaster in the end. Meanwhile it is one of the wonders of the world. Recently it has been cleaned and modernized. In the old days it was more homely and cosy. There was no strip-lighting, but a lamp for each desk to be turned on as the reader desired. And lamps hung aloft from the dome, friendly and soothing in the winter dusk and dark. The atmosphere was less spick-and-span than now. The Room is in the form of a huge circle; the design best imagined by thinking of a wheel; the spokes as the rows of desks; the hub providing the space for the largest catalogue in the world.

Many great men from all parts of the world have used this mine of knowledge, and indeed it is associated with many mighty names, historic figures who have risen from their seats to go out into the world and change it. Karl Marx sat there for years planning the overthrow of capitalism, while both Lenin and Trotsky used the Room as quite a home from home until they were ready to blow up homes. Samuel Butler went there every day, always sitting in the same seat. In his early years Bernard Shaw did most of his reading there, and met William Archer who helped to start him on his

461

career. It was pleasant to enter into such an atmosphere, and now and then look up to see some legendary figure lost in the anonymity of the place. I once found G. K. Chesterton beside me taking down a book from a shelf, and I noted his formidable head, his concentrated eye, and purposeful movement. I saw the classic profile and amazing head of hair of Havelock Ellis. I saw Cunningham-Graham consulting a catalogue; standing very erect, well-dressed, with sharp beard, every inch the gentleman, and Hero as Man of Action not unwilling to lend a hand to Literature. One of the habitués was Rose Macaulay, who had the face of a nineteenth-century governess combined with that of a lost child, and whose reputation as a novelist was second to her reputation as the worst driver that anyone had ever known; and personally I support this finding for she drove me once, and her lethal jerkiness in progression made me amazed that she continued to live.

John Stewart Collis, *Bound Upon a Course* (1971)

Preferring London to the Lake District

I need not describe to you the expectations which such an one as myself, pent up all my life in a dirty city, have formed of a tour to the Lakes. Consider Grasmere! Ambleside! Wordsworth! Coleridge! I hope you will. Hills, woods, lakes, and mountains, to the devil. I will eat snipes with thee, Thomas Manning. Only confess, confess, a *bite*.

P.S. I think you named the 16th; but was it not modest of Lloyd to send such an invitation! It shows his knowledge of *money* and *time*. I should be loth to think he meant

> 'Ironic satire sidelong sklented
> On my poor pursie.' – BURNS.

For my part, with reference to my friends northward, I must confess that I am not romance-bit about *Nature*. The earth, and sea, and sky, (when all is said,) is but as a house to dwell in. If the inmates be courteous, and good liquors flow like the conduits at an old coronation, if they can talk sensibly, and feel properly, I have no need to stand staring upon the gilded looking-glass (that strained my friend's purse-strings in the purchase) nor his five-shilling print, over the mantel-piece, of old Nabbs the carrier, (which only betrays his false taste). Just as important to me (in a sense) is all the furniture of my world; eye-pampering, but satisfies no heart. Streets, streets, streets, markets, theatres, churches, Covent Gardens, shops sparkling with pretty faces of industrious milliners, neat sempstresses, ladies cheapening, gentlemen behind counters lying, authors in the street with spectacles, George Dyers, (you may know them by their gait,) lamps lit at night, pastry-cooks' and silversmiths' shops, beautiful Quakers of Pentonville, noise of coaches, drowsy cry of mechanic watchmen at night, with bucks reeling home drunk; if you happen to wake at midnight, cries of 'Fire!' and 'Stop thief!' inns of court, with their learned air, and halls, and butteries, just like Cambridge colleges; old book-stalls, 'Jeremy Taylors', 'Burtons on Melancholy', and 'Religio Medicis', on every stall. These are thy pleasures, O London! with thy many sins. O City, abounding in w . . . , for these may Keswick and her giant brood go hang!   C. L.

Charles Lamb, Letters (1909)

The fairest capital

> Rank abundance breeds
> In gross and pamper'd cities sloth and lust,
> And wantonness and gluttonous excess.
> In cities vice is hidden with most ease,
> Or seen with least reproach; and virtue, taught
> By frequent lapse, can hope no triumph there
> Beyond th' achievement of successful flight.
> I do confess them nurs'ries of the arts,
> In which they flourish most; where, in the beams
> Of warm encouragement, and in the eye
> Of public note, they reach their perfect size.
> Such London is, by taste and wealth proclaim'd
> The fairest capital of all the world,
> By riot and incontinence the worst.
> There, touch'd by Reynolds, a dull blank becomes
> A lucid mirror, in which Nature sees
> All her reflected features. Bacon there
> Gives more than female beauty to a stone,

And Chatham's eloquence to marble lips.
Nor does the chissel occupy alone
The pow'rs of sculpture, but the style as much;
Each province of her art her equal care.
With nice incision of her guided steel
She ploughs a brazen field, and clothes a soil
So sterile with what charms soe'er she will,
The richest scen'ry and the loveliest forms.
Where finds philosophy her eagle eye.
With which she gazes at yon burning disk
Undazzled, and detects and counts his spots?
In London: where her implements exact,
With which she calculates, computes, and scans,
All distance, motion, magnitude, and now
Measures an atom, and now girds a world?
In London. Where has commerce such a mart,
So rich, so throng'd, so drain'd, and so supplied,
As London – opulent, enlarg'd, and still
Increasing, London? Babylon of old
Not more the glory of the earth than she.
A more accomplish'd world's chief glory now.

    She has her praise. Now mark a spot or two,
That so much beauty would do well to purge;
And show this queen of cities, that so fair
May yet be foul; so witty, yet not wise.
It is not seemly, nor of good report.
That she is slack in discipline; more prompt
T' avenge than to prevent the breach of law:
That she is rigid in denouncing death
On petty robbers, and indulges life
And liberty, and oft-times honour too,
To peculators of the public gold:
That thieves at home must hand; but he, that puts
Into his overgorg'd and bloated purse
The wealth of Indian provinces, escapes.
Nor is it well, nor can it come to good,
That, through profane and infidel contempt
Of holy writ, she has presum'd t' annul
And abrogate, as roundly as she may,

The total ordinance and will of God;
Advancing fashion to the post of truth,
And cent'ring all authority in modes
And customs of her own, till sabbath rites
Have dwindled into unrespected forms,
And knees and hassocks are well-nigh divorc'd.

William Cowper, *The Poetical Works* (1963)

All that life can afford

I suggested a doubt, that if I were to reside in London, the exquisite zest with which I relished it in occasional visits might go off, and I might grow tired of it. JOHNSON. 'Why, Sir, you find no man, at all intellectual, who is willing to leave London. No, Sir, when a man is tired of London, he is tired of life; for there is in London all that life can afford.'

James Boswell, *Life of Johnson* (1791)

Bibliography of
Works Consulted

ACKROYD, Peter, *Hawksmoor* (Hamish Hamilton, 1985)

ADDISON, Joseph, and others, *The Spectator* (J. J. Chidley, 1843)

ALLINGHAM, Margery, *The Tiger in the Smoke* (Chatto & Windus, 1937)

AMIS, Martin, *London Fields* (Cape, 1989)

ARMITAGE, Gilbert, *The History of Bow Street Runners, 1729–1829* (Wishart & Co., 1939)

ASQUITH, Lady Cynthia, *Diaries, 1915–1918* (Hutchinson, 1971)

AUBREY, John, *Brief Lives*, ed. Oliver Lawson Dick (Secker & Warburg, 1949)

BABINGTON SMITH, Constance, *Rose Macaulay* (Collins, 1972)

BELLOC, Hilaire, *Complete Verse* (Pimlico, 1991)

BENNETT, Arnold, *Riceyman Steps* (Cassell, 1923)

BENSON, A. C., *Edwardian Excursions* (John Murray, 1981)

BERNARD, Jeffrey, *Low Life* (Duckworth, 1992)

BETJEMAN, John, *A Nip in the Air* (John Murray, 1974)

– *Collected Poems* (John Murray, 1970)

– *First and Last Loves* (John Murray, 1952)

– *Summoned by Bells* (John Murray, 1960)

BLAKE, Robert, *Disraeli* (Methuen, 1966)

BLAKE, William, *The Poetry and Prose of William Blake*, ed. Geoffrey Keynes (Nonesuch Press, 1939)

BOOTH, Charles, *Life and Labour of the People of London* (Avalon Press, 1902–3)

BOSWELL, James, *Life of Johnson* (Oxford University Press, 1966)

– *London Journal*, ed. Frederick A. Pottle (Heinemann, 1950)

BOWEN, Elizabeth, *Collected Stories* (Penguin, 1983)

– *The Death of the Heart* (Jonathan Cape, 1938)

BRIDGES, Robert, *Poetical Works* (Oxford University Press, 1912)

BRIGGS, Asa (ed.), *They Saw It Happen* (Blackwell, Oxford, 1960)

BROWN, Craig (ed.), *The Agreeable World of Wallace Arnold* (Fourth Estate, 1990)

BROWNING, Elizabeth Barrett, *Letters of Mrs Browning*, ed. F. G. Kenyon (Macmillan, 1897)

CAMDEN Society, *The Chronicle of the Years of Queen Mary* (1849)
CARLYLE, Thomas, *The Life of John Sterling* (1851)
CASANOVA, Giovanni, *My Life and Adventures*, trans. Arthur Machen (Joiner & Steele, 1932)
CECIL, David, *The Cecils of Hatfield House* (Constable, 1973)
CHANNON, Henry, *Chips: The Diaries of Sir Henry Channon*, ed. Robert Rhodes James (Weidenfeld & Nicolson, 1967)
CHESTERTON, Mrs Cecil, *In Darkest London* (Stanley & Paul, 1926)
– *The Chestertons* (Chapman & Hall, 1941)
CHESTERTON, G. K., *Autobiography* (Sheed & Ward, 1936)
– *The Man Who Was Thursday* (1908)
COBB, Belton, *Murdered on Duty* (W. H. Allen, 1961)
COLLIS, John Stewart, *Bound Upon a Course* (Sidgwick & Jackson, 1971)
COLVILLE, John, *The Fringes of Power* (Hodder & Stoughton, 1985)
CONRAD, Joseph, *The Secret Agent* (Penguin, 1990)
COOPER, Duff, *Talleyrand* (Cape, 1938)
COPE, Wendy, *Serious Concerns* (Faber, 1992)
COWARD, Noël, *The Lyrics of Noël Coward* (Heinemann, 1965)
COWPER, William, *The Poetical Works* (Oxford, 1963)
CRAWFORD, Marion, *The Little Princesses* (Cassell, 1950)
CREEVEY, Thomas, *A Selection from the Correspondence and Diaries of the Late Thomas Creevey MP*, ed. Herbert Maxwell (John Murray, 1923)

DARBISHIRE, Helen (ed.), *The Early Lives of John Milton* (Constable, 1932)
DAVIDSON, John, *Fleet Street and Other Poems* (Grant Richards, 1909)
DEFOE, Daniel, *A Tour Through the Whole Island of Great Britain* (Oxford University Press, 1910)
DE SAUSSURE, Ferdinand, *A Foreign View of England in the Reigns of George I and George II* (1902)
DICKENS, Charles, *The Fireside Edition*, 22 vols (Chapman & Hall, 1911)
DOSTOYEVSKY, Fyodor, *Winter Notes on Summer Impressions*, trans. Kyril Fitzlyon (Quartet, 1985)
DOUGLAS, Alfred, *Poems* (Mercure de France, Paris, 1896)
DOYLE, Arthur Conan, *The Adventures of Sherlock Holmes* (Macmillan, 1892)
– *The Memoirs of Sherlock Holmes* (Newnes, 1893)
– *The Return of Sherlock Holmes* (Newnes, 1905)
DRIBERG, Tom, *Ruling Passions* (Jonathan Cape, 1977)

ELIOT, T. S., *Collected Poems, 1902–1962* (Faber, 1966)
ELWES, W., *They Saw it Happen* (Geoffrey Bles, 1950)
EVELYN, John, *Diary* (Oxford University Press, 1971)

FALKNER, J. M., *Poems* (Westminster Press, 411A Harrow Road, London W9, no date)

FARSON, Daniel, *Limehouse Days* (Michael Joseph, 1991)
– *Soho in the Fifties* (Michael Joseph, 1987)
FIELDING, Henry, *Jonathan Wild* (1743)
– *An Enquiry in the Causes of the late Increase of Robbers* (1752)
FLETCHER, Geoffrey S., *The London Nobody Knows* (Hutchinson, 1962)
FROUDE, James Anthony, *Carlyle's Life in London, 1834–81* (Longmans Green, 1885)
FULFORD, Roger, *The Prince Consort* (Macmillan, 1949)

GASKELL, Elizabeth, *The Life of Charlotte Brontë* (1857) (World's Classics, Oxford, 1947)
GAY, John, *Poetry and Prose*, ed. Vinton A. Dearing (Oxford, 1974)
GIBBS, Philip, *The Pageant of the Years* (Chapman & Hall, 1946)
GOLDSMITH, Oliver, *The Complete Works* (Oxford University Press, 1949)
GRAEME, Bruce, *The Story of Buckingham Palace* (Crawlboys and Smith, 1928)
GREVILLE, Charles Cavendish Fulke, *Leaves from the Greville Diary* (Eveleigh, Nash and Grayson, 1929)
GROSSMAN, Leonid, *Dostoyevsky: A Biography* (Allen Lane, 1974)
GROSSMITH, George and Weedon, *The Diary of a Nobody* (1892)

HAIGHT, Gordon, *George Eliot: A Life* (Oxford, 1969)
HAMILTON, Patrick, *Hangover Square* (Constable, 1941)
HANNINGTON, Wal, *Unemployed Struggle 1919–1936* (Lawrence & Wishart, 1936)
HARDY, Thomas, *Collected Poems* (Macmillan, 1974)
HARE, Augustus, *The Story of My Life* (George Allen, 1896)
– *Walks in London* (Macmillan, 1878)
HARE, Kenneth, *London's Latin Quarter* (Bodley Head, 1926)
HAYDON, Benjamin, *The Diary of Benjamin Haydon*, ed. William Bissell Pope, 4 vols (Harvard, 1960–3)
HAYTER, Alethea, *A Sultry Month* (Faber, 1965)
HEATH-STUBBS, John, *Collected Poems* (Carcanet, 1988)
HERRICK, Robert, *The Complete Poetical Works*, ed. The Revd Peter Mackay (Oxford University Press, 1913)
HERZEN, Alexander, *My Past and Thoughts*, 4 vols (Chatto & Windus, 1968)
HICKEY, William, *Memoirs of William Hickey, 1749–1809* (Hutchinson, 1960)
HOUSMAN, A. E., *The Collected Poems* (Jonathan Cape, 1955)
HOWGRAVE-GRAHAM, H. M., *Light and Shade at Scotland Yard* (John Murray, 1947)

JAMES, Henry, *Selected Letters*, ed. Leon Edel (Belknap Press, Harvard, 1987)
– *The Golden Bowl* (Macmillan, 1904)
– *The Wings of the Dove* (Modern Library, New York, 1946)
JOHNSON, Samuel, *The Lives of the English Poets* (1779–81) (World's Classics, Oxford, 1949)

KAVANAGH, P. J., *Collected Poems* (Carcanet, 1992)
KEATS, John, *The Letters*, ed. Hyde E. Rollins (Oxford University Press, 1958)
KING, Mrs Hamilton, *Letters and Recollections of Mazzini* (Longmans Green, 1912)

KIPLING, Rudyard, *Rudyard Kipling's Verse: Definitive Edition* (Hodder & Stoughton, 1940)

LAHR, John, *Prick up Your Ears* (Allen Lane, 1978)
LAMB, Charles, *Essays of Elia 1823* (World's Classics, Oxford, 1961)
– *Letters* (R. Rivière & Son, 1909)
LAMPSON, Frederick Locker, *London Lyrics* (W. Isbister & Co., 1874)
LANCASTER, Osbert, *All Done from Memory* (John Murray, 1963)
LARKIN, Philip, *Selected Letters of Philip Larkin*, ed. Anthony Thwaite (Faber, 1992)
LAWRENCE, D. H., *Assorted Articles* (Martin Secker, 1932)
LEVY, Amy, *A London Plane-Tree and Other Poems* (1893)
LINEBAUGH, Peter, *The London Hanged* (Allen Lane, 1991)
LOCK, Joan, *Marlborough Street: The Story of a London Court* (Robert Hale, 1980)
LONGFORD, Elizabeth, *Wellington, Pillar of State* (Weidenfeld & Nicolson, 1972)

MACAULAY, Rose, *The World My Wilderness* (Collins, 1950)
MACINNES, Colin, *City of Spades* (MacGibbon & Kee, 1957)
MARIE LOUISE, Princess, *My Memories of Six Reigns* (Evans Bros, 1946)
MARKINO, Yosuo, *A Japanese Artist in London* (1910)
MAYHEW, Henry, *Mayhew's London* (1851) (Spring Books, no date)
MILMAN, Henry Hart, *Annals of St Paul's Cathedral* (John Murray, 1868)
MILNE, A. A., *When We Were Very Young* (Methuen, 1924)
MILTON, John, *The Complete Poetical Works*, ed. Helen Darbishire (Oxford University Press, 1931)
MITCHELL, R. J., and Leys, M. R. D., *A History of London Life* (Longmans, 1958)
MOORCOCK, Michael, *Mother London* (Secker & Warburg, 1988)
MORTIMER, John, *Rumpole à la Carte* (Viking, 1991)
MORTON, H. V., *In Search of England* (Methuen, 1927)
MORTON, James, *Gangland* (Little, Brown, 1992)
MOSLEY, Diana, *A Life of Contrasts* (Hamish Hamilton, 1977)
MOSLEY, Nicholas, *Beyond the Pale* (Secker & Warburg, 1983)
MOUNT, Ferdinand, *The Man Who Rode Ampersand* (Chatto & Windus, 1975)
MURDOCH, Iris, *A Word Child* (Chatto & Windus, 1975)
– *The Black Prince* (Chatto & Windus, 1973)
– *Under the Net* (Chatto & Windus, 1954)
MURPHY, Robert, *Smash and Grab* (Faber, 1993)

NESBIT, E., *The Phoenix and the Carpet* (Puffin, 1978)
NICOLSON, Harold, *Diaries and Letters, 1930–1939* (Collins, 1966)
– *Diaries and Letters, 1939–1945* (Collins, 1967)

OLSEN, Donald J., *The Growth of Victorian London* (Batsford, 1976)
ORTON, Joe, *Diaries*, ed. John Lahr (Methuen, 1986)

PANKHURST, Emmeline, *My Own Story* (Eveleigh, Nash, 1914)
PARRIS, John, *The Lion of Caprera* (Arthur Barker, 1962)

PAYNE, Robert, *The Life and Death of Lenin* (Heinemann, 1963)

PEAKE, Mervyn, *Selected Poems* (Faber, 1972)

PEARSON, Hesketh, and Kingsmill, Hugh, *Talking of Dick Whittington* (Eyre & Spottiswoode, 1947)

PEPYS, Samuel, *The Diary of Samuel Pepys*, ed. Robert Latham and William Matthews (Bell & Hyman, 1970–83)

POPE-HENNESSY, James, *Queen Mary* (George Allen & Unwin, 1959)

POWELL, Anthony, *A Buyer's Market* (Heinemann, 1952)

– *Books Do Furnish a Room* (Heinemann, 1971)

– *Casanova's Chinese Restaurant* (Heinemann, 1960)

– *The Military Philosophers* (Heinemann, 1968)

POWYS, John Cowper, *Wolf Solent* (Jonathan Cape, 1929)

PRAED, W. M., *The Poems* (Moxon & Son, 1864)

QUENNELL, Peter, *The Wanton Chase* (Collins, 1980)

READ, Herbert (ed.), *The London Book of English Verse* (Eyre & Spottiswoode, 1949)

RICKERT, Edith, *Chaucer's World* (Oxford University Press, New York, 1948)

RIDLER, Anne, *New and Selected Poems* (Faber, 1988)

RIMBAULT, E. F., *Soho and Its Associations* (Dulau & Co., 1895)

ROBERTS, Brian, *The Mad Bad Line* (Hamish Hamilton, 1981)

ROGERS, Kenneth, *The Mermaid and Mitre Taverns in Old London* (Homeland Association Ltd, 1928)

ROSE, Kenneth, *King George V* (Weidenfeld & Nicolson, 1983)

ROSS, Julian Maclaren, *Memoirs of the Forties* (Alan Ross, 1965)

ROUTH, C. R. N., *They Saw it Happen, 1485–1688* (Blackwell, Oxford, 1956)

SCARMAN, Lord Leslie, *Report on the Brixton Disorders of 10–12 April 1981* (HMSO, 1981)

SEWELL, Anna, *Black Beauty* (1877) (Puffin, 1966)

SHAKESPEARE, William, *The Histories and Poems of Shakespeare* (Oxford University Press, 1949)

SINCLAIR, Iain, *Downriver* (Paladin/Grafton Books, 1991)

SITWELL, Edith, *The English Eccentrics* (Faber, 1933)

SMITH, Dodie, *The Hundred and One Dalmatians* (Heinemann, 1956)

SMITH, James, *Comic Miscellanies* (Lowood & Abbott Ltd, 1873)

SMITH, Stevie, *The Collected Poems of Stevie Smith* (Allen Lane, 1975)

SMOLLETT, Tobias, *Humphrey Clinker* (Lippincott, Philadelphia, 1895)

SPENDER, Stephen, *Journals, 1939–1983* (Faber, 1985)

SPENSER, Edmund, *The Collected Works* (Macmillan, 1897)

STENDHAL, *Memoirs of an Egotist*, trans. David Ellis (Chatto & Windus, 1975)

STOW, John, *A Survey of London* (Oxford at the Clarendon Press, 1908)

STRACHEY, Lytton, *Queen Victoria* (Chatto & Windus, 1921)

SWIFT, Jonathan, *The Nonesuch Swift*, ed. John Hayward (Nonesuch Press, 1968)

TENNYSON, Alfred, Lord, *The Poems of Tennyson*, ed. Christopher Ricks, 2nd edition (Longmans, 1987)

THACKERAY, William Makepeace, *The Works*, 20 vols (Thomas Nelson, 1900)

THOMSON, David, *In Camden Town* (Hutchinson, 1983)

THORNBURY, Walter, *Haunted London* (Hurst & Blackett, 1865)

TRENCH, Charles Chevenix, *Portrait of a Patriot* (William Blackwood, 1962)

TREVELYAN, G. M., *England in the Age of Wycliffe* (Longmans, 1899)

– *English Social History* (Longmans, 1944)

TRISTAN, Flora, *London Journal* (1840)

VOLTAIRE, François, *Letters on England*, trans. Leonard Tancock (1980)

WALLER, Edmund, *Complete Poetical Works* (Oxford University Press, 1953)

WATKIN, David, *Thomas Hope and the Neoclassical Idea* (Batsford, 1968)

WAUGH, Auberon, *The Diaries of Auberon Waugh, 1976–1985* (Andre Deutsch, 1985)

WAUGH, Evelyn, *Scoop* (Chapman & Hall, 1938)

– *The Letters of Evelyn Waugh*, ed. Mark Amory (Weidenfeld & Nicolson, 1980)

WEBB, Beatrice, *My Apprenticeship* (Penguin, 1971)

WEDGWOOD, C. V., *The Trial of Charles I* (Collins, 1964)

WELLS, H. G., *Kipps* (Martin Secker, 1905)

WELLS, John, *Rude Words* (Macmillan, 1991)

WHARTON, Michael (Peter Simple), *The Stretchford Chronicles* (Macmillan, 1980)

WHITTEN, W. (ed.), *London in Song* (Grant Richards, 1898)

WILDE, Oscar, *De Profundis* (Methuen, 1949)

WILMOTT, Peter, *Adolescent Boys of East London* (Pelican, 1969)

WILSON, F. M., *Strange Island* (Longmans, 1955)

WOOLF, Virginia, *Mrs Dalloway* (Hogarth Press, 1925)

– *The Diary of Virginia Woolf*, ed. Anne Olivier Bell (Hogarth Press, vol. III 1980, vol. V 1984)

WORDSWORTH, William, *Poetical Works* (Chapman & Hall, 1903)

WROTH, Warwick, *The London Pleasure Gardens in the Eighteenth Century* (Macmillan, 1896)

YOUNG, Filson (ed.), *The Trial of Hawley Harvey Crippen* (William Hodge, 1920)

Acknowledgements

For permission to reprint copyright material the publishers gratefully acknowledge the following:

PETER ACKROYD: from *Hawksmoor* (Hamish Hamilton, 1985). MARTIN AMIS: from *London Fields* (Cape, 1989); reprinted by permission of Random House UK Ltd., and Peters Fraser & Dunlop Group Ltd. HILAIRE BELLOC: 'Ballade of Hell and Mrs Roebuck', 'The Telephone' and 'George' all from *Complete Verse* (Pimlico, a division of Random Century, 1991); reprinted by permission of the Peters Fraser & Dunlop Group Ltd. A. C. BENSON: from *Edwardian Excursions: Extracts from A. C. Benson's Diaries* by David Newsome; reprinted by permission of John Murray (Publishers) Ltd. JEFFREY BERNARD: from *Low Life* (Duckworth, 1992); reprinted by permission of Gerald Duckworth & Co Ltd. JOHN BETJEMAN: 'For Patrick Aetat LXX', 'Parliament Hill Fields', 'Devonshire Street', 'Monody on the Death of Aldersgate Station', 'The Arrest of Oscar Wilde at the Cadogan Hotel', 'In Westminster Abbey', 'Business Girls', 'The Cockney Amorist' and 'Song of a Night-Club Proprietress' from *Collected Poems*; extract from *First and Last Loves*; reprinted by permission of John Murray (Publishers) Ltd. ELIZABETH BOWEN: from 'The Demon Lover' from *Collected Stories*; and from *The Death of the Heart*; reprinted by permission of Random House UK Ltd., and Alfred A. Knopf Inc. A. S. BYATT: from *Possession* (Chatto & Windus, 1990). DAVID CECIL: from *The Cecils of Hatfield House* (Constable, 1973); reprinted by permission of Constable Publishers and David Higham Associates. HENRY 'CHIPS' CHANNON: from *Diaries* (Weidenfeld, 1967). MRS CECIL CHESTERTON: from *In Darkest London* (Stanley Paul, 1926). JOHN STEWART COLLIS: from *Bound Upon a Course* (1971); reprinted by permission of Sidgwick & Jackson. JOHN COLVILLE: from *The Fringes of Power*; reprinted by permission of Hodder & Stoughton Ltd. DUFF COOPER: from *Talleyrand* (Cape, 1938). WENDY COPE: from *Serious Concerns*, copyright © Wendy Cope 1992; reprinted by permission of Faber and Faber Ltd., and Faber and Faber Inc. NOEL COWARD: 'London Pride', copyright © 1941 by the Estate of Noel Coward, by permission of Michael Imison Playwrights Ltd. MARION CRAWFORD: from *The Little Princesses* (Cassell, 1950). LORD ALFRED DOUGLAS: 'Impression de Nuit:

London', copyright © The Estate of Lord Alfred Douglas. TOM DRIBERG: from *Ruling Passions* (Cape, 1977); reprinted by permission of David Higham Associates Ltd. T. S. ELIOT: extract from 'The Waste Land' from *Collected Poems 1909–1962*; reprinted by permission of Faber & Faber Ltd, and Harcourt Brace Jovanovich Inc. DANIEL FARSON: from *Soho In the Fifties* (Michael Joseph, 1987) and from *Limehouse Days* (Michael Joseph, 1991). GEOFFREY S. FLETCHER: from *The London Nobody Knows* (Hutchinson, 1962). ROGER FULFORD: from *The Prince Consort* (Macmillan, 1949). BRUCE GRAEME: from *The Story of Buckingham Palace* (Hutchinson, 1928). MICHAEL HAMBURGER: 'London Tom-Cat', copyright Michael Hamburger, reprinted in *More Comic and Curious Verse*. PATRICK HAMILTON: from *Hangover Square* (Constable, 1941); reprinted by permission of Constable Publishers and A. M. Heath & Co. Ltd. ALETHEA HAYTER: from *A Sultry Month*, reprinted by permission of Quartet Books Limited and the author. JOHN HEATH-STUBBS: from *Collected Poems* (Carcanet, 1988); reprinted by permission of David Higham Associates Ltd. JAMES POPE HENNESSY: from *Queen Mary* (Allen & Unwin, 1959). H. M. HOWGRAVE-GRAHAM: from *Light and Shade at Scotland Yard* (John Murray, 1947). P. J. KAVANAGH: 'Blackbird in Fulham' from *Collected Poems* (Carcanet Press, 1992); reprinted by permission of Carcanet Press Ltd. JOHN LAHR: from *Prick Up Your Ears* (Allen Lane, 1978). OSBERT LANCASTER: from *All Done From Memory*; reprinted by permission of John Murray (Publishers) Ltd and Houghton Mifflin Co. PHILIP LARKIN: from *Selected Letters of Philip Larkin 1940–1985*, edited by Anthony Thwaite; reprinted by permission of Faber & Faber Ltd. JOAN LOCK: from *Marlborough Street, the Story of a London Court* (Robert Hale, 1980); reprinted by permission of Laurence Pollinger Ltd. ELIZABETH LONGFORD: from *Wellington, Pillar of State* (Weidenfeld, 1972). ROSE MACAULAY: from *The World My Wilderness* (Collins, 1950); reprinted by permission of the Peters Fraser & Dunlop Group Ltd; COLIN MACINNESS: from *City of Spades* (Allison & Busby); reprinted by permission of Reg David-Poynter. PRINCESS MARIE-LOUISE: from *My Memories Of Six Reigns* (Evans Bros., 1946). ERIC MASCHWITZ: from *A Nightingale Sang In Berkeley Square*, copyright © Eric Maschwitz Musicals Ltd. R. J. MITCHELL & M. R. D. LEYS: from *A History of London Life* (Longman, 1958); reprinted by permission of the Peters Fraser & Dunlop Group Ltd. MICHAEL MOORCOCK: from *The Angered Spirit* (Secker & Warburg, 1988). JOHN MORTIMER: from *Rumpole à la Carte* (1991); reprinted by permission of Peters Fraser & Dunlop Group Ltd. H. V. MORTON: from *In Search of England*, copyright © 1927 H. V. Morton, published by Methuen; reprinted by permission of the publisher and A. M. Heath & Co. Ltd. JAMES MORTON: from *Gangland: London's Underworld* (Macdonald, 1992). DIANA MOSLEY: from *A Life of Contrasts* (Hamish Hamilton, 1977). NICHOLAS MOSLEY: from *Beyond The Pale* (Secker & Warburg, 1983); reprinted by permission of the Peters Fraser & Dunlop Group Ltd. FERDINAND MOUNT: from *The Man Who Rode Ampersand* (Chatto & Windus, 1975). IRIS MURDOCH: from *Under the Net* (Chatto, 1954), copyright ©

Iris Murdoch 1954; from *A Word Child* (Chatto, 1975), copyright © Iris Murdoch 1975; from *The Black Prince* (Chatto, 1973), copyright © Iris Murdoch 1973; reprinted by permission of Random House UK Ltd. ROBERT MURPHY: from *Smash and Grab* (Faber and Faber, 1993); reprinted by permission of the publisher. HAROLD NICOLSON: from *Diaries and Letters 1930–1939*; reprinted by permission of HarperCollins Publishers. JOE ORTON: from *The Orton Diaries*, edited by John Lahr, copyright © Joe Orton, published by Methuen; reprinted by permission of the publisher and Casarotto Ramsay, London. E. J. PARRIS: from *Lion of Caprera* (Arthur Barker, 1962). MERVYN PEAKE: 'Victoria Station, 6.58 p.m.' from *Selected Poems* (Faber and Faber, 1972), reprinted by permission of David Higham Associates Ltd. ANTHONY POWELL: from *Books Do Furnish a Room, A Buyer's Market, The Military Philosophers* and *Casanova's Chinese Restaurant* (all published by Heinemann); reprinted by permission of David Higham Associates Ltd. JOHN COWPER POWYS: from *Wolf Solent* (Cape, 1929). ANNE RIDLER: from *New and Selected Poems*; reprinted by permission of Faber and Faber Ltd. BRIAN ROBERTS: from *The Mad Bad Line* (Hamish Hamilton, 1981). KENNETH ROSE: from *King George V* (Weidenfeld, 1983). PETER SIMPLE: from *The Stretchford Chronicles*, copyright © The Telegraph plc, London 1980; reprinted by permission of Ewan MacNaughton Associates. IAIN SINCLAIR: from *Downriver* (Grafton Books, 1991). DODIE SMITH: from *The Hundred and One Dalmatians*, copyright © Dodie Smith Laurence Fitch Ltd. STEVIE SMITH: from *The Collected Poems of Stevie Smith* (Penguin 20th Century Classics); reprinted by permission of James MacGibbon. STEPHEN SPENDER: 'In Long Acre' from *Journals 1939–83* (Faber and Faber, 1985). STENDHAL: from *Stendhal, Memoirs of an Egotist*, translated by David Ellis, copyright © David Ellis 1975 (Chatto & Windus Ltd, 1975). JULIAN SYMONS: 'A Forgotton Man of the Thirties', *Times Literary Supplement*, 26 March 1993. DAVID THOMSON: from *In Camden Town*; reprinted by permission of Random House UK Ltd., and Mrs A. M. Thomson on behalf of the Estate of David Thomson. CHARLES CHENEVIX TRENCH: from *Portrait of a Patriot* (William Blackwood, 1962); reprinted by permission of David Fletcher Associates and the author. G. M. TREVELYAN: from *English Social History*; reprinted by permission of Longman Group UK. VOLTAIRE: from *Letters on England*, translated by Leonard Tancock, copyright © Leonard Tancock 1980 (Penguin Books, 1980). DAVID WATKIN: from *Thomas Hope and the Neoclassical Idea*; reprinted by permission of John Murray (Publishers) Ltd. AUBERON WAUGH: from *The Diaries* (Deutsch, 1985). EVELYN WAUGH: from *Scoop* (Chapman & Hall, 1938); reprinted by permission of Peters Fraser & Dunlop Group Ltd. C. V. WEDGEWOOD: from *The Trial of Charles I* (Collins, 1964). H. G. WELLS: from *Kipps*; reprinted by permission of A. P. Watt Ltd on behalf of The Literary Executors of the Estate of H. G. Wells. JOHN WELLS: from *Rude Words* (Macmillan, 1992), copyright © John Wells 1992. PETER WILMOTT: from *Adolescent Boys of East London* (Pelican, 1969). ARTHUR WIMPERIS: 'Gilbert the Filbert', copyright © Francis Day & Hunter Ltd 1914; reproduced from Music Hall, Programme Number Three, copyright © International Music Publications 1984. VIRGINIA WOOLF: from *The Diary of Virginia Woolf*, edited Anne Olivier Bell (Hogarth Press); reprinted by permission of Random House UK Ltd.

Every effort has been made to contact or trace all copyright holders. The publishers will be glad to make good any errors or omissions brought to our attention in future editions.

Index of Authors

General Index